THE JEWISH
EXPERIENCE OF TIME

THE JEWISH EXPERIENCE OF TIME

PHILOSOPHICAL DIMENSIONS OF THE JEWISH HOLY DAYS

ELIEZER SCHWEID

translated by
AMNON HADARY

JASON ARONSON INC.
Northvale, New Jersey
Jerusalem

This book was set in 11 pt. Weiss by Alabama Book Composition of Deatsville, AL and printed and bound by Book-mart Press, Inc. of North Bergen, NJ.

10 9 8 7 6 5 4 3 2 1

Library of Congress Cataloging-in-Publication Data

Schweid, Eliezer.
    The Jewish experience of time: philosophical dimensions of the Jewish holy days / Eliezer Schweid.
        p.   cm.
    Includes index.
    ISBN 0–7657–6105–X
    1. Fasts and feasts—Judaism.   2. Jewish way of life.   3. Judaism—
Essence, genius, nature.   I. Title.
BM690.S377   2000
296.4'3–dc21
                                                                99–27863
                                                                    CIP

Printed in the United States of America on acid-free paper. For information and catalog write to Jason Aronson Inc., 230 Livingston Street, Northvale, NJ 07647-1726, or visit our website: www.aronson.com

CONTENTS

PREFACE

This book is about the philosophical contents of the Jewish calendar. It presents a systematized overall view of how the sequence of time is structured through *mitzvot*, symbols, and prayers, as well as weekly, festival, and holiday Bible readings and study. Each chapter is concerned with the dominant ideational theme of a single festival or holiday; each theme is but a component in the totality of the calendar. The totality should not be regarded as a closed system in the philosophical sense; it certainly ought to be seen as an overall outlook that relates to the core issues of human life, applying insights through symbols that shape life-style, feelings, and reason.

For whom is the book intended? For those who are involved with the Jewish calendar in their daily life, either because they want to structure the life of their families or community Jewishly, or because they serve as transmitters or receivers of the Jewish heritage: parents and children; teachers and pupils who wish to gain more profound insights; cultural coordinators in their community centers; anyone exercised by the question of how to design a holiday celebration or a festival ceremony; anyone who wishes to examine the substantive issues that transcend technical chores. Moreover, this book is directed to people who ask about the unique essence of the Jewish world view and because of their commitment to it are perplexed by the difficulties of coming to terms with problems of the Jewish people's existence and with the existential situation of contemporary Jews.

For those who ask what is Judaism and who is a Jew and for those who care about how Judaism can persist as more than an idea—as a modality for living, there is an integral connection between the pragmatic questions of practitioners and the theoretical queries of those who require a definition of Judaism as an outlook on life. Neither of these aspects can stand alone without being informed by the other. Professionals cannot act without knowing what they themselves profess or without articulating it. Transmitting a value system necessarily depends on believing in it. In effect, such a transmission process means acting out the principles of one's convictions through the way one lives. This is the premise that underlies the book's theme—the calendar with its Sabbaths and festivals—for we are dealing with a world outlook contained in a way of life, and a way of living that shapes a world outlook. In any case, this book is intended as a resource for professional educators in the broadest sense of the term or for those who inquire into the aspects of the principles of a Jewish world view. Although all the target groups mentioned above can be assisted by this work, neither definitive solutions nor decisive answers will be found for we are dealing with a living calendar that is still in the process of evolving, an organism engaged in assembling its constructions and renewing itself through them.

The assistance this book would like to offer can be summed up as renewing the link with an all-encompassing and emerging historical process, as forging the necessary intellectual tools that a contemporary person needs so that—through a living contact with the Sources—he can derive applicable solutions. Such solutions can be instructive for community leaders, for individuals in their families, indeed for every creative person in the course of his life.

The book joins an extensive library. The assumption that the Jewish calendar, its Sabbaths, holidays, and appointed times is the most definitive articulation of a Jewish outlook has long been accepted among Jews; certainly there is no more appropriate educational introduction to Judaism as a living heritage than learning about and experiencing the holidays and festivals. Holidays and festivals are essentially *institutions* meant to educate, and since the learning aspect has always been an integral part of the festivities themselves, Jews did not need to suffice with teaching their attendant *mitzvot* and regulations. The philosophy that interpreted the sense and significance of the holidays clung to them as a flame to a burning coal. Throughout the generations, a rich multi-faceted literature grew up around the philosophical essence of the calendar and its rhythms; in modern times, marked as they are by the scientific method, there has been a proliferation of systematic works that present the calendar as a subject in and of itself. This book owes a great debt to that extensive library which it now joins, indeed it could not have been written without it. Nonetheless, it differs from the majority of previous studies, including those with a great affinity to modern philosophical writing. The author feels that this work fills in a strongly perceived lack on the part of educators and students who are seeking the essence of Judaism. The distinctiveness of this work stems from an attempt to arrive at an ideational overview by means of a detailed analysis of the literary and ceremonial/symbolic content of each holiday and festival; and along with that to add as exact a description as possible of the heritage, layer upon layer. While subjectively interpreting the material, this is an approach that seeks objectivity; it is the outcome of personal experience with the historic/cultural reality of contemporary Judaism as well as reflections on a renewed creative design of holiday themes.

Such an effort involves complex questions of methodology, but for a number of reasons it seems preferable to postpone the discussion of these to the Afterword. Anyone whose particular interest is not methodology is thus spared by this leap-frogging; whereas anyone who is keenly interested will benefit if the discussion follows on the actual application of methodological principles. Therefore we go directly to the matter at hand (which is also at the very heart of the methodological quandary), the first chapter. This chapter, which serves as an ideological infrastructure for the entire book, is possibly the most problematic because it attempts to encompass all that emerges from a broad-spectrumed, many-faceted cultural creation. Is it possible to speak about the philosophical meanings inherent in the structure of the calendar as an overall design for the sequence of time?

ONE

THE JEWISH CALENDAR:
THE SIGNIFICANCE OF TIME CYCLES

THE JEWISH CALENDAR:
A COMPREHENSIVE LIFE PLAN

In all cultures the yearly calendar is of central importance as a permanent blueprint for the ordering of time. Culture, as the totality of the voluntary and purposeful functioning of human society, expresses an ongoing effort on society's part to apply its evaluations, aspirations, and goals to the natural environment. From this standpoint, culture is an inclusive world view that interprets man's self-image, his understanding of his place and role in the universe, and the significance he attaches to his existence through his actions. Establishing a time cycle is like determining the parameters by which a given society wishes to apply its standards. The time cycle is a necessary element of a society's culture. Without a specified time sequence, man cannot have an overall view of how his life unfolds in relationship to other members of his society; collective consciousness depends on the realization of existence in the same locality and at the same time. Every society "decodes" the tempo of natural occurrences on which its existence depends and, in harmony with that rhythm, frames the institutions which express the meaning of its beliefs and values. Conse-

1

quently, the calendar is one of the major keys to understanding any society as a comprehensive structure of meanings. For the Jewish people the calendar holds a particular importance. There are two reasons for this. The first stems from the unique destiny of the Jewish people, and the second from the priority of values imposed, from within, by the Torah, on the Jewish people's way of life.

The destiny of the Jewish people is the destiny of a diaspora people, the majority of whose time was spent living outside its land; that is, for most of their history the Jewish people lacked the second principle that determines a people's consciousness of mutuality—the underpinning of living together in the same circumscribed locality. The importance of the first principle—existing together in the same time sequence—took on additional importance. By strictly maintaining the same order of time, Jews in communities that were dispersed throughout the world could live events in common, investing them with the same meanings by using the same symbols. As a result, the course of time broadened to fill, insofar as possible, the role of the missing spatial dimension. At this point, one can take issue with an opinion that is especially prevalent among spiritual leaders in the Diaspora. This view—originating in the profound thought of the great Jewish philosopher, Franz Rosenzweig—holds that the Jewish people relinquished the dimension of *place* retaining the dimension of time alone. Should one choose to interpret this maxim not as a flight of poetic expression whose purpose is to call attention to a certain truth by flowery overstatement, then it is absolutely meaningless because it is impossible to separate the notion of time from the notion of place.

The natural unfolding of time cannot be cut off from the tangible impressions of a specific territorial environment because the timing of events is fixed by observing the rhythms of that environment. The observations are landmarks used to divide time and impose shape on its flow, and of course these events occur not only in time but also in space. Every calendar reflects a local landscape, and an examination of the Jewish calendar shows that its seasons are those of Eretz Israel, and the seasons of Eretz Israel also mark the historic events that determined the Jewish people's attitude to its land. Moreover, from a *halakhic* standpoint, the sole authority for sanctifying the year for Jews in the Diaspora resides in the Bet Din of Eretz Israel; Eretz Israel is therefore the organizing principle of their annual cycle. It was through a common annual cycle that the Jewish people drew the presence of its land into its diasporic existence (which is what was meant by the statement that the course of time broadened so as to fill the role of spatial dimension, too). One way or another, the dimension of time gains the upper hand over the dimension of space.

However, even preceding the Exile, Jewish culture emphasized historic memory as the central motif of national experience; without this, the Jewish people would not have been able to exist in the Diaspora even expanding its perception of time to include space. In order to know who it is and what its goal is, the Jewish people need to preserve specific historic events in its memory: the journeys of the Patriarchs, the enslavement in Egypt, the Exodus, the presence at Mt. Sinai, the wanderings in the desert, conquest and settlement in Eretz Israel, the kingdoms of David and Solomon, the establishment of the Temple in Jerusalem, its destruction, Exile, the return to Zion, and once again, destruction and exile. This procession of events was set in the consciousness of the people by a constant effort to renew memory—repeatedly instilling it with an immediate relevancy, interpreting contemporary occurrences in its light. Jewish holidays are *appointed days;* appointed in the sense of occasions for assembly, times for encountering historic memories and expectations. It is the overlay of immediate events on the background of history that determines self-perception and the direction of life. In every holiday, even more on commemorative days that are not holidays, the people encounter its past and its future. The people remember what has been and anticipate a longed-for future, thereby stretching the present as a midway station on the ongoing journey. The expression of such a world outlook and set of values is particular to Jewish culture. The noblest creation to typify the Jewish way of life was distilled in the process of shaping the time pattern: the Sabbath, the holidays and festivals, and the latent and overt connections between them. The Jewish calendar incorporates a comprehensive life-plan for the people, its communities, families, and individuals.

These things were so obvious in the past that they were taken for granted. The Jewish people was isolated from its non-Jewish environment by the way in which it marked its years, and the structure of its calendar. It numbered years from the time of the Creation and the Exodus from Egypt, whereas others counted time from the birth of their Messiah or the migration of their Prophet. Jews apportioned months by coordinating the solar year and the lunar month, whereas for other peoples it was either by lunar months or by solar year alone. The Jewish people rested on the Sabbath, others on Sunday or on Friday; holidays were celebrated by each people according to their own calendar. During the same cosmic time, three distinct time cycles co-existed—existed; so long as Jews maintained their isolation within their own cycle, they did not assimilate—even when they absorbed many of the influences of their surroundings. Actually there is no better indication of assimilation than the departure of Jews from their own time cycle, marking their years—as well as their months and days—according to the Common Era. The different calendar was the carrier of a different culture. The return to Zion reinstated the dimension of space into the life of the Jewish people, but this has not brought a commonality in which the people live exclusively within a Jewish time dimension, a condition that characterized them during most of the Diaspora years. Arguably, the return of the people to selfhood calls for a comprehensive amalgamation so that the parameters of time and the parameters of space become as one.

THREE STRUCTURAL PRINCIPLES
OF THE CALENDAR

How does a people establish its calendar? It does so by fixing events or acts in a recurring cycle. Initially, the focus is on natural occurrences that appear in a set rhythm that mark equal units of time: the daily cycle of the sun, the monthly cycle of the moon, the cycle of the seasons. Society has obviously chosen to recognize these natural events as its measure of time. With the broadest possible consensus, this measure of time appears to be so taken for granted that it enjoys universal human acceptance, as though it were a law of Nature, for these are the occurrences that shape the permanent conditions of man's existence. These natural events are like a structure in which man establishes his home; at the same time, it is the consensus itself that utilizes the delineations of time, and it is the consensus itself that interprets the meaning and structure that is created. (This notion will be examined below.) There is another kind of natural cycle that marks the organization of time—the episodes of biological growth that are part of an individual's life: childhood, maturity, old age, and the course of generations, in keeping with the Aristotelian concept "when things arise upon the passing of former ones." In this context, even if the cycle of biological time is a given and imposed upon man as fate, an a priori consensus is implicit because the intervals between the episodes are inexact, their determination is consensual and particular to each culture.

We are, in any case, confronted with time determining events in an impersonal cycle: cosmic time; and time determining events in personal life: biological time; these two categories are joined by occurrences whose sequence is a purely consensual matter. These are occurrences or deeds that express goals and outcomes that man himself has chosen to fix, milestones that mark a triumph or a defeat in the people's struggle for a goal it has set itself. The people superimposes these events on the cycle of cosmic time, and as the cycles recur, they emphasize them, thus placing them in the progression of history. There are three structural principles of the calendar and annual cycles as units of time: the cosmic principle sets the measured units of night and day, month, year, and season; the biological principle determines a course for individuals as they develop and change, and marks communal times in the tempo of the generations; and the historic principle marks events that symbolize the goals and aspirations of the people, events that express the value judgments that determine a way of life.

There is a strong tension between the first and second principles. No culture can disregard either of them, but there are important differences between cultures regarding what is appropriate and what is emphasized. This can be experienced either as external determinism or as the exercise of free will. The former is man's fate as imposed on him by the facts of his life; the latter is man's ability to decide freely. On the one hand, life is shaped from without by objective and concrete conditions of existence; on the other hand, life is molded from within by a subjective competence. In the first case, a cyclical structuring of time revolves along a permanent mechanical course:

> One generation passeth away, and another generation commeth;
> And the earth abideth forever.
> The sun also rises, and the sun goes down
> And hastens to his place where he arises.
> The wind goeth towards the south
> And turneth about unto the north;
> It turneth about continually in its circuit,
> And the wind returneth again to its circuits...
> That which has been is that which shall be,
> And that which has been done is that which shall be done;
> And there is nothing new under the sun.
>
> Ecclesiastes 1:4–10

But contrary to this perception, there is a different kind of linear progression of time, which flows from the past to the future. Each station between them carries within it the uniqueness of ever new singular events and takes note of accomplishments and goals. It appears that the biological course binds these two time structures together for it describes a course of progressive growth toward maturity and an objective datum of the nature of things as perceived through the internal experience of the self as a natural "given." Even if it were possible to underscore the linear-developmental aspect of growth in time we would still be confronted by the cyclical nature of these events, which is invariably deterministic. This then is the tension that exists between two poles: the cosmic time of a culture as opposed to its historic time.

The clearest expression of the deterministic world view linked to the dimension of cosmic time is a belief in the influence of the planets and stars. (It should be stressed that in and of itself belief is an act of will, a choice, an agreement; it is the mode that man chooses when he interprets the meaning of the facts of his life.) This belief interprets the notion that the movement of the heavenly bodies has a shaping influence on the way the world looks and the processes that become the conditions of human life as an articulation of absolute determinism. All of man's events and deeds become subject to a predetermined cyclical principle. Thus the positions of the stars can be read as a map of events that are preordained. Regardless of what man may think or desire, the disposition of the stars will decree what happens by a system of cause and effect. As we have noted, to accept this is to negate man's free will. One can opt for determinism and shape one's life accordingly. Will the historic dimension then disappear? Certainly not, since every choice, including acceptance of determinism, calls for decisions and concretizes a historic process. But the aspiration to conceive of a fixed course, even in something that appears to be open and emerging, repeatedly invokes myth from within the historic narrative and subordinates the historic process to predesigned patterns.

Consequently, myth fashions linear time into a cycle. This is indeed the characteristic perception that the cultures of pagan peoples hold about time. The zodiac and the various forces of nature govern events in time, shaping its course by means of myth. The Jewish people has an opposite belief. It does not deny the palpable effect of heavenly bodies and other forces of nature on man's life, nor does it completely uproot myth from every corner of life. But the belief in one supra-cosmic Creator of the world banishes sovereignty from the zodiac and from natural forces, and linear historic time is superimposed on cyclical deterministic time. In this way a vista is opened to the freedom of man's willed choice in shaping the content of his life and determining his fate. This first hallmark characterizes and singles out the Jewish calendar from calendars that are typical of pagan peoples: the Jewish calendar is linear shaped time, the shape progressing from past to future in a straight (or spiraling but progressing) line that stands out in contrast against the background of the cyclical time of the zodiac.

UNITS OF TIME

Again and again, historic time is emphasized yet not made exclusive. According to its own conception, the historic shaping of time interprets the consensual characteristics of events that mark the annual calendar; the intent here is not only historic events, which are celebrated at the same time from year to year, but also the manner in which there is a consensual shaping of cosmic time. Ostensibly the transitions from day to night, the waning and waxing of the moon, and the change of seasons are givens over which man has no control. But this is not so. The meaning attached to these cosmic events can completely alter the sense of existing in time. The various orientations that cultures possess have shaped vastly different time frames. Take, for instance, the consensual observation of the transition from day to night. One can measure a 24-hour period beginning at sunset, or one can measure it from dawn onward. The factual data remain unchanged but there is a definite difference in the significance of the event for the person who experiences it. Another example: when measuring larger units of time one can prefer either the lunar or the solar cycle; the cosmic data remain unchanged. Their meaning changes. Ultimately, it is clear that short time frames, those which extend between a twenty-four-hour period and a month, are the result of consensus: the month is divided by the moon's cycle—half as it waxes and half as it wanes, and each half is further subdivided into a half, giving one units of a week. This is an intentional division of time in a harmonious, symmetrical structure that gives man an inclusive grasp of time as well as an orientation to time. Not only is the division consensual, but so is the way in which the days are joined into units of a week. The day of rest as a marker of time can be set in a number of places, and one can count the days toward the end of the weekly cycle in an ascending order, or from the end of the cycle in a descending order. Of course, such differences in the manner of counting are symbolic, but they do provide a concrete perception concerning the shape of time.

Another consensual way of formulating the units created by markers of

cosmic time is by introducing specific content into special days—
holidays and festivals—and consolidating those special days as symbols.
Focusing attention on a phenomenon of nature fosters the sense of a cycle
that repeats itself and is interpreted in myth. But it is also possible to
invest the delineators of cosmic time with historic content and utilize
natural phenomena as a means that will invoke cultural/historic memory.
This method does not break the cyclicity; on the contrary, cyclicity has
to be maintained. It is only that from year to year a linear progression
becomes intertwined within cyclicity; the result is a special dimension of
"newness." This quality of novelty is superimposed on the progression of
the past toward a future, which is both an end and a goal.

Ultimately, every culture has its own forms by which the consensual
transition from one age to another age is arranged in the course of
biological time: rituals of birth, maturation, marriage, burial, and so forth.
These ceremonies do not have set stations along the cosmic course, for
they relate to the individual. Each individual has a personal, biological
time; the culture only sets the applicable form for each event. But
biological time does infiltrate the permanent calendar, and the calendar
has ceremonies prepared for these occasions (specified days in which the
public customarily takes note of events and whose permanent arrangements have a consensual form). These events, too, become part of the
permanent cycle, even if each time it is other individuals who celebrate
their own occasion in the public life cycle; the large outer perimeter of
cosmic time remains the cycle of the year and its seasons.

Society recognizes more extensive groupings of time: periods, eras;
indeed, these break out of the annual calendar. Their boundaries are not
set, nor do they adhere to a cycle. They are set in the historic course only
ex post facto; only then are they commemorated in the fixed annual round
of the year. Nonetheless it is possible to stretch natural time beyond the
confines of cosmic time by an objective symbolization of the rhythm of
the generational cycle. According to an inclusive view, biological time is
not exclusively an individual's time. Since it is the time of all individuals,
it is also the time of an entire public that is changing, even if the
individuals do not all change at the same time. Thus the public sounds the
rhythmic beat of the historic process of growth (or decline) by penetrating the natural events which determine the lives of individuals. There are
cultures that extend the calendar in this direction as well. Jewish culture
is one of these, and it is characteristic of it: the cycle of sabbatical and
jubilee years pulses to the rhythm of generations. True, it measures this
cycle by broadening the unit of consensual time created between the day

and the month in order to design the new symmetrical structure of the week. Weeks of years, and weeks of weeks of years, a sabbatical year and a seven-fold sabbatical year. The unit that specified the day as a symmetrical cycle of cosmic time span also sets the symmetrical cycle of biological time. (This is in harmony with the principle that will be expounded below: the principle of renewal along the path that leads to a goal.)

COMBINING TWO COSMIC RHYTHMS:
LUNAR AND SOLAR

As alluded to earlier, the Jewish calendar has certain latent ideational aspects. In examining the calendar's design from the aspect of demarcators of cosmic time, two predilections stand out. When compared to the calendars of the two peoples among whom the Jews lived throughout the period of their exile, what first becomes apparent is the tendency to harmonize two cosmic rhythms that are not identical, the rhythm of the new moon and the rhythm of the solar year. The Christian calendar is a priori fashioned by the rhythm of the solar year; the Moslem calendar by the rhythm of the moon. By means of a constant corrective effort (through leap years and leap months) the Jewish calendar is accommodated to coordinate these two rhythms. The months are reckoned according to the moon while ensuring that the holidays that mark changes in the solar seasons take place at the appropriate time of the year. This strategy probably has historic reasons as well as reasons based in belief and world outlook. Maimonides summarized this matter in *Hilkhot Kiddush HaHodesh* I, 1. "The months of the year are lunar months for it is written, 'A monthly sacrifice each month' and it is written, 'This month shall be the first of your months.' And the sages have said, 'God showed Moses the shape of the moon in a prophetic vision' and said, 'Thus it is—observe and bless it.' Whereas the years that we count are solar years for it is written, 'Observe the month of Spring.'" However, beyond the suppositions that could be made concerning the reasons for this strategy, one fact, whose meaning is authentic for all generations, stands out clearly: the annual calendar that requires correction, mandated by the need to coordinate two types of cosmic time, cannot be understood as the projection of a mechanical sequence of events. It is true that Nature operates according to its laws, but coordinating the units of time that result from its various heavenly bodies is a human operation. This means that it is man who designs the correlation of time sequences according to which he lives his life. For this reason, there is a need for an institution whose decisions will, from time to time, adjust the progression of the calendar; there is a prescribed form for these decisions and a specified ceremony for their enactment. This has been explicitly recognized as early as the period of the first return to Zion.

One of the most important responsibilities of the Great Court in Jerusalem was the intercalation and sanctification of months and years, which called for the insertion into the calendar of additional days and months. Intercalation depended on eyewitness evidence of the appearance of the new moon, on a permanent ceremony for sanctifying the time, and on notification to all the people in Eretz Israel and the Diaspora. Both the process and the ceremony were an expression of the aim to involve the entire people in the dual event of renewal and sanctification; that is, the people were expected to participate in, and experience, the arrangement of time as an activity that must be reconstituted by human beings: the Sages and the evidence of the common people. There were circumstances in which the implications of this concept could not be avoided: what would happen should there be an error in bringing and accepting the evidence? What would happen if there was a disagreement between the Sages on intercalating the month and year? In the well-known dispute between Raban Gamliel and Rabbi Yehoshua in which the date for Yom Kippur was in dispute, Rabbi Akiva's incisive words summarized the Law, "'These are God's appointed times, sanctified days as you shall declare them' whether they occur in their season or not, I have no festivals but these" (*Rosh HaShanah* 24–25).

That is, God undertakes to abide by the decree of the Sages and they have the sole prerogative in the matter. In order to grasp how far-reaching this is, it is important to realize that by this period the Sages already knew how to intercalate months and years using a mathematical formula. Had they wanted to, they could simply have applied a mechanical, mathematical procedure in order to forestall any deviation between the lunar and solar years. They avoided such a step, choosing to maintain the ceremony of soliciting eyewitness testimony, discussion, decision, sanctification, and notification. The transition to a mathematics-coordinated calendar was unavoidably arrived at once the dispersion grew and it was no longer possible to maintain a single calendar for the entire Jewish people according to the traditional practice. Nonetheless, despite the difficulty, from a *halakhic* standpoint there was still a reliance on the High Court's decree, which accorded mathematical adjustments the same validity as sanctifying the month in accordance with testimony; that is, the adjust-ment was still regarded as a human endeavor. This then is the overriding significance that flows from the synthesis of two measurements of time which man is called upon to reconcile. Man is enjoined to sanctify the course of his time. In the relationship between a cosmic course of time and a historic course of time, the cosmic notion carries great weight. Man internalizes this by superimposing a construct on the arrangement of time.

The other tendency, also discerned by means of comparison, is to "flatten" the circular course of time as it moves from past to future, making it linear. Thereby the recurrent cycle symbolizes a road that proceeds in a straight line to a goal. The symbolization is first effected by how small units of time are measured: a day begins on the evening which precedes it, the week is measured from Sunday to the Sabbath. The day, the light, the Sabbath are symbols of a purposeful expansion. The path of time rises in anticipation through the course of days in a week, and Sabbaths in the month, returning to a cyclical course. But the road also points to a linear direction, which subsequently breaks the cycles of the month and the year at sabbatical years and jubilees. Indeed, the jubilee symbolizes the aspiration to a distinct strand upon which all the cycles seem to be threaded from the beginnings of Creation to the End, which is Redemp-tion. This gives rise to the statement that in the Jewish people's grasp of time, more emphasis is put on the historic principle than on the principle of cosmic time. The historic principle dons the cloak of the cosmic principle as it activates the corrective and coordinating mechanism, and shapes the inner flow, which joins the segments. The foundation of the calendar is perforce composed of cycles of months and years but it con-tains a mooring for linear historic time where segments of the cycle can unite, granting perennial recurrence a meaning of perpetual renewal—man's purposeful and believing enterprise.

HARMONIZING THE NATURAL
AND THE HISTORICAL

In examining the relationship between the principles of cosmic and historic time, an additional structural phenomenon is demonstrated. Just as a synthesis was found in the Jewish calendar between computing the solar year and computing the lunar months, a synthesis was found between two principles that determine the starting point for the annual cycle, and consequently a starting point for numbering the years. The

Mishnah speaks of four New Years in the Jewish calendar. Two of them are particularly noteworthy as the start of a reckoning whose impact may be felt throughout one's life and whose significance transcends a limited ritual matter. Indeed these two—whose perimeters intersect each other precisely at midpoint—were also set as starting points for the beginning of the year and for numbering the years. Rosh HaShanah, which falls on the first day of Tishrei, is the New Year of Creation; the year that begins on the first day of Nissan is called the New Year of Kings. Consequently, the Jewish year begins twice, once every six months. In the middle of one cycle, a second cycle begins, and in the middle of the second cycle the first one begins again, and so on; the two numberings intertwine.

Setting the start of an annual cycle and the numbering of years is consensual; it stems from the values on which cultural life is founded. A symbolic significance that interprets the flow of time is contained in this. Examination shows that starting the year and starting the numbering of the years on the first of Tishrei links the enumeration to the beginning of a cosmic cycle, the Act of Creation; to be more precise (the significance of this precision will be understood later), the creation of man. The significance that Rosh HaShanah imparts to the count is both personal and universal: the Day of Judgment; whereas, beginning the year and the numbering of the years on the first of Nissan initiates the enumeration of a historical process, the exodus of the Jewish people from the Egyptian house of bondage. (This is despite the fact that the natural background of the season, Spring, is very much felt and strongly emphasized.) Passover imparts a national and historic significance to the counting, which begins with the first month of Spring, for it registers the Jewish people's emancipation and its aspiration to redemption.

While the distinction between the two new years that are intertwined in an annual cycle and in the numbering of years points up the synthesis between cosmic and historic time, it also directs our attention to the sacred sources on which both new years are based, the books of Genesis and Exodus of the Five Books of Moses. Genesis establishes and interprets the numbering according to the cosmic principle; Exodus interprets the numbering according to the historic principle.

The first chapters of Genesis are, in effect, an interpretation of the basis for counting time since the Creation. One is easily convinced that the purpose of the book is not merely to satisfy curiosity about what happened in the past. The event that took place in the past was the establishment of an order that persists into the present; an order of beings and an order of times, and the book proposes to illuminate the meaning of a constant present, which renews itself in us. The sequence of time that is fixed in the Genesis of today is no less than that of yesterday, as it will also be tomorrow. It testifies to the rhythm of days that begins on the evening before, on the continuum of days that leads to the Sabbath, on the establishment of the sun and the moon that mark time in the cosmic cycle. Only afterward do we move on to biological time, the order of generations as expressed in Noah, the second weekly Bible portion in Genesis that begins with "These are the generations of Noah."

The initial seven days of the created world constitute the world as we experience it daily, heaven and earth and all they contain. The count of seven days is a time frame set by a consensual recurring cultural pattern; consequently, this has become the context for our experience of the spatial and temporal world. The distinction between light and dark is what defines the smallest measure of cosmic time; light is day, and darkness is night. The transition from night to day and from day to night holds a symbolic meaning. It is the distinction between the world as "unformed and void" and orderly existence, between what is shrouded in mystery and what is revealed, between the partial and the complete. By these distinctions, time acquires its direction of flow from evening to day. Scripture testifies "there was evening and there was morning," and this testimony is repeated six times. Six times for six days, named as the days of the week in the unchanging tempo of time—to this very day. Day one, second day, third day, to the seventh day. This is the sequence of the continuing, consecutive relationship from day to day; the exception is Sunday, which is called day one. The commentators take note of this.

Apparently the role of this day is not only to serve as the first day of the week but also to serve as a model for the measure of what a day is, by which all other days are measured. However, when day one is counted as part of the days of the week, it is referred to as all the other days are, the first day in the sequence that marks a continuity which ends on the Sabbath. Here another distinction must be made. The Sabbath is sanctified; in this it is as distinct from the other days as light is different from darkness. It symbolizes the intended perfection of Creation, "and the heaven and the earth were finished and all the host of them, and on the seventh day God finished his work which He had made" (Genesis 2:1–2). It is not a cosmic event that is responsible for the singularity of the Sabbath. Although the seventh day encompasses the same measure of time from evening to day as the other days do, it is sanctified and set apart by God through rest. Rest is the completion—or the perfection—of doing. It is the pulse beat of purposefulness. It ratifies the direction of time's flow to a future and to wholeness.

In its first chapter, the Book of Genesis is instructive about how to live in time, with what intent, and with what understanding. There is commentary and amplification of this notion in the Yotzer benediction of the morning prayer when the worshipper greets the new day. The prayer is both a cognitive and experiential enactment of the Creation story. Morning is conceived of as symbolizing the renewal of Creation, "Blessed art Thou, O Lord, Master of the universe, Creator of light, Author of darkness, Architect of peace, and Creator of all that exists, Who grants illumination to the world and all who dwell in it, Who mercifully and bountifully renews the act of Creation on each day." In this context, the term "renews" reveals an ideological principle that is important in understanding the sensation of time in the Jewish calendar. On one hand, the days add on to one another creating a continuity; the weeks assemble one after another creating a continuity, as do the months and years. They constitute a trajectory, not merely a repetition, because though each day comes after the one that precedes it, and before the one that follows, it is also inherently autonomous. It is one alone, unrepeated and unrepeatable, in its singularity. In this sense only is it new as it joins a totality in which every point along the way is both autonomous and integrated in a purposeful design.

Historic time is therefore firmly rooted in cosmic time. The symbolic commentary that orients the alignment of time both confirms cyclicity and departs from it. The cycles do not repeat themselves. They progress one cycle after another. The Book of Genesis embodies this continuity in its stories too, though it does not introduce historical dimension but remains on its fringes. The transitional segment is, as noted, the biological measure of time, or the sequence of generations. From the Creation story, which reaches its peak in the creation of man, the Book of Genesis goes on to tell the story of the first generations, and in this connection the narrative form carries great weight. The Book of Genesis is presented as part of "these are the generations." Nature exists through the fruitfulness and multiplicity of every plant and living thing. Man too exists through the continuity of the generations. But man is responsible for his fate. His life is not merely a continuation and repetition of those who preceded him. Each man is unique and each generation is singular, and it is on this singularity that they are judged. Consequently the continued existence of human generations is the continuation of a story, whereas the other creatures of nature repeat a permanent cycle and have no story. The historical narrative thus originates in the association of the generations.

Admittedly, a precise reading of this narrative of beginnings uncovers a somewhat cyclical structure. Each generation is like a circle that completes itself, and an additional cycle departs from it to repeat a parallel course. The biblical narrative describes a progression of generational cycles, each cycle containing ten generations: Adam and his generations, Noah and his generations, Abraham and his. The fate of these generations is analogous. When the generations of man are replete with sinfulness, they are drowned in the flood; the world once again becomes unformed and void. Once again there is a first man—Noah, but the generations of Noah too are filled with sin; although the world is not sentenced anew to be unformed and void, a new beginning must be made after the debacle of that generation. Abraham is again a founder of a different humanity, which will descend from him within the continuity of generations. Yet it is clear that this is not a cycle that repeats itself like the cycle of those who give birth and those who are born. Generational time is not exclusively cyclical, it moves forward. Noah withstands a trial that Adam failed, and Abraham is tested and succeeds as no man before him. Abraham is the first to undertake living in anticipation of a promised— yet not concrete—future.

In this decision to cut himself off from the aspiration of returning to a lost Garden of Eden at the beginning of time, to strive instead toward an envisioned future, Abraham establishes the dimension of history. This is actually the significant literary fact: in the transitional process from the narrative of Adam to the narrative of Noah, and from the narrative of Noah to that of Abraham, we depart from a prehistoric mythical stratum to enter into the sphere of historic narrative. The figure of Abraham is possessed of historic characteristics, whereas that of Noah is still bound by mythic characteristics. Abraham is the founder of a people. A people is a continuous unity of generations; therefore there is no people who does not possess a history as such. History is the dimension in which the people exist. At narrative's end in Genesis, the story of the generations has come to an end, and the annals have begun. It is at this point that the Book of Exodus takes up its burden.

Just how the constitutive narrative of Genesis is reflected in the renewing life cycle of the people remains, however, to be examined. As has been noted, the *Yotzer* benediction of the morning prayer introduces Chapter One of Genesis into the perpetual life cycle, which is renewed daily and weekly. Where does the annual cycle come full circle? On Rosh

HaShanah, which occurs on the first of Tishrei. This is the New Year of Creation. While it is true that the Rosh HaShanah prayer mirrors the Book of Genesis, it is rooted in the second chapter, which is a kind of retelling of the Creation story, whose concern from here on is not the establishment of a cosmic progression but rather the creation of man and the continuity of his generations. Rosh HaShanah marks the creation of man rather than the creation of the world. The weekly cycle is linked to the Creation and the Sabbath is a testimony to the act of creation in the sense of Genesis, Chapter One; whereas Rosh HaShanah occurs on the sixth day of Creation, the day on which man was created. This is the shift from a cosmic time cycle to a biological time cycle.

The books of generations begin with the creation of Adam and Eve, and the chronicles of their lives. The narrative of Adam's deeds in the Garden of Eden, and of subsequent deeds, are part of this shift. This is a story of trial and sin, a story of failures. The world of Nature obeys its Creator's will and is true to itself, always whole never judged; whereas man, who is intended for a higher perfection because he is dependent on his own will and deeds, is judged. Rosh HaShanah is also a day of judgment, a day when man's actions are assessed and his fate decreed; is he entitled to an existence or not? This concept, which has its origins in the Book of Genesis, is expressed in the integrated liturgy of Rosh HaShanah. It is also found in the biblical portion read on both days of Rosh HaShanah abstracted from the narrative of Abraham's life—the banishment of Hagar and Ishmael as well as the binding of Isaac— underscoring man's perception that the context in which man is judged is in the continuity of his generations. (In a subsequent consideration of the elements that compose Rosh HaShanah, this matter will be dealt with in greater detail.)

Historical time, which shapes the Jewish calendar, is anchored in the cosmic and biological concepts of time in Genesis, but it becomes institutionalized according to the narrative in Exodus. The historical narrative is, of course, set in a specific time that occurs within the scope of cosmic time. Passover, when the story of the exodus from Egypt is recalled, comes in Nissan, the month of spring. The Festival of Shavuot, which recalls the Jewish people's settling in the Land as well as the Time of the Giving of the Law, occurs during the period when the first fruits are gathered. The Festival of Sukkot in which the people's wandering in the desert is recalled takes place at the autumn harvest season. Rooted in the natural cosmic cycle, the symbolic significance of the seasons transcends that context and enters the historic course. Indeed, the course opens with

Passover, which marks the second beginning of the year and is the more important of the two beginnings from this standpoint. The exodus from Egypt is the event that constitutes the existence of the Jewish people. The people's annals as a people begin here, and the memory of this event is intended to give concrete shape to the Jewish people's consciousness of historical time from generation to generation.

This statement bears emphasis and explanation. The cyclical picture of cosmic time arises in human consciousness as a direct response to the natural occurrences that determine the conditions of human life on earth. It is generally organized by Myth, and indeed Myth conceptualizes, in images, the experiential material of natural occurrences into a specific shape and lends them meaning, but Myth does not generally require the raising of human experience to a higher supernatural and supersensory sphere. Moreover Myth does not return man to a non-immanent point in the past nor does it project on to a non-immanent point in the future. For pagan Myth, the past and the future view of the cycle become identical as a perpetual now. The past is a future that may recur, and the future is a past that is about to recur, just as the present has already been and shall be. Contrary to Myth, historical time is an undertaking of memory and hope. Historical time begins with a memory of a one-time past, which has happened never to return and comes full circle in a hope of a one-time unprecedented future. Necessarily, the sensation of the present must also become different than that of the cyclical picture of time. The present is the span of activity that stretches between an event or action in which we start and a point in time in which we expect a conclusion. Thus it too is shaped by memory and hope. Past and future are not cut off from the present, and are not foreign to it. Interest in them is not merely curiosity. The past and the future are the two poles that define the present and dictate its direction.

Just as the space in which we operate acquires an organized structure by the objects which are placed in it and which we traverse; similarly, the time in which we function acquires an organized form as a result of certain events we negotiate. The past and the future are parallels to what lies behind us and what is ahead of us, but of course only a living memory, and only a living vision, can construct a picture of historic time as a present that stretches before us from past to future. This then is the role of the exodus story in shaping the historical time frame of the Jewish people. It begins the year and the historical counting of years. By invoking the memory of the event that established the people, it sets a direction for the people's history and its enterprise. Furthermore, it positions that memory at the furthermost horizon of time and denotes the direction toward which the people strive; on the horizon of the future it radiates a vision of the teleological future conclusion. This story shapes the image of the course of time in which the people stride. Throughout its history, the people go from Egyptian bondage toward a perfect redemption in its homeland.

As we have noted, the historical track is not a product of experiencing direct and tangible events in Nature. Man perceives the historical track when he remembers and hopes; more precisely, man comes to this perception when memory and hope become more than truncated flashes or passing glimpses. When memory and hope consolidate, they become a continuity, a living reality in which man attempts to shape his deeds and way of life in accordance with this continuity. In order to live in the historic track, man must transcend the sensory present and actively live the events preserved in his memory as well as the vision that radiates from memory toward his future. This is an ongoing effort to create an additional strata of reality above sensory experiences in the natural cycle. It is not, of course, isolation from experience in the natural cycle, which, in any case, is impossible. On the contrary, man strongly relies on natural events so that he may rise to a sphere that is exclusively a product of man's willed enterprise. Collective memory is the arena of continuous existence in such a sphere. It is only by understanding the implications of this that the way in which Jewish holidays and festivals are shaped as markers of historic time can be well understood.

In light of this, one turns first to the literary character of the Exodus narrative as a story that is intended to shape the structure of time. This is clearly the story of an actual historic event, and it is solely as such an event that it has meaning. But it is also clear that the *story* cannot be construed as history in the conventional sense. It is a guidepost emblem-atically designed to articulate the importance that the people ought to attach to the historic event. It is only thus that the event can remain vivid in memory and it is only thus that the event can point a direction for future deeds and endeavors, which will carry forward its importance and purpose. In other words, as it is narrated in Exodus, the event is remembered and repeatedly recalled anew by the people who were established as a result of it. It is the ceremonial formula that one generation recites to another so that each generation will regard itself as having left Egypt and going to its own land. What are the details of this process and what is the structure of meanings which rise from the story? These questions will be dealt with in the chapter devoted to Passover.

Here, however, we are dealing with the shaping principle from the perspective that historic time assigns to the formation of the calendar. The cycle of cosmic time proceeds from the New Year on the first of Tishrei through permanent cyclical coordinates that recur in a measured, steady rhythm: the beginnings of months, Sabbaths, transitions from day to night, the changing seasons of the year—spring, harvest, and the bringing of the first fruits. From the New Year on the first of Nissan, a cycle stretches out that connects the cycles of time to the historic dimension: Passover, Shavuot, Sukkot, Shemini Atzeret. These are followed by the holidays and festivals that were initiated with the Jewish people's significant happenings in its later history: Hanukkah, Purim, and Yom HaAtzmaut as redemptive events; Tisha B'Av, the Tenth of Tevet, and Holocaust Remembrance Day as events of destruction and mourning. How do these two tracks combine without canceling each other's uniqueness? That is, how can a two-tiered system of holidays and festivals be simultaneously maintained while underscoring the different points of departure and distinction with equal emphasis?

The cosmic cycle that opens on the first of Tishrei and is subsequently marked through Yom Kippur, beginnings of months, and Sabbaths, has both a personal existential and a universal spiritual meaning that permanently relates to man. The historic cycle adds the three pilgrimage festivals as well as holidays and days of commemoration, but it is transmitted through the Sabbath as well. Despite the distinction between the cycles, there is no marking of cosmic time that does not have a historic dimension; nor is there a marker of historic time that is not linked to a cyclical event in nature to which a symbolic meaning has been attached.

The seam that binds the two cycles and places them in equilibrium is the cycle of Sabbaths, which proceeds in a steady and equal rhythm throughout the years. This is the reason that the Sabbath enjoys a special emphasis in the Jewish calendar, and of course this distinction stems from the frequency of the Sabbath. The distance between Saturdays is brief and fixed, and before the impact of one Sabbath has waned, the impression of the next Sabbath rises. The Sabbath creates an unbroken thread between holidays and festivals, a thread whose continuity is palpable though this is not the only reason for the prominence of the Sabbath. A no less important reason is the intensity and richness of its content. Here, too, we defer detailed discussion to a later chapter, which deals specifically with the Sabbath; at this point only its relationship to the overall structure and meaning of the calendar is emphasized. The Sabbath is mentioned initially at the beginning of Genesis in a very specific place: the end of the Creation story; and again, at the beginning of Exodus, also in a very specific place: the end of the narrative of the people's departure from Egypt. Admittedly, it is mentioned several more times in the Book of Exodus, entering the calendar from both its cosmic and historic strata. The formula for the Sabbath *kiddush* in the prayer book reflects and balances them both. "Thou hast graciously given us Thy holy Sabbath as a heritage, in remembrance of the Creation. The Sabbath is the first among the holy festivals which recall the exodus from Egypt." Sabbath is a commemoration of both the act of Creation and the exodus from Egypt. The depth and wealth of elements in the Sabbath derive from this dual strata, and from the important role of keeping this duality in balance.

A meeting between the two strata and a mutual utilization of the elements of each can also be found in the structure of every important holiday in the Jewish calendar. There is no holiday with historic content that is without a distinct basis in a nature holiday. It is a fixed and structural phenomenon. The Torah drew on an existing infrastructure of natural life, which was observed among the Israelites but also among environing peoples. The Festival of Passover is a spring festival. Shavuot is a holiday of gathering the first grains, perhaps also firstlings among the flocks; and Sukkot is a harvest holiday. Moreover, a thorough examination of the sources of holidays that were inaugurated in the post-Torah era, such as Hanukkah and Purim, reveals that natural events, already observed, were also at their root, "liberated" by historical memory when it transposed their significance. The Oral and Written Law created a historical strata that was superimposed on the natural strata. It is instructive that this addition did not shunt aside the previous strata of important holidays or eclipse it; quite the opposite, it was emphasized by transforming its meaning. The tangible natural event is seen as a supporting symbol for giving new life to historic memory, and the ceremony that animates the memory is anchored in a previous ceremony that marked a natural occurrence. Thus the historical layer rests on the natural layer, deriving palpable strength as it redirects meaning by introducing a natural festival to the memory and vision of the historic course of time.

ALIGNING THE CALENDAR
AND EXPERIENCING MEMORY

So far the complex character of the Jewish calendar has been observed from two aspects: harmonizing the lunar and solar year, and harmonizing the cosmic and the biological cycles on the linear historic track. We have seen that such a consonance has continuously played a creative, cultural role. It is involved in a permanent effort of aligning the calendar and a constant effort of recalling and experiencing memory. The Jewish calendar is a creation renewed on permanent foundations, which brings us to another aspect of the effort to harmonize the ordering of time. The cyclical track aspires to the permanent. It refuses to change, choosing to contend with it; it is inherently conservative. But the historic track traverses change and cannot overlook it. The historic track cannot exist without constant notice of these two tendencies, which are of course mutually dependent but also subject to an intense tension between them. On the one hand, there is a tradition that strives for a punctilious conservatism; on the other hand, there is a historical consciousness that tends towards the novel as it is expressed in the singular event. In its evolution over the generations to the present, the Jewish calendar is a creation that has been shaped between these two tendencies. There is probably no need to stress the conservative tendency. The contemporary generation whose daily experience is characterized by rapid and radical change is predisposed to the novel and rejects conservatism; it is therefore quite aware of the inflexible conservatism of the tradition both insofar as the calendar is concerned and in other aspects of life. Differences are not detected so that the annual cycle appears to revolve around an unchanging axis. One Sabbath resembles another, every Rosh HaShanah resembles every other, as does every Passover. The same cycle of prayers, the same liturgical poems, the same Haggadah.

Is it feasible to live the progression of historic time in this manner? In comparing the Jewish people's way of life, ostensibly petrified at the foot of Mt. Sinai, to other peoples in their environs poised to compete on the same historical course, one of the greatest Jewish thinkers of this century, Franz Rosenzweig, developed an approach that says that the Jewish people exists in an eternal dimension of time, which transcends history. Its biographical cycle ended when the Jews went into exile; since then it revolves in a perpetual, annual cycle, from Egypt to Sinai and from Sinai to its land—as opposed to the biography of contemporary time, which can only be transient. Cyclical permanence is undeniably sharply marked in the Jewish calendar. This permanence is not only a natural tendency of tradition, it is also an absolute need of cultural life—the basis of sequential identity. In no way is this the only and singular characteristic. Close examination reveals that there is also a dimension of how things are designated as historical events and how they become transformed with

regard to changes in the way the calendar is set (e.g., the transition from
sanctification of the year according to eyewitnesses to sanctification
based on computations), as well as the changing design and content of
every holiday.

Two types of events become markers of time in the calendar: holidays
whose intent is to highlight a sense of having been rescued, and days that
commemorate destructions and decrees. Since the history of the Jews
during its generations of exile was inundated by events of the second type,
there was a surfeit of such days to the point that some were displaced by
others. A measure of permanence and special prominence was assigned to
those commemorative days connected to destructions of the Temple,
particularly the Ninth Day of Av. From the biblical period to the present
day Hanukkah and Purim are events of the first type, which have been
added to the calendar. These holidays hold a special status. In addition to
historical memory per se, to marking historical periods that have differing
conceptual values and aspirations than those of the biblical period, these
two holidays represent a principle of the calendar's openness to incorporate signs of change. Hanukkah and Purim testify to the notion that even
in exile the Jewish people did not exit from history. Purim connotes the
historical sense of reality of a people in exile. The people live and
confront each historical hour. Actually there is no more conspicuous
evidence of this claim than developments in the last generation. Within a
thirty-year span, a number of new holidays and days of commemoration
were added to the calendar that our forefathers could not have conceived
of.

The entire unit of time stretching from Passover to Shavuot has been
refashioned by these additions: Holocaust Remembrance Day, Memorial
Day for the Fallen of the Israel Defense Forces, Yom HaAtzmaut, and
Jerusalem Day. The rejuvenation and heightened emphasis placed on Tu
B'Shevat, Lag B'Omer, and Tu B'Av—whose profiles in the tradition were
flaccid and pale—must be added to these totally new days. The return to
Zion served to pour new content into these vessels, activating and
accentuating them at least for a large segment of the people who sought
a fuller expression of its Jewish national identity.

Similar insights arise from an examination of the content and form of
each individual holiday in its process of crystallization. As transmitted by
the contemporary tradition, each is multi-faceted. There is no holiday
that has not undergone a number of transformations, some quite decisive.
Indeed, there are holidays whose character so changed at a certain stage
of their consolidation as to become unrecognizable. It is, however, a

surprising fact that despite changes in character, the process is generally one of accretion, which does not delete that which has already been accepted and sanctified. Of course this is not the case when decisive internal considerations prevent the continuation of certain forms (e.g., the termination of the sacrifices when the Temple was destroyed), but even then there is not a complete displacement; rather substitutions that retain at least a memory of what once was, with some new amendment. All of which results in a multi-layered composition that flows from the Bible through the Mishnah, the Talmud through the rabbinic literature, the literature of Kabbalah and Hasidism to contemporary writings. Granted, certain generations excelled in their creative contributions while others made almost no additions or deletions. As a rule those generations that experienced a historical juncture were the ones that surpassed in creative contribution. In recent time, the formational impact made by the Kabbalists of Tsfat, on the one hand, and Zionists, on the other, stand out. (This topic will be examined in greater detail in the chapters dealing with each holiday.)

On the strength of this, it must be said that the calendar is not only the manifestation of a life cycle that revolves around a permanent axis but alternatively it is a collection of impressions of the history of the Jewish people. From the creative materials gleaned at each new hour in its biography, the Jewish people designs a monument. The public that lives according to the cycle of the calendar passes through all the strata of this creation: the Bible, Mishnah, Talmud, rabbinical literature, prayer book, liturgical poetry, Kabbalistic and philosophic literature, and modern Hebrew literature. It experiences the people's long journey through them: as though they left Egypt themselves, stood at the foot of Mt. Sinai, wandered in the desert, occupied the land, established the monarchy, and built the Temple; as though the Temple crumbled upon them and as though they were exiled and returned to rebuild it, and the Temple was destroyed again, and they went into exile once more. As though while in exile they dreamt the redemptive dream, and in the exile went through the Holocaust, as though they fought the people's War of Liberation in their land, and as though in their own day, they devote themselves to the redemptive enterprise.

For a person who lives the Jewish calendar in such a way, it is as though he links the entire historic course within his personal life. He does so by virtue of recognizing the uniqueness of the historic hour that is his. This is his period because the past is only the direction from whence he came to the present, according to which he will yet continue. Just as the calendar was open to contemporary events of the past, so it is available to the present and will be available to the future. The maintenance of the calendar—as is apparent from all that was said above—is an ongoing role, a creative endeavor. This calendar is bound to the pool of its sources as a wheel rests on a fixed axis but like the revolving wheel it must renew itself with every revolution of its cycle.

TWO

INDICATORS OF TIME:
HOLIDAYS AND FESTIVALS

SANCTIFYING TIME

Indicators of time are days that are highlighted by specific acts in order to remind, experience, and interpret changes in Nature, in the individual's course of life, or in the biography of a people. They differ from one another not only in content but also in their modes of expression, and in the extent to which they have become differentiated from the daily routine in which humans beings are immersed, particularly in their work and ordinary interactions. There are indicators that last several days while some are limited to one day only. Some have a wealth of content, some are sparse; some are highly regarded, some hardly felt. This is true of changes in the calendar. Indicators that were once considered most important become forgotten, almost abandoned, while others are charged with new value. For example, Tu B'Av, which was important in ancient times, was almost forgotten after the Exile, whereas Tu B'Shevat, which initially had merely formal *halakhic* significance, has been rejuvenated in the present era. Clearly, there are differences in form and prominence between old holidays rooted in primary sources and holidays of more recent origin, and between holidays constituted in a natural/historic stratum and days dedicated to a specific historical memory alone. Several indicators of time in the Jewish calendar: the Sabbath, Rosh HaShanah and Yom Kippur, and the three pilgrimages—Passover, Shavuot, and Sukkot—have been accorded the highest degree of prominence. These are followed by Hanukkah and Purim inaugurated in the early period, and Hag HaAtzmaut—Israel Independence Day—in the present era. Alongside these are days of commemoration for tragedies that befell the people—most outstanding, the Ninth of Av and Holocaust Memorial Day.

These are the indicators that shape the compass of the Jewish calendar in the modern period. The existence of such holidays as Rosh Hodesh, Tu B'Av, the Tenth of Tevet, Lag B'Omer, and others can be felt in the diversity of the calendar but they have a low profile, virtually not rising above the horizon of ordinary days. Nor are secular days without moments of anticipation and specialness—unconnected to holidays—punctuated as they are by prayer, and mealtime blessings. Consequently the time sequence is sensed by means of the day, week, month, and year, through many ascents and descents, changes, and varieties. In this chapter, the aim is to examine the mode in which indicators of time are shaped in the Jewish calendar. What sets them apart and how do they differ from general days? To this end, we apply ourselves to the more important time indicators, those that shape the overall structure of the Jewish calendar: the Sabbath, Rosh HaShanah, and Yom Kippur, and the three pilgrimage holidays.

Such days are of course holidays but the consideration here is more with how they were crystallized than with the quality of ritual that ennobled them with the title *hag* or *hagigah*, celebration or festivity. What is a celebration? A day whose separation from other days is most decisive and apparent, a day with an elevated ritual status. A holiday is a sanctified day. To understand the significance, the notion of sanctity must first be examined. Sanctity is the particular status with which humans invest a spiritual or physical presence: God, humans, objects, places and times, deeds, thoughts, and feelings as differentiated from all other days, deeds, feelings, and thoughts. Two actions affect this special status. First, a distinction that detaches and sets apart; second, elevation to the highest degree of importance—that is, attributing sanctity to that which is regarded as above the sanctifier and at the peak of his scale of values.

We begin with the action of separation. A sanctified thing is something that has been differentiated so that it stands alone, but not every separation is a distinction and not every distinction is a step in the direction of sanctity; after all, there is nothing that is not separate and distinct from every other thing. The act of sanctification has a quality of severing or, more precisely, it is absolute. The sanctified matter is perceived as totally different from all other things, at least in one specific aspect. Therefore one can distinguish between gradations of sanctity. Believers say that in the full sense of the term the *truly* sacred is absolutely distinct in every aspect and different in purpose than all other essences in the world, that is to say, God. All other sacred things relate to Him, are elevated toward Him, or symbolize Him, and it is in this sense that they possess sanctity. The notion of sanctity then belongs essentially to the sphere of religious experience. One could, however, apply the concept to matters that are *relatively* separated and *relatively* elevated in that they are subject to the verdict of the sanctifier who perceives himself as supremely sovereign in his life, but it would be proper to remember that this is a borrowed sanctity. True sanctity can only be found where man recognizes a presence that stands above him absolutely, and serves as the source of all his assessments. Therefore, if a holiday is a sanctified day it is a priori a religious institution. This does not mean that the *secularization* of a holiday is utterly untenable but that secularization converts the holiday into a day of borrowed standing, and experience shows that this is a problematic status difficult to maintain over an extended period of time. This, however, is a topic that requires special attention.

How does a day become consecrated? First of all by its being made distinct. A holiday is a day that is cut off from the consecutive flow of other days and is set apart. This is accomplished by expropriating the day from the domain of ordinary human activity, at least in so far as voluntary, directed activity is concerned. If on all other days time is consigned to man to do anything he desires, or all of his labor, on this day time has been sequestered from his authority. He is not entitled to do as he wishes but is specifically required to do certain things. Indeed, the most important holidays and festivals, Sabbath, Rosh HaShanah, Yom Kippur and the three pilgrimages, are set apart by prohibition of labor. But note that what is in question is not a mere day of rest—a day on which man may rest if he wishes—but a day where a cessation of work is total; work is forbidden even if it is very necessary to man, or if he enjoys it very much, or it is required for his relaxation and recreation. It is this clear and unambiguous decree that grants the act of distinction its character of absolute separation. True there is severity in this, indeed this severity is the essence of the sanctifying experience that is not a priori intended for the gratification and satisfaction of man. It holds an element of awe.

Anyone who presents himself before the sacred stands before a boundary that may not be trespassed; the prohibition is concretized through a threat or punishment suspended from above. The threat is inherent in the absolute otherness itself. Anyone who does not adequately prepare himself in anticipation and does not fulfill its conditions may be dangerously injured when he comes in contact with the sacred or the sanctified. This is the case in the prohibition of labor. The prohibition is a tangible boundary that one may not cross. By this clear demarcation of a boundary line that expropriates time from man's will, the perception of a different time is realized, a time qualitatively different from the time of other days.

This time is infused with a presence so powerful that it thrusts aside the presence of the mundane. The one separate day is formulated as a different presence of time, an *objective* presence which cannot be overlooked. Just as a wall built across a field cannot be overlooked because if it is disregarded one will certainly and painfully collide with it, so time that has been sanctified cannot be overlooked otherwise one will painfully collide with it. Ostensibly we are not dealing with ourselves or our subjective assessments, but with the objective validity of this special time. To the extent that the prohibition of work is accepted as an absolute and unquestionable law, a holiday is characterized as a religious institution. Secularization of a holiday, even when the prohibition of labor is voluntarily retained as a desirable tradition, cancels the objective authority of separated time, which then disintegrates and quickly disappears into the flow of regular time.

Still another question arises that is inherent in the world of religious philosophy. In the previous chapter we saw that the Jewish calendar was purposely structured so as to require decisions of the highest *halakhic* authority, the *Bet Din HaGadol*, to sanctify time. Does this not imply that the sanctity of time is a subjective evaluation that changes nothing in the *quality* of time itself even from a religious perspective? To clarify the question, a distinction must first be made between two orientations related to understanding the concept of sanctity that are found in sources of Jewish thought, beginning with the Bible. One orientation is essentially ritualistic and may be termed the priestly code. According to this orientation, sanctity is the presence of something tangible in the sanctified object. Everything consecrated is charged with the same presence, not unlike a strong radiation that emanates from a godly presence. Anyone not adequately prepared, who has improperly touched a consecrated substance, will be injured much as a person who touches a charged object is shocked because he has not properly insulated himself.

In keeping with this view, sanctified time is time that is charged with a godly presence. Its essence is charged with holiness. An instructive theoretical development in understanding the concept of sanctity can be found in the thought of Rabbi Yehudah HaLevi, author of *The Kuzari*. According to this, sanctity is reserved for the Eretz Israel time-frame, for time began at the start of Creation, and Creation began in Eretz Israel. This applies to the Sabbath as well, which God sanctified by His presence. The Sabbath begins as it enters the borders of Eretz Israel, on Friday at sunset, and continues until it exits that boundary twenty-four hours later. This is the circle of sanctified time in its essence. Anyone who observes the Sabbath in Eretz Israel is therefore in an essentially consecrated place, in an essentially consecrated time. The second orientation is primarily ethical and can be characterized as the prophetic code. In this sense, sanctity is the noble status that attaches to earthly objects, emanating from a consecrating behavior. God alone is essentially holy, elevated above all things and differing from them absolutely. Anything that we individuate in order to express our belief in one God and our obedience to His will becomes sanctified. It is sanctified through thought, feeling, and deed. But inherently, as an object, it holds no sanctity.

According to this concept, sanctified time is time through which man expresses his belief in God and obedience to His will. It is the performance of deeds (or the avoidance of forbidden deeds) that sanctifies time. An instructive theoretical development of this orientation on the notion of holiness is found in the thought of Maimonides, particularly in his *halakhic* tract, *Mishneh Torah*. Maimonides fought bitterly against the assumption that objects, places, or times could be inherently sacred. Everything flows from sanctifying behavior. One can easily see therefore that the question raised earlier is answered differently depending on the different point of view of those who maintain either of the two orientations.

From the position of those close to the objective priestly view, sacred time is clear and simple. God, from whose essence sanctity emanates, wants to take the verdict of the Sages into account and applies His sanctity as if it has been determined by them. From the viewpoint of those close to the prophetic position, what is simple and clear is the connection between sanctity and the decision of the Court. But once the Court has given its decree, obedience to that decree is an assertive, objective demand. God's will is that man shall not disobey it and the threat of punishment, whether social and institutionalized or anchored in the order of the universe, validates it absolutely. That is, even if sanctity is not the essence of time, it is the essence of the obligation that limits that time and defines it from the moment that it becomes sanctified through the Court's decree. One way or another, in both these approaches the prohibition of work expropriates the day from man's sovereignty and presents the sanctified day as an entity possessed of a palpable specialness that truncates the flow of ordinary time, raising it to another horizon.

We come now to a second stage, one of affirmation. A holiday is dedicated to God through service, service in its religious sense: worship of God. The day is freed through the prohibition of labor and refilled with a content of service, and the service of each holiday has a content that delineates its special nature: prayer, Torah readings, the *haftarah*, and the *megillah*, and special requirements such as the seder at Passover, and the sukkah at Sukkot. The service dedicates the day to God and particularizes it, elevates it to a higher plane. If one aspect of sanctifying a day is its expropriation from the realm of man's will, and its element of severity, then the other stage, the affirmative one, returns the day to man as an act of grace from above. By aiming his deeds upward, man is granted a bounty of spiritual life, a bounty of gladness. In this aspect the holiday is genuinely a *yom tov*, a goodly day, a joyful day that is marked by man's emancipation from the slavery and worries of existence that characterize the earthly plane of everyday life.

The opening verses of the special blessing that sanctifies the pilgrimage holidays clearly underscores these two elements in the shaping of the holiday as a sacred day. "Blessed art Thou, O Lord, King of the universe Who has chosen us from among all the peoples, elevated us above all languages and sanctified us through His commandments; And has given us, O Lord, lovingly appointed days for rejoicing, holidays, and times for gladness." Initially the benediction stresses sanctification through a commandment, putting into place the obligation that expropriates the day from the realm of man's desires. Then the blessing notes that holidays and festivals were granted to us. This is the grace that fills the day with gladness and rejoicing whose source is from above, from the sphere of sublime life. Thus the second stage is not feasible if it is not preceded by the first restrictive stage, which separates the day, cutting it off from a previous continuity and directing it toward the other, differentiated continuity.

SYMBOLIC ACTIONS

As a sanctified day, the holiday expresses an aspiration to the absolute perfection of that which is beyond. This aspiration is felt both in the decisive separation and in the injection of positive content. Separation seemingly severs the bonds of man's everyday activity, whereas propelling positive content seeks a fullness that leaves no space for a vacuum in the cut off time. This is—need it be said—an ideal aspiration to which one can strive, but it cannot be enacted in its entirety. Clearly it is impossible to totally sever the physical, mundane bonds of man's life. Natural man exists physically in his body's needs and satisfactions, and unavoidably also in his worries and pain. All these continue to exist during holidays as well. Suspension of work on Sabbaths and holidays, and even more the fast that sanctifies Yom Kippur, are merely symbolic deeds that represent perfection and wholeness beyond man's possibilities of realization in his natural existence. By means of a symbolic detachment from the worries of everyday life, one can, however, lend man's natural needs—eating and drinking, recreation and rest, and social intercourse—a significance that derives from the spiritual content of the holiday. If in everyday life, man eats, drinks, rests, and interacts within his society for the sake of the satisfactions inherent in those deeds, on the holiday he employs them as symbols that express gladness and the grace intrinsic to human existence. Ceremonial meals, socializing, recreation, and rest are transformed into instruments by which to experience the difference linked to the prayer service. Again, this is clearly a symbolic shaping of activity whose basic natural character has been reinterpreted, resolutely maintaining the effort to ennoble.

It is an additional consideration that characterizes the holidays as markers of time and as sacred days: the aspiration to fill time to its maximum by means of symbolic activity. Ordinary secular days are themselves days of activity that fulfill life's demands. But from the standpoint of man's status or his destiny, they are days that do not contain an ongoing scrutiny into the meaning of deeds; they include many moments of mechanical routine, many moments of utter happenstance, many moments of undirected motion, many vacuums in which the momentum of physical activity is not accompanied by attention to design or an intentional orientation of specific significance. Holidays aspire to days of density and the fullness of deeds laden with meaning. All the activities vital to man are like matter on which symbols must be imposed, and it is desirable that, insofar as possible, such symbols not allow for routine emptiness, chance, and absence of intent. In this sense, a holiday is an elevation to a life of significant deeds, both in general and in detail.

As we noted, significant activity calls for a density of symbolic deeds that follow in close proximity on a wide spectrum leaving but a few empty spaces for chance or undirected routine. Such activity also calls for a turn toward observation and reflection, which can raise deeds to the conscious level, interpreting their significance. Each deed requires one to intensively direct one's attention at the start and to conceive a meaning at the end. Indeed this is the thought that shapes the forms of worship that fill the holiday with positive content. The blessing is basically a form of directing the will to a specific action; whereas interpretation, Torah discussions, and homiletics are a way of raising the significance of the action to a level of consciousness. But elevating matters to the cognitive level involves prayer and devotional poetry as well, and all these are distinct attributes of the culture of the holiday.

The Passover seder is a most illuminating example. Here is a festive meal that coalesced as a symbol where the very feast enacts the exodus from slavery to freedom—the assembled guests sitting sumptuously as free men in the midst of their people; where every detail of the feast: the matzah, the bitter herbs, the wine—are all emblematic; where each symbolic action is directed and invoked through a blessing that is immediately interpreted by the Haggadah. The seder meal is an example of a design so copious as to fill symbolic action to its ideal fullness, but every holiday aspires to such a fullness. It may be compared to a monumental work of architectural art in which anyone entering the space that has been designed to express a symbolic meaning senses that none of the component parts remain as they were originally, but each one is so crafted that in its placement it also expresses a certain aspect of the significance of the entire structure. The intense nature of life during the holiday is a deeply felt elevation, and the symbolic actions that are inferred from this elevation have a spillover of meaning for man's life in general.

MONUMENTS OF TIME

In considering the holiday as a sanctified day, we noted that it is separated and differentiated from other days. It now becomes clear that the day is set apart from other days only to be returned to their sequence in a transposed form. Holidays coalesce into their own succession; taken together they comprise an aggregate, while the other days are mediating days within the pattern of the year. The mediating days fill out the pattern and find their rationale within it. If holidays are days carved as monuments of time, replete with symbolic deeds and their interpretations, then clearly they are not intended to interpret themselves alone but to give meaning to man's actions in general. The Sabbath symbolizes and bestows significance on the week; Rosh HaShanah and Yom Kippur give meaning to the annual cycle; the pilgrimages illuminate the significance of activity throughout the seasons. Together they interpret the year in its entirety, and the years merge into seven-year cycles and jubilees.

For people to feel that the holidays symbolize an intended objective for their activity in daily life too, there certainly ought to be a tangible connection between holidays and other days. This link is mentioned during the holidays. It is recited and studied. Study as a mode of observation, as well as man's accountability, are important and positive aspects of a holiday, important and outstanding parts of the service. (This statement will become clearer as each holiday is dealt with individually.) In itself, however, this is not sufficient. The connection must be felt in the activity that shapes both holidays and ordinary days. Ordinary days are indeed interspersed with many signposts where man can pause and glimpse the beyond: prayer times, and mealtime blessings. But these are fleeting moments that do not vanquish routine, nor is it proper that they should.

Routine is vital and desirable in its proper time; nonetheless, these moments are reminders that accord secular days a connection to the Sabbath. In addition to the brief reminders, there is also the preparation before holidays and Sabbaths. Jews count days in anticipation of the Sabbath and prepare themselves for it, beginning early in the week. Much preparation is involved for each of the major holidays. Housecleaning in anticipation of Passover; the count of the *omer* between Passover and Shavuot; the recitation of *slikhot*, the penitential prayers in the period before the Days of Awe; and the arrangements for constructing the sukkah—all these activities orient ordinary days toward the holidays and illuminate the secular days with the anticipated crown of the holiday's radiance. To this must be added those markers of time whose prominence differs in degree from that of the Sabbath—Rosh HaShanah, Yom Kippur, and the pilgrimages. Days such as Hanukkah and Purim mediate between ordinary and sanctified days. They close the gap between one holiday and another, diversifying the quality of deeds and feelings, and they constitute varying degrees in the transition from daily life to the elevated plane of the holiday.

A bond is also created from the thrust of the holiday itself. The activity that fills the holiday with content requires the public's direct and active participation as well as that of the individual within it. The performance of symbolic deeds is not a task for the select alone, and the integrity of symbolic deeds does not demand perfection in the aesthetic sense; the perfection required is one of faith, not necessarily of esthetics. In other words, expectations are suited to each individual's ability, including those whose ability is only modest, for in any case the substance that shapes the forms and symbols of the holiday is the stuff of deeds, customs, and the requirements of ordinary man in his daily life. That is to say, the elevated plane of the essence and significance of the holiday is not so sublime as to disappear from the ability of performance, of experience, and of understanding by the entire house of Israel. In this way the holiday is returned to everyday life in the context that shapes it, directs it, and symbolizes its significance.

Holidays hold a salient position as a means of applying significance and values to the entire scope of a people's cultural activity. This refers, of course, to holidays that remain within the operative life-style and therefore impact on every aspect of daily life as well. A holiday only exists and impacts when two conditions are met: the authority to separate and sanctify, and the authority to shape the course of the overall way of life through the symbols that the holiday employs in order to transmit meaning.

To summarize, at their highest degree markers of time are consecrated days. They are rigorously separated from other days by canceling work and are elevated toward the absolute Being, which is above man and commits him through the prayer service. The positive elements of the holiday are a granting of grace by God to His worshippers after He has freed their time and dedicated this time to Himself. As a grace granted to the people, holidays are *yamim tovim*—goodly days—days of gladness and rejoicing. Indeed, the gladness is expressed through a significant shaping of all man's natural activities. The holidays are monumental structures of time through which man acts purposefully, testifying to the significance that is intended for man's existence. Since this is so, the days that were removed from the routine flow of time recur in order to channel the flow of time into a directive frame whose meaning is in its unity. From this standpoint there is a close and continuous link between holidays and general norms that shape the people's way of life.

So much for the holidays in general. In what follows we take up each indicator of time individually, beginning with the first among them, the first to be mentioned in the Bible, the first experienced by anyone entering into the Jewish people's life agenda; first and primary from the standpoint of the design of the perfected form intended for a holiday: Shabbat.

THREE

THE SABBATH:
RECALLING THE CREATION—
REMEMBERING THE EXODUS

PROHIBITION OF WORK

The most prominent indicator of time in the Jewish calendar is the Sabbath. Its distinction is certainly due, at least in part, to the frequent and rhythmic cyclicity of its appearance, comparable perhaps to the heartbeat in a living organism. The Sabbath endows the life span with a sense of continuity as week after week, throughout the months, during all the seasons, embracing all the holidays, it recurs in its set form. Admittedly, there is diversification by virtue of certain Sabbaths' proximity to holidays when specific portions are read from the Torah and *haftarah*, and particular additions made to the prayer service, but in its parameters and content the Sabbath remains the same. This is not merely a result of frequency. The Sabbath is a primary junction between the cosmic cycle and the course of history as they are both marked in the calendar. By its very repetition, the Sabbath accords cyclical cosmic time a purposeful direction from Creation to Redemption, setting sabbatical and jubilee years. The Sabbath has acquired special attention because it directs the flow of time but its wealth of forms and excellence of structure also contribute to its distinction as a marker of time. It is likened to a bride in the ritual poem, *Lekhah Dodi* and welcomed in song by Jewish communities throughout the world. The metaphor is firmly anchored in the verses of Genesis that describe the Sabbath, "Thus the heavens and the earth were finished and all their host, and God completed his work," an expression that testifies to the beauty and goodness that was concluded, containing a symbolic unity and perfection. During all the generations, Jews diligently guarded the Sabbath so that its beauty would be complete—greeting it as a bride, as a day of perfection; indeed, as a day on which people are elevated toward the perfection of life for which they are intended. The Sabbath symbolizes this perfection and interprets its significance. As a recollection of Creation, it testifies to the wholeness of Creation; as a memory of the exodus from Egypt, the Sabbath is itself a departure from slavery to freedom, and from bondage to redemption.

These two intertwined motifs are seen in the very designation of the day and its endowment with sanctity. In this sense, the Sabbath not only possesses primacy—it is the first day consecrated by God—but it also precedes all others, serving as a paradigm for consecration. It is on the Sabbath that the *kiddush* makes its appearance as a central motif, important in and of itself. This is apparent in the opening lines of the *kiddush* where the Sabbath is individuated from other days by expropriating it from the sphere of man's autonomy to do as he wishes. The Ten Commandments require that we "Remember the Sabbath day to keep it holy." How then is the Sabbath sanctified?

> Six days shalt thou labor and do all thy work but the seventh day is a Sabbath unto the Lord your God; in it thou shalt not do any manner of work; thou, nor thy son, nor thy daughter, nor thy man servant, nor thy maid servant, nor thy cattle, nor the stranger that is within thy gates.
>
> Exodus 20:8–11

It is a day consecrated by total and absolute abstention from work. No manner of labor is to be performed by anyone capable of working in the household of a Jew. The prohibition is entirely inclusive and the day is sanctified by it. Nonetheless, the a priori abstention from work is not merely meant to free time for an alternate endeavor; rather, it is the primary and main content of the day. The Sabbath is a day of non-work, and that is the meaning of *Shabbat*: He rested from the labor of Creation; man rests with Him. It is the day on which a Jew is commanded to realize the abstention from work as an experience of inherent value. He must rest. The realization that rest is not paralysis, but a specific form of spiritual activity, is the outcome of a rigorous understanding of what is intended by Sabbath rest. It is an active abstention, a relinquishing of the activity that naturally clings to man when he is in an unmediated relationship with his environment. In order to rest on the Sabbath one must intend not to do any work, to postpone any activity that has an aspect of labor; in such a way an affirmative infrastructure of experiencing the day is assumed through a consciousness of the prohibition and its observance.

It is true that anyone wanting to learn about the special dimension of the Sabbath from the quotations above, or from other biblical quotations alone, could reject an interpretation of the prohibition of labor as exaggerated sermonizing. This is no longer the case when attention is directed to the full range of *halakhic* deliberation of the Sabbath in the scholarly literature, particularly the Oral Law. The fact is that matters concerned with the prohibition of labor account for most of the *halahkic* discussion in the Mishnah and the Talmud. What tasks are prohibited? What is included in the category of work, and what is not? And what limitations are placed around work on the Sabbath so that there is not even an inadvertent transgression of the prohibition of labor, while at the same time the day is one of joy, of both physical and spiritual pleasure? The main thrust of the meticulously detailed discussion that makes minute distinctions and puts numerous "fences around the Law" attests primarily to the objective of abstaining from labor and of raising that objective to full consciousness. It also attests to the hardships one must constantly be aware of since—without close attention to each detail—difficult situations could arise even on a day meant as a day of rest. Not infrequently, matters are perceived as so urgent that to refrain from doing them could involve suffering. In such an eventuality, it is proper to decide when suffering goes beyond the limit to the point of danger, thereby permitting a particular task. All these considerations illustrate the active aspect found in rest; that is, an intentional and perpetual alertness that is a volitional, heartfelt abstention from all work so as to experience—in contradistinction to labor that is ordained for the six secular days of the week—the non-labor of Sabbath. The Sabbath is distinguished from all other holidays including holidays in which labor is prohibited; the exception is Yom Kippur, the Sabbath of Sabbaths.

The question that arises in this connection is whether a mitzvah, which is essentially a prohibition, can also have an affirmative significance. Can there be a positive connotation to consistent abstention from labor? If there is a practical answer to the question, it must be sought within the two contexts in which the Sabbath commandment is found: "A recollection of Creation" and "A remembrance of the exodus from Egypt." Maimonides's position is that by the prohibition to refrain from work, the Sabbath testifies to the fact that the world was created ex nihilo. In his judgment if the world pre-existed, that is originated in itself, of itself, it precludes the possibility of a sabbath in the Creation, for the action of becoming and of growth, of growth and multiplication, of withering, old age, and death goes on uninterruptedly. It also continues on the Sabbath, for Nature does not stand still, nor can it. One can speak of a sabbath-in-Creation only if one posits that the world has been newly created; if one assumes that the natural movement toward becoming had a precursor in the invention of things, and their introduction into Nature. The act of Creation ended once the world was, essentially, completed. Man demonstrates this when he rests on the Sabbath; that is, when he abstains from labor, which creates things that did not exist before, and refrains from supplementing that which Nature continues to produce and bring into being according to its own natural order. The deliberate cessation from labor is thus made into a symbolic enactment of a profound religious idea, the symbolic enactment of a wondrous, absolute potential that invested Creation as a perfected reality.

In returning from such Maimonidean thoughts to the actual text of Genesis, Chapters One and Two, an additional element is discovered. Each day of Creation is marked by a unique attainment that adds something to the Creation. In this sense the seventh day is not different, it simply heralds—in an especially elevated style—the fact that the world is now complete. What was created new on the seventh day? Nothing; nonetheless, something is new. On the seventh day, the achievements of Creation were finished and consummated, and now—at a time of rest that is the fulfillment of the deeds or the abundance that overflows from the deeds—a pristine unity and perfection is generated. This is what He "finished."

On the Sabbath God completed Creation and having perfected it, took it on to Himself, for now it had become worthy of the intended perfection; this is its consecration, so He also blessed it, that is, granted the Sabbath an autonomous permanent existence. While it is true that no new essence was created on the Sabbath, everything that was done in the six days of Creation is perceived as a unity by virtue of the view that encompasses and transcends it. In this sense, repose rises from the midst of work whose purpose has been achieved, if only to enjoy its benefit; this is the positive value of inaction. In this construction, rest is not idleness, nor is respite the opposite of work. The same applies to man's labor, man who was created in the image of his Creator. In the initial aim of Creation, labor was not imposed on man as punishment, rather it was as participation in the act of Creation. Therefore, even in the ordinances regarding the Sabbath, in the Ten Commandments, man is enjoined to work six days, and the enjoyment of the Sabbath is contingent on this. The Sabbath is the realization of the week's labor.

Such sublime statements evidently idealize labor so that it would be appropriate were man to work for the full satisfaction inherent in Creation, and the importance of this motif in man's labor is undeniable. Work is destiny; in its absence personality disintegrates and the meaning of life is lost. Yet one cannot overlook the curse that accompanies labor, turning it into a wearying burden in the socio-historic reality, exhausting the body and stifling the soul, at times leading to enslavement. Man becomes enslaved to the fulfillment of his vital needs and consequently he is in bondage to those who have amassed the resources of labor. This aspect of labor, its transposition into toil, is not overlooked in the narrative of the Torah or the commandments. As early as the book of Genesis, a distinction is made between the ideal aspect of labor—man's work in the Garden of Eden—and the aspect of labor as a curse. In the reality of history, which turns the Garden of Eden into a distant dream, man struggles to overcome obdurate Nature, whose soil is miserly in its produce, and struggles with an ongoing anxiety about existence that brings competition, jealousy, war, and enslavement in its wake. From this standpoint, the Sabbath is not only the completion of work during the six days of Creation, it is also a liberation from the oppression and enslavement of toil in order again to grace man with the original reason for life, his stature as a free being.

The significance the Sabbath acquires in the context of "a recollection of the exodus from Egypt" is easily seen. The story of Egyptian bondage is intrinsic to the story of man's enslavement to existential anxiety. It is famine that impels the Israelites to go to Egypt. Indeed, it is hunger that then enslaves Egypt itself. Those who hold the grain treasuries take control of the means of labor so that all of Egypt is enslaved to them. Ultimately, the Israelites, too, are enslaved and the rigors of their toil become emblematic of labor's curse. The Israelites cry out from their labor, and it is from toil that they are redeemed. In this respect the Sabbath symbolizes, perhaps even more than Passover does, the primary human meaning of liberation; this is how it is engraved in the Tablets of the Law. The termination of work on the Sabbath is the pronouncement of liberty and therefore it is the core of the commandment.

Initially, this seems simple. It is not. One could describe the Sabbath as a day free of labor if it was found that the biblical commandment obliges a Jew to desist from his work on the seventh day. Which is to say—as it is for many today—a day in which a man is released from the duty of work and may do as he wishes. That would be so only if the Sabbath was not a day that was expropriated from man's sovereignty, but conversely a day given to him to be used at his discretion. That is not how the Torah grants Sabbath to the Israelites. It is not simply a day on which one can rest. It is primarily a day on which it is forbidden to work, and in this prohibition there is an ostensible limit on human liberty no less than in the obligation to work on the six secular days. It is a surprising paradox; anyone examining it is persuaded that the paradox did not go unnoticed by the biblical narrative. When the commandment of the Sabbath is first enunciated to the Israelites fleeing Egypt, it is given to them as a *trial*.

Then the Lord said unto Moses, "I will rain down bread for you from the sky, and the people shall go out and gather each day that day's portion—that I may thus test them, to see whether they will follow My instructions or not. But on the sixth day when they apportion what they have brought in, it shall prove to be double the amount they gather each day." So Moses and Aaron said to all the Israelites, "By evening you shall know it was the Lord who brought you out from the land of Egypt; and in the morning you shall behold the Presence of the Lord, because He has heard your grumblings . . ." In the evening quail appeared and covered the camp; in the morning there was a fall of dew about the camp . . . And Moses said to them, "That is the bread which the Lord has given to you to eat. This is what the Lord has commanded: gather as much of it as each of you requires to eat, an *omer* to a person for as many of you as there are; each of you shall fetch for those of you in his tent."

The Israelites did so, some gathering much, some little, but when they measured it by the *omer*, he who had gathered much had excess, and he who gathered little, had no deficiency: they had gathered as much as they needed to eat. And Moses said to them, "Let no one leave any of it over until morning." But they paid no attention to Moses; some of them left of it until morning and it became infested with maggots and stank. And Moses was angry with them.

So they gathered it every morning, each as much as he needed to eat; but when the sun grew hot it would melt. On the sixth day they gathered double the amount of food, two *omers* for each; and when all the chieftains of the assembly came and told Moses, he said to them, "This is what the Lord meant: tomorrow is a day of rest, a holy sabbath of the Lord. Bake what you would bake and boil what you would boil, and all that is left put aside to be kept until morning." So they put it aside until morning as Moses had ordered; and it did not turn foul, and there were no maggots in it. Then Moses said, "Eat it today, for today is a sabbath to the Lord; you will not find it today on the plain. Six days you shall gather it; on the seventh day, the sabbath, there will be none."

Yet some of the people went out on the seventh day to gather but they found nothing. And the Lord said to Moses, "How long will you refuse to follow My commandments and My teachings? Mark that the Lord has given you the Sabbath; therefore He gives you two days food on the sixth day. Let every man remain where he is: let no man leave his place on the seventh day." So the people remained inactive on the seventh day.

Exodus 16:4—30

In this passage, the first mention of the Sabbath in the Book of Exodus, in the context of Egyptian bondage, God tests the people to see if they will keep his commandments; in contradistinction to most of the trials connected with the exodus, this one does not involve withstanding hardship and danger to life; on the contrary, it is a test in which the people confront conditions of plenty given to them almost effortlessly. It bears emphasizing that the narrative of the falling manna is clearly a didactic story. First God educates the people not to covet the amplitude He has given them, an amplitude that exceeds their needs. Every man is a guest at the Lord's table; He sees to all their wants in accordance with their needs. It is at this point that the conflict begins with people's natural inclination to exceed what they truly need, amassing as much they can. After each person gathered the manna according to his ability, it was reapportioned to the head of each family in accordance with the family's needs. Here is the attribute of ideal justice observed through dividing the munificence that God gives man; man himself need add nothing.

The next trial is somewhat more difficult. The people have to overcome a natural tendency to save, to put aside for the morrow. It is a natural inclination because one cannot rely absolutely on the expectation that the plenitude found today will be renewed tomorrow. Concern for the future is most vexatious; in order to have confidence in the future, one saves and stores. But this means that the people do not have faith in the promise that was given to them. They want a different assurance, the certainty that one has in hand what will be required tomorrow. Indeed, it is on this point the aim of the story becomes manifest, the link between it and the Sabbath. The Sabbath becomes the third test: the people are required to trust that, contrary to its nature, the manna will not spoil.

They must trust that the manna, which usually spoils and becomes infested with maggots if kept to the next day, will remain wholesome from Friday through the Sabbath. This is the difficulty of adapting a miracle: it does not perform in natural ways. The people, it appears, would like to have their needs fulfilled through ordinary avenues. There is an immense advantage to Nature. One depends on Nature as on an axiom; it provides a feeling of steady reliability. This is not the case with miracles. One has to believe in the miracle. It is belief that God is testing in this didactic story, and throughout the length of wanderings in the desert. The intention is to educate the people to a way of life founded on belief, in place of the existence they endured in Egypt, which was grounded in the tangible, in man's actual possessions.

Two opposing paths of life—the way of Torah and the way of Egypt—are in confrontation here. Man can aspire to total sovereignty over the conditions of his existence and over Nature's potential; alternatively he can realize that man has no sovereign control over Nature and that such a situation is impossible to achieve. Consequently man's existence and his freedom are contingent on the trusting person's belief and ethical certainty that if he acts righteously as he is commanded and if he does not covet more than what he really needs, he will never lack in the future nor will any harm befall him. Here is the crux of a paradox: as a result of desiring certainty, a certainty based on controlling Nature, Egypt became a house of bondage; whereas it is only by foregoing certainty, only with the acceptance of living through belief that man can be granted freedom. In this context, the Sabbath is intended to symbolize the way of life of the believer, and the freedom gained through faith.

But it appears that the paradox of slavery—inherent in man's aspiration to control Nature—is also the explanation for a converse paradox, that of liberty acquired at the cost of a limitation on man's arbitrary will. The motive of those who wanted to gather manna on the Sabbath is also the driving force of those who cannot rest on the Sabbath. They are concerned for the future and have no trust in a miracle. Anxiety about their future enslaves them to their toil. They cannot rest until they are sure that they possess enough for their needs today and tomorrow and the day after tomorrow. When can they be sure? Fear and craving never end. Even the greatest material gain only serves to reinforce the primary fear that what they have amassed will be appropriated by someone who is covetous and cunning. In truth, does man unequivocally desire to be free?

Apparently the answer to this question is ambiguous, which is why an uncompromising commandment expropriates the Sabbath from man's arbitrary will and prohibits labor, even against his wishes, only to return the day that has been taken from him as a benefaction. The grace of freedom. In the context of recalling the exodus from Egypt, this is how the Sabbath is understood as liberation. It is not only a day on which one does not work, it is a day on which it is forbidden to work; in other words, it is a day in which man confronts the trial which can be withstood only through belief. The intended benefit of this repetitive trial is to discipline man so that he is released from the internal element that enslaves him—the aspiration to hold on to a guarantee of future security. The Sabbath day requires the believing person's ethical certainty, and such a certainty is the freedom that can be man's portion.

THE SABBATH AS METAPHYSICAL VISION

The two positive meanings in the prohibition of labor—the concept of rest as the completion of labor and the concept of rest as liberation from a spiritual slavery to labor—are complementary. By liberation from a compulsive enslavement to work and concern for the future, man can reassess his labor during the six days of the week as the fulfillment of the goal that grants life its meaning. If he can free himself from a tendency to regard the fruits of his labor as a guarantee of his security or his sovereignty over Nature, then man can view work as the potential peculiarly available to man—the creative ability, which adds something to Nature that only man can add. That is, if man can free himself from the slavery of work, he can experience something of the presence described in the story of Creation, something redolent of the Garden of Eden. If an individual can achieve this as an actual experience in his life, not only as a sublime idea, then the Sabbath has been granted him as a metaphysical vision that has been realized.

Of course this remark, which says too much, must immediately be qualified. Paradisiacal reality is an unachievable vision in human historical reality as we know it; it cannot be made applicable to the full gamut of human cultural institutions. One can only aspire to the realization of such a vision in order to bring it closer. The highly blemished socio-cultural arrangements in which man finds himself cannot be entirely even on the Sabbath. They remain in force. Nonetheless, on the Sabbath this vision impacts tangibly on the life of a Jew so that he can actually taste it, not merely as a sublime thought or as something imagined but as a living reality that also has a shaping influence, if not on all the arrangements of his life, on the direction in which, to the best of his ability, he tries to move those arrangements. The Sages said that on the Sabbath a Jew tastes the flavor of Paradise; it would appear that this is also the extent of the profundity of the statement. Sabbath is a utopia that touches reality and shines its light upon it.

All of which means that on the Sabbath a process occurs that results in a change of direction not only in how things are observed and the emotional expectation of individuals but in the network of social relationships as well. The social arrangements of the six secular days are not annulled but they are suspended; they are replaced, if only symbolically and by implication, with a different texture, a different network of relationships, one that is decreed. In great measure, the social relationships of the six days of the week reflect man's aspiration to sovereignty over the means of his existence. These relationships are based on private ownership, and the rule of power upheld by it. Even when one speaks of an enlightened society that places limitations on ownership, subordinating it to the rule of law, such a society is permeated by exploitation, enslavement, and a diminished self-view of the individual who ideally sees himself as someone for whom the world has been created. Even in such a case, there is no end to the confrontation rooted in jealousy, competition, and fear.

The Sabbath is intended to suspend—if only for one day—this system of relationships and to superimpose on them—if only implicitly and symbolically—a different set of relationships. While abstention from work removes the day from man's possession, it also serves to limit man's ownership over his property. What is property? It is the sum of objects that man can employ to gratify his satisfactions as he wishes. Property is consequently the utilitarian use of objects for a specific benefit. My land belongs to me exclusively, and only I can plow and sow and reap its yield for myself; the house belongs to me so that I can dwell in it or rent it; mine alone is the implement I own and its use is for my benefit exclusively. If any limitation is placed on my ability to use the object in my possession, willy-nilly my ownership of it has been reduced. This is also the extent to which my ownership of it has been restricted. The very fact that anyone has the authority to circumscribe my right to use an object limits my sense of absolute ownership, making it relative. Indeed the idea that man does not have absolute proprietorship over objects necessary for his existence, that ownership is relative or contingent, characterizes the entire Torah law; it stands out most prominently in the "seven" series of the time cycle: the Sabbath, the sabbatical year, and the jubilee. Man's ownership is suspended for a specified period. He is prohibited from tilling his soil in the seventh year, which limits its bond to him, though it does not cancel it.

Thus a different system is introduced into the regular social system—the result of a compromise between justice and love, and man's nature. This different system represents the social relationships that should be man's ideal destiny as a creature made in God's image. The general prohibition of work on the Sabbath limits the use of property. No longer is man permitted to exploit either his land or his tools as property, neither he himself nor those in his household, "You shall not do any work—you, your son or daughter, your male or female slave, or your cattle, or the stranger who is within your gates" (Exodus 20:10). With this limitation on one's assets, what is stressed is the basic fact that—beyond inequality, which is a necessary product of relationships based on property—in God's eyes all creatures are equal from the standpoint of their essential worth, and the relationships between them on the Sabbath reflect, if only implicitly, the equality of their intrinsic value as human beings, as God's creatures. On the Sabbath they all stand together, as peers.

Of course this common abstention from toil is only a starting point, a departure from the track of relationships based on property. From this starting point, a set of relationships arise whose foci are the family on one side, and the congregation and community on the other. These are actually the two social hubs around which the Sabbath as a positive life content coalesces. Family and kehillah are the two primary building blocks of the people. Observation shows that these units fill a number of diverse functions, among them conspicuous roles in property-based relationships. As such, they are far removed from the ideal respect of an individual's inherent value. Even when such an idea informs a formal legal framework, it is still quite a way from directing interpersonal and intersocietal relationships as they actually work themselves out. On the contrary, there is a natural tendency to dominate and enslave not only in larger units of organization, but in the smaller, most intimate ones as well. A man can regard himself, indeed behave, as the baal, the master, of his wife and family, and act in the high-handed manner of a ruler in his community.

A differentiation must be made, therefore, between the family and kehillah in their everyday being and functions, and between the family and kehillah in their ceremonial roles practiced particularly on the Sabbath, holidays, and festivals. In ceremonial roles, the family is structured around the symbol of the Sabbath table; the community is arranged around the symbol of a prayer service in a minyan at the synagogue. A different kind of social reality is forged around these symbols, one that tacitly touches the sublime plane of the ideal. Standing before God, all the members of the family and all those who join the *minyan* as individuals become equals. This does not mean that there is equality in their ritual functions, or even in their positions of honor. On the contrary, the roles that are intrinsic to the social unit as such—father, mother, sons, and brothers in the family; Cohen, Levi, and Yisrael; scholar and rabbi; and ordinary householder in the synagogue—are all emphasized according to their degree of "purity," and honor is extended to each one in accordance with the functions that constitute the social partnership devoted to the service. From the standpoint of personal worth, it is precisely here that each individual finds his place. A clear, symbolic expression of this is found in the *minyan* where each individual adult joins the quorum and is counted as one.

The special cultural pattern of family togetherness, and of the community praying together, are elements of both the Sabbath and festivals; the Sabbath is particularly important from this standpoint because its repetition maintains the pattern with sufficient frequency and prominence. The sociology of the ritual bears noting; that is, the rich and complex nature of interpersonal relations that is enabled by ritual and so made an integral part of it. The ritual superimposes itself on the network of social roles in the family and the synagogue; it creates such an organic composite that it is not possible to determine the line between a sacral activity and the experience of interpersonal meeting that is enabled by and for it. Those who assemble at the family table do so in order to be with one another—to express love for one another, to reveal themselves to one another—each in accordance with his nature and position in the family, sit together sanctifying the day; those who congregate at the synagogue come to see and be seen, to converse, to recount and hear even as they come to pray. Though this fellowship can occasionally cause a disturbance (calls for quiet and decorum are part of the prayer setting) the actual disruption is reasonable. It is an unavoidable feature of the style of prayer characteristic to a synagogue without which something essential is lost, brothers "sitting together" before the Lord, in the totality of their human presence.

Though this is not the place to develop the principles and laws of sacra-sociology, a number of main points, at least, do need to be identified. First, notice the emphasis placed on the way in which the covenantal basis of the social/sacral framework is constituted. A covenant is a compact of mutual responsibility and commitment by individuals who voluntarily take on worship in common. As soon as they voluntarily undertake to do so, they require each other to fulfill the roles that stem from that "faithful" worship; it is not for financial compensation but through the vigor of their loyalty and the trust that the public has in them. Thus Jews who live in the same locale are obliged to set up a synagogue, maintain it, ensure a permanent *minyan* and prayers; they must insure that the synagogue has the necessary functionaries for prayer service, and should they err in the performance of their duties—such as when the Torah reader makes a mistake or when the prayer leader stumbles over words—everyone is responsible for correcting the error, and they do so enthusiastically. An entire network of mutual obligations is created; as well as expectations and pressures and, as opposed to these, an entire network of support and honor. Since this is so, tensions arise between individuals and groups in the congregation. The sociology of the synagogue depends on a delicate and tenuous balance that is typical of a voluntary society in which both unifying and dislocating forces are present. Occasionally a quarrel breaks out that reverberates throughout the community but if there is a faithful leadership, unity prevails and the service goes on.

The support and honor network is inseparable from the ritual, reflecting the need to evaluate each individual according to his contribution. This expresses itself particularly in ceremonies connected with reading from the Torah: lifting the Torah scroll out of the ark, bringing it to the lectern, opening it, being called up to the Torah in turn, raising the Torah scroll, dressing the Torah, and returning it to its place; and of course the blessings recited while fulfilling each of the tasks. It is a long—sometimes quite tiresome—list of honors but popular social pressure maintains it with great care so that each individual is assured the honor and blessing to which he is entitled. No one forgoes these honors, and no one evades the obligations they entail. For purposes of this social ritual, the choice of the ceremony that surrounds the reading of the Torah on Sabbaths and holidays is not an accidental one. The ritual is a remnant and renewal of the Ceremony of the Covenant. On that occasion the Jews united as a people, and as a people sealed a covenant with the Lord according to the Torah. Following on the covenant, the Tent of Meeting was erected through contributions from the entire people, symbolizing both the unity of the people and the bond between the people and their God. Synagogue society is structured on this model. The congregation, by virtue of its unity and consensus, is made into a divine chariot for sacred worship. The ceremonial Torah reading is symbolic of this; in its celebration the unification of individuals into a congregation is actualized.

With this framework, based as it is on the covenant, each individual is important according to his station and ability to contribute to the common spiritual life of the congregation, and as such each individual is honored. But individuality does not transcend the congregational framework, rather it is rooted in its unity as a setting that energizes, pressures, and unifies. Where does the authority come from? On one hand, from the consent of the individuals; and on the other, from the supra-social role which they have undertaken, worshipping God in common. The complete union of social process and ritual depends on this.

Still another matter needs to be noted in this context: the social/ritual ceremony creates a setting that not only relates to congregational occasions, and celebrations of the people in general, but to all the important events of individuals within the congregation. This is the setting for marking births, for bar mitzvahs, and for weddings, as well for recalling the loss of loved ones on the anniversary of their death. This is also the setting in which a person notes the deliverance and mercy that he has experienced or a tragedy that has befallen him; this is the setting for prayers for the safety of all sacred communities and of the people, its leaders and government ministers; and this is the setting for blessing the nation's soldiers and defenders. Again, one cannot distinguish between the congregational/social or social/national aspects, and the ritual/religious aspect because they are intertwined, which is why this framework naturally becomes the enabling setting for the responsibility of the community toward its individuals. Indeed there were communities in which an individual could insist on the redressing of an insult within the synagogue by halting the service, obliging the entire congregation to mediate a dispute, and so grant him justice. Yet again, such a principled demand is based within the ritual itself, for the entire public is implicated in the wrongdoing of its individual members, and they are obligated to protest an injustice done to one of them, remonstrate against any wrong doing of any of the individuals, and demand its correction. This motif, especially apparent in the Yom Kippur service, will be dealt with in the chapter devoted to Yom Kippur, but it is important to recognize that no motif that is particularly emphasized in any holiday is without an ongoing expression in synagogue life. It is only natural that the synagogue should serve as a highly intensive focus of interpersonal concern.

Finally, we note how the broad institutionalized structure of the community is reflected in the atmosphere of the synagogue, and the impact of the synagogue on that structure. Organized institutions of the community were dependent on the socio-economic stratification and the

political order in every country where Jews lived. Differences of class and
the internal struggle between the classes were reflected in the atmosphere
of the synagogue where the wealthy, the notables, the powerful insisted
on the lion's share of the customary honors. This distorted the non-
property-based, popular character of the ritual that was a concomitant of
the covenant ideal and of the Sabbath as utopia. But even in communities
in which there was a compelling class consciousness, the idea of a
Sabbath-like covenant had an impact that transcended the domain of the
synagogue.

The most salient expression of this influence could be seen in
charitable institutions. From a *halahkic* standpoint, *tzedakah*—charity—is
founded on the idea of covenant. All Jews bear a mutual responsibility and
are obligated to protect one another. Should one of them suffer a reverse
in their socio-economic status, the public is required to assist him in
returning to his previous status so that he continues to live in accordance
with his accustomed position. This concept is a broadening of the sacral
social framework, and the mechanism that operated the charitable
institutions actually functioned in the synagogue. A wealthy person who
wanted to retain his honorable place in the congregation had to
contribute heavily to *tzedakah*, and a major part of the charity was solicited
and pledged at prayer time, particularly on being called up to the Torah.

Consequently, the societal style that evolved in the synagogue,
particularly on Sabbaths and holidays, establishes the community as a
"sacred *kehillah*," a term that should be regarded as a concrete expression
of the idea of the Sabbath. The Jewish Socialist movement, which also
sought somehow to be grounded in elements of the heritage, would
proudly point to the Sabbath as a "social achievement"—one weekly day
of rest for the worker. Ex post facto the Sabbath was indeed a social
achievement, but a priori it aimed at something of greater grandeur and
importance. The Sabbath was intended to establish a network of human
relations that liberated individuals from enslavement to property and
placed them side by side as fellows, allies in the name of a common
spiritual goal that served to make them each other's equal. Not merely a
day on which the laborer is entitled to rest but a day on which all are
prohibited from working, when the use of their property is expropriated
so that all stand as free men and, in this sense, equal before their Maker.
The Sabbath religious service virtually established such a society, if only
implicitly. That is what Franz Rosenzweig meant when he said that on the
Sabbath the Jewish people "anticipated" the redemption. Anticipated in
the sense that it firmly planted the future in the present as though it had

already materialized; as though it had materialized but nonetheless is still expected, hoped for—because perfect realization remains forever in the realm of hope. But if man desires it greatly, then he "leans" forward from the moment, living his hopes in the actual dimension of the present, thus "utopia" becomes a reality contiguous with life itself, illuminating it with its envisioned splendor, pulling life toward itself.

THE SABBATH AS QUEEN

Up to this point, the discussion has focused on the positive significance of a day sanctified through the prohibition of labor. We now come to the affirmative elements, symbols, and customs that are *mitzvot aseh*, positive commandments of the Sabbath. Two contending, yet complementary, approaches are seen in the Torah's grasp of the sanctity of the Sabbath. One concept finds sanctity in the consecrating deed; the other locates sanctity as an inherent attribute that permeates consecrated times and objects. Sanctification of the Sabbath, through the prohibition of labor, is a pronounced example of the first approach; whereas the symbols that stand for the positive elements of worship on the Sabbath are outstanding examples of the second concept. On the one hand, there is a *halahkic* construction that is measured, exacting, and strict; on the other hand, an *aggadic* creation that is richly imaginative, winging upward to the heavens. As it has come unfolded through the generations, the image of the Sabbath is a shared creation of both approaches, which provided one a framework for content, and the other content for a framework. There were periods when the *halahkic* creation was stressed, and periods for stressing the *aggadic* creation. The *halahkic* image of the Sabbath crystal- lized primarily in the work of the Sages, whereas the *aggadic* image of the Sabbath crystallized mainly in the work of medieval scholars. Their greatest contribution was that of the Kabbalists who imbued the Sabbath symbols with a brilliant emanation drawn from the upper spheres.

Again, what distinguishes the Sabbath from the six work days? Different than the *halahkic* determination that differentiated the day through a prohibition of labor, the *aggadic* creation fashioned an impres- sive setting of symbols that resembled a garland of gold—greeting the Sabbath on Friday evening; taking leave of it on Saturday evening. The ceremony of greeting the Sabbath begins in the home with the family, moves to the synagogue, then returns to the family home. It is intended to be a sharp shift from the humble level of workaday reality to an elevated Sabbath plane of reality; here the Sabbath performs, shaping the patterns of deeds and detailed behavior in the social areas of home and synagogue. Everything is directed toward emphasizing and illustrating the qualitative transition in time. The feverish preparations in anticipation of the Sabbath come to a peak since everything must be finished by sunset Friday when all labor ceases.

Suddenly tranquility descends, and the mother who has freed herself from the Sabbath preparations lights the candles and blesses them. Lighting the candles is the very last activity, after which no labor is permitted. Finale. Having lit the candles, the blessing is said beyond the threshold of light that separates one kind of time from the other. For a moment, the times stand arrayed across from one another, secular time on one side and sanctified time on the other, past and future on either side of the intervening present: the light of the flames counterpoised between them. The weekday afternoon service, *Minhah*, slopes downward toward the conclusion of Friday; the *Ma'ariv* evening service, beginning with *Kabbalat Shabbat*, ascends ceremoniously. The Sabbath now reigns over the time of the entire congregation. Everyone's time. When the Sabbath has been sanctified inwardly and outwardly, people return home to the Sabbath table. When the *Kiddush* is said over the wine, and the two loaves of bread are blessed, when one breaks into song and begins the meal, people are already in the very midst of sanctified time. The secular has retreated and disappeared.

At the end of the day, one approaches the setting from the opposite direction. It begins with *Seudah Shlishit*, the third Sabbath meal, which is redolent of wistful sadness, a foretaste of the approaching ordinary week. Again, this transition between one day and the next is accomplished in the context of secular time, once the eve of the following day has begun. It is here that the last partition can be found marked by the light of the *Havdalah* candle. Negotiating this partition, one finds oneself again in the six days of work.

The *Havdalah* ceremony that marks the separation between times illuminates a special state, the sanctity of the Shabbat as a presence that emanates from above. It is sanctity in its essence, touching a different sphere of existence more sublime than the terrestrial. For the mythical imagination, however, this is insufficient. It continues to mold the presence of the Sabbath, endowing it with shape and image; it is perhaps the greatest achievement of the Kabbalists, particularly the Kabbalists of Safed, though they themselves drew on a previously existent store of aphorisms by the Sages. The Sabbath is a guest from another world, the intended bride and queen. Kabbalistic concepts embroider on these symbols. The Sabbath is emblematic of the Jewish people in its unity. In its unity, the people rises to become *Knesset Yisrael*, the assembled Jewish people, and in this unity that is raised above the earthly sphere, the Jewish people is the bride toward whom God "the bridegroom" goes in welcome, at the very moment that the Jewish people welcomes the Sabbath. The bride and the bridegroom unite in loving embrace, and on the Sabbath, the *Shekhinah*—Divine Providence, who is personified as a queen—descends and dwells with the Jewish people who have separated themselves from all that is secular in order to be in her presence. The theoretical interpretation of these symbols is beyond the scope of this study, but it is important to note the incorporation of this symbol into the popular heritage of the entire Jewish people who welcome the Sabbath, whether they are privy to Kabbalistic secrets or people whose hearts and minds are distant from the Kabbalah. Both these strata have accepted the personalized image of the Sabbath; all Israel greets the Sabbath with the lofty poetry created by Rabbi Shlomo Alkabetz, the Kabbalist of Safed.

> Come my friend to greet the bride
> To welcome in the Sabbath eve

And when they arrive at the poem's last stanza, they rise and face west where the sun has just set, and from where the Sabbath is said to step forth, toward them.

> Come in peace, O bridegroom's crown
> Come in joy and gladness
> Amid the faithful of the chosen people
> Come O bride! Come O bride!

With no connection to the Kabbalist view so strongly expressed in this poem, the figure of the Sabbath as a regal being, a guest from on high and a bride, shapes the positive sacral experience of the seventh day. The day's worship, the meals, the hymns, the repose, the conversations with friends—all these are conducted as though in the presence of another. It is a majestic presence. One puts on the best clothes, the best manners, chooses the finest prayers—all out of respect for the honored guest that has come to visit, who joins the people for the entire day. This personalized presence is the essence of sanctity.

THE JOY OF THE SABBATH

The Sabbath has been considered in each of its aspects. Combining the two creates the overflowing feeling of abundance that marks the Sabbath; the fullness is expressed in a special motif, independently emphasized, with which a discussion concerning the conceptual significance of the Sabbath ought to be concluded: the Sabbath is called *oneg*—joy.

Earlier in the chapter, it was noted that the day is expropriated from man's will by suspending labor. From this standpoint, there is a rigorous element to the Sabbath that derives from the awe that is inherent in faith. This severity is sensed as a discomfort that attends the Sabbath; indeed, discomfort is one of its distinguishing marks, and it ought not be concealed. There are people for whom the discomfort calls forth rebellion, people who are accustomed to gain satisfaction through a release of their energetic nature. Such people claim that the Sabbath is limiting and is thereby oppressive and boring. Those who accept the Sabbath as a day of rest and a societal achievement, though not as a sanctified day, feel all the more discomfited for the affirmative elements of sanctity do not "compensate" them for the unaccustomed limitations imposed on them. In truth, along with the bothersome limitations, the Sabbath as a sacred day is also a joy. Once its time frame is removed from the domain of man's will, the day is returned to man so that he can rejoice in it; just as abstaining from labor is a commandment, so enjoyment of the Sabbath is commanded. It is through joy that we experience abundance and wholeness, and the Sabbath symbolizes the fullness and wholeness of the Creation, and of history.

What is joy? It is the enjoyment of superabundance in the provision of one's existential needs, that is enjoyment of luxury. The provision of needs in the proportions required by man for his actual existence and health has an element of enjoyment, but it is not joy. Joy begins in becoming liberated from the need to confine oneself within the bounds of necessity, in the permission granted man to extend himself without the fear of future want. At the same time, enjoyment is not merely a perception that accompanies the fulfillment of vital needs; it is something sought and felt in its own right. Joy reaches its peak in a sense of overflowing abundance. It is an abundance that does not serve only to satiate deficiencies. Rather, it is a flood that courses beyond the rim of fullness, a high tide that symbolizes the absolute, that which exists, the steadiness of the flow of life.

It is true that the word *oneg* relates to the physical aspect of the sense of abundance, yet the spiritual aspect is linked to it as a flame to an ember. Joy symbolizes gladness while it comprises its source as well. Gladness is the overflowing of spiritual powers that validate themselves in their own abundant stream. It is nurtured by the high tide of physical powers and is parallel to them, which is why physical joy fuels gladness while being emblematic of it; it is one of its sources and one of its principle expressions. Where does joy come from? Who grants man abundance, liberating him from a sense of constriction? The spiritual significance of physical joy stems from the faith of the believer that his Creator provides for his needs in abundant generosity without limit. From this standpoint, joy testifies to God's grace, and those who feel such grace know they are loved.

The concept of *Oneg Shabbat*, the Joy of the Sabbath, relates precisely to the physical aspect of the celebration, and it is *halakhically* so defined. The Joy of the Sabbath is primarily an abundant meal, and a Jew is commanded to savor at least three full meals on the Sabbath. Such a commandment may appear incomprehensible to anyone seeking an ideal spirituality in the Sabbath, but it is actually deeply rooted in the notion of the Sabbath as a day that testifies to the comprehensiveness of Creation and of its permanence. The meal restores man's natural vigor. It revitalizes him, at least physically, bringing him to a starting point from which he can begin to function. The abundant meal symbolizes the continuity of Creation, which was completed in the first six days. It testifies to the blessing, a kind of persistent force that renews itself, eternally pervasive, and it testifies to the comprehensive will and love of the Creator who made the world in its fullness and blessed it. Just as the bounteous meal has its roots in the profound ideal of the Sabbath as a recollection of the act of Creation, to the same extent it is deeply rooted in the recollection of the exodus from Egypt. Leaving slavery for freedom is linked to the secure existence that is promised the Jewish people by God, by virtue of its faith. We are reminded of the bond that links the appearance of the manna to the commandment of the Sabbath. But more than this memory, one must keep in mind the goal toward which the Jewish people travel through the desert as they leave Egypt—the land of Israel, which is a land of milk and honey, a land in which they will not want for anything.

What, after all, is the blessing that the Patriarchs pronounced over their sons?—an abundance of choice fruit, a lushness of harvests. And what crowns the good life in the days of redemption according to the prophetic vision, "And the mountains shall drop sweet wine and all the hills shall melt"; and of Sukkot, the feast of gathering in the abundant harvest, "And thou shalt be altogether joyful." Repeatedly, one finds abundance renewing physical life, affirming it as being good, nourishing the sense of overflowingness inherent in gladness as well as symbolizing it. Repeatedly, the abundance that bursts out is the most impressive testimony of God's grace and perfection in the Creation; consequently the Sabbath is called joy. It is as though the full extent of that joy has been removed from God's province and now resides in the abundant meal, the meal that renews the forces of life. But the Sabbath meal is not merely eating, it is eating together, and this is what nourishes the gladness that bursts forth, rising to its peak in song. The grace after the meal is the finale. All of the conceptual elements noted above are included in the blessings of the grace. Reciting them consciously articulates the blessings, and when they are sung in unison, it gives an elevated expression to the feeling of gladness, gratitude for life in its fullness and for God's grace, which is their source.

All the components that mold the image of the Sabbath are found in the other holidays and festivals, sometimes in their totality, sometimes in part. These then are the modes of observing and marking the holiday as a sacred day. The uniqueness of the Sabbath is that these components are accentuated for their own sake, not as an internal backdrop for the emphasis of another idea. The Sabbath is the sanctity of the sacred day, the fullness of the full day, the joy of the day intended for gladness, the quintessence of celebration of the holiday. Therefore the Sabbath deserves to be considered the holiday of holidays and the appointed day of days—simultaneously an underpinning and a purpose.

FOUR

Rosh HaShanah: The Holiday of Creation

THE DAY OF JUDGMENT

There are four new years noted in the first chapter of the *Rosh HaShanah* tractate of the Mishnah—the first of Nissan, of Elul, and of Tishrei; a conflict revolves around the date of the fourth with the School of Shammai favoring the first of Shevat, the School of Hillel the fifteenth of the month. Only two of the four are significant beginnings in the calendar of the Jewish people. The first of Nissan is the New Year of Kings, and it designates the historic-national course. The calendar new year for counting sabbatical years, jubilees, tree plantings, and the seeding of vegetables, according to this tractate, is the first of Tishrei. To understand the annual cycle of a year, and the cycle of a collection of years, it is clear that the new year that begins on the first of Tishrei takes precedence over the others. Indeed, this reflects the reality practiced by Jews for hundreds of years. As the starting point for counting days, weeks, and months of the year, Rosh HaShanah begins on the first of Tishrei. A different picture, however, is depicted in the Torah where it is the first of Nissan that begins the count of the months of the year, while the first of Tishrei is referred to as "the first day of the seventh month." There is no hint here at either the starting point for counting time, or the Day of Judgment. The first of Tishrei is referred to as the day of sounding the shofar. Nor does the Mishnah designate the Rosh HaShanah of the first of Tishrei as a Day of Judgment. It notes four junctures where the world is judged, each juncture relating to specific matters. It is nonetheless clear from this Mishnah that the judgment of the first of Tishrei carries a special importance because it is on this day that living things are judged; which is to say that it is on this day that their actual existence stands in judgment. And it is here that the principal notion that distinguishes Rosh HaShanah in its conceptual aspect is touched on. This, in any case, is how it was viewed from the period of the Second Commonwealth onward. Since the thrust of this book is not to conduct a historical study but rather to analyze the wealth of conceptual strata of each holiday as it has been consolidated and sanctified to the present period, this will be the book's focus.

The narrative of the holiday begins here: on the first of Tishrei the cycle of days comes to an end and begins again, as do the weeks and the months of the year. Why explicitly on the first of Tishrei? Because it is the day that signals Creation, the coming into being of the world, and of time, or at least the coming into being of the enumeration of time—in modern terms, the birthday of the world. To be exact, it is a birthday because its enumeration begins not on the first day of Creation but on the sixth day when God said, "Let us make man"; that is, the first of Tishrei is the birthday of mankind. The story continues and recounts that this day on which we note that the creative process was initiated—particularly when the creation of man began—is the Day of Judgment, the day God sits in judgment on all human beings and determines their fate in accordance with their deeds. The existential, emotional, and cognitive content of the day derives from the assumption that the day that begins time is the Day of Judgment.

The first issue to be addressed arises from this statement. What is the link between Rosh HaShanah and the Day of Judgment? Jewish tradition posits such a link as though it were to be taken for granted. Indeed? If one compares the conceptual modes by which new years are perceived in various cultures and religions, it is doubtful that such a link is axiomatic. But, within the context of the belief in which the Torah makes the Jewish people unique, the link is substantive. Though the holiday of the first of Tishrei is not legislated in the Torah either as the beginning of the year or as a Day of Judgment, nonetheless the link between the beginning of Creation and judgment is decidedly biblical. It could be said therefore that the later portrait of the holiday as it became realized in *halahkic* sources and in the prayer book, interpreted that which is only vaguely and obscurely stated about the holiday in the Bible. This was done, however, in the spirit of very distinct core ideas in the Bible. It will subsequently be seen that biblical literature constitutes a major component in the description of the special worship for Rosh HaShanah, and that study of the Bible is the primary source for understanding the elements of the holiday. In other words, the form of Rosh HaShanah as it took shape in later *halahkic* sources is a kind of homily on the Scriptures.

CREATION AND JUDGMENT

What then is the connection between the beginning of Creation and judgment? Such a question turns one naturally to the Book of Genesis where, from the onset, the linkage is found to exist. God creates the world in pronouncements couched as decrees. Things come into being by virtue of their Creator's command, who then sits in judgment on them. Of every single object that was created on each day of Creation, it is said, "And He saw that it was good." "He saw" denotes examination and evaluation; "good" denotes approval. And the blessing is the conclusion that derives from approval. Everything found to be in accordance with God's will is endowed with existence and permanence. This applies even more to man. Man, who was created in God's image, acts in accordance with his own judgment and will, and consequently warrants constant re-evaluation. At the moment of his creation, his natural state was to be good and he was blessed. Yet as soon as he comprehended his ability to act by choice, man sinned. He was judged. Man's eldest born sinned, and he was judged. Ultimately the sinfulness of humans became so grievous that God regretted creating them, and returned chaos to the world. One man, Noah, was found innocent, and so it went. The entire biblical narrative is the story of recurrent trial and judgment. "God established the world in justice" is the earliest idea. Man in particular, who is the pinnacle of the world as well as its end purpose, must prove his right to exist. Consequently the day that marks his creation is also the Day of his Judgment.

Here we have the first formulation of the notion of God's sovereignty over the world. God, who created the world and sustains it, holds unlimited sway over it; the world can exist so long as it obeys His absolute will. Such is the meaning of the verse noted above, and this is how it is repeatedly defined in the Bible, as the totality of the function of sovereignty. Indeed this formulation shows the internal relationship between the vagueness of "the first day of the seventh month" in the Torah and the projection of Rosh HaShanah in the Oral Law. *Yom Truah*, the Day the Shofar is Sounded, is the day God's sovereignty is accepted; God appears as a King upon His throne, and sovereignty is expressed in the execution of the Law.

But, this conception of sovereignty is grounded in a prior assumption that is the principal singularity of the biblical belief. Creation precedes God's sovereignty just as the giving of the Law precedes justice, as though, from the standpoint of molding the Laws of Nature, Creation parallels legislation whose essence is to set forth a moral order, an order from which good emanates. This kingdom is not an arbitrary one because capriciousness and arbitrary rule are incompatible with law; it is rather the rule of moral law. Through Creation, God ordained the rules for the world's existence and made them permanent. The legislative act was bound up with the law, and examination of the text shows that the Bible views the laws of natural existence as an expression of Monarchy because they are viewed from a moral perspective: an absolute Will to beneficence manifested itself in these laws. Assuming that at the time of Creation man was singled out as having been given independent intellect, will, and self-leadership, clearly man also required a unique legislation that would point him in the direction of doing that which was intended by the moral will of his Creator.

This is the basis of God's commandment that begins as early as the story of the Garden of Eden, is repeated to Noah and his post-diluvian sons; its highest expression is in the giving of the Torah to the Jewish people. According to this perception, there is not only a *parallel* between the event of the Creation and the event of the legislation—that is, the time at which arrangements were determined according to which the world would exist and according to which human society would be conducted—but there is also an initial *identity* between these two occurrences. A priori, the natural order is interpreted as the expression of beneficent Will. It is organized, harmonious reality that is *the good*.

There is, therefore, a substantive link between the moral injunction incumbent upon man and the law upon which the world is based. Both stem from the same Will, and both are directed toward the same end. Sin injures the world's order and destroys the world. And the simple conclusion that stems from this is that sin itself is the destruction of life. Alternatively, punishment is the direct result of sin. When human society becomes morally corrupt, the natural order bursts and the world returns to chaos. The first time this idea was sounded was in God's words to Cain after the murder, "The voice of thy brother's blood crieth unto Me from the ground." That is, the earth does not conceal the blood. The universe protests the terrible deed of fratricide. It is a blow to the order of the universe. Similarly, Israel's prophets castigate their people warning that if they do that which is evil in God's eyes, Eretz Yisrael will disgorge them from itself. Briefly then, in the biblical view Creation is legislation, and the sovereignty of God over Creation is in the execution of justice. Man is judged by his deeds. He must justify his existence by shouldering the yoke of divine sovereignty. If he fails, he is punished; and the punishment is an undermining of existence and its destruction. This is the substantive link between the commemoration of Creation and law.

The view that identifies the existence of the world with the moral order is, as noted, what distinguishes the prophetic Jewish world outlook from paganism. To understand the ideational content of Rosh HaShanah, one must also take account of basic motivations whose impact can be observed in man's behavior, and the quality of the determinations that man must make in his deeds. What prompts man to sin? Why does he disregard the law on which his existence hinges, just as it does for all living creatures who submit themselves naturally to the law that was decreed for them? The answer, undoubtedly, testifies to man's possession of a faculty that distinguishes him from all other natural creatures; he alone has intellect and will. He alone has choice. Indeed, there is in man, too, a natural inclination to the good. His intended perfection as a man is achieved only by doing the good, and inherently man aspires to perfection. This notion is expressed with a special clarity in Psalm 1, "Happy is the man" who walks in the paths of God and performs His commandments. Happy because he is blessed with an authentic existence.

But freedom of choice is in man's nature; consequently man's nature also becomes an inner obstacle that he must surmount in order to achieve perfection. As a creature of free will, man first has a natural tendency to individuate and concentrate on himself. Will is expressed when it activates the ability to desire—even in contradiction to what has been commanded. In other words, there is an arbitrary element in freedom that is rooted in emphasizing one's selfhood. It is the contrariness flung at a command, even a just command, which springs from an external authority. From another aspect man, as a natural creature, would like to live as all other creatures, exempt from the moral responsibility of his actions, responsive solely to his natural drives. As a natural creature, man would like to find the existential conditions he requires ready and waiting for him, and the instructions that orient his deeds imprinted as natural instincts and not as painful choices among a variety of tempting options whose precise significance are not available to him, just as their future outcomes are unknown.

There is a conflicting tension between these two natural inclinations; in concert they shape man's special status in the world. Man's uniqueness as a willed, choosing creature grants him a certain sovereignty in nature while broadening the scope of his needs. The immediate result is to take man yet one more distancing step from a natural existence responsive to drives and instincts. To the extent that he is a creature who chooses, man is a fearful creature. A growing anxiety for the future is his lot. He would like his status as a willing and choosing individual to be commensurate with an ability to ensure that he has the same instinctive security that lower forms of life possess. Yet he is unable to have such dominion. The more he strains, the more the gap grows between his needs, and what nature and he himself can provide. This is how the awful contradiction is created in the midst of man's life, and this is the source of sin.

According to the biblical perception, from the beginning man is confronted by a choice in principle that will determine his life's aim. The first choice is to validate the two natural inclinations of man's metaphysical status; that is, to aspire to an arbitrary dominion over nature, to absolute assurance that everything he requires today, tomorrow, and on the day after, throughout the span of a foreseeable future, will be secured. How? Simple: by holding the collateral in his hands. He must amass treasures. He must acquire today what he will need tomorrow. He must rely on what is actually his, which he can immediately realize. This, according to the Bible, is the orientation of paganism, which manifests itself practically in the cultures of the largest instrumental nations, the cultures of the river civilizations—Egypt at one end, and Assyria and Babylonia at the other. But it is not accidental that these civilizations, motivated by a desire to reign supreme over nature, ultimately bring about man's self-enslavement. The enslavement of man to man, and the enslavement of the rulers to their hunger to rule.

What is the alternative? It is to accept the yoke of the dominion of the Heavens through belief. In this sense, belief is man's inner readiness to rely on a moral certainty that is evidenced both in the order that reigns in Creation, and the characteristic of enlightened human will. Man, who is certain that God created the world for the good and set an aim of goodness for man, can relinquish an aspiration for external assurance. He does not look for dominion but for actions that express an ethical tendency to construct the core of his selfhood from within. He must be sure that if he acts in such a manner, he will benefit, first from a standpoint of essential destiny—he will achieve his perfection as a man; but also from the standpoint of his external fate, even though he has no practical surety that tomorrow he will find all he needs for his existence. This is because he relies on the beneficial proclivity by which God rules His world. In its essence, moral certainty is belief, and when man relies on it he gains liberty and the meaningful essential destiny that sets him apart. Of course, this is an ongoing test. In every new situation man confronts conflicting choices, and he must decide—and preceding every such decision a struggle is conducted between the natural tendency to dominion and the believing will. Consequently man is judged at every moment, and his deeds determine his fate.

Through its symbols Rosh HaShanah, as it became crystallized in the later tradition, reflects the bases of the biblical outlook: God founded the earth on justice, and He safeguards His creation through justice. The commemoration day of Creation is the Day of Judgment in which man is required to take on the yoke of God's rule. Man is judged according to his deeds; he is punished for sins and rebellion, whereas belief justifies his life in the eye of the Creator, and this effects bounteous life for eternity.

ROSH HASHANAH AND THE BIBLICAL OUTLOOK

Celebrated as it is in later tradition, how does Rosh HaShanah express the biblical outlook?—through a reflexive, abundant, complex exploitation of the biblical source. Early on, the process is apparent in the ritual symbol that separates Rosh HaShanah from other holidays—the sound of the shofar. The commandment is found in the Torah, "And in the seventh month, on the first day of the month, ye shall have a holy convocation: ye shall do no manner of servile work; it is a day of blowing the horn unto you" (Numbers 29:1). The blast of the shofar is clearly implied in the biblical quotation though the Torah does not spell out the significance it attributes to the act. Later *halakhic* tradition, however, does just that as it institutes the sounding of the shofar in the special Rosh HaShanah service: the prayer of *malkhuyot, zikhronot, and shofarot*—the kingship of God, remembrances, and trumpets. Undoubtedly composed later than the Bible, the prayer was structured entirely as a mosaic of biblical verses. Finally, the biblical reading and the *haftarah* that were chosen to be read on this day bear mentioning. Here are entire biblical chapters that need to be understood in their direct context, but the act of choosing precisely these chapters for recitation on Rosh HaShanah is clearly an interpretive act, and the interpretation is in keeping with the perspective of a late tradition that returns reflexively to the Bible. The intent of the interpretation is revealed through the liturgical context in which these narrative chapters are placed. The worshipper is required to find the moral that stems from the chapters on his own through his participation in the day's prayer service; that is, he is called to an investigative, homiletic understanding that is integrated in the very act of prayer.

The contribution of the biblical readings from the *haftarah* and the *parashah* to the ideational content of the holiday present entire segments of the *Mikra*, the Five Books of Moses, for study in the course of the day's prayer service. During both days of Rosh HaShanah (according to the *Mikra* there is only one day; the *halakhah* subsequently doubled this because of considerations connected with the sanctification of the month), Chapters 21 and 22 of Genesis are read. The first day's *haftarah* is from the Book of Samuel I; Chapter 1 is read in its entirety and Chapter 2 through verse 11. The *haftarah* for the second day is from Jeremiah, Chapter 32:1–19. The *parashah* for the first day describes Isaac's birth, circumcision, and weaning; Ishmael and Hagar's banishment due to Sarah's determination, and their deliverance; the story of the Covenant among Abraham, Avimelech King of Grar, and his army Chief, Picol, regarding the wells Abraham dug; and the story of the tamarisk tree Abraham planted in Be'er Sheva. On the second day, the story continues and comes to a climax with the *akedah*—the binding and near sacrifice of Isaac. The *haftarah* of the first day recounts the tale of Elkanah and his two wives, Hannah and Penina; Hannah's entreaty before Eli at Shilo, and her vow; the story of how Hannah's plea was answered and the fulfillment of her vow; and it concludes with Hannah's hymn of thanksgiving. On the second day, the *haftarah* is composed of Jeremiah's prophecy of comfort, which recalls Rachel the matriarch lamenting the fate of her children, and the promise God made to remember the affection of His people and to keep the Covenant made with the patriarchs.

First observation might suggest that this is a strange choice. What connection can there be between Rosh HaShanah and a story that begins with Isaac's birth and the expulsion of Hagar and Ishmael? What connection does Rosh HaShanah have to the story of Samuel's birth and consecration? Furthermore, if Rosh HaShanah is the day that commemorates the creation of man and the Day of Judgment, wouldn't one expect that the chapters to be taken from the Book of Genesis would be those that relate the story of the Garden of Eden, a story of sin and decree that rouses one to prayerful return? A number of homilies from the Sages attempt to explain this quandary. One *midrash* says that both Sarah and Hannah conceived on Rosh HaShanah so the stories of their conception are recalled on this day.

Another *midrash* relates to the *akedah*: Why does the Torah command the shofar to be sounded on Rosh HaShanah? It is to remember the binding of Isaac through the blast of the ram's horn, a story that ends with sacrificing the ram, whose horns were caught in the thicket, instead of Isaac. Clearly these homilies are intended to link a wealth of motifs to Rosh HaShanah, something that the Bible itself does not do. There is apparently nothing here but a homiletic rationalization, the ex post facto rationalization of a decision with a profound reasoning behind it. Why does God remember Sarah and Hannah precisely on Rosh HaShanah? In the Sages' view—which greatly broadens the scope of the holiday's content—Rosh HaShanah is the Day of Judgment, and it is precisely in this personal, individual context that there is a link to the fate of the people as a whole. Invoking these stories raises tangible feelings in the worshipper that his fate as an individual is bound up in the generational continuity of his people, a continuity that is about to be decreed, and which is his judgment as well.

In other words, using biblical portions, the *midrash* authenticates the notion that Rosh HaShanah is the Day of Judgment of each individual Jew, and of the people as a whole. In the process a detailed narrative illustration of the notion is provided. In applying this to the *akedah* story, the *midrash* connects the blast on the ram's horn at Rosh HaShanah to the horns of the ram entangled in the thicket in order to repeat that here is something to reinforce the worshipper's belief on the Day of Judgment. Fear of the judgment is great. How can a person justify himself before his Creator? The story of the *akedah* evokes the virtues of the patriarchs whose lives and deeds—in a distinction which rebounds to the credit of the people—set the people's faith throughout its history. May the virtue of Abraham and Isaac, who withstood the terrible trial of the *akedah*, protect the worshippers on their day of judgment. Such tying of the *parashah* to the prayers of Rosh HaShanah arises from the context of the day's service. The central prayer of Rosh HaShanah is *malkhuyot, zikhronot, and shofarot*, which, as noted, incorporates the sounding of the shofar. Indeed in the *zikhronot* portion, the prayer attaches great importance to the story of the *akedah*.

From the flow of these remembrances in the prayer, one understands why the Sages chose this portion for the reading of the day, instead of the story of Adam and his sin; it is precisely because it is a day of judgment, and all the recollections called up deal with judgments actually conducted on this day. An accused person is not inclined to remind his judge of past sins, either his or his ancestors. On the contrary, the person seeks to recall anything he can that might lessen the sentence. Consequently the zikhronot prayer recounts the story of Noah who, through his righteousness, saved the human race; and Abraham and Isaac whose akedah story is evidence of the highest degree of belief. This is a central and prominent theme in the service as it was formulated in the Oral Tradition. The story of the akedah is found in the daily morning prayer, and the explanation for this is evident in a sentence that comes near the end of the story. "Master of the universe, may it be Your will, Lord our God and God of our fathers, that our fathers' covenant be credited to us, just as our father Abraham overcame his mercy toward his only son when he was ready to sacrifice him in order to do Your will, so may Your mercy overcome Your anger and may Your mercy surmount your other attributes and may You mitigate the strict letter of the law for us."

In their selection of readings, the Sages keep in mind a consideration that stems from the worshipper's actual situation, which, though the prayer holds educational elements, is not a didactic one. It is a psychological event that occurs simultaneously with its very articulation. If it was a lesson meant to deal with the ideational significance of Rosh HaShanah, it would have been suitable to select chapters such as the creation of man, his sin and judgment; but it is prayer that is the issue. The worshipper is meant to regard himself as standing, actually at the moment, in judgment before his Creator. What is to be said should arouse within him, and arouse, as it were, in the One he stands before, thoughts and feelings directed at his situation, at that moment. The chapters selected, therefore, must shape feelings within the worshipper that are proper for the Day of Judgment, chapters that will actuate within him the significance of his position, and yet be supportive. If this is the perspective, then the selection may be said to be judicious. The stories of God's remembrance of Sarah and Hannah concretize the condition of the supplicant as an individual within the people. The story of the akedah situates the worshipper in a position of merit and empowers him to beseech a mitigating mercy from his Judge. If one continues this line of reasoning, yet another perspective is opened. The stories of the Bible are presented to the worshipper as examples and omens, or in the words of the Sages, "the fathers' deeds are an omen for their sons." It is from reading the Torah that one can learn how to withstand the trial of belief, and what unsuspected power true prayer has to change God's decree for man.

THE SACRIFICE OF ISAAC—
A GESTURE OF ABSOLUTE FAITH

Viewed in the context of the day's prayer, what is the interpretation of the *akedah* story? The first thought that occurs is that from the standpoint of "the fathers' deeds are an omen for their sons," the *akedah* illustrates for the worshipper a level of exemplary faith of which only Abraham was capable. It is doubtful that that is what was intended. It is doubtful that anyone who relies on the merit of the Fathers regards himself as being able to achieve that same degree of belief—which is why the cognitive shift that occurs in the prayer close to the *akedah* story, in the daily morning service, is so interesting. Abraham's exemplary deed is regarded by the worshipper not as applying to himself but to his God, Who is about to pass judgment on him. That is, if Abraham was able to suppress his mercy toward his son, it is expected that God will withhold His anger. In this instance the deeds of the Fathers are a sign to the Holy One rather than a sign to the sons. The worshipper alludes to the absolute merit that derives from the Fathers, and applies to the sons, because a deed like the *akedah* persists through the generations, and it obligates God when judging the offspring of the Fathers. Nonetheless, the story also holds a portent for the sons, and this becomes clearer if the *akedah* is studied in its broadest context. In the opening sentence of the story, the Torah itself testifies to this. "And it came to pass after these things that God did prove Abraham" (Genesis 22:1), signifying that the events that preceded the trial serve as a background to understanding the test itself. The prayer book accepted this association when it placed the background of the *akedah* story in the position of a self-sufficient Bible reading on the first day of Rosh HaShanah.

Detailed examination of both parts of the story indicates that whatever preceded the *akedah* was itself a test; at the same time, Abraham's feelings and thoughts as a person of belief during these trials may be clarified. Abraham had two sons and he was tested regarding each of them. The expulsion of Ishmael—in Abraham's preference for Isaac—in keeping with Sarah's will, is a great test. It is important to note that Abraham does not give up his son without argument in the story of Ishmael. He sees it as wrong, and he remains unconvinced until God grants him two things that appear to be totally missing, or totally absent, in the *akedah* story: an explanation of the reasons for the deed and its necessity, as well as the promise that no harm would befall the son.

The explanation is "For it is through Isaac that offspring shall be continued for you" (Genesis 21:12). The handmaiden's son must be driven out so that he will not be a co-inheritor with Isaac. It is the Divine plan. And in the name of this plan, Abraham is expected to overcome a father's feelings for his eldest-born son. But the plan does not extend to sacrificing the first-born son. Immediately afterward Abraham is told to have faith, not to be apprehensive because "as for the son of the slave woman, I will make a nation of him, too." One sees then that Abraham does not acquiesce in the expulsion of his son until the morality of the deed is clarified and until his responsibility as a father for the fate of his son is guaranteed.

This is the background of the *akedah* with one highly significant verse that joins the two parts of the story into a thematic whole: "For it is through Isaac that offspring shall be continued for you." Without this verse, the *akedah* story is sealed and impenetrable. Could the same man who did not relinquish his eldest-born until he was promised that no harm would befall him abandon a son of his old age without a word? Furthermore, could the same man who did not agree to expel his eldest-born without explanation sacrifice the son of his late years without demanding a reason for such an awful commandment?

Against the background of the expulsion of Hagar and Ishmael, it would appear that this short sentence holds the answer to both questions: the justification for Ishmael and Hagar's expulsion does not stem from the father's preference for either of his sons, nor of one of the mothers. If this were merely Sarah's preference for her only son because of her love for him, and because of enmity for her rival and her son, it would be purely and simply a case of moral injustice. The justification is seen in the specific destiny for which Isaac was found suitable by God. From the standpoint of unfolding events, it was best to favor Isaac and separate him from Ishmael. It is clear then why Abraham had to have proven, even to himself, that this was not a preference due to his feelings as a father, and that even vis-à-vis Isaac he only carried out God's will. If it is proper to sacrifice his fatherly feelings for Ishmael, he must show the same readiness vis-à-vis Isaac. And in this way he also sets Isaac on the path leading to the role for which he has been chosen. Here is the implicit reason behind "For it is through Isaac that offspring shall be continued for you," and it is the great assurance that accompanies Abraham on his way. He is certain, though he does not know how, that no harm will befall Isaac. Simply, it is out of the question because it is God's will—"For it is through Isaac that offspring shall be continued for you."

And it is between these two opposing truisms that Abraham stands as a man of faith. He knows surely that he must sacrifice the personal father's love he has for Isaac, and give him to God, for Isaac was given to him only so that he might, with full heart, consecrate him to God. Abraham knows with certainty that it is totally impossible for God to want to harm either him or his son. How will these two truisms co-exist? That Abraham does not know. This is his trial, and Abraham confronts it successfully because he makes the determination as a believing person. It is incumbent upon him to fulfill his role and offer up his son. How will the promise be kept? For that, he expects God to do His part. Consequently going to the *akedah* is an act of absolute faith.

Abraham goes to the brink, which he can do only because he believes with a certainty that stems from an absolute moral affirmation; even standing at the brink, his belief is unshaken, his belief that God will fulfill His part. He offers his son to God. He has enacted what he has been commanded to do, and in the same hair's breadth between fulfilling the aim by an unstinting deed, God responds and gives Abraham his son. In the situation thus created one sees the explanation for the dilemma Abraham confronted as a believing person: Isaac was indeed given to God—but not as a sacrifice; rather as a living person to fulfill the mission God set him. The historiosophic issue this statement brings one to is, however, beyond the scope of the present discussion.

What can the worshipper at Rosh HaShanah learn from the trial of the man of faith? Standing trial before his Creator, being judged, it would appear that one should understand the significance of the gesture of faith to be made. Like Abraham, he must present himself in absolute moral faith before Him. Whatever the outcome, the believer depends totally on God, and this inner gesture, by which the defendant accepts God's will in advance, is what vindicates him. It is only an internal, absolute devotion to God's will, within a life of faith, that guarantees that the good which God intends in all His acts will be revealed in the course of the believer's life. Abraham's stance in the *akedah* is a model of self-justification through a gesture of absolute belief. It is the believer's faith that such a gesture holds the potential to actually oblige the God one believes in, because ". . . His deeds are perfect, yea, all His ways are just" (Deut. 32:4). Examination shows that because of this certainty the worshipper can utter the most audacious statement in the daily prayer, calling on God to take an example from Abraham's deed as a man of faith. The gesture of absolute faith obliges God to respond with a gesture of love.

PRAYER AS AN ACT OF BELIEF

Should there be room for doubt that this is the profound meaning of the *akedah* story as part of the Rosh HaShanah service, the *haftarot* displace it. Generally there is a thematic correlation between the *parashah* and its related *haftarah*, and generally the choice is an interpretive or homiletic one. The very conjoining of portions that are far from one another in the Bible in the same prayer service calls for understanding each portion from the perspective of the other. What is it that the Sages want to stress in the Torah portion by means of the *haftarah* they append to it? What common theme do they see between them? In the present case, the thematic parallel is very pronounced even at the narrative level: a son is born after extended barrenness as a gift from heaven. There is tension between the beloved wife and her rival. The son born as a heavenly dispensation is dedicated to the Divine will. Of course, following on the story of Abraham, Hannah, and Elkanah, her husband, know that consecrating their son to God does not call for an *akedah*. Instead, the child will be dedicated to God's service. It will be his life's mission. Thus, the dilemma of a life in faith that is revealed in Abraham's trial is not found here, and because of this the story comes within the scope of every Jew's experience.

The tension of the whole test is focused now in another place; that is, the way in which the believing person strives to influence his fate in something that is undetermined between him and his Creator. Prayer is a gesture of belief, and it is an active effort by man to justify himself in God's eyes and alter His decree, if indeed the decree is severe. Consequently, Hannah's story is one of changing a Divine decree through prayer. From the perspective of the man who is standing before God, this is the added dimension that this story has over the tale of the *akedah*. One does not see Abraham at prayer; rather, he is engaged in an act of devotion. Nonetheless, from what follows we can see that prayer, as a process that changes the worshipper, is also an act of devotion. In Hannah's case, it is a devotion that can be expected of anyone, and her prayer underscores the moral available to the worshipper from the *akedah* story.

What is the psychological reality out of which Hannah approaches prayer? She is indeed the beloved wife, but what has been given to her by her husband is appropriated by God and given to her rival. Hannah is barren. It is this decree that she must change. It appears that the annual pilgrimage to Shilo is a recurrent attempt to change the decree by means of a devotional act. Admittedly a routine devotion. Nor has it succeeded. After years of disappointment and frustration, Hannah is seen to be close to the turning point. On the verge of despair, she retains but a remnant of hope to which she clings for a final effort. That decisive effort brings about a change between the two forces that operate in her environment. Penina, the rival wife, goads Hannah to respond rebelliously. "Moreover, her rival, to make her miserable, would taunt her that the Lord had closed her womb" (I Samuel 1:6); that is, Penina tries to push Hannah into the sin of rebellion against her husband and against God, with the result that Penina will emerge victorious. The opposing force in Hannah's environment is Elkanah, who in his love for Hannah, tries to reconcile her to her condition. "Her husband Elkanah said to her, 'Hannah, why are you crying and why are you not eating? Why are you so sad? Am I not more devoted to you than ten sons?'" (I Samuel 1:8).

Hannah is thrust into the middle between her husband's love and her rival's hatred, each functioning ostensibly out of personal motives. The motivation, if basically selfish, appears all too human, easily understandable. This is true not only of the rival's hatred, but of the husband's love, which seeks to gain all the devotion of the beloved wife. The two use her for their own emotional gratification, and from her viewpoint, regardless as to which of them she heeds, the result is the same. She would sink into the bitter disappointment of a love that bears no fruit. Hannah's choice is to escape both these controlling influences. The decision is entirely her own, and it thrusts her into a new direction, which brings the ultimate transformation. The nature of the decision is revealed in prayer. More accurately, prayer is converted into a process in which a decision can be made, and it takes place in a direction that opposes not just the influence of the husband and rival wife, but runs counter to the selfish psychological intent that is the basis of their influence.

The verbal content of Hannah's prayer is not given in the story; it notes only that "she kept on praying before the Lord" (I Samuel 1:12). But this was a silent prayer. "Now Hannah was praying in her heart; only her lips moved, but her voice could not be heard" (I Samuel 1:13). As to the content of the prayer, we hear simply the essence of her petition, and her vow. Nonetheless, the story gives a vivid reflection of the psychological process in which Hannah is engaged. At the beginning of the prayer, one reads that she was "wretched" and it is out of this wretchedness that she wept. Wretchedness is the state from which she must free herself. Indeed, she escapes from it through a psychological conversion, which she expresses in a vow. As Hannah rises from her prayer it appears that she knows full well, not only through the words of the High Priest, Eli, but also inwardly, that her prayer has been answered; she becomes a different person. This is indicated in a short but highly significant expression, "So the woman left, and she ate and her countenance was no longer sad" (verse 18).

How does Hannah know that her prayer has been answered? How does Eli know it? One learns of the nature of the psychological change Hannah has undergone from her reply to the stern chiding of the High Priest. Though an individual generally reacts to such a reprimand by a meekness born of weakness and awe, or in a rebellious retort, Hannah reacts in neither way. She changes Eli's attitude toward her rejecting his words, not in bitterness but with perfect deference. She accepts his authority without, however, giving in to his judgment. From this response, Eli senses that she had offered a genuine prayer and that her petition had been granted. Indeed, the reaction to Eli's speech is but a continuation of the emotional conversion that emerged in her vow. Hannah neither rebels nor concedes. In her vow, she promises to consecrate the son who will be born to her, should she be granted a son, to God, turning her entreaty to God into a pledge to Him. It is not for herself alone that she beseeches a son. The fulfillment of her prayer will be realized in her son, and he will be the fulfillment of the Divine will.

Here is the inner meaning of a prayer that can abolish a decree. Neither passive acquiescence nor the hyperactivity of revolt, but rather elevating that which is personally sought into a loving gesture that is attuned to the Divine will. Hannah's readiness to give lovingly that which she will receive invests her with the merit to receive in love that which she had been prepared to give. The transformation that takes place in her gives her the assurance that her prayer has been heard because now she has made her desire as the Divine desire, and the Divine desire will be done.

Hannah's prayer is like Abraham's deed; it is a gesture of belief; her trial takes place during her prayer to God. She had become worthy of the fulfillment of her petition because it was no longer merely her desire, but had become God's will too. She knows now that if she has undertaken to accept God's will in practice, God, who examines man's heart, will grant her desire. In the ceremonious announcement, said aloud as she completes her vow, Hannah says this explicitly. It would appear that confronting God in this way—out of complete readiness to do His will and complete certainty that His will, which is identified with the doing of good and justice in the world, will triumph—is what makes the story of Hannah analogous to the story of Abraham. Hannah's prayer can serve as a model for all men.

GOD'S PRESENCE IS EXEMPLIFIED BY THE SHOFAR

The special prayer for Rosh HaShanah is the prayer of *malkhuyot, zikhronot, and shofarot*. The shofar is sounded at the end of *shaharit*, the morning prayer, invoking these three basic elements of the day's service. At the completion of *musaf*, the late morning prayer, the shofar is sounded again preceded by the words of a prayer that interprets the themes of *malkhuyot, zikhronot, and shofarot*, words that are, in effect, homilies derived from the Torah, the Prophets, and the Writings. And in a ceremonious gesture they encompass three core ideas concerning belief contained in the outlook of the Bible and the Sages. *Malkhuyot* is the first and the most general. The congregation accepts God as its King. It recognizes and professes that God rules the universe. Even if all men do not acknowledge His sovereignty, the day will come when they shall and all creatures will unite to serve Him in awe. The subject of the prayer is Kingship itself. The congregation describes God as a Monarch and unconditionally subordinates itself in awe to the Sovereign's will. Humility vis-à-vis the Divine, and the acknowledgment of His sovereignty is the beginning. This is testified to by the first sounding of the shofar.

The *zikhronot* prayer interprets the role of the Monarch in ruling His world. The King makes Himself transcendent to the world so as to rule it. His will is directed at the world; He knows all that transpires; He remembers all creatures and deeds. Examining the *zikhronot* prayer in detail reveals that God is described as the Judge of all man's deeds, past and present. In other words, in this instance the meaning of *zikharon* as memory is to pay attention—a constant presence, complete concern. Everything that occurs in the world is known and is ever present before God. Every deed endures; having been done, it must effect change; it cannot but produce effects. Human beings tend to forget certain deeds and thus imagine that they were not done; God does not forget. The deeds persist before Him and have outcomes.

The worshipper is expected to remember this. In standing before his Creator, all his deeds are disclosed; nothing is forgotten, and judgment will be passed on all. Consequently, after assuming the burden of monarchy, the worshipper approaches the judgment of his King. But, it should be noted, this is not a passive appearance. In presenting himself before the Creator for trial, the worshipper not only reminds himself that God remembers everything he has done, he ostensibly reminds his God of certain things pertaining to the history of mankind, to the patriarchs, and to the Jewish people. It is an energetic effort to have the Heavens recall that man has amassed merits in God's reckoning, the credit of Noah, the virtue of Abraham.

From the standpoint of the individual worshipper, this is an attempt to project the best that is in him before his Judge at the moment of judgment, the most perfect image to which he can aspire, which he now embraces, which he has reason to hope he can achieve because in the past it was once achieved by man. In other words, in the presence of the trial the worshipper struggles to elevate himself to a level that might justify him in the judgment. He is mindful of being in the presence of his Judge and recounts himself at his best, if only from the standpoint of his absolute desire to renew himself and be as worthy as he can be. The second blast on the shofar arouses one to this aspiration.

Ultimately the *shofarot* prayer highlights the aim toward which God rules the world. The sound of the shofar symbolizes the great events at which God was revealed to men, particularly the revelation at Sinai, and future occurrences in which He will be revealed to them. The sounding of the shofar is the tiding of redemption. God's revelation to man bespeaks His love for their existence. These are the occurrences of perfection at which creatures can raise themselves to be worthy of their Creator's will—the revelations of perfection, or the heralding of redemption. God, Lord of the universe, judges his creatures in order to make them pure and lead them toward that goal. The third sounding of the shofar testifies to this, and it encompasses within it the two previous testimonies. The symbolic meaning of the blast on Rosh HaShanah is interpreted as marking God's presence in the midst of His people. Anyone who hears the sound of the shofar is reminded that God's kingdom is present here and now. Here and now one stands before his God. Anyone who directs his attention to the sound of the shofar is as someone in the presence of God, momentarily and eternally. When one is fully intent, when one assumes the yoke of the Kingdom of Heaven, when one presents himself at his best before his Creator—his Judge, it is as though one undertakes the yoke of Divine government. It is then that he will have a change of heart, and should this occur he will feel as Hannah "and her countenance was no more sad." In his heart, he knows that he has been acquitted.

As one stands before the Royal Throne as a Seat of Judgment, the cycle of the year draws to a close. As one stands in the renewal, before the future when the Kingdom of Heaven will reign, the new cycle begins: "May an old year and its afflictions end, a new year and its blessings begin."

FIVE

YOM KIPPUR:
CONFESSION, ATONEMENT,
AND REPENTANCE

REPENTANCE—A SPIRITUAL PROCESS

As it developed in Jewish tradition following the destruction of the Temple, Yom Kippur was a Day of Atonement dedicated to repentance. In the sequence of the Days of Awe, man is first judged by God on Rosh HaShanah, but the judgment is not yet final. Indeed, the fear of punishment that hangs over man prompts him to regret his evil deeds, atone for them, and make repentance. With the gates of repentance still not sealed, it may be that if a person wholeheartedly repents his sins they will be atoned for and his sentence alleviated. Yom Kippur, which falls ten days after Rosh HaShanah, is dedicated to expiation and repentance. According to the Torah, the day is intended to atone for the sins of the community as a whole, and for its leaders. However, the community is the sum total of its members, and they are accountable for each other even in the spiritual and moral sense. It is to the account of the community as a whole that the sins of individuals are charged. Therefore atonement for the sins of individuals was aggregated as they stood with the community before the Seat of Justice and Mercy, asking for each other's forgiveness and for the forgiveness of their Creator, in addition to atonement for the polity.

Thus the Yom Kippur concept that requires clarification is the notion of repentance. There are two concepts here whose relationship appears at first glance to be somewhat unclear: atonement and repentance. According to the Torah, the day is called *Yom HaKippurim*, and the theme of the day is repentance. The question is whether or not these two concepts are identical. It may be useful to start the discussion with the succinct *halakhic* summary offered by Maimonides in *Hilkhot T'shuvah*, the "Laws of Repentance" chapter of his book, *Mishneh Torah*. While this segment relates to the concept of repentance in general, Maimonides himself applies it to Yom Kippur in particular. As early as the first section, mention is made of the scapegoat (Mishnah 2) and Yom Kippur as a day that atones for sins (Mishnah 4). In the second section, Maimonides expressly states that "Yom Kippur is a time of repentance for the individual and for the community, and the final stage of forgiveness and pardon for Israel. It is therefore incumbent upon each individual to make repentance and to confess on Yom Kippur" (Mishnah 7).

Three concepts are present here in a single sentence: atonement, repentance, and confession. Can these be considered a single theme? Careful study shows that in his attempt to summarize the *halakhah*, Maimonides was somewhat hard-pressed in this respect. He intended to discuss the commandment that deals with repentance; the question is, does such a commandment actually appear in the Torah? "If one has infringed on a commandment in the Torah," Maimonides opens, "whether it is a positive commandment or a prohibition, whether transgressed deliberately or in error, when he repents and is contrite, he must confess before God, blessed be He. As it is stated, 'And if any man or woman commit a sin, etc., they shall confess the sin.' This is confession, and confession is a positive commandment" (Mishnah 1).

It is then confession that is the commandment, and Maimonides introduces the theme of repentance while discussing the commandment of confession (". . . he must, when he makes repentance and is contrite, confess"). As far as the Torah is concerned, the requirement of confession is literally related not to repentance but to atonement. The confession is heard as one's hands are placed on the head of the sacrificial animal. But does the subject of repentance go unmentioned in the Bible as a whole, or the Torah in particular? On the contrary, the concept appears frequently. Repentance is the very life mission of the prophets who are sent to exhort the people of Israel and its individual members to repent so that they may be saved from the terrible punishment that awaits them. The fact remains, however, that if one looks for substantiation for a commandment to repent—i.e., for a binding legal norm—no such source can be found, at least not expressly.

This is the quandary that Maimonides as a man of *halakhah* sought to resolve and, in so doing, raised a profound problem that goes beyond the formal legalistic issue. Just how profound this question is becomes clear if one examines the inner context in which the concepts of atonement and confession appear in the Bible, and where the notion of repentance appears in the Bible. Atonement and confession, phrased in mitzvah-like or legal terms, are located in the Priestly Code. The sources clearly show that atonement is a highly ritualistic act that involves the offering of sacrifices. The sinner who wishes to be exonerated brings an animal offering, places his hands on its head, and confesses. The priest slaughters the offering and sprinkles its blood on the altar. The act of sprinkling the blood atones for the sin. In contrast, there is no reference to ritual in the prophets' call to repentance; rather, it is religious and ethical.

The people as a whole, and each individual member, are exhorted to stop their evil deeds, particularly in the moral realm. They are charged to do that which is good in the eyes of their Creator; this is the meaning of repentance. Moreover, a certain tension can be seen between the atonement ritual and the prophetic call for repentance. While the prophets are not opposed to the ritual itself, they are opposed to the belief that the ritual per se can effect atonement without repentance. Wherever they see a natural, human tendency to rely on ritual atonement without repentance, they strongly oppose it. The ritual act has no value unless accompanied by psychological, social, and moral deeds. In the absence of repentance, a clear distinction, even dichotomy, can be seen between these concepts.

Since the subject of the present discussion is the ideational theme of Yom Kippur, it should be noted that this dichotomy was also given prominence in the development of the day's liturgy. In this respect, it is worthwhile examining the Torah portion read on Yom Kippur, and the *haftarah*, which stands in apposition. The Torah portion is taken from Leviticus (the Priestly Code), Chapter 16, and includes a detailed description of the sacrificial offerings on Yom Kippur. The word "atonement" appears repeatedly throughout the chapter in connection with the description of the sacrifice of the bulls, the sacrifice of one goat and the dispatching of the second, the scapegoat, to Azzazel. The chapter reaches its climax with the commandment, "And it shall be a statute forever unto you: in the seventh month, on the tenth day of the month, ye shall afflict your souls, and shall do no manner of work, the home-born, or the stranger that sojourneth among you. For on that day shall atonement be made for you, to cleanse you; of all your sins shall ye be clean before the Lord" (verses 29, 30). What is striking is not merely that the word "repentance" does not appear even once in this chapter, but that there is no hint of the concept. The chapter does not include even the slightest allusion to a psychological or moral effort.

In contrast, the *haftarah*, which is taken from Isaiah 17:14 and Chapter 58, is devoted entirely to spiritual endeavor and moral self-correction. The strongly worded language relates explicitly to the dichotomy between the purely technical ritualistic concept and the moral approach of the prophets. "Is such the fast that I have chosen? The day for a man to afflict his soul? Is it to bow down his head as a bulrush, and to spread sackcloth and ashes under him? Wilt thou call this a fast, and an acceptable day to the Lord? Is not this the fast that I have chosen? To loose the fetters of wickedness, to undo the bands of the yoke, and to let the oppressed go free, and that ye break every yoke? Is it not to deal thy bread to the hungry, and that thou bring the poor that are cast out to thy house? When thou see the naked, that thou cover him, and that thou hide not thyself from thine own flesh? Then shall thy light break forth as the morning, and thy healing shall spring forth speedily; and thy righteousness shall go before thee; the glory of the Lord shall be thy reward" (58:5–8).

In juxtaposing this *haftarah* with the Torah portion, the sages created a typical *midrash* whose aim was to interpret a ritual act of atonement in the light of the prophetic concept of moral reform; it was in this spirit that they sought to shape the liturgy of Yom Kippur. This is also the spirit that pervades Maimonides's even-handed and precise *halakhic* discussion. Where does he find a connection between the ritual act of atonement and the psychological or moral act of repentance? The answer is in confession. In the Priestly Code referred to earlier, the matter of confession is mentioned in the following terms, "And Aaron shall lay both his hands upon the head of the live goat, and confess over him all the iniquities of the children of Israel, and all their transgressions, even all their sins; and he shall put them upon the head of the goat, and shall send him away by the hand of a designated person into the wilderness" (Leviticus 16:21).

This confession is an overt pronouncement—articulated in the hearing of the congregation and before God—of the sins committed by the people (and it is therefore also a personal confession). True, in this case there is no mention of remorse or corrective action. The pronouncement of sins is ostensibly intended to transfer them from the sinners to the goat, which supposedly takes these sins with it into the wilderness: "And the goat shall bear upon him all their iniquities unto a land which is cut off; and he shall let go the goat in the wilderness" (Lev. 16:22). Nevertheless, the overt pronouncement and recounting of the sins contains within it a kernel of the psychological and moral process. Through confession the sinner takes responsibility for his sins, recognizing that he has sinned and that he requires atonement. It is compelling to see how Maimonides takes this tiny seed hidden in the ritual act and develops it into a complete concept of repentance. "How does one confess? One says, 'Oh Lord, I have sinned and transgressed and done wrong before You, and I have done such and such acts; I am ashamed of my acts and will never do this thing again.' This is the main aspect of confession" (Laws of Repentance, 1:1).

Three themes are included in this concise formula, only one of which appears in the Bible: the overt confession of one's sins, the expression of regret, and the decision not to repeat such acts. In effect, this is Maimonides's definition of repentance. "And what is repentance? That the sinner shall abandon his sin and shall remove it from his thoughts and shall resolve not to do this act again, as it is said: 'A wicked man shall leave his ways, etc.' And also, that he shall be remorseful that he sinned, as it is said: 'For after my repentance I was remorseful,' and shall swear by He who knows all secrets that he shall not commit this sin again, as it is said, 'And we shall no more call our handiwork a god, etc.' and he must confess aloud and speak aloud these things that he has resolved in his heart" (Lev. 2:2).

Clearly Maimonides shifted confession from embodiment in the ritual act toward an orientation of psychological and moral repentance; in so doing, he followed in the footsteps of the Sages who interpreted the ritual act as symbolizing a spiritual process with moral significance. The transfer of sins from an individual to a sacrificial animal is a purely symbolic act; the more important dimension is that the confessor separates himself from the sin through his readiness to take responsibility for it, to repair that which can be repaired, and to refrain from such acts. It was in this spirit that Yom Kippur developed in the tradition after the destruction of the Temple. Sacrifices were no longer offered. Self-affliction through fasting was considered a form of sacrifice, but in so doing the act reverts to man himself. Moreover, the emphasis of confession as the core of the day's worship, and the reinterpretation of this concept in light of the idea of repentance are clearly evident in the prayer book.

Maimonides's comments, in this respect, summarize the process of the development of Yom Kippur in Jewish tradition following the destruction of the Temple. The confessional prayer is indeed the central prayer of Yom Kippur, repeated no fewer than six times. In place of the early short formula, a formula emerged that was to extend it considerably within a few generations both in length and complexity. It was as if the confession absorbed the entire ritual act, which could no-longer be performed and in so doing internalized the process and transformed it into a spiritual one. Further on, we will examine the confessional prayer as it developed in the prayer book to illustrate how it reflects the spiritual process. First, however, a fact must be conclusively stated—as Yom Kippur developed in Jewish tradition after the destruction of the Temple, it can be seen as a homily on the Priestly Code's ritual tradition in light of the prophetic concept of repentance. Initially, the concept of atonement was not synonymous with repentance, but later it was considered a symbolic act that reflected repentance as a spiritual process. With this fact in mind, these concepts and the relationship between them must now be re-examined, this time in a systematic, theoretical manner.

THE BIBLICAL BASIS FOR ATONEMENT AND REPENTANCE

A systematic study returns one to the common biblical basis for the concepts of atonement and repentance. Some familiar axioms need to be restated: God created man in His image so that man could rule the world in accordance with his Creator's commands. The description of man as created "in the image of God" is designed to stress that which differentiates humans from all other creatures—man has the capacity to think and to will. Man acts from intention and choice; in other words, the human being is free to act in accordance with the purposes he sets for himself. This freedom is also reflected in man's relations with his Creator, perhaps above all in these relations. Man can choose to obey his Creator's command, but he can also reject it. He can choose good, and this is what God commands him to do; but he can also choose evil. In certain circumstances, evil may appear to man—from his viewpoint—to be the good, despite its running contrary to God's will. It is here that the capacity for sin lies.

What is sin? According to the Genesis story, sin is the act that a human being knowingly performs against the command of God. God commanded man not to eat from the fruit of the tree of knowledge, but man was tempted and knowingly disobeyed the command. This is the initial sin, and since this is a typological story, the initial sin is a prototype for sin in its entirety. Does it therefore follow that sin is the refusal to obey, regardless of the nature of the act itself from man's standpoint? While this may appear to be the case at the beginning of the story, it is not so subsequently. The forbidden act is evil from the standpoint of the man, causing him to betray his destiny. In his sin, man loses that which distinguishes him, his moral freedom. It is through sin that all the relations between the man and his wife, and between them and nature, are distorted. What, then, is the motive for sin?

It emerges from the Genesis story that while man indeed knew at the outset that his act was wrong in terms of its disobedience, he was nevertheless tempted by some good that he imagined in the act from his point of view. First, the forbidden fruit was pleasant to behold. It emitted a sensual stimulation and held redolent promise of enjoyment. So it emerges that man's physical nature, the carnal urges that he shares with the animals, are the initial cause of sin. Man is tempted to satisfy his physical urges and thus neglects the destiny that relates to his spiritual and psychological being. It is important to be precise here: it is not the satisfaction of bodily needs that is considered a sin. Enjoyment of most of the fruits of the garden is permitted. But man, precisely because he has a conscious spirit and is capable of inclination and of purposeful action, is likely to regard himself and his physical and sensual enjoyment as desirable purposes in their own right, with the result that he may become enslaved to his urges. Sin lies in an utter enslavement to sensual enjoyment, which causes man to deviate from his moral destiny; this is the evil that God's commandments are intended to prevent.

Evidently then it is something more than the mere delight of the senses that causes sin. Hunger and thirst do not lead to sin; it is the desire for the enjoyment inherent in satisfying hunger and thirst that precipitates sin. What is the source of this desire that goes beyond the natural instincts of all living creatures? For human beings, enjoyment as such appears to have some kind of significance beyond the normal maintenance and function of the body. Man vindicates his joy of life through pleasure, and the natural needs of the body are no more than a pretext for this. In pleasure, man is actually seeking the gratification of a deeper desire that is unique to human beings as creatures with souls, thus reflecting his ability to choose for himself what is good for him. The Genesis story mirrors this motif: Eve is tempted by the snake, and man is tempted by Eve. The temptation that the snake adds to the sensual delight of the fruit lies in a psychological motive—if man eats from the forbidden tree, he will be "as God, knowing good and evil." The temptation is to disobey a divine command in order to realize an autonomous human capability. In this context, God's command appears to have been arbitrary from the outset, or designed to make man obey Him without regard for the nature of the action.

Man believes that his best interests lie in an act that is in opposition to the commandment since it is through this act that he reaffirms his autonomy. As seen by man, the forbidden act is counterpoised to his liberty. He interprets his freedom to choose to obey, or to disobey, as a decision between affirming his ability to choose by disobeying the commandment or forgoing this ability to choose by obeying a commandment which he finds arbitrary and discriminatory. This is the origin of the paradoxical duality of the act. Man sins because of his desire to reaffirm his liberty, but the act through which he reaffirms his liberty is no more than a surrender to the sensual delight that enslaves man and dissolves his will. As man learns from experience, the sensual pleasure in the excess of drink is an apparent good that is actually evil, and it emerges that the act that appears to be good before it is played out carries within it the moral death that follows on it. In his desire to reaffirm his liberty, man chose enslavement to his natural urges as an aim, thus effectively forgoing his liberty. Here is the twofold meaning of sin: disobeying the command of God, and failing the moral and spiritual destiny of man by submission to bodily drives that are regarded as a goal.

Thus it is evident that sin lies in wait for man at every opportunity. One might say that sin is inherent in man's physical and psychological existence, that it will always be present as a ready temptation, an incessant pressure, a constant test. Moreover, one cannot imagine that the Genesis story could have been any different; that is, it is impossible to envisage that Adam would not have sinned. By their very nature, humans are prone to sin, and while it is not inevitable that they will commit a particular sin, it is inevitable that they will sin. The trial is permanent and renewed at each moment, and human beings are too weak to resist at each occasion. A single failure is always on the horizon and will eventually occur; and when it does, it deprives man of his liberty. Herein lies the dilemma.

Man is born free, his moral responsibility and his existence as a human being is conditional on his freedom of choice, but he is also bound to fail through sin, and the weight of sin distorts his relationships and enslaves him. His sin becomes his fate and he is unable to escape it. There is no way out of this dilemma unless there is a way of maintaining freedom of choice even after sin, and eliminating the fateful and compulsive basis of sin even when failure is inevitable. The only solution is for man to be able to use choice not only with respect to acts that he has not yet committed, but also with regard to acts that he has committed, opting to want them and take them on or to reject them and remove them from himself. This is the psychological and moral experience that underlies both atonement and repentance. Atonement and repentance enable man to free himself from the burden of sins, which weigh down on him and threaten to enslave him. Atonement and repentance enable man to return to the primal state before he sinned and to once more face the tests of life as a free being.

In a culture based on the moral–religious values of the Bible and the Sages, atonement and repentance can be seen as an indispensable mechanism that is religious and ritualistic on the one hand, and psychological and moral on the other. Without a way of freeing oneself of sins that have already been committed, the Torah way of life would collapse under the accumulated weight of feelings of guilt and impurity. This is evident both in the context of the priestly or ritualistic literature, and in the prophetic or moral literature. In the former, sin offerings occupy a central role; atonement is one of the most essential functions of the priest. In prophetic literature, perhaps the central theme is the demand for repentance, which purifies and cleanses. Moreover, in the rule of life established by the Torah, we find an entire structure of laws for renewing and returning human beings to an initial starting point, based on the assumption that the ordinary lives of individuals and of the community inevitably lead to spoiling and desecration. The Sabbath, the sabbatical year, and the jubilee year are the foci of this system, and Yom Kippur is integrated into it through its definition as the Sabbath of Sabbaths. Yom Kippur symbolizes the axis of the renewal of life through purification, which explains the particular sanctity of the day. In the Oral Law, though not in the written law, Yom Kippur became the holiest day, the day on which man is purified and stands before his Creator as on the day of creation.

THE PATH OF REPENTANCE

The common ideational basis of atonement and repentance is reflected in confession. Confession is a central theme in both the ritual of atonement and in repentance, stressing the primary moral significance of atonement. In order to be cleansed of his sin, man must acknowledge that he has sinned. Such a statement might appear simplistic and superfluous—could a human being knowingly commit an act that is contrary to what he has been commanded to do without "acknowledging that he has sinned"? It is important to note that the reference here is not to acts committed in error such as an unknown prohibition or something meant to lead to a different result. The purview here is those cases that were committed deliberately, through conscious choice. Nevertheless, "recognizing that one has sinned" is a highly significant step, but sin cannot be overcome and the individual cleansed unless this step is actually taken. If one considers the psychological state of the sinner, a highly complex mechanism of concealment can be seen to be employed. The human conceals his act from the eyes of others and, in so doing, represses it or represses acknowledgment of its significance from his own consciousness. The sinner chooses not to see, or chooses to rationalize his act in a manner that relieves him of full responsibility for what he has done: circumstances led him to do it, or it was the fault of others, as well as other ways in which he can skirt the issue. Even if the sinner is aware of his connection to the forbidden act, even if he knows that the act is indeed forbidden, it does not mean that he has "recognized that he sinned."

Such recognition comes only when he actually accepts complete responsibility for his actions, without concealment, without hiding, and without excuses. This is the essence of confession. The sinner confesses his sins aloud in the presence of others. Doing this, he establishes his own responsibility as an objective fact that cannot be evaded, even by himself. This is the explanation of the statement by Maimonides in the halakhic definition quoted above: ". . . and he must confess aloud and speak aloud these things that he has resolved in his heart." In other words, until the words have emerged from their hiding place in the soul of the sinner and been stated before others, they are not a total and binding fact for the sinner himself. He could still hide from his own responsibility. However, if he does recognize that he sinned and takes responsibility, a possibility is opened that was not present until now. Only now, when he no longer hides his sin, can he be freed from it. Those who hide their sin can never be freed from the double guilt they bear—the guilt of the sin itself and the guilt of its concealment. In this respect, confession is indeed a decisive step.

However, confession may lead to two distinct options—the path of atonement and the path of repentance. The path of atonement involves a ritual act of physical cleansing, as if the individual had washed his soul of its abomination as he washes his body in water; the water takes the filth and carries it away. The person who confesses by placing his hands on the head of a sacrificial animal eliminates his sins as if they were foreign objects that had adhered to him from within himself. The priest then sprinkles the blood of the sacrifice on the altar and, in the presence of sanctity, cleanses the sinner of the impurity that has been eliminated along with his sin. The description of these acts in the chapter of the Priestly Code appears to be mechanistic and external, with no place for the soul itself. Can this really be the case? Can a person confess and be cleansed without feeling guilt and remorse and a desire to be purified? It is difficult to see that it could be possible. It is difficult to see sacrifice as anything other than a symbolic act, which, for its completion, requires a psychological process of involvement on the part of the sinner.

The fact remains, however, that in the legal description a psychological process is neither mentioned nor required, and that this act is perceived as part of the ongoing routine of life. The offering of the sacrifice and the atonement are not seen as a form of change, or as an effort to achieve change, in the individual's life. Man sins and atones and sins and atones, accepting as a fact of life that sin is part of ordinary reality and cannot be changed. The sinner's emotional participation in the act of atonement is therefore minimal, confined to a recognition of the obligation to do something in order to atone for the sin. It is this fact that appears to provoke the criticism of the prophets. They are not opposed to the ritual itself; they are furious at a ritualistic act with a mechanical perception of atonement that does not lead to correction but to a perception of sin as part of a taken-for-granted routine of individual and communal life.

The path of repentance goes in a different direction. Repentance, as understood by the prophets, is an internal, psychological process that aims to achieve comprehensive change in human behavior and thus change the personality that develops through an individual's acts. While ritual atonement is a permanent and cyclical base in the routine of life, and effectively accepts sin, repentance is an attempt to take a different path—the path of good deeds and purity, free from sin. Can man free himself completely from his natural tendency to sin? Is there in the world "a just man who will do only good and will not sin"? The Hebrew prophets and Sages knew full well that in the temporal life there is no complete expurgation of the tendency to sin. So repentance itself, as the ongoing effort to proceed along the path of good deeds and purity, was seen as the alternate route. Repentance, as distinct from atonement, was seen as a single act within a complex of several acts. Repentance is defined as an entire way of life, and the repentance is present in every segment of the path. An act of atonement is always an ongoing psychological process rather than a single event.

Once again the reference is to Maimonides's summary of the Sages' opinion. Repentance begins with confession, as the sinner accepts responsibility for his sin; it continues with an expression of remorse: the sinner regrets what he has done and actually changes his will. He no longer wants that which he desired when he sinned. He then tests the sincerity of his remorse through a decision not to sin anymore. He now faces the future with a psychological intention that is different from what it was at the time he sinned. The contrast with the act of atonement is shown once more: in atonement, the human concentrates on the atoning act itself—on the present; in repentance, man faces the future. He recognizes that the future is his test. As Maimonides concludes in his *halakhic* language, "What is complete repentance? It occurs when a person has the opportunity to commit a transgression that he committed in the past and determines not to do so because of his repentance. Not because of fear and not because of inability" (Chap. 2, I).

If an individual is indeed ready to stand the test, then a genuine change has taken place in his behavior and in himself. There is an essential difference between ritual atonement and repentance—the manner in which the sinner is freed from his sin. Atonement removes the infection of the soul caused by sin, whereas repentance is a psychological immunization process by which the sinner distances himself from sin. Through repentance, he becomes a new person. If his innermost will is changed, he is no longer the person he was when he sinned. Maimonides: "It is characteristic of repentance that the person who repents always cries out before the Lord in supplication, and does good deeds according to his ability, and distances himself completely from the matter in which he sinned, changing his name, as if to say 'I am someone else, I am not the person who committed that act,' changing all his acts to the path which is good and just" (Chap. 2, IV). Thus, the trial is in choosing the path that consistently seeks a tireless effort toward a wholeness of life, of good deeds, and of purity. As it emerged in the tradition of the Sages, Yom Kippur is the day on which the community and all its individuals place themselves on the path of repentance. It is not an isolated event, but rather the beginning of a trajectory.

THE BOOK OF JONAH

The service on Yom Kippur includes a number of sections that call for the study and examination of the nature of repentance as an essential part of

the process of atonement. One of these sections—the Torah reading and
haftarah, and the tension between the two—has already been discussed.
Another section that relates to a similar theme is the Book of Jonah, which
is read in the *Minhah* service, the afternoon prayers, of Yom Kippur. What
is this reading intended to arouse in the soul of the worshipper? The
simplest answer is that the story bears witness to the power of heartfelt
atonement, even if the sins are as grave as those committed by the city of
Nineveh. God does not wish to see the sinner punished; He longs for his
repentance, and if the sinner genuinely repents, he is immediately
forgiven. Such is the lesson to be learned from the behavior and fate of
the inhabitants of Nineveh. It is also the lesson that God teaches the
prophet Jonah, who is more stringent in his judgment of the sinners than
is God. A second answer to the question is based on the first. The
worshipper learns that just as the gates of repentance are not sealed to
him, neither are they sealed to others. Even if he observes people steeped
in transgression, he should not harden his heart with the thought that
they are beyond hope; on Yom Kippur, he must regard them as repentant
and their sins as atoned for and forgiven.

Does the reading of Jonah, however, represent a testament? Is the story
designed to influence the listener by relating an event that actually
happened? Was there an actual occurrence in which all the inhabitants of
a large and sinful city such as Nineveh genuinely returned to the path of
righteousness the moment the prophet's warning was heard in their
streets? Is it likely that such a story could be believed as a testimony and
could influence people as a version of real events? A measure of naivete
that goes beyond that possessed by most adults would be necessary to
regard the story as evidence. Any mature reading of the text reveals that
this is not a naive tale; rather, it is one that plumbs the most complex
depths of the human soul. Thus the story should be read as a prophetic
dream that illuminates the intricate relationship between the prophet and
his moral mission and, at the same time, as a mirror in which the
worshipper—in self-affliction and contrition—can find himself in his
repentance. If the worshipper sees the story in this manner, it may be that
it will yield a richer lesson than that mentioned at first.

The prophet's flight from the mission imposed upon him is actually his
dream, revealing a hidden dimension in the just and honest man who is
worthy of his mission. In reality, as a private and selfish individual whose
selfishness is related to his mission, the prophet does not want his mission
to succeed; such success would prevent him from realizing two very
human aspirations. First, he wants to see the sinners punished. He wants

to see a revenge that compensates the righteous man for his sufferings. Second, he wants to be recognized as telling the truth; if his mission is successful and the sinners repent, his prophecy will not come to pass. Some might point out that the prophet did not indeed know what was to happen. This is the painful yet droll paradox of the prophet's mission: only if it does not achieve its real purpose will it be successful on the personal level—the prophet will be seen to have spoken the truth and the righteous will be seen to gain vengeance over the wicked. Jonah's dream of escape thus reveals to Jonah the sin that follows from righteousness; the unadorned root of this sin, which anyone, and all the more so a self-righteous person, tends to repress and hide from himself. This is the mirror facing the worshipper, since who is more likely than a repentant worshipper to see himself as self-righteous?

Just as the prophet's flight is a dream that relates to his mission, so the story of the upstanding behavior of the sailors on the ship on which Jonah flees is a naive dream, as is the story of the immediate and full repentance of the inhabitants of Nineveh. Yet at the deepest level this naivete is permeated by a highly realistic perception. Despite the fact that as a selfish individual the prophet does not desire the total repentance of the people of Nineveh, such repentance is a credulous aspiration without which no one could set out on such a mission. If there were absolutely no chance, if the sinners were doomed to cling to their sins, what would be the point of the mission? Could the purpose really be to give the prophet the sense of satisfaction at the disaster he foretold? Accordingly a prophet could not set out on a mission unless, at the depth of his sober perception based on extensive experience with people, lay a kernel of innocence. The hope that his chastising produces results is hidden in the veils of his despair. The naivete would appear to feed on the utter simplicity and total clarity of prophetic knowledge. And indeed, what could be more simple or obvious than the repentance of sinners on the brink of certain and imminent doom? Surely the sinners have a desire to live? The sinners themselves appear to be conscious of the gravity of their transgressions. They are apparently aware that they are sinners and that a dreadful punishment awaits them. This knowledge does not result from any special powers; the internal collapse of the sinful society points to the inherent disaster. In the depth of their souls, each one realizes that a society such as theirs is doomed to annihilation, and that in the process of annihilation they as individuals will also perish.

Why, then, should it seem so extraordinary that, at the last moment, the sinners acknowledge what they know, and do the one elementary thing that can save them? After all, there could be nothing easier than to admit sin, repent through fasting and prayer, and decide not to sin anymore. That is all that is required of them. This simplicity and ease is the source of the naive hope without which no one could set out on a prophetic mission. Within his innermost self, however, the prophet realizes that the occurrence of the simplest act, precisely because it is so simple, is a utopian dream that has never come true. Indeed, the Book of Jonah presents a unique version of Utopia. Utopia is usually the vision of a state of perfection beyond the capacity of human activity. In the Book of Jonah, the vision presents the most obvious situation, but one that is almost beyond the possibility of realization. The question is why is this so?

Before attempting to answer the question, another issue requires examination. Jonah is a prophet, and a prophet is a righteous person. Yet from the outset the story depicts him as a sinner fleeing from God like a thief in the night. Careful reading indicates that Jonah is aware that he is a sinner. When the sailors urge Jonah to pray to his God, he replies that it is because of Him that misfortune has befallen them all. Yet he refuses to repent his sin. Though he receives sign after sign and call after call, he hardens his heart and falls into sleep—the last refuge of the conscience as it seeks to hide from itself. He does not want to know that which he knows. Only in deepest sleep does he once more encounter his lurking conscience through the oblique means of the dream; and only as distress engulfs him in the depths of the ocean, in the stomach of the fish, does he pray and receive salvation. Even so, his repentance is incomplete, and it is despite himself that he performs his mission. What is it that prevents Jonah from performing the simple act that the inhabitants of Nineveh perform?

If this riddle can be solved, it may be possible to understand why sinners do not perform the apparently simple, easy act that will bring them the sweetest reward of all—life. Jonah knows that he is a sinner, but he hides his sin from himself as he hides from the voice of God that commands him to embark on his mission. His behavior is not without reason. He hides his sin because he considers himself a righteous man. He has a quarrel with God, and he stubbornly clings to his self-image as a righteous man until the end of the story, when he is left naked and without shelter in the heat of the burning sun. Jonah is convinced that he is in the right—the sinners should be punished with full severity. His mission must not succeed. It is this thought that is his sin; but this sin is bound up with his self-perception as a righteous and innocent man—the perception that a human being has as he consorts with his ego as it stands in the world demanding its happiness.

What is it, then, that prevents the sinner from repenting despite his recognition of the fact that he is a sinner? The story of Jonah reveals that it is the sinner's self-perception of his righteousness and innocence as he examines himself in the context of his desires, longings, and expectations as an individual. Egocentric life rejects any guilt. Life is the promise of the gratification of desires that stem from the core of man's physical and psychological being. Life is the promise of happiness. Nevertheless, the egocentric man knows that it is his egocentricity that is the root of his sin. Man created in God's image was not created for this. Only if he learns to judge himself, as his Creator judges him, will he himself be prepared to repent, and to have mercy on sinners. To judge himself as his Creator judges him—could there be any more difficult task than this? Is it not beyond man's capacity?

Man's primal sense of justness and innocence is reflected in various ways; the prophet reflects it in his way, and the sinners to whom he is sent reflect it in their way. The repentant worshipper on Yom Kippur may also hide from himself under the soft, comfortable cloak of his good deeds. He fasts and prays and seeks repentance. Yet the heart of man is a complex and deceptive structure, with one chamber inside another. Even as man stands and reveals his innermost self, he may still be hiding. This is the reminder served by the Book of Jonah during the afternoon service—a warning that comes before the final effort of the day's prayers, in the Ne'ilah service.

CONFESSION

Yom Kippur was not intended for reflection on the subject of repentance, but for repentance itself. This repentance takes place in the confessional prayer. Reciting the confession with inner reflection and intent encapsulates a psychological process comprised of thought, feeling, and the desire to change oneself and to embark on a new path free of sin. The confessional prayer is indeed the main prayer of Yom Kippur, and is recited six times, from the afternoon prayer on the eve of Yom Kippur through the concluding Ne'ilah service. Each time, it is recited at length and with emphasis.

The centrality of the prayer is the result of historical continuity. When the Temple was in existence, sin offerings formed the center of the day's worship, and the confession was said over the offerings. Thus the confession is the only element of the Temple worship for Yom Kippur that could be maintained after the destruction. The context of the order of worship changed, bringing with it a shift in meaning from an emphasis on ritual atonement to a concentration on moral repentance. In place of an animal sacrifice, the worshipper symbolically offers himself through the self-affliction of fasting and confession. Since confession is the only ritual element that continues to be present, it has been lengthened exceedingly. From a single sentence, over the generations the prayer has grown into a complex formula comprised of a number of sections. It is as if the prayer had taken on itself the goal of expanding to fill the total span of time and action—and of the experience that accompanies action—that the sacrifices filled when the Temple existed. Be that as it may, the confession is the continuation of the ancient worship of Yom Kippur, and this worship was supposed to include the atoning act itself.

Let us therefore examine the prayer in order to observe the nature of the cognitive and emotional process that is supposed to occur in the soul of the worshipper who prays with complete devotion. The confession begins with a compact and considered introduction. The full quote is, "Our God and God of our fathers, let our prayer come before You and do not ignore our supplications. For we are not insolent and stubborn, saying to you 'Our God and God of our fathers, we are righteous and have not sinned'—nay, we and our fathers have sinned." This introduction is an attempt to overcome the internal obstacle felt by every worshipper as he comes to confess his sins before the Seat of Justice. All and all, the worshipper is submitting himself to the Judge, revealing his secrets and casting off the protective wall behind which he has been hiding. The worshipper must also overcome the sense of shame and disgrace that comes from revealing his weaknesses and imperfections, which explains why the first step across the threshold of confession is the most arduous one, requiring an internal crumbling that is effected through an intensification of willpower.

The introduction is designed to assist the worshipper in crossing this threshold: it begins with a supplication that creates a sense of intimacy and privacy between the confessing worshipper and God, his Judge, and continues on to provide a positive addendum to the negative impression that he will give through the confession. The fact that the worshipper is prepared to confess and, by so doing, prove that he is neither "insolent" nor "stubborn" but is ready to admit his sins, is a point in his favor that he introduces before the difficult act he is about to perform, in order that he may be able to perform it. This addendum is like a pole that enables the worshipper to soar over the thorny hedge below. Having emphasized the positive aspect of his very willingness to confess, the worshipper finds himself already into the confession.

It is, however, only the beginning. The confession is phrased in the plural, "We have been guilty, betrayed, usurped," etc. The list appears the first time in alphabetical order—a poetic device designed to express the desire to exhaustively cover the subject. The confessor must disclose all his sins, hiding nothing, and the concept of "all" is embodied in a recitation that goes from "A to Z." The first paragraph includes all the variations and sub-variations of the sense of guilt before God. It does not yet include details of the acts themselves—these details will follow; but before reaching this section, the worshipper takes a second step designed to overcome his internal difficulties. At this point, he is ready to genuinely submit himself before the Judge, accepting the sentence against him: "We have veered away from Your just commandments and laws and we have been unworthy. And You are righteous for all that befalls us, for You have acted in truth and we have been evil."

It may now appear that the worshipper divests himself of all protection. He confesses that he has no merit before God since he has deliberately transgressed God's commandments, which were designed for his own good. However, it is precisely his ability at this point to justify the sentence meted out to him that enables him to reveal his innermost self. Once I myself have accepted the sentence there is no point hiding anything—in any case, You know everything. "What shall we say before You, who sits on high, and what shall we tell You, who dwells in the heavens? You who know all matters, hidden and revealed." Since everything is revealed, man can rediscover aspects of himself. However, the feeling that relief comes from the knowledge that everything is known would appear to be illusory. The main facet is that the worshipper confesses—i.e., admits full responsibility for what he has done. Where does the strength to confess in this manner come from?

Examining the remainder of the confession shows that as the confessor justifies the sentence against himself, he is imbued with a strong sense of certainty—a certainty that originates in the positive point raised by the worshipper in the introduction to the prayer, his very willingness to confess. What is the certainty? It is complete belief in the justice of the Judge and His bountiful mercy. "I no longer pity myself," the worshipper says to himself. "I justify the sentence against me, but in so doing I am confident that, for Your part, You will forgive me." In the language of the prayer: "You know the secrets of the world and the mysteries of all creatures. You reveal the innermost self and examine emotions and intellect. Nothing is ignored by You and nothing is hidden from You. May it therefore be Your will, O Lord our God and God of our fathers, that You forgive us for all our sins and pardon all our transgressions and grant atonement for all our iniquities." It is interesting to note that this complete confidence in forgiveness and mercy comes precisely as the worshipper reaches the stage of justifying the sentence against him; since he has reached this stage, he can observe himself at an objective distance and confess his sins in detail.

The next section is the longest part of the confession, an alphabetical "catalogue" of transgressions designed to include all the sinful possibilities that the variety of individuals may have added to the conscience of the community. (We will return below to the fact that the confession is phrased in the plural rather than the singular.) In any case, while each confessing individual shares a portion in the sins of the entire community, through the all-inclusive and exhaustive list laid out before him, each individual must remind himself of his own particular sins. He does not recite them in detail in public, but as he recalls them he recognizes that they are his sins and so he states them before his Creator.

Arranged first in alphabetical order, and then in order of gravity and severity of punishment, the list of sins is lengthy and oppressive. Between sections of this part of the confession, however, a short sentence appears, almost like a refrain: "And for all these, O Lord, forgive us, pardon us, atone for us." The line is not only a request and supplication; it is also a remembrance through which the worshipper can draw strength. Only through inner confidence that God is indeed the God of forgiveness can the worshipper endure the oppressive text, which describes human existence as a vale of tears. Indeed, this section of the confession ends with the optimistic declaration: "For You are the One who forgives Israel and the Pardoner of the tribes of Jeshurun in every generation, and but for You we have no forgiving or pardoning King." However, the description of man's vale of tears takes its toll on the individual's conscience. A gulf opens between the forgiving, pardoning God and sinful man, a gulf that man, from his lowly position, can never bridge. The confessor plummets to dust and ashes, descending to the lowest depths of human existence. "My God, until I was created I was worthless, and now that I have been created it is as if I had not been created. In life I am but dust, and all the more so in my death; I stand before You like a vessel filled with shame and humiliation."

It would seem that in these comments the opposite pole of the confession's opening mood has been reached. In the opening, strength is afforded by the positive fact that the worshipper is willing to confess his sins. Now, at the end of the confession, the worshipper is left naked, with no merit, "a vessel filled with shame and humiliation." On his own, he cannot be saved from the depths. Yet it is precisely from this distance that the confessor finds the strength to draw close to his Creator and rely on Him. It is now great weakness that justifies the clinging that carries with it anticipation and expectation. "May it be Your will, O Lord my God and God of my fathers, that I will not sin anymore. And that which I have sinned before You wipe away in your abundant mercy, but not through suffering and disease."

There are two requests here, and each of them contains a double message. First, the confessor asks that he not sin anymore. In this way, he expresses the decision that Maimonides defines as the third and last stage of repentance; after the remorse inherent in the recognition of the evil of sin, the confessor expresses his desire not to sin anymore. This is his decision, but the manner in which it is expressed is somewhat surprising, based on the humble recognition of man's inability to trust in his own decision. This line of thought would appear to depart from Maimonides's logic. Is it really God who needs to guarantee that man will not sin anymore? Surely this is the sole responsibility of man? Partially, but not entirely, true. It is man's obligation to want to be freed of his sins; however, the recognition of the lowliness of the human condition, which stems from the experience of sin, shows that in the circumstances of his existence, it is impossible for man not to sin. Only God, the Forgiver and Creator, can save man from his inherent inclination to sin. This is the abyss between God and man, and precisely because he cannot overcome it, the worshipper believes that not only can God do so, but by His very essence He must do so. It is God who created man and placed before him a test beyond his capacity, and it is God who will support him in this unendurable trial beyond his strength, so long as he expresses a genuine desire not to sin and tries with all his might. Just as the father who anticipates his infant's inability to stand on his own guides and supports him, so God will offer His help.

Thus the confession has led man, step by step, to a recognition of the limits of human ability, breaking human pride, in order to open, bit by bit, the gates of faith and of nearness to his Creator. If the worshipper began the confession in terror and in awe of the Judge, he concludes it quiescent and docile before the merciful Father, the Father who must pardon him, since man cannot but fail to sin unless God assists him. It should be noted that the starting assumption of the confession is not blurred at its conclusion. Man is responsible for his acts. The decision to repent is his obligation and his decision. This is the content of the second request: "And that which I have sinned before You, remove in Your abundant mercy." It is here that the worshipper expresses his willingness to accept the cleansing punishment. Now he is willing to accept suffering, which he does not see as a harsh sentence but as the concern of a guiding Father and as a reflection of His love. By virtue of this intimate knowledge, he knows that his willingness to accept suffering will save him from the worst.

The worshipper who has prayed with devotion has, therefore, undergone a highly complex emotional, conceptual process. There has been a change that proceeds from a posture of human pride that includes a refusal to confess to a self-view of enlightened humility; in this, the division between man and his Creator has been destroyed. The child within man has been released from its many layers of protection to discover a compassionate Father who has been cloaked in the appearance of a King on a Seat of Judgment. Repentance thus takes on a double significance—in terms of man's consciousness and in terms of renewing the primal relationship between man and God his Creator. The entire process is characterized by ambivalence—ambivalence in understanding man's position in the world, and ambivalence in God's attitude toward man. Just as sin results from ambivalence, so ambivalence enables and reveals repentance, not only as a concept but as an existential experience. Confession is a conscious emotional experiencing of man's position vis-à-vis his Creator.

MUTUAL RESPONSIBILITY

The concept of confession as a prayer of the individual has been discussed in previous sections. It should be noted that while it is an individual prayer, it is not said in the singular but in the plural. Moreover, it is said not only on behalf of those gathered for prayer at the particular time, but on behalf of all the preceding generations of the Jewish people, "we and our fathers." The confessing individual presents himself for prayer within his community and in the midst of his people, and assumes responsibility for the sins of the entire public. In this context, it should be recalled that the Torah's original intention was that Yom Kippur would atone for the sins of the nation's leaders; from this notion, an atonement evolved for sins for which the entire community was responsible. Though a sin committed by an individual on his own was atoned for at any time, the individual decided to offer a sacrifice. As it developed in the Oral Tradition, Yom Kippur came to include atonement for the sins of individuals without obscuring the public nature of the day. The individual stands as part of the community and as part of the people.

This is so because the sins of individuals accumulate and add to the sins of the public; the doctrine that all individuals are accountable for each other applies in this instance, too, which is the explanation for the use of *anachnu*, the first-person plural, in the prayer. Each individual accepts not only his own sins, but also all the sins committed by his peers and fellows. He, too, has a part in these sins. In this lies the answer to the astonishment shown by many who only come to the synagogue on Yom Kippur—why does each individual confess to such a long and serious list of sins? Is there any individual who has committed all these offenses? Certainly not, but within the community as a whole all these sins have been committed, and each individual is considered a partner therein, not only in terms of his own "contribution" but also in the "contributions" of his fellows. The entire community must be found pure. The same principle applies with regard to the generational connection. The formula whereby God is addressed as "Our God and God of our fathers," and where the confession is expressed as "we and our fathers have sinned," indicates an awareness that the fate of the Jewish people is determined by the acts of all the generations. The children are accountable for the sins of their parents, just as they rely on their merit.

Another comment should be made here concerning those who only attend the synagogue on this day, and who are astonished by the language of the prayer. It is this very language that explains why they are attracted to the synagogue on the High Holidays and particularly on Yom Kippur. Perhaps this appears to be a paradox. Of all the Jewish holidays and feasts, none has a more "religious" nature than Yom Kippur. The entire day is devoted to relations between man and God; even man's behavior toward his fellow man is being judged with respect to his commitment to God's commandments. It may appear that this day could not hold any significance for someone who considers himself removed from the purely religious bond between man and God. Why, then, does such a person come to prayers? The standard answer is that participating along with the whole of the Jewish people on Yom Kippur is an obligation to beloved parents (and the Yom Kippur service includes the *Yizkor* memorial prayer) or that participation in the day, along with the whole of the Jewish people, stems from a sense of national affiliation. Yom Kippur is considered the holiest of days. In the past, no one was absent from the assembly on this day. Here, then, is the nub of the paradox: familial or national motives lead to participation in a purely religious festival that lacks the national elements found in Passover, Hanukkah, or Sukkot.

In considering these comments, however, the meaning of the apparent paradox, and the fact that it is not in fact a paradox at all, becomes evident. On Yom Kippur the entire people is in attendance and stands together in unity. There is a national basis here that permeates the religious basis and identifies with it. The unity of the people is realized in the mutual accountability of all individuals to each other and to the public, and in the accountability of the public to the individuals in terms of the religious and moral way of life that unites them. The sanctity of the day and the central importance attached to it stems from its public nature as a unifying force for the entirety of the Jewish people no less than from its purely religious significance. On this day, the connection between the generations, and between individuals and the people, is more tangible and fateful than on any other day. An individual must not, therefore, be absent on this day. Individuals who distanced themselves from the life-style of the Torah and the commandments, but who did not want to cut off familial or national links, continued and continue to sense the inner motif that draws them to prayers on Yom Kippur. However, their distance from a Torah way of life and the commandments prevents them from perceiving the faith and the experience that fuel the sensation of national unity, the result of which is a discrepancy between their motive in coming to the service and what they can identify as the essential theme of the day.

National unity as sensed in this manner clearly reflects a unique perception of inter-human relationships. Here the same "sociology" of the synagogue is faced that was remarked on in the discussion of the Sabbath. The foundation of this "sociology," which is based on the idea of the covenant, need not be repeated except to recall the unique status given to the individual as an explicit component of the polity, and the function of the polity as guarantor for the liberty and value of the individual, and at the same time, the agent that defines its personality through the roles that the polity allocates to the individual. On Yom Kippur, a special dimension becomes apparent in this network of relationships. From the point of view of a society that perceives its existence as a mission, and as having a role that goes beyond this—the worship of God—there is a public significance not only to sins between human beings which directly challenge societal order, but also for sins committed by an individual to himself or between an individual and his Creator. The sinner shirks from bearing the weight of the supra-societal role that unites the society and maintains its unique quality, and he therefore has ceased to fulfill the obligation that the people took upon itself in the covenant at Sinai that is renewed in every generation. This is the basis for the unique form of mutual responsibility. The sins between individuals and God also enter into the account of the sins of the community and, in any case, all individuals are participants in each other's sins. Thus it follows that individuals must help each other not to sin, by warning and forgiving each other, and above all, by considering their behavior not only in terms of their own individual interest and righteousness, but also in terms of their responsibility for the fate of the entire public and the people.

In summarizing this idea, Maimonides has adapted the words of the Sages: "Thus, each person must throughout the entire year consider that he is one half innocent and one half guilty. Similarly, the entire world is one half innocent and one half guilty. If he commits a single sin, he has tipped his own scales and those of the entire world to the side of guilt and caused destruction. If he performs a single commandment, he has placed himself and the entire world on the side of innocence and caused salvation and redemption" (Laws of Repentance, Chap. 3, IV). Notice the equation Maimonides creates between the individual and the world. Both accounts—that of the individual and that of the polity—are one, and a single act of an individual may determine the fate of the whole.

Naturally, there is reciprocity between the individual and the whole. The individual is responsible for the polity, and the polity guarantees that the individual will be able to live in accordance with the commandments of the Torah. The community also provides the individual with opportunities to repent; indeed, it draws and educates the individual to do so. Without the public, which institutionalizes the times and forms of repentance, it is doubtful whether individuals would be able to repent on their own. The specific designation of Yom Kippur as a time for confession and prayer, according to God's commandments, is a concrete expression of the assistance God provides for the individual who wishes to become pure and not sin anymore. Consider the confession once more. It is a private and personal act; an individual must motivate himself to confess. But the community provides the individual with the actual opportunity to realize this desire. Above all, confession is the removal of a sin that weighs on the individual conscience from his own private domain to a presentation before others. Only in this way does the confession acquire the force of a fact that the individual can no longer deny and from which he can no longer hide. Naturally it is true that matters declared before God have also left the private domain, but the fact remains that for most individuals the awareness that this has transpired comes only if the matter is declared in the presence of peers with whom he lives and who are his witnesses.

Maimonides expresses this idea saying,

It is highly praiseworthy that the repentant man should confess in public and relate his transgressions and reveal the iniquities between himself and his peers, and say to them: "Indeed, I sinned against such-and-such and did this to him, and today I repent and regret what I did." He who is proud and does not reveal his transgressions, but conceals them, has not fully repented; as it is said: "Anyone who tries to hide his transgressions will fail." To which sins does this refer? To transgressions between man and man. Concerning transgressions between an individual and God, the person need not make a public admission, and it is insolence for him to do so. He needs to repent before God, blessed be He, and detail his sins before Him, and confess them before the public only in general terms, and he is fortunate that his iniquity has not been uncovered; as it is said: "Happy is the sinner whose sin has been covered." [Chap. 2, 5]

In this section, Maimonides distinguishes sins between man and man, which must be confessed in detail and in public, and sins between the individual and God, even the declaration of which is considered "insolent." Maimonides appears to believe that the declaration of sins between man and man is necessary for these sins to be corrected, whereas declaring sins between an individual and God will have a negative impact. Note, however, that Maimonides requires that even these sins be stated before the public "in a general sense." The confessional formula in the service makes clear what is meant by the expression "in a general sense." The individual declares his sense of guilt but does not provide details of his sins. He expresses his sensation of being a sinner and his submission—sensations that require a public statement in order to be reinforced. Only after such a statement does the confession become a *fait accompli*.

In this way, the public provides the individual with an opportunity to confess before his Creator, to feel that the confession is a truly binding event. Moreover, for most humans, the institutionalization of repentance at set times and according to a fixed formula used by the entire community is a condition without which they would not achieve repentance. Even if the desire to repent was awakened in individuals, they would tend to be swept along by the flow of other events and the pressures of their own problems, desires, and difficulties. By providing a day when the entire community stands and prays together, and by offering the individual ways in which to express himself, the public provides individuals with a chance to break away from the tide of routine life and engage in moral stocktaking. Once again, we may quote Maimonides: "Although repentance and crying out [of one's remorse] are always desirable, they are particularly so during the ten days between Rosh HaShanah and Yom Kippur, and are immediately accepted; as it is said: 'Seek the Lord where you may find Him.' To whom does this refer? To the individual. As for the public, any time they make repentance and genuinely cry out [their remorse], they are answered; as it is said: 'As the Lord our God whenever we cry out to Him'" (Chap. 2, VI).

It is worth considering the preferential status that Maimonides attributes to the public. The public as a whole can confess at any time, and its prayer is accepted at all times, whereas the individual requires the specific occasion of Yom Kippur. The explanation for this seems to be that it is on Yom Kippur that the individual has before him the entire public, providing him with forms of repentance, which explains why Maimonides goes on to comment that "Yom Kippur is a time of repentance for all, individuals and public; it is the ultimate opportunity for pardon and forgiveness for Israel. Therefore, all must repent and confess on Yom Kippur" (Chap. 2, VII).

SUPPLICATION

The confessional prayer is indeed the central prayer of Yom Kippur; however, there is another prayer that is related to the confession, no less striking, that seems almost to follow directly from it. This is the prayer of supplication. The confessor throws himself down before the Seat of Judgment and begs for mercy. While he knows that by right he is not innocent, he nonetheless believes that God should pardon him. The worshipper begs and cries out, tearfully reminding God of His promise to the forefathers to pardon Israel. The emotional force of this prayer is felt particularly in the concluding—Ne'ilah—service. Here it appears as a last-minute effort to change the harsh decree, if, God forbid, such a decree has been issued. The fact that it comes in the last minutes imbues the prayer with particularly dramatic effect. Wave after wave, the weeping comes, in an effort to pry open the gates of heaven:

> Open a gate for us at the time of sealing the gates, for the day has turned;
> The day will turn, the sun will come and turn, and we shall enter into Your gates.

Powerful emotion speaks in this prayer, rather than intellect. Emotion overtakes intellect and strides far beyond its horizons. The heart knows what is hidden from the mind and carries the worshipper on to a final effort. Precisely because of the tremendous emotional force of the supplicational prayer, it is all the more remarkable that this prayer actually brings us back to the starting point of the confession where emotion and intellect are in balance. At the end of the concluding *Ne'ilah* service, the cantor and the congregation cry out once *"Shma"* — "Hear, O Israel . . ."; three times "Blessed be the name of His glorious kingdom for ever and ever"; and seven times "The Lord is God." After the *kaddish* prayer, the shofar is blown and out of the silence that follows, the congregation wish each other "Next year in rebuilt Jerusalem."

The significance of this sequence is strikingly simple: the crying out reaches its climax with a dramatic about turn as the worshippers lovingly accept the yoke of God's dominion. They no longer implore God, but rather accept wholeheartedly and lovingly the sentence that has been determined; whatever it may be, it expresses the justice and transcendency of God. It is precisely this ultimate willingness to accept the verdict that raises man to the highest possible level, only an instant after he had been writhing in his baseness and sin. This is a moment of holiness; a moment when the individual stands straight before his Creator. If he feels the sublime sanctity of this moment, he has sensed something that transcends forgiveness; he has reached the ultimate significance of his existence. And so it is that hope for the future breaks forth as the last sounds of the shofar fade away.

SIX

TEACHING JOYFULNESS
IN THE FESTIVAL OF SUKKOT

JOY AS A COMMANDMENT

Sukkot, the Festival of Tabernacles, is a meeting of two continuities in the Jewish calendar, each of which stems from a different start of the Jewish year. Based along the continuity that begins with Creation, Sukkot is the third holiday after Rosh HaShanah and Yom Kippur; it epitomizes the rejoicing that follows after the fear of judgment. It is also the third festival in the sequence that begins with the Exodus; that is, the third of the pilgrimage holidays—Passover, Shavuot, and Sukkot—and in this context it symbolizes the Israelites' sense of being under Divine providence, having left Egypt and received the Torah. Added to their historical significance, the three pilgrimage festivals also serve as agricultural festivals (the Festival of Spring, the Grain Harvest, and the Autumn Harvest) so that a third continuity, the annual agricultural cycle, is added to the first two, finding its expression in joy at the harvest and in the prayer for rain. This third continuity is the single symbol that relates both to the historic/national significance of Sukkot, and to its universal/existential meaning. In both these contexts, Sukkot reflects joy at the renewal of life.

It is hardly surprising that this festival is distinguished from others by profound rejoicing. Indeed here are a trio of notes in a joyous chord: the joy of the farmer who brings home a bountiful harvest; the joy of the worshipper who feels that his sins have been atoned for and his life begun again in purity; and the joy of the chosen people sensing the mercies of its God as it moves to freedom. Subsequently a fourth note was added. The holiday adjoining Sukkot marks completion of the annual cycle of Torah readings and the joy of the people who not only were given the Torah, but received it, is added. It is a joy that comes with the integration of the Torah to a fullness of spiritual life in which the soul is uplifted.

Among the Jewish festivals, Sukkot stands out as a festival of joy. Of course every festival is a joyous occasion. Even the Day of Atonement, celebrated in stern solemnity and requiring self-affliction, is nevertheless a day of joy; the Sages, in fact, commented that in the period before the Temple this day was one of the two most joyous occasions of the year. Sukkot is unique in that it elevates joy to the level of a commandment. Alone of all the festivals, the commandment, "You shall rejoice on your festival and be exceedingly joyful" was made with regard to Sukkot, the implication being that while in the case of other festivals joy is a by-product of the various activities associated with the holiday; in the case of Sukkot, joy is a theme in its own right. At Sukkot, one should consciously intend to rejoice; joy is brought to the consciousness of the celebrator as a desirable state of mind. The notion could be suggested that at Sukkot, Jews rejoice in the joy itself that flows from the natural and historic life force of the Jewish people. Joy is thus not only a spontaneous emotion, but also the very basis of a world view. In discussing the ideational themes of the festival, this feature needs to be given close attention.

First, however, another element in which Sukkot is unique in its conscious emphasis of a characteristic common to all festivals. Every Jewish festival is marked by commandments and symbols that relate solely to the particular occasion, and Sukkot is blessed with a number of such commandments and symbols; this is not the atypical facet of the holiday. The unique aspect of Sukkot lies in the type of commandments and symbols, particularly the sukkah itself—the thatched booth—and the four varieties of plant life—the "four species"—as they are used in the *hakafot* ceremony. These elements form a rich and highly colorful totality that is remarkable for its distinctiveness from the daily routine and its reversion to primal and archaic roots. Moreover, the commandments related to symbols of other festivals represent relatively brief actions that are integrated into the overall structure of the holiday: the lighting of candles, the blessing over two loaves on the Sabbath, the blowing of the shofar at Rosh HaShanah, and so on.

Sukkot, in contrast, has one symbol—the sukkah—in which all the other symbols are present. The sukkah is raised to the level of a framework for all the activity during the seven days of the festival. The whole festival seems to be brought together in the sukkah as other festival activities form a part of this whole. Lastly, these are symbols whose primary existential meaning is expressed through the picturesque and tactile language of movement, rather than through verbal interpretation. Other Jewish festivals typically articulate their meaning through the verbal context that envelops them. Existential gestures effected through particular objects, such as lighting candles or blowing the shofar, are complementary to prayer. Indeed, these gestures often appear to be a rationale for articulation, for a blessing or a prayer that not only interprets the meaning of the gesture but also forms a principal part of the symbolic gesture itself.

At Sukkot, the element of speech is reduced and becomes a rationale for the existential gesture: sitting in the Sukkah, holding the four species and shaking them ecstatically, and the *hakafot*. Expression through experience, rather than speech, is the essence of Sukkot. It can therefore be said that at Sukkot we bring into our consciousness the significance of the use of symbols as a fundamental and primal form of expression, which releases something in the human being that precedes speech—something that usually remains silent under a layer of words. Is there a connection between the emphasis on the element of joy as an independent theme of the festival and the symbolic shaping of a primal, existential gesture?

RITUAL SYMBOLS

The question arises, what is a ritual symbol? What role does it play in the festival? And what role does the sukkah, as the key symbol of Sukkot, play?

The ritual symbol is a certain sensual quality imbued with significance through internal and external actions that relate to that same quality. The expression "sensual quality" refers to an object that we see and touch—a picture; an area of color; a sound; smell, or taste; even a movement of the body; significance is an idea that we link directly with this sensual quality in such a manner that the quality comes to represent the idea, granting it an independent "objective" existence. The ritual symbol expresses a guiding idea—a binding truth—and concretizes it so that we encounter it and experience it in more than thought alone. The ritual symbol always activates at least two of our mental faculties, usually three, directing them to a single focus—a sense, thought, and an awakening sensation that bridges the sensual and the ideational. Naturally, by pointing out a symbol we indicate an idea; but the conscious confrontation of a symbol is first and foremost a total spiritual occurrence for the individual who experiences his idea by thinking it, sensing it, and being emotionally moved by it at one and the same moment.

The distinction between symbol as a regular means of communication and symbol as a means of experiencing an idea is crucial to understanding the role of symbols in the ritual acts that form the Sukkot framework. Festivals, as said, are tightly built units of symbols whose use is a continual and routine human activity. However, we know that any process of thought or will, and any form of inter-human communication, takes place through the use of symbols: words, pictures, sounds, movements, gestures. The difference lies here: in the routine use of symbols we tend to "parenthesize" the autonomous presence of the sensual quality that serves as a mediator within ourselves, or between ourselves and others. This quality is seen as a simple device for information that we wish to absorb or to transmit. Since these are routine actions that transmit information that is already known—which is only partially innovative—in the new context the transition from means to idea is rapid and almost mechanical. The symbolizing sensual object falls away from our consciousness immediately after performing its function, like a typewriter key that rises, leaves the letter marked on the paper, and falls back into place.

This is not the case with a ritual act. Here, the symbols are placed before us and their essence examined. There is no omission of the sensual quality's direct functioning in all its dimensions of size, scope, and intensity; visual color; picturesque nature; and rhythmic structure. Indeed, while directing our constant attention to the sensual and emotional process, we simultaneously concentrate on absorbing the nuances of the sensual activity and the responsive emotional awakening. Further study shows that during observance the unity of the symbol undergoes an internal division; the single idea divides into a myriad of ideas composed of each other or combined with one another—an ever-growing family.

When symbols are confronted in this way, it is evident that there is a break in the everyday activity designed to respond to stimuli within the immediate environment and so achieve immediate goals, chiefly the satisfaction of various physical and mental needs. Experiencing meaning, and only this, is now the goal. Thus the branching myriad of meanings is not distracting. On the contrary, the transition from one idea to the next, around the axis that unifies these ideas in a widening spiral, is part of the essential, rich nature of the symbolic experience. The experience becomes ever richer and more laden, increasing the intensity of the experience; life is enriched—more forceful and self-conscious—through an inherent subjective symbolism rather than serving to satisfy something external in the objective world. Moreover, through this activity of experiencing inherent meaning in the concrete presence of symbols, we re-enact a primal process of how an idea is created, its breaking forth through direct experience, and its manifestation through the means used for its expression.

In the routine use of symbols in daily life, we repeatedly raise part of an existing lexicon of known ideas, and the connection between these ideas and the symbols used to express them is familiar and consensual. This is a long way from the primal experience of identifying a thing, or the discovery of an idea; this is the heart of the matter. *This* is what truth is! Only when innovation of thought or judgment is achieved, when there is an innovation in the expressive symbol that is defined by the living experience from which the new truth springs, is the primal force of recognition of reality and discovery of truth felt. At such moments, experience is primal creation; only then is all our being aware of the full significance of the discovered truth, the innovation brought into our world, which, from now on, is a different world than it appeared to us yesterday.

Subsequently everyday life returns, and the recognition of the renewed truth also becomes part of the lexicon of memory and routine. The force of its presence fades, as does its shaping and directing influence on our attitude toward ourselves, our environment, and our behavior. This fact holds a latent danger with regard to the basic foundations and values that should inform the whole order of human life. Every culture takes as its foundation truths that will establish the objectives and aims of human activity. These truths attribute meaning to human existence. The age in which these truths are discovered is the period when that culture is established; it is also the time when key ritual symbols are instituted, drawing their sensual qualities from the experience out of which the truth was discovered. In order for the culture to survive, it must not only define its truths, phrase them, repeat them, and implement them in behavioral norms; it must also institutionalize their installation through a web of ritual symbols. In this context, establishment means a permanent, cyclical return of the public, and of individuals, to the primal experience—a constant actualization of the moment of discovery, out of which the members of a single culture face the truth of the truisms that guide their lives, and their binding factual cogency. Thus, the establishing events of culture and its fundamental truths are experienced through ritual symbols. There is a return to the beginning, to the earliest foundations, so as to rebuild the comprehensive cultural structure in which we now live and function. It is the process of regeneration and reorientation without which no culture can exist.

Lastly, having clarified the primal and archaic nature of establishing symbols of culture, we may explain the possibly embarrassing fact that these symbols are often obscure, even bizarre, their language not directly comprehensible given the context of the cultural present, which embodies a long and winding process of historical development. Ritual symbols—above all the most eminent and important ones—often arouse amazement and surprise. They are sometimes even off-putting since, in the context of the present, they may be interpreted as antithetic to the recognition of truth, or to modern morality. Nevertheless, each culture tends to cling stubbornly to primal symbols since it is these that represent and maintain its unifying kernel of personality. To forget these symbols would be to forget the moment when the culture was born, when it came into the world with its separate being and identity. Clearly, however, preserving the vitality of such symbols is possible only if they are reinterpreted in each generation. Symbols require fresh observation and understanding each time they are placed in the context of a new present.

The truth needs to be stated: it is not possible to achieve a fine distinction between the primal meaning of a symbol and its later interpretations. Even the first experience of a symbol includes an interpretation—the repeated observation of an experience that has already been undergone. As the historical distance between the establishment of symbols and the time of experiencing them grows, however, interpretations will require increasing measures of historical knowledge. Symbols are transmitted in accordance with a tradition that also accumulate them and passes on the new interpretations. Talmudic sages interpreted biblical symbols in a particular way, and Gaonim and medieval scholars added other ways. The tradition does not negate any of the interpretations it accumulates, though it sometimes adds an interpretation to an interpretation; we learn from all these interpretations, interpret them, and arrive at our own interpretation. The element of study enters here vis-à-vis primal symbols; it is a phenomenon particularly notable in the case of Jewish festivals. Study is an inseparable part of celebration, not only in the activities that precede the festival, but during the festival itself. Study, interpretation, and homily are vital elements of the prayer service and of festival activity. Notice the components of this process—reviewing what has been previously explained, sermonizing, and discovering a vital present relevance.

There are those who regard the learning process as a disturbing element, arguing that it prevents us from forming our own impressions and expressing a spontaneous emotional response. To this one might respond that academic study and research based on a deliberate effort to achieve emotional restraint and personal detachment might indeed impair the experience of a festival. This type of study has a place, but it is during the preparations for the festival, not during the holiday itself. During the holiday, a very different kind of study is appropriate—an attempt to identify with and fathom the thought being examined and the emotion that accompanies it. Such study attempts to appreciate the experience that fuels thought, as the student makes an effort to live this through as if it were his own, and in this way to understand it from within. Such study enables the student to acquire an internal experience of the greatest importance even if it is evident that this is not his final deliberation, but only his opinion at the moment.

Mentally, the student recreates a process of the development of those truths that unify and direct his culture; he discovers truths that in his own time may already have been covered over, experiences that may already have dimmed but which continue to exist, covertly or overtly exerting influence at a depth usually ignored by a consciousness rooted in the present. Sometimes this vital element in the depths of the individual, as in the depths of the national culture, is represented by that which is foreign and even repulsive. The individual cannot know himself or live in all the strata of his personality unless he reaches into and rekindles these depths, unless he brings them up to be expressed again in the context of the actions, emotions, and thought of routine life in the present. The process of study from which the new understanding springs is precisely the process of regeneration and reorientation. It follows that this process does not detract from an emotional response to the symbol but actually develops, directs, and completes the reaction.

THE SUKKAH AS AN ACADEMIC MODEL

It is because of the multitude and density of its ritual symbols, drawn from an ancient strata, that Sukkot was chosen as the chapter for an in-depth examination on the role of the ritual symbol. There is something particularly obscure and perplexing about the rituals of this festival— especially those that relate to the four species and the "rejoicing of Beit HaShoeva"—and the act of leaving the house to live in a sukkah, which is a specifically sharp deviation from routine life. The ritual and symbolic action is considerably prolonged, producing what could be seen as an extended play. Without examining its strange nature, an individual could not avoid examining himself during this play, which appears suitable for children. What is this activity—which to an impartial observer might appear as a deliberate and utterly serious return to childhood—intended to express?

The reference to Sukkot in the Book of Leviticus clarifies the importance of dwelling in the sukkah as a recollection of the Exodus from Egypt. "Ye shall dwell in booths seven days; all that are homeborn in Israel shall dwell in booths; that your generations may know that I made the children of Israel to dwell in booths, when I brought them out of the land of Egypt" (Leviticus 23:42–43). In references to the festival in the Books of Exodus and Deuteronomy, the emphasis is on the agricultural element: ". . . and the feast of ingathering, at the end of the year, when thou gatherest in thy labors out of the field" (Exodus 23:16). "Thou shalt keep the feast of tabernacles seven days, after that thou hast gathered in from thy threshing-floor and from thy winepress . . . because the Lord thy God shall bless thee in all thine increase, and in all the work of thy hands, and thou shalt be altogether joyful" (Deuteronomy 16:13–15).

Though these verses do not explain the custom of dwelling in the sukkah, a hint may be discerned in the definition of the festival as a harvest festival of field crops, since the celebration of the crops takes place in the fields from which the bountiful harvest has come, outside the home. The references are oblique; there are no details from which one could learn either just what a sukkah is or its nature is as a symbol. With only the passages in the Torah, it would be difficult to imagine how this commandment of dwelling in the sukkah was to be performed. This is one of the cases which the Sages quote when seeking to prove the absolute necessity of the Oral Law. The question as to whether this commandment could be observed on the basis of a general, conventional understanding of the word "booth" is a moot one; it is certain, however, that observance

of the sukkah commandment—in all its details, symbols, and meanings—
as it has been accepted by the Jewish people since the Return to Zion up
to the modern period, is the work of scribes and sages, a product of the
Oral Law. The symbolic quality of the sukkah, like the shaping of Rosh
HaShanah and Yom Kippur, can be seen as the commentary of Sages
formulated on biblical foundations. The web of ideas that the Sages
stretched across the symbol of the sukkah and its design have their origins
in the Bible, albeit not necessarily in the commandment regarding the
sukkah. It was a web spun by the Sages who brought it to a splendid state
of consummation.

The *Aggadah* is a good place to start a discussion on the significance of
the sukkah; however, since the intent here is to examine the function of
its symbolic quality, we begin with a *halakhic* definition. What is a sukkah?
How is it to be made? Why were limits set on what can be considered a
religiously proper sukkah? Do these delimitations, directed at its finest
details, provide any enlightenment as to the significance of the activity?
The discussion that follows is based on the extensive and highly complex
halakhic deliberation that appears in the Mishnah, Tractate *Sukkah*. The
focus here, however, is not on each detailed ruling; rather, it is on the
underlying principles and concepts of what a sukkah is. For these
purposes, the concentrated and concisely structured discussion in the
Mishnah is most appropriate. From it, the theoretical model that stood
before the Sages can be drawn, and its significance considered. What is
the thought that directs the making of the sukkah and the experience of
dwelling in it?

In the mishnaic discussion, details are not preceded by a general
definition; that is, beginning with the details, a general concept is
constructed on their foundation. What is a sukkah? First and foremost, it
is a thatched structure, a structure covered with *skhakh*, with thatch, which
is of course the origin of the name sukkah. Thatch is the main element of
a sukkah. For purposes of discussion, if the question is, what separates a
covered dwelling in which human beings customarily live in modern times
from a thatched structure, the concise definition, summarizing the entire
halakhic discussion is: a sukkah is a temporary dwelling place. All the
details in the mishnaic discussion are designed to explain what a
temporary dwelling place is—i.e., in what way it is a home, a place where
humans beings live, and in what way it is temporary; i.e., not intended for
permanent habitation.

Through a systematic analysis of the detailed mishnaic discussion one
can draw the characteristics of the sukkah as a residence and the factors

that distinguish it from a permanent residence. Above all, the sukkah is a structure that humans *make* for themselves. The word "make" is repeated several times in the first two paragraphs in Chapter One. "Anyone who has made it . . . But if he made it for the sake of the festival . . . He who makes his sukkah," and so on. Thus the sukkah as a residence is not a random collection of natural features; rather, it is an artificial structure created from materials taken from the natural environment and intended for the purpose of a structure. Second, the sukkah is a residence in that it is a standing structure offering a certain measure of protection against the natural elements. The sukkah provides shade and protects against wind; it moderates heat and cold and even provides a measure of shelter against the rain that is liable to fall at this time of the year. Last, as a residence, the sukkah is a place where there is enough room to perform the necessities that sustain a working person. It is a place where one can sleep (Chap. 2, Mishnayot 1 and 2); and where one can rest and eat (2:5–7).

What distinguishes a Sukkah from a permanent residence? In general terms, the difference is in its unfinished nature. The sukkah is erect and provides protection, but it is not stable, and it cannot withstand violent shaking (such as a strong wind or rain). It does not provide complete refuge from cold, heat, or dampness, and the vital needs referred to above can be met in a limited manner only. Moreover, while it is made from materials designated for the purpose, the degree of processing is limited. Thus it is the lack of wholeness that distinguishes the temporary from the permanent. The "model" offered by the Mishnah provides more details.

When referring to the designation of natural materials for the structure, the Mishnah insists that the branches used for the sukkah must not be attached to a tree or to roots in the ground. The branches are to be cut (Chap. 1, Mishnah 4), but, the Mishnah also insists, the materials used for the thatch, which is the main part of the Sukkah, must not be processed after being cut. Even bales of straw or bundles of wood or twigs may not be used—the bales must be opened (1:5). What is the permitted limit of processing? From the detailed discussion, the answer that emerges could be phrased as follows: if the raw material taken from natural flora has become an object in its own right, i.e., if it has been specified by some action for a purpose other than thatching, it is not permitted; if, however, the processing was for the purpose of the sukkah, it is permissible. The material for the sukkah should be clearly designated; the most minimal and essential act of processing required to express this designation is the act of detaching the material from the ground and adding it to the thatch.

The detaching stops the material's natural function, and placing it with the thatch signals its artificial function.

Shelter is still another area in which the Mishnah distinguishes between permanence and transience. The Mishnah maintains that the sukkah must divide a person from outside space, and this division is to be achieved by the sukkah itself, not by any other element (such as a tree or beam; see Chap. 1, Mishnah 2). Equally, however, the division should not be completely opaque (1:6; 11; 2:2). What are the limits in either direction? The mishnaic answer is that the covering should be more than half the roof of the sukkah; that is, the shade should be more extensive than the area exposed to the sun at midday. On the other hand, the parts fashioning the thatch should not join together to form a single, solid unit. If a certain quantity of thatch is concentrated in a particular part of the covered area and covers more than half of that area, if it is only potentially, the sukkah is acceptable. If the thatch is extremely dense and there are no spaces between the branches or planks, but these are not tied and could be separated by force, the sukkah is still acceptable. These are the extremes. The preferred definition of the sukkah lies between the two extremes.

A third question is concerned with the existence of the sukkah as a separate unit (see Chap. 2, Mishnayot 2,3,4). The Mishnah requires that the sukkah be a unit that stands on its own base, otherwise it is not the sukkah that is the dwelling place but the structure on which it leans. At the same time, the sukkah should not be a structure based on a permanent structure. Once again, borders are set. A sukkah that leans on another object (such as a bed) is acceptable as long as it remains erect after the supporting object is removed. If the sukkah rests against a permanent structure, the structure must be destabilized by removing some element, even if this is merely a relative instability.

Lastly, there is the question of fulfilling the necessities of living in the place (Chap. 2, Mishnah 6–9). The sukkah should be high and wide enough for a man to be able to sit, lie, and eat in it. It should not be too high, however. The minimum height is such that a man can sit and eat in the sukkah with most of his body enclosed within it. At the other extreme, a sukkah taller than twenty cubits is invalid (1:1).

A person who wants to observe the commandment of the sukkah properly studies before acting, and acts before dwelling. It is a single continuum of activity in which the study that accompanies the person as he acts and dwells imbues these with significance. The individual deliberately puts himself in a defined situation, aware of the fact that his dwelling in the sukkah is dwelling in a temporary place under specific conditions. The function of this act is to create these conditions of life around himself and to reflect on their significance. Thus action is accompanied by thought; the special emotions of the festival lie between action and *halakhic* thought.

What significance is there to a situation defined according to these limits? All the precise *halakhic* rules mentioned above appear to point to an intermediate state between natural existence and cultural existence. Natural existence means life within given environmental conditions, without change. Animals require caves, burrows, and crevices in order to find shelter; they feed on the flora and fauna that are available, without processing. A human being who lived this way in his environment would be little more than an animal. His humanity emerges when he starts to process his environment, creating tools and beginning to produce results from nature that nature itself does not grant. This is the condition of culture. Culture aims to construct a level of human existence that is above the level of natural existence through the use of artificial means. The cultural ideal is that the artificial achievement which enables an individual to secure his well-being and a certain control of his destiny, be a stable one, enduring and no less permanent than the natural cycle of life. In other words, when a human being leaves the natural state his aim is to achieve a higher level of that same certainty which exists in the constancy of natural phenomena. The factor spurring him on in the development of his culture is a sense of anxiety lest that which he has managed to extract from nature by artificial means, laid as the foundation of his well-being and happiness—perhaps as his very existence as a human being—might not still be there tomorrow or the day after.

This is the explanation for the desire to constantly consolidate cultural achievement and make it more enduring in the face of the forces of nature that are liable to destroy it. A structure, a permanent dwelling made of solid rows of stone, symbolizes the aspiration for a stable culture, as stable as is found in nature to which the human sphere is superior. Notice the precision with which the sukkah marks the intermediate stage. The permanent structure is left behind, but there is not a return to the natural environment. For a limited period of time the individual lives in conditions that, though cultural, still do not have the appearance of stability. The fact that cultural achievement is only temporary—that though it stands, the structure is weak—does not escape the sukkah dweller who is aware of the point and whose study directed him to build the sukkah in this manner. Why is the Jew required to return to this intermediate state of the beginnings of culture precisely on this festival? What is the truth that he is supposed to understand and live under these circumstances?

TEMPORARY DWELLING PLACE

Having discussed the sukkah as an academic model, let us now examine the immediate impression made by the transition from a permanent, organized home to a sukkah. Perhaps the initial response is excitement at the change from routine, at the element of innovation. The freshness of the thatch, the beauty of the colorful and engagingly shaped decorations, heighten the sense of something new, and excitement is swelled at being directly within nature. The breath of fresh air, the stars above twinkling through the thatch, the abundant foliage—it is as if a renewed friendship is struck up with the natural environment. All this contributes to the festive excitement of the transition, and it is a state filled with beauty and happiness. After a short while, however, the individual begins to feel a lurking dissatisfaction at the absence of comforts to which he is accustomed. Since the time of year is autumn in the Land of Israel, the lack of comfort could become actual suffering on particularly hot days, or when rain falls. Though one has only just left the house for the sukkah, there is a desire to return to it with its comfortable and stable shelter, to think about the charming sukkah while safely ensconced in one's home. But in the sukkah one must remain, unless the rain, cold, and wind are persistent and forceful. The Mishnah states that "For all seven days, one makes the sukkah one's permanent home and the house one's temporary abode. If it rains, when may one leave the sukkah? If the food is rancid. What is this analogous to? To a slave who comes to pour a glass of wine for his master, and pours the entire jug on him" (Sukkah, Chap. 2, Mishnah 9).

The experience of dwelling in the sukkah may, therefore, be highly unpleasant—during a festival in which the people are commanded to be "exceedingly" joyful. It is precisely at this point that the reason the Jew is commanded, at Sukkot, to return symbolically to the intermediate state of the beginnings of culture is most clearly seen. Dwelling in the sukkah is not only a renewing and refreshing experience, it is also a simple test—in the biblical sense of the word—an examination that reveals something about the human being, to the human being. A legend of the Sages casts an amusing light on the nature of this test. The story is quite long and talks about a future controversy between God and the nations of the world when He questions them as to whether they have observed the Torah. At the end of the controversy, the nations plead with God.

"Offer us the Torah anew and we shall obey it." But the Holy One, blessed be He says to them, "You foolish ones among the nations, anyone who took the trouble to prepare on the eve of the Sabbath can eat on the Sabbath, but whoever has not troubled on the eve of the Sabbath, what shall he eat on the Sabbath? Nevertheless, I have an easy command which is called sukkah, go and carry it out" . . . and why does He term it an *easy* command? Because it does not effect one's purse. Straight away will every one of them betake himself and go and make a booth on top of his roof; but the Holy One, blessed be He, will cause the sun to blaze forth over them as at the summer solstice and every one of them will trample down his booth and go away as it is said, "Let us break their bands asunder and cut away their cords from us." (But earlier it was said, "The Holy One, blessed be He, does not deal imperiously with his creatures." True! But this happens occasionally to the Israelites too when the summer solstice extends to the Festival of Tabernacles and they are vexed by the heat. Does not Raba say: He who is vexed thereby is freed from dwelling in the sukkah? Granted, in such circumstances they would be freed, but would Israelites contemptuously trample it down?) Thereupon the Holy One, Blessed be He, laughs at them, as it is said: He that sitteth in heaven shall laugh. [*Avoda Zara*, 3:3]

In other words, through dwelling in the sukkah—a temporary place that does not offer complete shelter—the extent of the individual's faith in the performance of the commandment is tested. It is a light commandment, filled with beauty. But it can also be very inconvenient, and if an individual does not have sufficient faith and willpower to observe the commandment, more than desisting from its performance, he may strike out against it in his anger at being deprived of his customary comfort.

While the Sages' tale is amusing, the seriousness of its message transcends humor. Here once again is a basic perspective in both biblical and Talmudic thought. Man's intellectual capacities, the quality that distinguishes him and makes him unique, grants him a measure of sovereignty over Creation. Man can, and indeed should, bend animal, vegetable, and mineral to his own advantage and welfare, should exercise "mastery" over them. Man can, and indeed should, process that which he finds in his environment, thus changing the natural existence of parts of the animal, vegetable, and mineral world, drawing from nature more than nature itself gives. Man can, and indeed should, build houses, lay roads, create tools, and insure himself against want, suffering, damage, and discomfort. Man can, and indeed should, do all this, yet he is not intended to have sovereign control over the universe that surrounds him.

There are limits to human domination and utility. Let no one imagine, therefore, that man's cultural achievements have granted him such control; in particular, let no one tender the achievement of such control as the purpose of life. Limited control was given to man only in terms of his being "created in God's image" in order that he might worship his Creator from this station. It is human destiny to worship the Creator; bountiful good is the reward, not the purpose. The nature of the striking distinction between the life of the believer and the life of the pagan is pointed out in the Bible. It is a distinction between human control of the conditions of one's existence as an end, and the worship of God as an end.

Those who choose the former path, which is certainly the one toward which man is directed by his natural urges, will eventually become enslaved to their own creations and cravings since the goal they have set for themselves, in attributing to human beings a level of Divinity that they do not deserve, cannot be attained. Those who choose the latter option do not delude themselves that they can ever be secure by controlling the conditions of their existence, freeing themselves from want and suffering. However, this direction does offer an inner certainty in the beneficent will of God, accepting all that is provided by nature itself, and all that can be drawn from nature as a gift of God. Precisely in so doing, man maintains his moral liberty and his dignity as a human being, and precisely in so doing he can be truly happy with the great bounty he has achieved through his labors.

A life of faith, then, is a life based on a sure reliance in God's bountiful will, which offers a reward to those who observe His commandments and do that which is good in His eyes. Even if the believer does not have any "guarantee" that he will not suffer want in the future, he is confident and happy with his lot. Those who wish to have some form of "guarantee" for their security live in a state of illusion and moral enslavement that eventually leads to the breakdown of the entire personality and, on the social level, to cultural collapse. Thus a return to the intermediate state of the beginnings of cultural existence, through the symbol of the sukkah, reminds man who he is and what his real position is in the universe; what the commandment is and how he shall perform it. It is a reminder that even the most developed civilization does not grant human beings control over the conditions of their existence, since the test of faith is a test of the choice between the natural desire for human sovereignty as a goal vis-à-vis the freedom that comes from accepting the yoke of the commandments. The sukkah is thus seen as a symbolic test of the believer.

Consequently it is not difficult to understand why on Sukkot, a harvest festival designed for rejoicing, the Jew is commanded to return symbolically to the intermediate stage of the beginnings of culture. The reminder comes precisely at the point when man sees before him, within his grasp, a bountiful harvest and full granaries. He is sated and quenched, and seemingly safe from want tomorrow and the day after. He apparently holds the key to his happiness. At this point, the sukkah reminds him that man has no stability in the world; his existence and achievements are flimsy since no civilization, however advanced its tools and means, is any more than a temporary dwelling place. All cultural achievements are fragile and transient, and have no place before eternity. A sad thought? Not really. Despite its frailty and lack of comfort, the sukkah is a symbol of a strong and confident joie de vivre. Precisely because we know that everything is transient and man may not continue to keep his treasures, which in an absolute sense are not his own, we can rejoice. On the contrary, were we to delude ourselves with an illusion of sovereignty, we could not truly rejoice at the bounty won through our labor. Worry and concern would seep through the illusion of stability. The commandment of the sukkah teaches the dweller within it that he should rely on the internal moral certainty of the Creator's bountiful will, and accept plenty—the blessing of the harvest of the fields—as grace, as a testimony of love.

Thus the significance of the sukkah as it marks harvest time in the cycle of the year's seasons. It is also significant as a reminder of the Exodus from Egypt, and in this context, the sukkah is seen as a counterpoint to the store-cities the enslaved Hebrews built for the Egyptians. The store-cities were evidence of the tremendous effort made by an entire civilization to insure itself against shortage by sequestering in advance all that it might require in a distant future. With their enormous buildings, these cities also represent the desire to overcome the cycle of existence and collapse, and to vanquish eternity. It is a culture symbolized by structures intended to last for generations; yet this pretentious effort transformed Egypt into a house of bondage. The rulers themselves became slaves to their lust for power and eternity. The Hebrews who left the store-cities for the desert dwelled in sukkot, flimsy structures that have a brief life. Learning to trust the shelter, a symbol of faith, is precisely what guaranteed their liberty. The sukkah also appears as a symbol in juxtaposition to the towns and villages the Jews built after settling in the Promised Land. The settlement of Eretz Israel and the bountiful harvest of the land were a provisional promise reflected in the commandments that relate to the land. If these commandments were observed, the Jews would dwell securely on their land, the rain would come in season, and the earth would yield its harvest. If they did not keep the commandments, there would be drought, the land would withhold its yield, and the Jews would be scattered from their land.

These commandments represent a recognition that man does not have complete and total mastery of earth and its harvest, and he must not attempt to achieve such mastery. Man must share justly with his fellows; precisely by overcoming the pagan instinct for domination will he insure his liberty and the protection of his God. The idea is reflected in a symbolic "retreat" to the temporary dwelling places of the desert period. Just at the season in which he grasps the bountiful harvest drawn from his inheritance, the Jew makes a gesture of departing from a solid house into a flimsy and transient structure. In this way, he acknowledges that the bountiful harvest is an act of God's grace. Two contexts are seen for the same idea: rejoicing intended to spring precisely from success in overcoming total materialism, and the desire for domination. So the symbol of the sukkah was developed in the Sages' halakha, like Rosh HaShanah and Yom Kippur, as an exegesis on the Torah. The Sages removed the Torah commandment from its ancient context, reinterpreting it within the broader setting of the biblical world view itself.

THE BOOK OF ECCLESIASTES

Still another halakhah from the Oral Law related to prayers at Sukkot supports an understanding of dwelling in the sukkah as a "retreat" to the early stage of civilized life, in order to stress the fragile and transient quality of human activity in nature. The Sages called for a different megillah to be read on each of the pilgrimage festivals. At Passover, it is the "The Song of Songs"; at Shavuot, "The Book of Ruth." These choices seem obvious, and the connection between these scrolls and the pilgrimage festivals on which they are read is simple and evident. At Sukkot, however, the Sages decided "Ecclesiastes" would be read—a choice that, at first glance, may seem strange. What does such a book, replete with sober, sad, and disillusioned wisdom, have to do with Sukkot, which is meant to be a festival of great joy, a festival when Jews are told to be "exceedingly joyous"? Is the reading not at odds with the festival?

The first hint of the thought behind the Sages' apparently strange decision comes in the name of the *megillab*, Ecclesiastes (in Hebrew, Kohelet). While it is true that the book itself states that this is the name of the sage whose sayings are collected here—Kohelet Ben David—it is not unreasonable to assume that a unique name such as this is in fact a nom de plume. A possible interpretation of the word Kohelet is "he who gathers in." How ever one interprets such an original name, certainly the Book of Ecclesiastes presents its contents as the harvest of an old king's bountiful wisdom, based on his rich life experiences. The king has had an opportunity to experience all that humans beings desire, all that is deemed worthwhile and purposeful on earth. He is about to close an entire life cycle—childhood, youth, and old age are drawing to their end, and this is the point at which he takes stock. What remains with him? What is his lasting harvest? The analogy to Sukkot, the festival of the ingathering, is immediately visible. Sukkot is also the closing of a circle. Spring and summer have come and gone, the autumn has arrived. The farmer gathers in his crops. Thus we are presented with a harvest of wisdom, the yield of a lifetime, on a festival when man gathers in the fruits of his labors from the fields.

The sad, jaded, disappointed tone that pervades the Book of Ecclesiastes is almost inevitable if one considers the point of view from which its author observes the world. An old man recalls all the joys of life that he desired, pursued, and indeed achieved. What is left of all these now that he has grown old? Everything is gone, nothing is left standing—and this is the meaning of the sentence that is repeated again and again with the weary rhythm of passing time. "This, too, is vanity." "Vanity of vanities, said Kohelet, vanity of vanities—all is vanity." Vanity is something that has no existence—it no sooner is, than it ceases to be; if it is replaced by something else, that, too, will not last; and the old man tastes the transience of it while it is still before him. The only thing left to the aging man is his wisdom. But is wisdom based on a knowledge that everything is vanity, anything more than vanity itself? Can there be any comfort in such wisdom? Proud of his wisdom; at the same time he despises it. He gathers in his harvest in order to establish a lasting monument to himself, hiding in his wisdom behind an oblique pseudonym. He foresees disappointment.

In this wisdom, which denigrates its own value, there is a certain sense of "nevertheless," but before attempting to probe this further, it is useful to examine again the place of Kohelet's sad, practical wisdom in the Festival of Ingathering. It goes without saying that the harvest is a joyous occasion; does that make it a completely inappropriate time for the perspective of a man at the end of a life cycle? Spring has gone; summer has come and gone; autumn has arrived. The harvest has been gathered, only the echoing memory of spring and summer remain. The harvest is before our eyes, nevertheless there is a fluttering of heart that everything is transient—the autumn and its bountiful harvest will also pass. Is anything permanent? It is vain to attempt to deny, to ignore or repress such thoughts in the consciousness of an individual who wishes to rejoice.

At this point, as the cycle of life is completed, a piercing sadness seeps into the heart. The great harvest which was anticipated, for which one lived, is no longer in the future but actively present, and as such seems already to belong to a past that is disintegrating, crumbling, vanishing. There is an attempt to cling to the present and stop the feeling of a devouring life flow. Can such a thing be achieved? Kohelet knows it is impossible. This is, perhaps, the first hint of a bittersweet optimism that lies beyond general disappointment. One cannot deny, however, that at the harvest festival people tend to cleave to the present, closing their eyes so as to see neither past nor future. Joy appears to be such a strong tide of the here and now that the movement of time is no longer felt. Ecstatic dancing to the point of oblivion, drunkenness, the sensual delight that wraps the human in a sensation of continual present, are devoid of a past or future. The question remains: Is this really joy? Deep within, does there not lurk a sadness at the sense of life slipping away—a sadness from which one attempts to escape through dance and drink?

Thus, with hindsight, the motif of Ecclesiastes is found in the atmosphere of the harvest festival; the reading of this *megillah* does not contradict the atmosphere of the festival—rather the natural human tendency to ignore the Kohelet motif and escape from it. The reading of Ecclesiastes is designed to remind us that beyond great joy we do indeed feel sadness, that there is a sedimentation of sadness in all joy in man's world since even in beautiful moments life continues to pass away. Perhaps, too, this is a reminder that all joy begins from sadness and rises above it, yet continues to carry it within. What need is there for the reminder? Surely it is not intended to spoil the festive joy, but to prevent an escape from sadness—the hallmark of life on earth—so that real joy may indeed be known.

The Book of Ecclesiastes carries a hidden message that rises up with reverse irony: the innocence of the believer in the guise of sober disillusionment. Notice that while Kohelet denigrates the value of his own wisdom, he has a high enough regard for it to gather its harvest and make it known to the public. "More than this, my son, beware of writing too many books" (12:12), he says at the conclusion of his work, but he does not apply this to his own book. The wisdom that knows that all is vanity appears to have a lasting value. What value? Some of the sages believed that knowing truth is the purpose of all human activity, for by knowing truth we achieve immortality. Kohelet does not share this view. He does not suggest that those who hear his lesson abandon the vanities of life and devote themselves exclusively to the pursuit of wisdom. Indeed, precisely when he sought to devote himself to wisdom, he discovered that this, too, is a vanity. So he abandoned that direction; then his wisdom was attended by the trials of everyday acts and their vicissitudes; reflecting and revealing human yearnings, almost cheerfully, he indefatigably restates the vanity of all these acts until the very end of his work.

Yet he does not advise his audience to refrain from all these acts, or to cease taking them seriously. On the contrary, he advises them to make the most of every moment of life for all that is special and good. "The light is sweet, and a pleasant thing it is for the eyes to behold the sun. For if man live for many years, let him rejoice in them all, And remember the days of darkness, for they shall be many. Everything is vanity. Rejoice, O young man, in thy youth; And let thy heart cheer thee in the days of thy youth, And walk in the ways of thy heart, And in the sight of thine eyes; But know thou, that for all these things God will bring thee into judgment. Therefore remove vexation from thy heart, And put away evil from thy flesh; For childhood and youth are vanity" (11:7–10). Thus childhood and youth are vanities, the light is vanity and even joy is a vanity. Nevertheless, the light is sweet to behold, and joy is good for man. Each period of time has acts appropriate to the moment, "A time for every need." Men should do that which is required at each time, experience everything, willingly live moments of joy and of sadness. One should not withdraw from life or despise life, but live it to the full.

Why, though, is the wisdom that knows that all is vanity critical? It is important to emphasize that the word "vanity" is not denigrating or scornful. In Hebrew, the word for vanity, *hevel*, means the breath that leaves the mouth—something that ceases to be as soon as it has come into existence; something that has no existence beyond the moment. But it does exist, and it should not be scorned since while it exists it is the being to which our lives are devoted. Even so, man should not believe that the present moment is the shape of all time. The knowledge that all is vanity prevents him from being bound to that which is finite and transient as if it were eternal. There is something beyond each hour that reaches out as each moment passes. Kohelet dwells on this point, repeatedly calling to mind that man is judged by God for all he does. That which is permanent and static always lies beyond the changing and transient view of the sights of the world and the highs and lows of life. The relative and transient should not be treated as anything other than relative and transient; only if this rule is obeyed will man be able to derive the most he can from what exists now. However, man is not able to treat the relative and transient in this way unless he roots himself in the transcendental knowledge of the believer—the last innocence of the man who knows that "all is vanity."

Thus the Book of Ecclesiastes aims to teach those to whom it preaches to abandon their natural tendency to dwell upon the transient present, and their attempt to possess the present so that it stands still, offering an illusory eternity. In order to rejoice in the present, man must both give himself over to it and yet remain beyond it, relying on a different certainty. In this way, perhaps a similarity can be seen between the message of Ecclesiastes and the message of dwelling in the sukkah as a symbol of an early state of civilization. In both cases, there is a retreat from the illusion of stability and strength inherent in mundane culture, and a return to the domain of sadness, fear, and longings that define the human condition in the world. Yet through this retreat and disillusionment, man's eyes are opened to see another truth, and this is what enables him to respond to all that the mundane present offers, in its fragile and transient beauty. One can be surrounded by sadness and yet break out into a well of joy if one approaches the sadness with the innocence of the believer.

Kohelet remains within the realm of reverse irony, but the truth to which he points is overtly stated elsewhere in the Bible, as a direct and strong message that apparently is the opposite of Kohelet, yet actually complements it. "Happy is the man who does not walk in the counsel of the wicked, nor stands in the way of sinners, nor sits in the seat of scorners. But his delight is in the Torah of the Lord; and in His Torah he meditates day and night. And he shall be like a tree planted by streams of water, that brings forth its fruit in its season; its leaf also shall not wither; and in whatever he does he shall prosper. Not so the wicked; but they are like the chaff which the wind drives away. Therefore the wicked shall not stand in the judgment, nor sinners in the congregation of the righteous. For the Lord knows the way of the righteous; but the way of the wicked shall perish" (Psalms 1). The sukkah is a symbol of fragile existence, yet to the person who dwells in faith within it, the sukkah symbolizes transcendental eternal existence.

JOY AND HOPE

We come back now to the starting point of the discussion, the unique nature of Sukkot as a festival when the Jew is commanded to rejoice. On this festival, joy is not merely an accompaniment of the festivities; it is a theme whose achievement is deliberately aimed at in its own right, experienced as an objective of the festival. Therefore it is only proper that joy be raised to the level of academic inquiry. What is joy? What place does it have in the way of life of a believer?

Joy is the feeling that one's spirit of life, one's soul has overcome internal or external obstacles. Joy is, of course, associated with achievements that involve the satisfaction of vital needs, the removal of dangers, the securing of well-being, peace, and so on. Yet the fact that obstacles were overcome in achieving these goals is of great importance, and intensity of joy is directly related to the question of how difficult it was to surmount obstacles before joy could be experienced. By overcoming hurdles, human beings reaffirm their inherent abilities. An inner, unbridled flow of life is felt, and this consciousness of life's events is joy. The way in which a sentiment is expressed is reflective of its nature. Joy is expressed in a liberating mental and physical movement that bursts through, no longer directed at any utilitarian purpose. It is declarative and demonstrative, expressive and revealing. Recitation and song show the outward movement of the soul; skipping and dancing, the movement of the body.

When joy is expressed in a directed and consummate way, it becomes song and dance and is raised to the level of an art form. In order to exhaust the sensation of achievement and overcoming obstacles, song and dance describes the stages of effort that preceded the achievement. In their songs and dances, those who till the land re-enact stages of plowing and sowing, and all the work in the field up to the time the crop is harvested; warriors re-enact the battle in their songs and dances; then comes the moment when victorious might overcomes its inhibitions and announces its achievement—it is the height of joy. Song and dance re-enact the effort that brought about the achievement, but the harmonious movements of song and dance are not intended to secure it. They are intended to reach a perfection that glorifies achievement and summarizes the sense of overcoming obstacles inherent in it. Joy carries with it the pains of the effort that preceded it.

Thus joy is an emotion that draws on a preceding confrontation; its memory is made an inner background for the release that follows. This is despite the fact that joy's innate tendency to bring the sense of overcoming obstacles to such a level of totality that the memory of struggles, difficulties, and limitations, which are inescapable and definitive elements of human existence, may be forgotten. Once a joyous person reaches a point of erasing the memory of effort and pain that preceded joy, he appears—through illusion or through a blurring of the senses—to have removed himself from the context of human existence, and to be bound by an emotion that is not joy.

In re-examining Sukkot as a festival of joy, elements of song and dance—the combination of movements of body and soul in the joint expression of overcoming obstacles—are found to play a prominent part particularly in this festival. Every festival brings joy; every festival therefore has song, and sometimes this song gives way to dance. At Sukkot, however, the singing and dancing are obligatory symbols of worship unique to the festival. Evidence of this is seen in the recitation of the *hallel* prayers with the four species held in hand, and in the *hakafot* around the synagogue—a reminder of the ritual in which worshippers circled the altar when the Temple was still standing. The singing and dancing reached their peak on Hoshanna Rabbah, the seventh day of the festival. As if to compensate for the loss of the Temple, the generations of exile added an eighth day, Simkhat Torah—the Rejoicing of the Law—in which worshippers perform *hakafot* embracing the Torah scrolls. Singing and dancing with the special symbols of the festival are expressions of joy, and in this context, it is useful to reflect on the four species: etrog (a citron), palm branch, myrtle, and willow. First, these symbolize achieve-ment—the choicest fruits of the land, the choice of its soil, air, sun, dew, and rain, of its wells and streams. The people that has been privileged to settle in its land and to enjoy its bounty raise the symbols of achievement, the symbols of the blessing that has been bestowed on their action, and singing and dancing express joy at the achievement. Popular tradition has attributed special meaning to the four species. The date palm is a common symbol of victory; the myrtle a symbol of the preservation and everlasting continuity of life; citrus fruits symbolize untarnished beauty; and the willow is a symbol of plentiful water. The symbols express the forces of life in their unlimited bounty, persistence, and ability to overcome all obstacles, so they interpret the meaning of the songs and dances.

At Sukkot, as a festival of overcoming life's obstacles, the individual returns to a primal level in the direct experience of struggle for human existence in nature. It is indeed remarkable that Sukkot preserved its character and its tangible symbols as an agricultural festival even during the period of exile and of separation from the soil. Moreover, it preserved the ancient character of the harvest festival, which reflects an ancient cultural infrastructure shared by the Hebrews and the agricultural peoples who preceded them in the region. Naturally there is a connection between a direct outburst of primal, emotional response that places a physical gesture before the speech that interprets it, and the preservation of an archaic ritual stratum that may even precede the stage at which a specifically Israelite ritual emerged. Wells of joy spring from the depths of the soul, and its earliest expressions are safeguarded in a primal level of psychophysical infrastructure that remains almost unchanged through the generation because one can barely distinguish between the emotion that is expressed at such "existential" moments and the patterns that shape and express this emotion. The basic experience remains archaic.

This essential conservatism in the primal patterns of expression would appear to explain the strangeness of some of the rituals of Sukkot. Other festivals also include curious rituals, but no other festival has retained such a broad and dominant stratum of ancient rituals that diverge so clearly from the standard prayers and blessings of the Jewish people. If a detached observer in the synagogue during *hallel* with the four species in hand, and during the Hoshanna prayers and the *hakafot* around the platform, were to compare these rituals with normal Sabbath and holiday prayers, he would be surprised by the extent of the differences. The ecstatic movements appear to hold a mysterious and foreign significance, reminiscent of descriptions or pictures of rituals in ancient nature-based religions. Can these strange movements be compatible with the usual perception of Judaism, particularly prophetic Judaism, as emphasizing moral and historical significance?

The festival of Sukkot offers a daring glimpse into hidden depths of soul and culture, a glimpse that is necessary for the very experience of the festival. Joy is an experience that sweeps personality along, laden with spiritual and physical expression, rooted in primal instincts. These instincts should be revealed and expressed rather than repressed if man is to feel the joy of the welling up of power. On the other hand, it is a daring glimpse because it removes certain limits that morality and social order impose on primal instincts in order to restrain them. The forces that spring forth could sweep away and destroy barriers without which there could not be a balanced personal or societal life. In other words, joy could become something completely different from what it is if impulses of passion were allowed to flow without checks and balances.

Joy, as a sensation based on overcoming internal and external obstacles, clearly tends toward total release and toward a limitless sense of confirmation so one might think that real joy releases the individual from an awareness of the limits of his ability and from fear of the future. One might think that to be joyous one must attain such a level of gratification as to be utterly sated and overflowing, that the mere sensation of want and hunger would be unthinkable. The image of happiness is the image of a present that fully realizes itself, symbolized by complete satiation of the sensual delights. Joy can reach its peak when man feels completely safe and satisfied, but in aspiring to a sense of absolute gratification, a human being is in danger of exceeding his humanity. In other words, joy entails an intrinsic danger of debauchery—the drunken satiation of sensuous pleasure, or a sense of magical dominion that ostensibly places nature at the control of humanity. In both of these interrelated ways, man can reach what the Torah defines as the essence of paganism. While this is a "natural" result of joy, it passes beyond the limits of joy, eventually destroying the structure of the personality and the social order.

For joy to be truly joy, therefore, the outburst should not be allowed to reach its outside limits. The feeling of release and of overcoming obstacles needs to be kept within proper boundaries, and an eternal tension maintained between the desire for self-affirmation and the memory of human suffering and effort that bear witness, even in joy, to the fact the humans beings are no more than human. Only if man is cognizant of the limits of his ability, of the sadness that has been and the sadness that is yet to be, is he capable of fully living the wonderful sweetness of the moment of achievement. Sadness is the internal background, or limit, for the experience of joy—the internal background for the experience of relative release that confirms the spontaneous impulse of life. In other words, joy exists only when happiness, as a total experience, appears as a vision, as a longing, as a future that can be contained by no present; when the wish remains a wish even at the time of its limited gratification.

In the patterns of behavior on Sukkot, one clearly sees the effort to contain, within well-demarcated borders, the impulses that rise with joy so that these do not degenerate either in the direction of sensual oblivion or of magical ecstasy. Primal forms of ritual may lie in the period before a distinct Israelite ritual evolved, but these have been interpreted and consolidated differently in order to maintain joy and keep it within limits.

In this context, the earlier comments on the significance of the symbol of the sukkah and the reasons for reading the Book of Ecclesiastes on Sukkot become clear. At the intellectual level and on the existential or symbolic level, the limits of human capability are thus definitely emphasized. If the flow of human capability tempts man with the illusion of eternity, the sukkah and the Book of Ecclesiastes are intended to remind him that, in the face of the truly Eternal, human actions and achievements are no more than "vanity of vanities." However, a reminder of the vanity of human life is not intended to drown joy with sorrow but to preserve joy, guarding it as the joy of the believer.

Pulsing strongly in the joy of the believer is his sense of overcoming obstacles and of inner vitality, yet he consciously restrains these feelings. He does not permit joy to spill over into either sensual satiation that leads to oblivion of memory and consciousness, or into a pride that claims a dominion of magic over the forces of nature. In his joy, the believer remembers suffering and is aware of his limitations. He is aware that even the sensation of overcoming all obstacles, for all its strength and charm, is no more than a "vanity"—something that is here today and gone tomorrow. Then what keeps him from sinking into anxiety, into worry and fear? How can he be happy while he still remembers and knows? Surely it is his success that supports him; even while he remembers his suffering, he sees the bountiful harvest before him. He is happy with the fruits of his labor; happy at the plenty and surfeit; happy, too, that something remains in his store-rooms for the days to come. For the present, achievement attracts the focus of his attention; however, the bountiful harvest also serves the believer as a symbol. He teaches himself to see in it not only the fruits of his labor whose plenty save him from want but also—and above all—an expression of God's grace. It is God who gave him the fertile land, and God who brought the dew and the rains at their appointed times. It is God who has wrought the miracle of growth. The sensation of love and grace that finds its expression in the bountiful harvest saves the believer from worry and sorrow. He trusts that the mercies of God will accompany him in the future, too, if he does that which is good in the eyes of his Creator.

Notice that he does not see faith as a kind of exemption from the effort required to bring forth bread from the land, to build houses, lay roads, improve his work tools, and perform the other tasks of civilizational construction. It is man's duty to bear responsibility for meeting his numerous needs—more numerous than those of any other creature, due to his unique nature as man. But the fact that nature responds to human effort to extract more and more from the land is seen as a repeated miracle, as an expression of God's grace, and the believer rejoices in the bountiful harvest as an expression of renewed grace.

How does the believer restrain the sense of overcoming all obstacles, addressing this sensation along the path he has chosen? The earliest expressions of joy are singing and dancing; on Sukkot, these are songs and dances that spring from the depths of the soul. Restraint is expressed in the inner gesture of the believer; a conceptual gesture that exerts an influence on imagination and emotion, breaking the flowing forces before they pass the limit. What is the gesture? It is the gesture of thanksgiving. The believer does not present his bountiful harvest as the fruits of his own labor and wisdom; he tenders them as a grace he has been granted, and as an expression of love. Therefore he bows down and offers humble thanks. Inherently, the gesture of thanksgiving implies humility, a recognition of the limits of relative human ability in the face of the total ability of God the Creator. In the humility of the believer, a breaking action takes place that prevents the sensation of overcoming all obstacles from overstepping its bounds.

In this context, it is worthwhile to reflect on the content of the *hallel* Psalms and on the Hoshanna poems recited at Sukkot. In these verses, man presents himself as impoverished and weak before his Creator. He thanks God for the good that He has mercifully granted him, and asks that he be saved and enjoy success in the future as well. A few examples will suffice: "Who is like the Lord our God . . . who raises up the poor out of the dust, And lifts up the needy out of the dunghill; That He may set him with princes, Even with the princes of His people" (Psalm 113). "I will give thanks unto Thee, For Thou hast answered me, and art become my salvation. The stone which the builders rejected is become the chief cornerstone. This is the Lord's doing; it is marvelous in our eyes. This is the day which the Lord hath made; we will rejoice and be glad in it" (Psalm 118). The *hallel* ends with the main content of the Hoshanna poems: "Please, O Lord, save us; Please, O Lord, grant us success." These are indeed thoughts, but when expressed in song and dance they exercise an effect on the imagination and on the emotion, melting the sensation of flowing forces and redirecting it to a flow of gratitude that is basically the response of love to the grace that expresses love.

While he knows that the present moment of flowing joy will pass, it is this feeling that enables the believer to regard the future with confidence. He realizes that he may expect want and pain, disease and death in the future. Despite this, he finds in his heart the strength to hope. Certainly the hope is not a specific knowledge that things will go well for him; neither is it the confidence that he has the means to annul any danger: the hopeful believer knows that human beings do not enjoy such control over their destiny. Hope is nothing other than a steady direction of life to which man remains faithful because he knows the commandment that applies to him, and because he believes in the good and merciful God who rewards those who follow in His path. Hope is certainty regarding the future; but it is a certainty that does not draw on actual control of the means of existence. Instead, this certainty bases itself on the moral validity of faith. If, therefore, joy entails a desire for victory and eternity, faith interprets this wish as hope, thus transforming the future into the domain of aspiration. Consequently, joy does not run over into an endless wallowing in the present. In fact, joy is a sure, steady look toward the future. The hopeful human being strides toward that which is good and whole as a vision; even if it never becomes the present within himself, it casts its light on every step he takes toward it.

To conclude, we return to the sukkah as the central symbol of the festival. It is also the symbol of redemption. In the end of days we hope God will spread the "sukkah of His peace" over us. In the end of days we hope God will re-establish "the fallen sukkah of David." These expressions from the traditional liturgy describe a hope for the future—not in terms of towering palaces, not in terms of a paradisiacal existence free from effort within a nature that provides for man's every want. Hope for the future is described as a sukkah: a brittle, vulnerable existence that has no solid, independent basis of its own. Yet precisely for this reason, we sense in the sukkah the grace that descends from on high. It is the sustaining grace; the sensation of gratitude becomes the essence of the sensation of life, its mystery and wonder. "It is not the dead who shall praise the Lord, Neither shall those who go down to the depths. But we shall praise the Lord, from now and for ever more, Hallelujah!" (Psalm 115). The verse expresses the human desire to cling to life, but the love of life is reflected in the sensation of gratitude to Him who granted life and gave life its eternal value, despite its essential and inherent transience.

This, then, is the essential basis of the teaching of joyfulness as reflected in the symbols and rituals of Sukkot: a retreat that limits and restrains the high tide of man's autonomous forces so as to direct the flow toward another sentiment, that of gratitude. Thus from a source of faith, man receives that which he could never receive (except through delusion) from his own perception of life—hope. In man's fleeting and transient life, hope is the feeling of the value of the present in the face of eternity.

SEVEN

THE TENSION BETWEEN MARTYRDOM AND WHO IS LORD OVER US (THE IDEATIONAL PROGRESSION OF HANUKKAH)

COMBINING THE OLD AND THE NEW

Despite the conservatism that generally characterizes religion, the holiday of Hanukkah demonstrates that the Jewish calendar is amenable to marking events that have been turning points in Jewish history. Moreover, though holidays stored form and content in the course of generations, there were times when the content was quite radically transposed. Not every event of national significance left a lasting impression on the calendar. However, when in retrospect it was seen that a particular occurrence indeed marked a noticeable change in the basic circumstances of national existence or in the overall comprehension of the people's situation regarding its relations to its surroundings and its God, that event was placed in the calendar. This is what transpired with episodes of redemption and liberation, and with acts of destruction. In time, the people interpreted the meaning of events differently, and the change found its expression in ways that memory shaped.

In the period between the return from Babylonian captivity and the end of the Second Commonwealth, days were established to mark destruction (which occurred twice) as well as redemption. Hanukkah and Purim are

two new holidays without basis in the Torah; they attest directly to a
historic background. The first, Purim, relates to a diasporic reality. The
second, Hanukkah, concerns the miracle of the Second Period of the
Jewish people in its land. The fact that no new holidays or memorial days
were added to the permanent Jewish calendar from that time to the
present should not be seen as proof that, in the popular perception, the
nation's status vis-à-vis other peoples and God remained unchanged.
Indeed there were such changes but a need did not arise to mark them by
opening the calendar to new days of observance. Existing holidays
sufficed, and changes were expressed through restyling, occasionally
through the addition of another stratum, and sometimes even by
superimposing one stratum on another so that a contemporary perception
changed an evaluation of the past as well. Hanukkah, for example,
changed from a holiday of the people's liberation in its own land to a
holiday that expressed the longings of an exiled people for its home. In
our own time, there has been such a far-reaching transformation in the
history of the Jewish people, and in its understanding of its fate and goals,
that the calendar was unfolded to commemorate events.

The process began with an emphasis on half-holidays—Tu B'Shevat
and Lag B'Omer—whose origins in the tradition were very hazy.
Redesigning these days was wholly an innovation of the Zionist movement, whereas the tradition had given them but scant notice. At the same
time, several holidays, well defined in the tradition, acquired an additional
stratum of content; the most far-reaching change can be seen in
Hanukkah, where content seems to have been thoroughly revamped. And
with the establishment of the State of Israel, the calendar has been opened
to mark Holocaust and Heroism Day, Independence Day, and Jerusalem
Day. This new, creative stratum has greatly impacted on the structure of
the Jewish calendar. The transformation of the Hanukkah content can
provide instructive evidence as to the nature of the spiritual encounter
that is inherent in this creativity, and the radical reshuffling of values it
brought about. In contradistinction to the indistinct shape of forgotten
days such as Tu B'Shevat and Lag B'Omer, Hanukkah retained a sharply
focused symbolic profile. Throughout the long generations Hanukkah
remained an unfinished holiday, distinguished from venerable holidays
heavily laden and densely packed with tradition. Though the gaps left by
tradition could be seized upon for the introduction of new content, the
audaciousness of the innovation could not be obscured. The old and the
new were forced to confront each other.

HANUKKAH—THE UNFINISHED HOLIDAY

Hanukkah, the beautiful, young, and gay, somewhat childlike holiday is, paradoxically, a holiday with a covert spiritual problem. The ideational message it transmits is somewhat blurred, the indication of an internal debate that the Jewish people has been conducting with itself for generations—an argument that remains unresolved. There is a sense of an unfinished dimension in the design of the holiday. It is a relatively long holiday, lasting eight days; longer than Passover, and like Sukkot with the addition of Shemini Atzeret. Despite this, it does not have a single day that is sanctified by a prohibition to work. Only as the candles are lit at twilight is work forbidden on Hanukkah. Actually, it is only during this brief period through the entire eight-day span that there is a sense of the holiday at all for from morning to dusk one hardly feels a holiday spirit. Weekdays have their own customs, as does the Sabbath. Hanukkah has a distinctive symbolic feature and a number of customs associated with it, but the single symbol that joins the eight days together does not infuse the days. Not only is the kind of density that characterizes the Sabbath, Rosh HaShanah, Yom Kippur, and the three pilgrimage holidays not felt, but one actually senses a void. Folklore and games try to fill the void, but clearly they are merely a substitute and do not touch directly in any way on the central motif of the holiday. Furthermore, despite the fact that the historic event that the holiday celebrates is mentioned specifically in the benedictions and prayers, nowhere is there a full presentation of the event. One detail is featured to such an extent that it obscures everything that preceded it; indeed, from the way in which the holiday developed in the tradition, nothing could be learned about what preceded it.

A short discussion about the holiday by the Sages, in the Gemara, is a good expression of this (*Shabbat* 21). The brief description mentions merely the miracle of the cruse of oil and leaves unanswered the crux of the question "What is the meaning of Hanukkah?" Scholars of later generations gave further evidence of this in the repetition and invention of far-fetched answers that stretched even to the meaning of the name (such as *hanu kha*—they encamped on Kislev 25; or *het' nerot*—eight candles, in which *halakhah* follows the House of Hillel), extending as far as the gist of the celebration: Is Hanukkah (literally, a dedication) a reference to the rededication of the Temple? or to the altar? or to the menorah? Even these questions do not touch the principle involved.

The main question is whether, beyond the miracle of the cruse of oil found in the Temple, the holiday is supposed to mark political and

military liberation from foreign rule, or whether it has been decreed that
the historical background be obscured by concentrating on the feeble
light of the small candles in a reference only to a miracle that occurred in
the Temple. It certainly cannot be said that there is no hint of the
historical occurrence in the story of the miracle. It is hinted at but only
just; it remains unexplained. Compared to the traditional pattern of
holidays, we are left almost entirely in the dark. Another instance of the
fragmentary nature of the holiday is found in its having been established
not as though it were a newly coined holiday but rather as a derivative of
a previous construct, seeking retroactive links with a stratum of ancient
historical memory so as to afford this secondary coining a traditional
"rational." According to one tradition, Hanukkah imitated the formula of
Sukkot and its concluding day of Shemini Atzeret, as the Maccabees—
unable because of the war to celebrate Sukkot at its appointed time—held
a delayed ceremony once they had liberated Jerusalem and purified the
Temple. Even the central symbol from which Hanukkah gained the name
Festival of Lights was said to be derived from the lights used at the Festival
of *Beit HaShoevah*, the water-drawing celebration. So much for one set of
traditions.

Another set links Hanukkah to the eight-day celebration at which King
Solomon dedicated the first Temple. This inner link is strengthened by
the allusion to an even earlier stratum—the dedication of the tabernacle
by Moses in the desert. Consider also that the common Hanukkah
menorah was designed primarily with reference to this tradition, and its
design is reminiscent of the description of the Temple found at the
beginning of Kings I. To repeat, it is as though the intent in this restriking
of a form linked to an ancient mold is to obscure the primary importance
of the historical event. Admittedly the purification of the Temple is a high
point of the narrative; its original meaning, however, cannot be understood outside the full national context.

In dealing with the shape and content of Hanukkah and its symbols,
what then is being expressed by their unfinished, unclear aspects and their
secondary status?

THE DEVELOPMENT OF HANUKKAH TRADITIONS

Let us first observe the profile of the holiday in greater detail as it
developed in the tradition of the Sages, through the tradition of later
scholars, to the present time. "Maoz Tsur," the hymn customarily sung

after the blessings and the lighting of the candles, refers to the dedication of the altar—the ritual significance of the holiday; the central symbol of the holiday, however, is the lighting of candles in a menorah that is reminiscent of the seven-branched candelabrum in the Temple. On the eve of the first day, one candle is lit (in accordance with the *halakhah* based on the House of Hillel), two on the second evening, and so on until the eighth and final candle. Undoubtedly this is a commemoration of the miracle that occurred in the Temple, and the formula for the blessings confirms this; at the same time, the main action of kindling lights in a menorah that resembles the menorah in the Temple, carries a decided symbolism. It represents the intimate, unending link that exists even in the gloom of exile between a believing people who light candles and God who is mindful of His people. By virtue of observing the ongoing link, hope is expressed in the kindled menorah whose light increases day by day. It is the hope that that which was done for our fathers in "those long days at this season" will take place again in greater measure for us or our children. The miracle of the ongoing existence of the people, the miracle of belief and hope grows to become the miracle of redemption.

Indeed this is the main thrust of the blessing over the candles: confession of the miracle. The confession has an aspect of a recurrent experiencing of the event itself. The candles were customarily lit in the window to announce the miracle, the symbolic expression of an enduring belief, a demonstration of faith. This is the nucleus of the celebration in a Jewish home. In the synagogue the holiday is noted in three ways, the first of which is the *Modim* benediction recited during the *Shmoneh Esreh* prayer: "In the days of the Hasmonean, Mattathias ben Yochanan, and his son, when a wicked Hellenic ruler rose up against Thy people Israel to make them forget Thy Torah and transgress the laws of Thy will, Thou in Thy great mercy did stand by them in the time of their distress. Thou did champion their cause, defend their rights and avenge their wrong; Thou did deliver the strong into the hands of the weak, the many into the hands of the few; the impure into the hands of the pure; the wicked into the hands of the righteous; and the arrogant into the hands of the students of Thy Torah. Thou did make a great and holy name for Thyself in Thy world and for Thy people Israel Thou did perform a great deliverance unto this day. Thereupon Thy children entered the shrine of Thy house, cleansed Thy Temple, purified Thy sanctuary, kindled lights in Thy holy courts, and designated these eight days of Hanukkah for giving thanks and praise to Thy great name." The formulation makes an oblique reference to the events that preceded purification of the Temple and kindling of the menorah, but the emphasis is on the wicked who tried forcing Israel to forget their Torah, and God who nullified their evil intent. The people continued worshipping their Creator, and for this thanksgiving and praise are offered.

The second way in which the synagogue takes note of Hanukkah comes at the end of the Morning Service, at the close of the *Hallel* prayer when a number of psalms are recited. These psalms have been designated for recitation on days when the Jewish people experienced a miraculous salvation. The third reference occurs on the Sabbath of Hanukkah when the *Nasah* portion is read from the Book of Exodus. The verses here describe the dedication of the tabernacle by Moses. The haftarah is from the Book of Zechariah (Chap. 2:14–4:7), in which the prophecies recall the reinstitution of the Temple service following on the return from Babylonian exile. The menorah is mentioned as symbolizing a future redemption and the portion concludes with verses laden with significance—an explanation of the holiday from the perspective of the Sages: "This is the word of the Lord unto Zerubbabel saying: Not by might, nor by power, but by My spirit, sayeth the Lord of hosts. Who art thou, O great mountain before Zerubbabel? Thou shalt become a plain; and he shall bring forth the top stone with shoutings of Grace, grace, unto it." Consider that it is not the heroism of human beings that redeems—neither "by might, nor by power"—it is the spirit of God. In other words, emphasis is again placed on the miracle.

Many customs are practiced at Hanukkah: foods, games, songs, and so forth; occasions for gatherings of friends and merriment; but these are in the realm of folkways. The Hanukkah meal, in distinction from the Purim repast, which is a commandment, is not sanctified. In this, too, one notes a diminution of the holiday's status. Of course this enables a broad range of spontaneous, popular initiative. In the absence of sanctity, the holiday can be filled with secular enjoyment, a fact well exploited by the Zionist movement.

THE MIRACLE OF HANUKKAH

From the preceding description one gathers that as the holiday developed in the tradition of the Sages, a single topic was emphasized: the miracle that occurred in the Temple, which enabled the renewal of the service. To penetrate the ideational meaning of the holiday, an examination of the notion of the miracle and the interpretation given to it is needed. In the popular mind, a miracle is an unnatural event that happens to people. This applies to the cruse of oil in the Hanukkah story since a day's supply of oil that lasts for eight days is not a natural event. Still, though there is a supernatural element, or at least something that is unexpected or goes beyond that which can be explained by a progression of given circumstances, the essence of the phenomenon is not adequately defined by it. A miracle is an event which is perceived by those to whom it happens as a direct divine intervention in their fate. The supernatural element is, perhaps, a necessary component but in itself it is not sufficient.

For a supernatural or unexpected event to be considered direct divine intervention, it must offer imminent testimony that it carries a specific intent that believers can attribute to divine will. In other words, only if what has occurred in an unnatural or unexpected way suits what the believers perceive as worthy of divine intent will the occurrence be regarded as a miracle. When justice is served for those who merit it despite their weakness and small numbers—that is, even though what has happened is unexpected, perhaps even impossible by virtue of the natural circumstances, it is when the event can be explicated from its moral aspect that it is in the realm of the miraculous. The words said during the prayers in the *Modim* blessing for Hanukkah clearly underscore such a definition: "Thou didst deliver the strong into the hands of the weak, the many into the hands of the few; the impure into the hands of the pure; the wicked into the hands of the righteous; and the arrogant into the hands of the students of Thy Torah." It is fitting that God should succor the pious and punish the wicked; regretfully this does not occur either naturally or regularly. On the contrary, in the natural order the wicked prosper and the righteous suffer. If the miraculous occurs and the pious are saved, in accordance with justice but against nature, that is a miracle.

The statement has additional consequences for understanding the significance of miracles in the Jewish people's thought and religious experience. The primary meaning of the word *nes* is a banner or standard that can be seen by everyone, an unfurled flag that people follow. For the believing person, an event that testifies to divine intervention in the name of justice belongs to the category of the miraculous for it testifies to something that transcends its having happened. Of course the pious person rejoices when he is saved from suffering in his hour of trial, but no less important to him is proof of the justness of his chosen way, the path of belief. The miracle ratifies belief and reliance on God's beneficent moral inclination; it is an inclination that God Himself chooses and insures in the world. Anyone who seeks to do that which is good in his Creator's eyes and live according to what has been commanded trusts that in doing the good he will be better off despite the fact that doing the good thing is not necessarily doing what is pragmatically useful for economic, social, or political success. A miracle confirms belief that must withstand the difficult trials of this world.

Moreover, when the miracle take place, the believer feels that God is close to him, God cares for him and loves him. The miracle removes the believer from his isolation, justifies him, and verifies that there is a meaning to his way of life. It is precisely these ancillary aspects of the miracle experience that are stressed when giving thanks, particularly in the *hallel* hymns. The believer gives thanks that he has received confirmation, that his righteousness has been proven in the face of all persecutors and belittlers, that God is close to him, and that he feels His active concern and love for him. In this sense the miracle is a genuinely peak experience.

A problem basic to the life of a believer is brought into focus by these things. There are generally few events that confirm belief and many societal trials that put belief into question, and what is true of the individual believer's experience within his people is all the truer for the Jewish people's experience among the nations of the earth. Step by step the question of the Jewish people's fate grows in severity. The consciousness that it is a people chosen to live in faith, to perform the Creator's commandments among the nations, becomes the axis of religious experience and thought. In the biblical period the question of why the righteous suffer while the wicked prosper was raised as a quandary of believers, particularly the prophets. The people do not heed the word of God as enunciated by the prophets who undergo great personal suffering in their mission. Feeling isolated within his people and abandoned by God as well, Jeremiah asks the believer's question, "Why does the way of the wicked prosper?"

Still, even Jeremiah has no difficulty explaining the Jewish people's fate among the nations. His heartfelt sense that justice is done in history is reinforced as he recalls the great miracles of the past—the exodus, the giving of the Torah, and the inheritance of Eretz Yisrael, on the one hand; his sense of sin in the present, on the other. Even when the worst happens—the destruction of the Temple, of Jerusalem, of the country, and the exile of Judah—his faith is confirmed. While the Lamentations scroll is a shocking dirge, it is nonetheless an expression of wholehearted justification of judgment. Paradoxically the later prophets found corroboration for their faith, even acquiesced to the bitterness of their personal lot, by observing the terrible historic justice that befell the people. The wondrous faith that shines forth from the prophecies of comfort they sounded, precisely when tragedy struck, stems from this. They have no doubt that justice will continue to be revealed in the kingdom of God. If punishment comes, so will recompense, a fact they felt was attested to in the awesome past as well as in the atrocious present.

After the Babylonian exile, a marked change is discerned. The question of the reason for the suffering of a people loyal to their God while in exile is raised by the second Isaiah, and it appears that the question becomes more insistent in the Jewish religious experience and thought of the Second Commonwealth: it is no longer a question asked by righteous individuals who suffer because of the wicked. It is also, perhaps mainly, a question of a people who testify to their faith yet suffer among the nations. This may be the cause of a marked sense found in the religious literature of a period in which God ostensibly distances Himself from His people, and His direct leadership is no longer felt. The redemptive interference that justice requires for saving the loyal from impious pagans is long in coming. The Return to Zion served to reinforce the faith even though, in signs and portents, it was not engraved in the people's memory as an event similar to the exodus from Egypt. If divine deliberate leadership was manifest here, it functioned indirectly, and it was followed by urgent internal and external events that brought into question the certainty that a just, divine leadership is apparent in the people's history. Are those loyal to God's message the leaders of the people? Has justice been dispensed to the people who, among the nations, has remained loyal to the Torah? These questions are at the center of the complex and multi-faceted disagreement between the religious streams that arose in Judaism.

It is against this setting that attention is focused now on the traditional background. This is the story of a miracle that occurred; a supernatural effect that confirms faith. But the dimensions of the miracle are surprising, particularly given the background that is known from other sources regarding what took place "in those days, at this season." Compare the miracle of the cruse of oil to miracles that the Bible relates regarding the exodus from Egypt, the desert wanderings, and the wars of conquest of Eretz Yisrael. In these stories, God is revealed through signs and portents, extracting a people from the house of bondage, "with a mighty hand and an outstretched arm." God saves his people from a pursuing army; God supports a numerous people in the desert; God grants his people the Torah; God leads his people in the desert; God routs His enemies and vanquishes seven nations for His people. Whereas in the story of Hanukkah, God enables the priests of His Temple to re-establish the Temple service by means of a single vessel of pure oil sufficient for one day's light, which nonetheless burns for eight days and so allows time for the preparation of new, pure oil to kindle the menorah. What is the meaning of this intended diminution? Was it really impossible to etch the event in the people's memory by employing all the hallmarks of a great biblical miracle?

It appears that was not the way the Sages who shaped the tradition interpreted events. They rejected the option of a biblical rendition; they did not confirm God's intervention in the unfolding events of the time within a broad national and political perspective. Choosing not to deal with what had transpired on the external level of relations with the surrounding nations, the Sages limited the scope of the event to the internal sphere—God's service. It seems that justice does not manifest itself on a national scope at this stage in Jewish history; it manifests itself only in the people's ability to turn inward and so sense the nearness of God in His house. The service of God has in and of itself become the goal. It is the ultimate good in which a believer senses that God loves him and chooses him. The small lights burning in the menorah became a symbolic expression of this experience of the believer, an experience totally different from the supernatural event found in the biblical narrative.

THE ZIONIST MOVEMENT AND HANUKKAH

There is an inherent paradox in what has been said above. The holiday that was established to mark the renewal of the Jewish people's independence in its land, its city, and its Temple crystallized, in the tradition, as a diasporic holiday. It is essentially diasporic to perceive of God as uninvolved in His people's national fate—absenting Himself—while His nearness is perceived in the seclusion "of one's tent" through prayer and the performance of mitzvot. This was clearly at variance with the perception of the Hasmoneans who revolted and established the holiday to commemorate their deeds. So it is also clear that a narrative that limits the significance of the event testifies to an intended ideological transformation. Details are not available, but there is some foundation to the supposition that the change is connected to the split that developed between the Sages at the head of the High Court in Jerusalem and the Hasmonean kings. The Sages were disappointed with the kings for imitating monarchy on a Hellenistic model thereby moving away from the Pharisaic interpretation of the Torah, and this could have been a convincing factor for withdrawing spiritual and religious endorsement of what had been essentially an act of Hasmonean daring.

Retroactively, the Sages then rescinded any religious significance from the military, political victory and concentrated exclusively on that part of the event that they saw as positive from the commandment/religious perspective—the renewal of Temple service. They did not regard the military, political victory in and of itself as divine intervention; it was seen as nothing more than a precondition for the cleansing of the Temple. The embodiment of the miracle is that God drew the people back to His service. This turn of events was not an a priori dropping of the national dimension, certainly not a surrender of national hope for the future, but in the religious delegitimation of the existing Jewish monarchy one can see the forging of diasporic tools. Apparently celebrating the holiday in keeping with such a tradition was essentially a preparation for creating a diaspora.

Indeed the intention of the Zionist movement, born of the new age of Jewish history, was to reverse the diasporic view that had molded the holiday in such an image. In its search for some mooring within the tradition to anchor the tremendous innovation it wanted to introduce to the exiled Jewish people, Hanukkah was found to be most suitable. And in truth until the establishment of the State of Israel and the inauguration of Independence Day, Hanukkah was the pre-eminent holiday of the Zionist movement. It was a natural development. There is a marked juxtaposition in the deeds of the Hasmoneans and the Zionist endeavor; the aspiration is the same: national independence in Eretz Yisrael. The fact that Hanukkah was never sanctified through the prohibition of labor and was not burdened by symbols but rather left available for popular creativity eased the reinterpretation and shaping of the holiday. Secular Zionism could celebrate it according to its lights without directly colliding with either the tradition or its guardians. Ostensibly nothing qualitative had changed. The symbol of Hanukkah was retained but verses that accompanied the lighting of the candles somewhat diverted the meaning of the symbolic act:

Hear! In those days of yore at this season:
A redeeming and saving Maccabee,
And in our time the entire Jewish people
Will unite as one, arise and redeem itself.

The Zionists retained the social practices of the holiday, enriching them at large convocations by means of readings and plays that recalled the historic act and its significance for contemporary Jews. But a serious examination quickly discloses the contradiction between a religious understanding and a secular national reading of the holiday. Here is one of the most successful expressions of a national secular orientation of Jewish culture that thrusts aside the religious stratum, substituting for the national stratum that had been covered by it. The Zionist movement uncovered the full history of the Hasmonean revolt that had been cloaked by the story of the miracle of the cruse of oil; it forged a link between the non-miraculous historic event and its aspiration for national and political independence. Was this linkage in consonance with the world outlook of the Hasmoneans? Was this, in fact, a genuine return to the sources?

THE SAGES' REACTION TO HANUKKAH

The variegated literature that has been preserved from the period of the Return to Zion to the end of the Hasmonean monarchy is illustrative of the great changes that occurred then in the political situation, way of life, outlook, and belief of the Jewish people. Though some note was taken of these changes while analyzing the significance of the cruse-of-oil narrative, to get at the ideational infrastructure in the conflict between the Hasmonean House and the Sages, it is necessary to go into the issues more thoroughly.

Two lacunae stand out in the Jewish literature of the Second Commonwealth as compared to that of the First. These attest to the qualitative nature of the spiritual transformation that took place. First is the disappearance of a prophetic literature perceived as such. Zechariah and Malachi, in the period of Ezra and Nehemiah, were the last prophets whose mission was accepted by the people and whose messages were included in the Bible. In the Apocrypha of the period that follows them, an effort can be seen to fill the prophetic role in a variety of ways such as the creating "solutions" to earlier prophecies or composing prophecies in the name of earlier prophets. But it is instructive that there is no direct pretension to speak with prophetic authority. What may be inferred from this is that even those who regarded themselves as continuing in the way of the prophets did not feel that they were worthy of prophecy, or that they would be accepted as prophets by the people. The interpretive literature of the Sages and scribes appears to have had that same awareness; namely, that they drew their authority from a prophecy that had already been canonized and gleaning from them a moral for their own day. Eventually it would be claimed that "a Sage takes precedence over a prophet." One way or another it seems that the Sages believed that prophecy had been terminated at least for the time being.

The second lacuna is the disappearance of a literature that transmits the history of the Jewish people and its leadership as it was related in the historic volumes of the Bible. This type of literature ends with Chronicles and Ezra/Nehemiah, which did find their way into the Bible. The Apocrypha of the period that follows displays a marked effort to fill the role of observer, interpreter, and recorder of events in different ways; for instance, apocalyptic literature and historiography similar to the Hellenic conventions (the compositions of Philo and Josephus Flavius). But this literature, too, though utterly different in its assumptions and biases from that of the historic literature of the Bible, was not preserved by the people nor was it generally written in its vernacular. Apparently composing annals of the times as a testimony of the people's journey under divine guidance also terminated, at least for the time.

There is a clear link between these two lacunae. The historic writing of the Bible, after all, was composed primarily by the prophets and was a projection of their experiences and beliefs, testifying to events that occurred in their sphere as carriers of the divine message. They described the circumstances of their mission and its results. They noted for subsequent generations how justly God guided His people; how He saved them when they were worthy; and how He punished the people when it transgressed. If direct prophecy was closed off then historic writing, in the prophetic mode, was also. What transpires hence forward is no longer illuminated by direct divine guidance for which prophecy is, of course, the means for its realization. Even if God watches over His people and is Cause of events, the people do not sense His direct intervention; consequently the assumptions and orientations can only be decoded through events mediated by a sacred literature that has already been canonized. Consider that even as great an event as the Return to Zion during the days of Ezra and Nehemiah is no longer described in the biblical style. True, it is noted as God's doing, but not by direct intervention. God stirs Cyrus's heart, and touches the hearts of the people's leaders, and the leaders realize from what occurs and from their knowledge of the Torah what they are obliged to do and what the people must do. In this transitional period they still have full trust in the divine direction of events; it is a feeling that is increasingly on the decline in the period that follows.

The Book of Maccabees describes the deeds of the Hasmoneans. Most scholars agree that especially Maccabees I was written originally in Hebrew soon after the events, probably by a scribe loyal to the Hasmonean House. Anyone who examines the Hasmonean literature discovers its uniqueness and significance. Against this background, one can also understand the significance of the fact that this literature, so close in spirit to the Bible, was rejected by the Sages, to be preserved only in a foreign language by non-Jews. Maccabees I was written in biblical style (one senses this even through the Greek translation) and tells of political and military events in a realistic, accurate, historic—rather than a visionary, apocalyptic—manner. It is composed with a burning sense that God does indeed intervene actively in the life of His people, and it is He that leads them to a national, political victory—to a renewed independence and sovereignty of the people in its land. Moreover, whoever wrote the book believed that in the light of these events prophecy would be re-established, and it is this prophecy from which the authority of a renewed political leadership would emanate. Consequently this is the declaration of a great hope for a restoration. Apparently this is the explanation for historical writing in the biblical prophetic mode—a foreword to the renewal of prophecy.

Still and all, the fact is that it is a hope for restoration and renewal. The background for this hope is an extended period of God's angry absence from history. In other words, one also finds in Maccabees I a response to the perception that the people have that their situation has changed, and that this change cannot be overlooked. The issue that the response focuses on is the source of the authority and the validity of the goals of Hasmonean leadership. That leadership had begun its campaign without benefit of prophetic validation, indeed had gone beyond the authority that should have been invested in the Hasmoneans by existing institutions of leadership—all this because the institutions had failed both the national and the religious challenge. Unquestionably this is an unusual situation. The Hasmoneans initiated their campaign by virtue of their own initiative. But they never pretended to prophesy. They interpreted the situation that developed as one in which the Torah obliged them to act as they did. They understood that their circumstances commanded them to refuse the decrees of foreign domination, to kill its collaborators, to rebel and engage in war to liberate the country from the yoke of a despot who sought to uproot the Torah from among the people. Since this was the case, they regarded their victory as divine vindication of their initiative, perhaps even confirmation that it was through them that God led His people. In this sense Maccabees I is not simply a book of biblical historic testimony; it is an expression of a highly significant rejuvenation.

A new religious concept that began at the time of the Second Commonwealth expresses this spiritual/religious stance: *Kiddush HaShem*, the sanctification of the Lord. The Hasmonean Revolt was an act of sanctification of the Lord; indeed the cast given to Hanukkah by the tradition is linked to this concept. Among the stories related to the holiday is the famous one of Hannah and her seven sons. The story is intended to illuminate the background that leads to the war of the Hasmoneans. A wicked Hellenistic kingdom prohibits the study of Torah and the performance of its commandments. At the risk of their lives, Hannah and her sons refuse to transgress the commandments. This is a sanctification of the Lord in the sense that they publicly demonstrate the extent of their faith in the face of the most demanding, the ultimate trial which a believing person may confront. Readiness to suffer and die for the sake of observing the mitzvot is a confirmation of the very religious truth that the wicked seek to undermine.

Consider that according to this perception, *Kiddush HaShem* is an existential response to the great religious issue touched on at the beginning of this discussion: How can individuals, and how can a people, overcome the historical trial that denies an underlying assumption of the believing experience? How can one believe when repeatedly there is an ostensible absence of a governing moral rule in the people's history—that is, when there is no just divine stewardship that gives the wicked their due and saves the righteous? The pious, who sanctify of the Lord, regard the allegedly disappointing reality as a trial. The believer's response must be to remain true to the covenant made by his fathers. Steadfastness in the covenant is a supreme religious value and calls for martyrdom if need be. It is the expression of pure love whose public demonstration proves the justness of the belief even when it is unlikely that the believer will know reward. Demonstrated in such a way, the belief holds an absolute value that gives a meaning to life that, in worldly terms, surpasses life itself. Still, it is understood that the believer trusts in the appearance of sublime justice. In maintaining the covenant, he is assured beyond doubt that God too will maintain the covenant, even when His ways are inscrutable.

This construction of *Kiddush HaShem* as a way of confronting a situation in which God absents Himself admittedly relates passively to the here and now. Nonetheless, *Kiddush HaShem* can be seen as an active mode, an energetic demonstration of the absolute validity of belief rather than an attempt to change the circumstances that cast the believer as powerless. Even when the notion of *Kiddush HaShem* goes back to a time when the people lived in its own land, this understanding is consonant with the perception of an exilic reality; indeed, the greatest historical manifestations of the belief occurred in exile. Maccabees I presents another view of *Kiddush HaShem*, a version that describes opposition that comes face to face with external circumstances. The Hasmonean war began with an initiative that originated in a personal uprising. Without benefit of an a priori religious sanction, an unknown leadership initiates a revolt disregarding the institutionalized elites that had acted treacherously and submissively.

Mattathias the Hasmonean is neither a prophet nor deputized by a prophet. He finds himself in a situation in which he understands himself to be constrained by the Torah to act in a particular way. Not only does he refuse to transgress the commandments of the Torah, but he acts "zealously" on its behalf as did his predecessor, Pinchas the High Priest. In other words, he forcefully opposes those who would transgress as well as their sponsors. He attempts to change a disappointing historical reality. If God does not save His faithful, Mattathias will rise to save them. He interprets God's "restraint" as a summons to him. But there is no human usurpation of the divine role. Convinced that he has been commanded, Mattathias must act in accordance with the command though in realistic terms there is no chance of success, and consequently God will do his part as the Redeemer. The impending victory of which he is certain, despite its uncertainty, will be the absolute proof of God's rule in the world; thus the heavens will be sanctified through the testimony of faith and its victory.

This ideational motif is found in the declarations of all the leaders of the revolt. The very fact that the heroes feel compelled to make so many speeches explaining their deeds to their followers is an interesting departure from the parlance of the biblical narrative. Nor is this merely a stylistic influence of Hellenistic historiography. It is an objective necessity that derives from the nature of the situation; in the absence of prophetic validation of the mission, a need arises for testimony that can explain it, and the explanation must be public. Mattathias began his activity with a declaration that was integral to the deed itself. "Though all the nations that are under the kings domain obey him, and fall away every one from the religion of their fathers, and give consent to his commandments, yet will I and my sons and my brethren walk in the covenant of our fathers. Woe to us if we abandon the Torah and its commandments" (Maccabees I, Chap. 2:19–22). The deed is then described. Mattathias slays the man who rose to sacrifice as the king ordered, and this is followed by another declaration. "And Mattathias cried throughout the city in a loud voice saying, 'Whoever is zealous for the Law and maintains the covenant, Let him follow me'" (Chap. 2:27).

Repeatedly the emphasis is on an absolute obligation to keep the covenant, not passively but actively, zealously. The most clear-cut description of this way of thinking is found in Mattathias's testament to his sons:

"Now malice and chastisement rule, it is a day of upheaval and wrath. And now my sons be zealous for the Torah and give your lives for the covenant of your fathers. Recall deeds that the fathers performed in their generations and you shall inherit great honor and a name in eternity. Abraham was found loyal in his trial and he was considered righteous. Joseph in his time of tribulation observed the commandment and became Overlord of Egypt. Our forefather, Pinchas, was zealous and received a covenant of eternal priesthood . . . Therefore understand that in every generation all who hope shall not falter, and of the wicked man's word have no fear for his honor is as dung. Today he shall be in the ascent, tomorrow he will disappear for he shall return to dust and lose his way. Be stalwart my sons, be strengthened in the Torah because in it is your honor." [Chap. 2:45–64]

From historical experience, Mattathias knows that anyone who upholds the covenant and is zealous for the Torah is doing God's will and is rewarded. He gains everlasting honor, and honor is but an expression of self-worth, an expression of a life that is not empty but has achieved its true goal. God does not abandon His followers but He expects them to act out their faith in deeds. The explanation proposed for the embarrassing reality of God's nonintervention in the face of the harrowing deeds against His Torah and against the keepers of his covenant was that it is a trial. The believer must endure the trial, and Mattathias does not doubt that salvation will come by means of the deeds of the faithful.

Mattathias's sons do indeed follow in his footsteps. Here are Judah's words before a crucial battle:

"How can our small force fight so numerous and mighty a host, exhausted
as we are today for lack of food? It is easy for the many to be delivered into
the hands of the few. Heaven sees no difference in gaining victory through
many or through few. Because victory in war does not lie in the wake of
numbers but rather strength comes from Heaven. They come against us
with the weight of their power for violence and for wickedness, intending
to destroy us and take our wives and children as spoil. We however are
fighting for our lives and our laws. And He will shatter them before us. You,
therefore, have no fear!" [Chap. 3:17–23]

Even more explicitly:

They assembled and marched to Mitzpeh opposite Jerusalem because there
had earlier been an Israelite place for prayer in Mitzpeh. On that day they
fasted and put sackcloth and ashes upon their heads and they rent their
garments. They spread open the scroll of the Torah at the passages where
the gentiles sought to find analogies to their idols. They took the priestly
vestments and the first fruits and the tithes and assembled the Nazarites
who had completed the periods of their vows. Crying aloud to Heaven
they said, "What are we to do with these? Where are we to bring them?
Your Sanctuary has been trampled and profaned and Your priests are in
mourning and affliction. The gentiles have gathered against us to destroy
us. How shall we be able to withstand them, unless You come to our
aid." . . . Then Judah spoke, "Prepare yourselves for battle and be brave.
Be ready early in the morning to fight these gentiles who have gathered
against us to destroy us and our Sanctuary for it is better for us to die in
battle then to stand by and watch the outrages against our people and our
Sanctuary. As He wills in Heaven so will He do." [Chap. 3:46–60]

It is a description of a prayer service. Since there is no prophet in Israel,
the people and the leadership are at a loss regarding God's commandment
at the moment. Nonetheless both the people and the leaders intuitively
understand their duty in light of the Torah. Consequently their prayer
resembles an appeal to a heavenly court. For their part they fulfill all the
commandments that are required of them, to the extent possible. The fact
that there are commandments that cannot be performed because idolaters
occupy the Temple while the Lord does not help His people is regarded
by them as a lawful claim against God. God is required to do His part.
Judah's final, powerful words are that we shall do what is required of us,
even if we fall in battle. There is inherent value in a deed that expresses
absolute faith. God will do as He wishes. But, do these words leave any

doubt as to what the Divine Will ought to be? Is there any doubt that the campaign will make the redeeming truth apparent?

When the few vanquish the many and the righteous overcome the wicked, it is seen as proof of the combatants' faith. They kept the covenant as did God. They fought, but the victory is the manifestation of God's leadership of the people. Was there a miracle? From the fighters' point of view, a miracle did indeed occur; the fact that they induced it is the embodiment of a miracle in a deed that is expressive of faith. Nothing supernatural happened. Faith proved its compelling power to overcome any other force. In any case, the certainty that what transpired through their intermediacy was a manifestation of God's leadership within his people is what caused them to feel that it should all be written down in a testimonial volume for the generations to come. It also gave rise to the sensation that they stood at the dawn of an era that would restore the times to their former glory. God would once again dwell among His people and in His sanctuary; God would once again lead His people in the fullness of national history.

The meaning of the Sages' reaction to both the Book of Maccabees I and the events described in it can now be properly explained. Rejecting the document while magnifying the miracle of the cruse of oil, is an indication that the Sages accepted neither the Hasmonean evaluation of the nature of their exploits, nor their version of their feats as *Kiddush HaShem*. In the Sages' view, neither the military victory nor the renewal of monarchy represented a departure from the state in which God absents Himself. God did not return to lead His people in the fullness of its national history. Hasmonean monarchy is not the redemption. The sole miracle that occurred was that of the cruse of oil; in other words, it is through the renewal of the Temple service that the people will return to God. It comes as no surprise that in the words of the later Sages it is the passive perception of *Kiddush HaShem* that is sanctified, a notion linked to the story of Hannah and her seven sons. Yet another story, that of the Ten Martyrs, had a crucial impact on the people's religious world outlook during the exilic period. The Sages' transvaluation of the significance of Hanukkah is therefore tantamount to the beginning of a profound roll back from a national initiative at the level of broad historic endeavor. The Zionist movement alone dared to confront this verdict, which found its ultimate crystallization following the defeat of the Bar Kokhba revolt. It was only the Zionists who attempted to overturn the verdict.

THE HOLIDAY WITH A MULTIPLICITY OF FORMS

The Zionist movement reinstated the entire historical narrative as told in the Book of Maccabees into the holiday of Hanukkah, giving it a central place in studies, discussions, dramatizations, and tableaux. No longer a humble story of a little cruse of oil alone, but rather the saga of a people rising against foreign domination, standing free on its own land. But was the Zionist assertion that it had reclaimed the original meaning of the holiday correct? A review of what has been said above shows that it is only partially true. The Zionist movement did return to the notion of selfhood and the people's aspiration for political independence in Eretz Yisrael. But the spiritual/believing element that was part of the Hasmonean enterprise was dropped completely (this, of course, applies to the secular majority among Zionists). For this majority, the return to Eretz Yisrael was not an instance of *Kiddush HaShem*, nor was its success testimony to a miracle that had occurred:

> "No miracle attended us
> We found no cruse of oil."

These short, well-known sentences of the poet, Ze'ev, written for Hanukkah, subsume the secular Zionist outlook on religious tradition, and the self-image of the secular Zionists colored their perception of the Maccabees' struggle. Not only is a sense of miracle absent, nor is there a belief that a miracle was likely, but much more: there is a rejection of dependence on Divine Will and guidance, a refusal to anticipate validation and aid from on high. In its trenchant negation of exile, secular Zionism rejected any expectation of heavenly grace. In its view, such an expectation is the embodiment of all that is negative and passive in exilic life. In point of fact, as opposed to the Hasmoneans' audacious belief of having put God to the test by their unstinting performance as their part of the covenant, one frequently hears in Zionist literature an aggressive, agitated note of rebellion towards heaven. Bialik's famous poem, "The Dead of the Wilderness," is a classic expression of this secular Zionist motif. Not coincidentally was it frequently read at Hanukkah performances.

> "We are the mighty!
> The last generation of slaves and the first generation of free men!
> Alone our hand in its strength

Tore from the pride of our shoulders the yoke of bondage.
We lifted our heads to the heavens, and behold their broadness was
                    narrow in our eyes,
So we turned to the desert, we said to the wilderness: 'Mother!'
On the tops of crags in the thickness of clouds,
With the eagles of heaven we drank from fountains of freedom.

And who is Lord of us?
Even now, though the God of Vengeance has shut the desert upon us,
A song of strength and revolt has reached us, and we rise.
To arms! To arms! Form ranks, Unite! Forward!
Despite the heavens and the wrath thereof.
Behold us! We will ascend
With the tempest!"

The revolt against exile is interpreted not as an effort to reinstall God's direct leadership but as a struggle to proceed "Despite the heavens and the wrath thereof." It is to rebel against a passive expectation of heavenly grace, rise up against a fate with which the Jewish religion conspired as though it was an immutable heavenly decree. Clearly, in this rebellious mode, there is no return to a Hasmonean point of departure by way of the miracle of the cruse of oil. This is a break from the continuity of a believing outlook in order to find support for an aspiration to modern, national independence in a pre-exilic tradition. If this is the case, then yet a third incarnation of the holiday's content can be observed. The difference between this incarnation and previous ones is no less than the difference between the Hasmoneans and their predecessors, nor smaller than the distance between the Sages and the Hasmoneans. Now, in the Zionist era, the majority of the people feels that it stands alone confronting a silent heaven with the responsibility for its fate falling squarely on itself, alone. The covenant has been abrogated or never existed at all. And again, if this is the case, then along with the disappearance of the miracle the question that the miracle answers is also rescinded, and the people have nothing on which to depend other than their own strength. The people are commanded to be stalwart and withstand their enemies by dint of political and military strength.

Quite properly a question arises as to whether Hanukkah is integral to the continuity of thought expressed in the calendar's time sequence from Rosh HaShanah to Rosh HaShanah and from one Passover to the next. Did the holiday perhaps detach itself from this progression so that it represents a consciousness of belonging in an altogether different sequence of time? Or, perhaps, still another turn is possible, one that will invest a sense of spirituality and faith in the difficult experience of a people wrestling by itself for its liberty and the uniqueness of its spiritual creativity. There are no cut-and-dried answers to these questions. In this respect, the Jewish people is still struggling internally, and the decision in this battle over the nature and the self-image of the people, and the nature of its orientation in relations between itself and other peoples, and between it and its God is still quite far off. Meanwhile, each sector of the people celebrates the holiday according to its own style and interpretation. All that is required from each person in the various sectors is to understand the depth of the problem and understand the weight of memories and historic experience that come to the fore in the variety of the holiday's expressions, so that in the very multiplicity of forms it will be the holiday of a single people.

All of which brings one back to earlier lines in the chapter: Hanukkah, the beautiful, young, and gay, somewhat childlike holiday is a holiday with a covert spiritual problem. There is here a subterranean disagreement lasting the entire length of Jewish history, that occasionally flares up from its depths, which has now burst into flame. The conflict demands that a portion of the festivities be devoted to a probing spiritual account of the people's attitude to its past heritage and to the vision of its hope for the future.

EIGHT

THE TWICE-AVERTED GAZE: PURIM, HOLIDAY OF EXILE

THE THEME OF EXILE

An engaging kinship exists between Purim and Hanukkah. Both holidays were initiated after the Return to Zion as days of thanksgiving for a miraculous redemption, though one deliverance occurred in Eretz Israel and the other in exile. Both holidays mark a new historic experience, both acknowledge a change in the relationship between the people and their God, and between them and the nations that were their neighbors or hosts. As for their status as holidays, neither is consecrated by a prohibition from work (though there is some disagreement on this score about Purim). Consequently there is an atmosphere of secularity mixed into the festivities that is emblematic of the essential nature of both Hanukkah and Purim. From the standpoint of sanctity and density of content, however, ostensibly Purim has the advantage despite the fact that Hanukkah lasts a full eight days and the *hallel* prayer is recited, while Purim is a one-day holiday without benefit of the *hallel*. Purim's advantage stems from the fact that *Megillat Esther* was added to the canon and consecrated. By virtue of reading the *megillah* in the synagogue, the recitation was raised to the status of a biblical mitzvah as enunciated by divine inspiration; and, though there is no prohibition regarding labor, sages recommended that one refrain from work so that the day could be filled with mitzvot. The meal itself is a mitzvah at Purim, even as is drinking extravagantly. Unlike Hanukkah, where the secular element offers a kind of leisure time for everyday pursuits, Purim has a distinctive atmosphere filled with unusual and lively customs. In other words, the secular element too has taken on special meaning, a specialness that is experienced by reflecting on the way in which the holiday has been fashioned. According to the Sages, ultimately, when all other holidays are abolished at the end of days, the Festival of Purim will go on to eternity.

In any case, there is a paradox here that bears looking into: the holiday marking a salvation that took place in exile is more prominent, more highly regarded, than the one that marks a redemption in Eretz Israel. The meaning of the paradox becomes clearer if one adds that for a period of time Purim and Nicanor Day (which occurred at about the same period and commemorated one of the Macabbean victories over the Hellenists) competed for popular acceptance, until Purim won out. By this time, despite the Return to Zion, exile had become a major historical experience in the consciousness of the Jewish people; it was this consciousness that shaped the people's image in their own eyes as well as their neighbors. A suitable expression had to be found that would explain the significance of exile and direct the people's reaction to it; this apparently was more important than the need to express the experience of becoming rooted anew in Eretz Israel. Did the people and its leaders already sense, as early as this period, that the situation of exile and dispersion was a more salient characteristic of the nation's life than living together in their own land; that this characteristic would become even more pronounced for a long period to come? Was this the reason that Hanukkah also developed—in the tradition—from a perspective of exile?

INTERPLAY OF MOTIFS

Looking more closely at the mitzvot that shaped the meaning of Purim, one discerns its importance in the fact that the one day holiday resonates throughout the month of Adar. The Sages remarked that "with the advent of Adar one rejoices abundantly," and the earliest tidings of the holiday, in effect a kind of ideational preparation for it, comes on the first Shabbat of Adar. On this Sabbath, *Shabbat Zakhor*, the closing portion of the Torah service is from Deuteronomy 25:17–19. "Remember what Amalek did to you on your journey, after you left Egypt—how, undeterred by fear of God, he surprised you on the march, when you were famished and weary, and cut down all the stragglers in the rear. Therefore, when the Lord your God grants you safety from all the enemies around you, in the land that the Lord your God is giving you as an inheritance, you shall blot out the memory of Amalek from under heaven. Do not forget!" Following the *maftir*, the *haftarah* is read from I Samuel 15:1–34 in which the story is told of the first attempt to perform the commandment of decimating Amalek, in the days of Saul. The bid failed because of insufficient spiritual strength. He was victorious in war, but Saul did not carry out the mitzvah that prohibits taking spoils and leaving any Amalekite alive; in fact, he and the people with him had mercy on the prisoners, and took booty. A breach then develops between Saul and Samuel because of the dereliction, and so the fate of Saul's monarchy is sealed.

This is the biblical, prophetic root to which Purim is bound though *Megillat Esther* spins the strand out in its own way. During the festival of Purim, Jews recall what Amalek did to them; on Purim, Jews remember that there is an eternal enmity between Israel and Amalek; and when the Jewish people is outside its land, it is abandoned to Amalek. Serving as the connecting link to *Megillat Esther*, the *haftarah* could be interpreted to mean that when the Jewish people lives in its own land it holds the upper hand over Amalek but if the nation recoils from doing what it has been commanded to do because it lusts for the spoils of materialism, it may find itself—outside its homeland, in exile—in a recurring confrontation with Amalek. In exile, the nation is weak and dependent. Here, it appears, is an allusion to a causal link between forfeiting the opportunity to fulfill a certain goal when the people lives in its homeland, and the exilic condition with its attendant dangers.

All this applies to the preparation for the holiday; on the holiday itself such a serious and relentless ideological motif seems to go underground. It does not, of course, disappear but its presence is veiled by merriment. Substantively this day is about gladness at being saved from the hands of Amalek and revenge, while in exile, against Amalek. The commandments that articulate this gladness begin with reading the *megillah* in an atmosphere of extreme revelry, unusual for a typical synagogue service, and the addition of a special version of the thanksgiving prayer during the *amidah*. There is, as well, a prescribed meal, which calls for drinking to the point of intoxication, the exchange of special foods between relatives and friends, and gifts for the poor. The last two mitzvot, especially the one of gifts to the poor, reinforces the unifying popular nature of rejoicing.

Rejoicing is meant to encompass the entire people so that no one suffers want or is unhappy on this day. Purim stresses mutual responsibility within the nation, both as a precondition for salvation and as a concomitant for true gladness. Consequently it could be said that in turning inward, it is this motif that is highlighted as opposed to a motif of remembering Amalek that turns outward; that is, the Jewish people retains its uniqueness through unity, which is mutual responsibility.

And this is the virtue that can save the people from the threats and dangers of exile. Maimonides stresses this truth. "It is preferable that a person be extravagant in giving gifts to the poor rather than holding a sumptuous feast and sending gifts of food to his friends. For there is no joy greater than the joy found in gladdening the poor, the orphan, the widowed, the proselytes. For anyone who gladdens such as these resembles Providence as it said, 'To revive the spirit of the downtrodden and uplift the heart of the distressed'" (*Mishneh Torah, Hilkhot Megillah* II, 17). In Maimonides's judgment, gladness is not primarily in a merriment of outward rejoicing at victory and revenge; it is rather in reinforcing a sense of the people's fraternity and the merciful feeling they have for one another.

Beyond all of these commandments, the Festival of Purim is replete with special and unusual practices, which—though they do not carry the weight of a commandment—hold such sway that no one is lax in their performance: the raucous sound of noisemakers each time Haman's name is mentioned during the reading of the *megillah*, burning Haman in effigy so as to eradicate his name and wipe out the "memory of Amalek," wearing Purim costumes and performing skits from the *megillah* narrative, the custom practiced by scholars of giving facetious renditions of biblical verses, etc. All these customs give Purim a boisterous character, a tendency to frivolity, as the holiday appears to go to extremes of unruliness in a phenomenon completely foreign to behavior at other festivals and certainly in the daily routine. It is as though the awe and self-restraint that generally characterize Jewish behavior suddenly depart for a day so that a Jew allows himself to act foolishly. It could be said that this is an extreme to which one goes by virtue of religious awe; it is not genuinely wild behavior, only make-believe with a trace of unaccustomed rejoicing at victory. This is the box into which the secularity of Purim is compressed in order to shape the holiday and give it meaning. The phenomenon requires an explanation regarding the interplay between the motif of remembering Amalek's deed, and remembering the uniqueness and internal unity of the Jewish people.

CASTING LOTS

The key to understanding the complex ideational contents of the Purim festival and how they are interrelated is found in the very first mitzvah that installs the holiday: reading the *megillah*. In examining the *megillah* therefore, one must first emphasize not only the story, but its interpretation.

The strange nature of Purim among the Jewish festivals is inherent in two distinctive features of the *megillah*, content and literary form. From beginning to end, the ironic tone that permeates the story is an internalized laughter and it differentiates *Megillat Esther* from all other parts of the Bible; it stands out in its departure from the prophetic style that is pervaded by pathos and a predilection for direct, overt, and serious discourse. *Megillat Esther* has a covert laughter that coils around itself, a latent glee encased within a manifest laughter. A number of other uniquely literary devices of the scroll are graced with irony. For example, the oblique allusions to the story of Joseph's success in Egypt, the story of the war against Amalek in the days of Saul, the perplexing fact that God's name is never mentioned in the narrative despite the fact that the plot has situations that any other biblical narrative would have attributed to God's direct intervention. Again, the uniqueness of the holiday is dependent upon the uniqueness of the *megillah*, another fact that grants the *megillah* a special status. Whereas the Sages assigned each of the Five Scrolls a holiday on which it would be read, *Megillat Esther* actually establishes the holiday; the only reason for its having been written is to explain the origins and significance of the festival. The ironic elements of the scroll fashioned an ironic holiday. It recalls what Amalek did to the Jews even as they imbibe "so much that they cannot distinguish between cursed be Haman and blessed be Mordecai." These paradoxically ironic elements invite a distancing perspective through an atmosphere of frivolity.

Since the holiday and the scroll are so inextricably bound to one another, the first clue to deciphering the latent strata of the *megillah* is found in the name that the scroll gave the holiday. What is the meaning of the word *purim*? According to the *megillah*, Haman, archenemy of the Jews, cast *purim*—that is, "lots"—to pick the month in which he would wreak vengeance on the Jews. But his plot was overturned by the Jews themselves who rose up, killing their enemies instead. "Wherefore they called these days Purim after the name of *pur*. Therefore because of all the words of this letter, and of that which they had seen concerning this matter, and that which had come on to them, the Jews ordained, and took upon themselves, and upon their seed, and upon such as joined unto them, so that it should not fail that they would keep these two days according to the writing thereof, and according to the appointed time thereof, every year" (*Megillat Esther* 9:26–27). What does the word "pur" mean? The *megillah* explains, "In the first month, which is the month of Nissan, in the twelfth year of King Ahasuerus, they cast pur, that is the lot, before Haman from day to day, and from month to month, to the twelfth month, which is the month of Adar" (*Megillat Esther* 3:7).

The verse also notes a common Persian practice. Apparently, to assure success, the time for carrying out important decisions was set by lot. If such is the case, it bespeaks a belief in keeping with a pagan outlook. Pagans did not attribute the success of their deeds to practical considerations of cause and effect, certainly not to ethical reasoning; but to blind fate, to nothing but arbitrary chance that paralleled the unrepressed reign of their passions, impelling them to act. Paradoxically, they wanted the arbitrary randomness to be consonant with their goals; therefore they needed to guess at it in advance and in order to do this they needed to assume that chance is the embodiment of uncompromising necessity. In any case, when one casts lots, one divests success of any reasoning— pragmatic or ethical—and the action of people who believe in fate does not tolerate any censorship of its capriciousness. This characterization of the socio-cultural reality practiced in the court of King Ahasuerus serves as a background to the story of the *megillah*. Notice that all the deeds of the king and his ministers are devoid of either pragmatic, utilitarian, rational, or ethical reasoning. The sole motivation is fulfillment of an immediate passion that makes no distinction between the drive and the deed other than fear of the "lot." Notice also that both the decision to annihilate the Jews and the decision to save them occurs in the same arbitrary, impulsive manner devoid of any moral consideration.

The irony of casting lots in this story is clearly directed at the non-Jewish surroundings. On the very day that was appointed for their destruction Jews rose up to kill their enemies. Fate was reversed. But it is not only a reversal of Haman's will; it is also a derisive refutation of the pagan outlook that underlies that will. Blind fate does not rule events; there is an ineluctable power that directs them. It does so not in arbitrary blindness but in accordance with a particular aim, and it mocks those who are unaware of it and who do not act in keeping with its aim. Here is the manifestation of prophetic irony vis-à-vis pagans. Still, one cannot overlook the fact that Jews in the Purim story do not seem to be so different than their neighbors. They too hold a *pur* and call their victory celebration by its name. We know full well that the Torah and prophecy posited a different truth that stands in contradistinction to a belief in the immutability of fate. God guides men and watches over their actions; His leadership and supervision is justice. Creatures are judged by the nature of their acts: if they act well, they are well compensated, and if they sin, they are punished. Religious, ethical consideration is what determines the unfolding of events, not blind fate that reflects arbitrary capriciousness. But in reading the story of the *megillah*, one gets the impression that the Jews who lived in Shushan forgot this truth. They do not act through the exercise of free choice, nor in accordance with the ethical, religious commandment that is incumbent upon them; instead, they await the king's permission to exact their revenge according to the same *pur*. Pluralizing the name of the holiday to "Purim" embodies the double aspect of the irony vis-à-vis the non-Jews, on the one hand, and the Jews, on the other. So the name of the festival serves as a key to explaining the story of the *megillah*.

EXCESS AND POWER

In its opening sentences, the *megillah* introduces the reader into the atmosphere of the royal court as the reflection of a world outlook symbolized by the casting of lots. It presents a king at the height of his powers celebrating with his ministers, advisers, and servants. What a value system is disclosed by the grandiose carnival—a feast that boasts excessive consumption, wastefulness, extravagance without end, pandering to sensual passions: eating, drinking, magnificent costumes, majesty of buildings and gardens, the satisfaction of sexual appetites. All of these represent success and achievement; they are the meaning of life; everything that is done to acquire them is taken for granted. But, it bears noting, the satisfaction of these sensual appetites is not exposed on the level of primal licentious drives. The bestiality that reigns in the court of King Ahasuerus is elevated to a plane of marked refinement; here is a highly developed culture that raises satisfaction of the senses to an art form. An unmistakable hallmark of this is the ostentatiousness that accompanies the pleasing of passions. Mere enjoyment is not sufficient; apparently the display of pleasure is more important than the pleasure itself. Everything is presented in public so that the populace may show its approval through amazement and admiration. It is the rationale for the prodigal superfluity of food and drink, the costumes and the magnificent structures that can never be fully enjoyed. Excess is a necessary part of the outward show and it leaves no room for doubt in the heart of the observer.

Why does a hedonist require external validation? Undoubtedly—and here again the story's ironic sting is sensed—to satisfy the notion that "man is superior to the beast." As a man, the hedonist cannot suffice with pleasure for its own sake. He seeks to regard it as emblematic of life's meaning, assuming that pleasure can have significance. In any case, this overpowering drive—greater than the natural drive to eat, drink, or engage in sex—breaks out into a search for significance precisely in a place where it is absent—the pursuit of power. In the story of the *megillah*, pursuit of power for its own sake is elevated to a supreme value that assigns meaning to all things. Ahasuerus celebrates the high point of his regime anxious about his sovereignty because of Queen Vashti's refusal to make an appearance. In every aspect, the prestige of the regime appears as a supreme value. In other words, the regime is not perceived as a means for achievement of the general good; that is, the social order, stability, tranquillity, or security in the face of an external enemy. The dominion is an autonomous value because it grants the ruler advantage over others and compels them to declare repeatedly that he is their master. Haman's rise to power, as the story continues, is not viewed as an accidental occurrence. His behavior symbolizes the pure will to power. Power for the sake of power. Power as the meaning of life. No other consideration, certainly not regard for the general or even the private good; no moral considerations exist for him. Finally, it must be noted that what seems to be utter folly in Ahasuerus's actions and Haman's behavior is not foolish when seen from a different point of view: rather, it is a reasonable deduction based on the value system of the society described. If the full satisfaction of one's impulses and the attainment of validation from all the observers is the meaning of life, then the absurd behavior of Ahasuerus and Haman is the height of wisdom.

Clearly it is also the height of foolishness. At least this is the position of the *megillah*. Only the *megillah* does not say so overtly, which brings one back to the ironic motif. Ostensibly, the narrator of the *megillah* does not present himself as being outside the picture he describes. It is as though he regards developments from within; as though the value system of his characters is his own, their logic his; as though he accepts the motives for their deeds because no other motives or considerations exist. Not one critical pronouncement is made. Indeed, it would appear that there is no external narrator as the figures in the *megillah* tell their own story. Nonetheless, the narrative looks like it pokes fun at its characters, and even at the narrator. At times they are so laughable and one-sided that one doubts the "realism" of the story. Are there such people? Do such situations arise? Are we not confronted by shadows or masks? Such questions suggest that the story has a latent, internal criticism. How is such a mocking tone transmitted without its being specifically articulated? Apparently it is achieved stylistically, particularly the use of a subtle counterpoint. The pratfalls of the characters, resulting directly from actions that reflect their point of view, produces constant laughter.

As early as the beginning of the story, we read, "Now it came to pass in the days of Ahasuerus—this is Ahasuerus who reigned, from India even unto Ethiopia, over a hundred and seven and twenty provinces." One cannot miss the linguistic mimicry that imitates the pomposity of a king who ennobles and magnifies himself—so important and elevated is "this Ahasuerus." But quickly one discovers that he does not even rule in his own household—the queen rebels, refuses to do his bidding. And it is immediately clear that even such a trivial refusal puts the well-being of the entire kingdom in question, and the upshot is that even the slightest compunction sabotages the principle of an absolute monarchy. Thus, inexorably, the deeds that cause Haman's downfall are precisely the actions meant to outwardly signify his exploits as an absolute ruler. Even more telling, as we observe the regime of rulers supposedly at the height of their power, it is clear that the passion to rule is so overpowering that it rules them rather than they ruling it. Their drive to power is so strong that they cannot restrain it in order to remain in power.

The irony is at its most trenchant as the story describes the king's status within his own court. His is only an apparent command of events that occur around him; actually he has no real impact on them. The instincts that rule him open the door to all those driven by similar instincts—who are stronger than he is—to intrude in his dominion. They are the movers; he is nothing but an apparent ruler, even the royal seal is held by his ministers. Is this an indication that in fact they are the rulers? Is Haman not the ruler? Quickly it emerges that neither does Haman rule his own household. Prey to his drives, all his aims are thwarted. The peak of the story comes close to the end of the plot when it becomes evident that the principle on which the monarchy is based overrides the rule of the king himself—the ability to make a decision according to what he wills. He must therefore entrust power to someone else so that his own decision can be changed: "Write ye also concerning the Jews as you please, in the king's name and seal it with the king's ring; for the writing which is inscribed in

the king's name, and sealed with the king's ring, may no man reverse"
(*Megillat Esther* 8:8). Thus the consequential logic of the regime turns it
into folly. The will of the monarch is so absolute that it becomes
impossible for the monarch himself to undo it! If this is so, who then is the
true ruler? If one does not acknowledge a supra-human force that directs
events to a desired end—employing people's actions, even foolish ones,
toward that end—it is natural for pagan rulers such as those in the *megillah*
to ascribe the success of their regime to fate. The idea of fate as some kind
of blind necessity symbolizes the instinctual, meaningless arbitrariness
that rules their actions.

THE IRONY OF THE *MEGILLAH*

Of course one is not surprised at the mockery to which *Megillat Esther*
subjects the reigning world view in the royal court of Persia. But there is
certainly a keen ridicule directed at the Jewish characters, too. Had the
Jews actually maintained their peculiar laws as Haman said they did, it
could be expected that they would have lived according to an altogether
different value system, and that there would be an overt confrontation
between their value system and that of their environment. This is not how
the *megillah* describes things.

There is an explicit literary clue in the names. Both Jewish characters
in the *megillah* have foreign names. Mordecai and Esther. Not ordinary
names, these; they are freighted with a decided pagan reference—
Mardukh and Ishtar. From a societal standpoint, it is an indication that
even if these worthy Jews do not inwardly deny their Jewishness, they
would like to disguise it from the surrounding population; however,
selecting names that have a pagan connotation could also betoken that at
least in their external behavior, they accept the value system of their
environment. Such an interpretation can be found in Mordecai's instruction to Esther; notice that the *megillah* repeats the instruction for emphasis.
The first time (*Megillat Esther* 2:10) "Esther had not made known her people
nor her kindred; for Mordecai had charged her that she should not tell it."
And the second time (*Megillat Esther* 2:20) "Esther had not yet made known
her kindred nor her people as Mordecai had charged her; for Esther did
the commandment of Mordecai, as when she was brought up with him."
It is true that hiding her background has a "tactical" aim, and contradicts
the fact that Mordecai himself reveals his Jewishness to good purpose
when the confrontation with Haman occurs (*Megillat Esther* 3:4). "Now it

came to pass, when they spoke daily unto him and he harkened not unto them, that they told Haman to see whether Mordecai's words would stand; for he had told them that he was a Jew."

This revelation precisely at the moment of confrontation bears looking into. It appears that up to this moment Mordecai has concealed his Jewishness; he reveals it for a reason known only to himself. If anything is to be learned about these heroes from their behavior, it is that Jews in Shushan did not customarily disclose their Jewishness to others. Even more important evidence concerning the value system is exposed through the actions of Mordecai and Esther. Esther is displayed with all the virgins for the beauty contest that leads to winning the queen's role. Something in her demeanor and bearing is quite different from that of the other women, which results in the approval of Hegai who guards the women, and in her favor in the eyes of the king. Mordecai is anxious indeed (*Megillat Esther* 2:11). "And Mordecai walked every day before the court of the women's house to know how Esther did and what would become of her."

All of which shows that while participation in a contest of sexual attractiveness leading to the position of queen was not something taken for granted by Jews, neither did they make an attempt to evade a contest that runs completely counter to the morality of the Torah. Knowing that at the end of the story the salvation of the Jews comes in such a strange way (though not before Mordecai has placed the people in mortal danger by thrusting himself into an open, personal confrontation with Haman), one cannot but wonder about the point of the irony concealed in this web of curious behavior, behavior that contradicts both the morals of the Torah and the law of the land. In what way had the Jews sinned to bring them to the brink of destruction? Does the threat itself indicate the nature of the sin? Perhaps what drove the Jews to the verge of disaster was their eagerness to participate in the life of the non-Jews among whom they lived and to play the game according to their rules and morals.

At this point the strata of latent significance concealed by the literary style of the ironic story should be disclosed. All interpretations of the *megillah* note that the confrontation between Mordecai and Haman is one between a scion of the house of King Saul (*Megillat Esther* 2:5), "Mordecai the son of Jair, the son of Shimei, the son of Kish, a Benjamite," and a scion of the house of Agag, King of Amalek (*Megillat Esther* 3:1), "Haman the son of Hammedatha, the Agagite," which means that Mordecai and Haman re-enact a mortal war—originally undeclared—between Israel and Amalek. Thus events are returned to their source in the Torah, where they are perceived as an implacable conflict between good and evil. The truth by which the Jews must live stands opposed to falsehood and evil-doing for its own sake that Amalek represents. If this is the case, then the *megillah*'s formulation of such an unfathomable dichotomy must be seen as extremely ironic.

The dichotomy begins under the leadership of personalities such as Moses and Joshua, continues through Samuel and Saul, and works itself out in a personal power struggle of two competitors for supremacy. It really appears that Mordecai's struggle with Haman is not very different than is Esther's in her efforts to infiltrate the royal palace. Not only are the rules of the game accepted, but failure and success are measured by the same yardstick. Haman puts on airs, seeking royal honors. Mordecai refuses to bow down to him. Haman sees the height of success in riding the king's horse while a herald publicly proclaims his honor, but it is Mordecai who gains that distinction, and Haman who is forced to proclaim it. Haman, who wishes to hang his enemy, is hung on the very same tree. And then the ultimate triumph: Mordecai is appointed to replace Haman. Nowhere is there the hint of any reservation about the function, its trappings, its methods, or its logic. There is a conflict around the question of who will rule. There is no contest as to the quality, the methods, or the goals of the regime. Therefore it seems that Mordecai enjoys the honor that befalls him to ride the king's horse not a bit less than Haman would have, had his plan seen fruition. So Mordecai's concepts, at least if he is judged by the manifest strata of the story, are not different than Haman's on such issues as honor and success.

Finally it should be noted that what is said about Esther and Mordecai's behavior in the affair applies to all the Jews. The people do not rebel against the arbitrary fate decreed for them through the king's minister, nor do the people protest against the decree itself, which has no correlation to any moral consideration; therefore, when fate is reversed, they gladly do to their enemies what their enemies thought to do to them. Thus the formula that equates the contending parties repeats itself: first, Mordecai and Haman, and then the Jews and their enemies. The game is played according to the precepts and laws of a pagan monarchy. In other words, not only in name and in visage do the Jews not display their singularity; neither do they do so in the behavior and morality that they act out. Consequently, the irony of the *megillah* is also aimed at them, illuminating their deeds in the light of a ludicrous pettiness.

IRRECONCILABLE VIEWPOINTS

Nonetheless there is not a complete parallel between the Jews and their adversaries. The difference exists and is felt; perhaps it is what explains the salvation of the people despite their sin. Notice first a pungent irony: the man who intimates that the struggle between the Jews and their adversaries is a conflict between two irreconcilable viewpoints is not Mordecai but Haman. Because of his hatred he knows that by their very existence the Jews stand for something utterly opposed to the spirit and laws of the kingdom: (*Megillat Esther* 3:8) [and Haman said unto King Ahasuerus] "There is a certain people scattered abroad and dispersed among the people in all the provinces of thy kingdom; and their laws are diverse from those of every people; neither keep they the king's laws; therefore it profiteth not the king to suffer them." There is something foreign and special about the Jews, something that puts them at odds with the "laws and customs of the king." And should they forget it or try to disguise it, the enmity of their adversaries is quick to remind them. It is true that if one looks carefully at their actions, at a certain moment some selfhood dependent on a different morality is discerned, and when that something is revealed, even obliquely, fate is turned around and the Jews are saved.

Where does the kernel of difference manifest itself? In Esther's act of deliverance—she is ready to endanger herself in order to save her people. When Mordecai speaks to her he lays bare the moral dimension that is diametrically opposed to the gross, selfish consideration that has convinced the king to agree to the annihilation of the Jews (*Megillat Esther* 4:13–16). "Then Mordecai bade them return answer unto Esther: 'Think not with thyself that thou shalt escape in the king's house more than all the Jews for if thou altogether holdest thy peace at this time, then will relief and deliverance arise to the Jews from another place, but thou and thy father's house will perish: and who knoweth whether thou are not come to royal estate for such a time as this?' Then Esther bade them return answer unto Mordecai: 'Go, gather all the Jews that are present in Shushan, and fast ye for me, and neither eat nor drink three days, night or day; I also and my maidens will fast in like manner; and so will I go in unto the king, which is not according to the law; and if I perish, I perish.'"

These words demonstrate two interconnected considerations: the first is Esther's moral responsibility for her people. She may not save herself while turning her back on their plight. Second, there is some other power that determines the flow of events, and that presence operates in response to moral worth. Mordecai alludes to the succor that will come from "another place" and Esther responds through prayer and fasting because she is about to go against the custom of the royal court. Indeed, this is a very subtle technique in the art of storytelling, both in the development of the plot and its stylistic exposition. Esther is about to go into the king's chamber, which is truly "not according to the law," thus putting her life in danger. In effect, though, she is playing brinkmanship according to the regime's own rules of the game. By those rules, the king may, if he is good-hearted, approve the daring. There is a chance for grace even in a kingdom devoid of morality. It is simply that the grace is not determined by moral principle but by a basic arbitrariness which can sometimes work out for the good. Should the king find Esther appealing, and should she stimulate his erotic affection, he will permit her visit, which is "not according to the law," and thus it will become "according to the law."

So from the perspective of the monarchy, Esther is gambling only on her luck, whereas from a Torah perspective her actions will be judged by the Ruler of all events. This is the point at which irony comes close to showing itself, displaying—beyond the laughter—a religio-moral prophetic pathos. That pathos is clearly sounded in Mordecai's admonition. It could be said that here the story reaches its peak, coming dangerously close to breaking its own rules of style and design. It is not accidental that precisely at this point there is an oblique reference to a Providence that lies beyond the play of fate, and that Providence is a law that operates by moral principles. The Name that remains unsaid throughout the story comes close to explicit mention. Only close. The Name is not mentioned and His grace is manifested by means of the king's "grace." Thus the story continues according to the same structure and the same ironic style.

Perhaps in summary it could be said that at the very last moment, confronted by the height of danger, Mordecai and Esther stand up to the test, validating the truth. It is a truth that is in confrontation with a hedonistic world view and the absence of ethical behavior in the monarchy. By virtue of their stance, they are saved and save their people. Still, their situation and their way of life and the extent of their acculturation into their environment all remain unchanged. Is it in any way conceivable that there could be a change in the situation of the Jewish people if, even in a time of danger, they do not consider leaving the diaspora and returning to their own land in a context of independence?

EXILE

The moment has come to unmask the irony. *Megillat Esther* proposes to tell the story of exile and denote its role in the course of Jewish history. From the historic, religious perspective of the Bible, exile is a condition of *hester panim*—God's turning away in anger. That is to say that God refrains from revealing Himself directly as one who leads his people. God conceals Himself abandoning the people to its fate. It is easy to see how the design of Megillat Esther's narrative embodies a situation of *hester panim*. This is a simple explanation for the fact that God's name is not mentioned in the *megillah* and that the *pur* appears, at least externally, to dominate the ups and downs of the plot. Indeed there is something wondrous in the internal logic of the combination of events. No event is truly accidental. On the contrary, a purposeful, moral logic links events to one another so that the righteous are saved and the wicked are punished. Everything is ordained. And although there is not a single *unnatural* occurrence, in no way can the connection between events be considered to occur naturally. It is precisely the apparent happenstance as it recurs with persistent regularity that shows an intended, highly integrated structure.

Unavoidably, the reader must ask, who is toying with the heroes of the story in such a manner? Who is the director hiding behind the scenes? The production itself does not point unambiguously to the director; it strives mightily to present each event as an independent occurrence; that is, an accidental event that neither stems from nor is inevitably linked to the previous ones. This is the interpretation given to a condition of *hester panim*. Divine providence has not totally disappeared. It retreats from observable intervention and appears to be operating through chance. The heroes of the story have no notion of the force that drives their fate; they think of themselves as being at the mercy of happenstance. This predicament of *hester panim* is, of course, a test. The characters really can influence their fate but only if they dare to run counter to the conventional rules of behavior in their environment, which appear to be the way in which success is insured.

It is by virtue of its human dimension that the profundity of the *megillah*'s description of exile is evident. How is exile perceived in the view of the heroes? The reader learns immediately, of course, about the awful danger that awaits them. A displaced and dispersed people has to rely on the grace of their rulers. These rulers have no aim other than power, and no ethical principle deters them. Precisely because their peculiar traditions cannot abide the world view that established the rules of behavior in their environment, the Jews foment hatred toward themselves, and because they are utterly dependent on the whim of their rulers, they can find themselves suddenly exposed to annihilation. It may be taken for granted that the Jews will respond in a way that grants them something of the regime's power. Indeed, Mordecai and Esther penetrate the royal precincts reaching the highest rank. Does this enable them to avert the terrible danger? Seemingly, the answer of the *megillah* story is affirmative. Mordecai and Esther save their people and kill their enemies. But following on the literary analysis above, the ironic aspect of the affirmative answer is easily seen. Even individuals who achieve fame do not act by virtue of their own strength or that of their people. They, too, are dependent on the grace of a sovereign who is ruled by arbitrary, instinctual drives. Today they are at the peak of power. Tomorrow they may be cast aside because it is only the sovereign's arbitrariness, not their own power, that has raised them to glory. What is more, the people who apparently have an opportunity to kill their enemy do not even consider the possibility of self-defense without first getting permission from the monarch.

Indeed, the fact that the power Jews in exile have emanates from others proves something even graver about the essence of exile. To achieve an imaginary power, Jews must act by the rules of their environs. In other words, their customs, demeanor, and actions and ultimately their value system must resemble their foreign surroundings. To achieve this they need to betray their own world view, belief, and Torah. Consequently, exile is also the people's *hester panim*. A people in exile is abandoned to an environment that may be dominated by Amalek, and this environment injects its value system into the Jewish people's way of life. Jews may wish to acculturate themselves in order to find respite and satisfaction consistent with the ways of the culture. They may forget their spiritual uniqueness. Amalek's hatred, which may be aroused at the very threshold of assimilation, is an outcome of what little specialness remains externally, and this carries the hallmark of an indirect providence. Should the people return to itself and discover its true face, it will be saved. But as long as it continues to prefer exile and rejoice in the miracle proclaimed as the "grace" of a foreign king, it is but a transient deliverance, a stay granted until the next confrontation.

There is an obvious historical background to the story of *Megillat Esther*. The reality that it reflects is of exile in the Persian kingdom. The story cannot however be regarded as history proper, neither can it be classified as literary interpretation; surely not as an exacting description of a one-time experience. It is meant to illustrate the nature of exile in general. The homiletic nature of the *megillah* alludes to this purpose as it points to the Amalek motif in the Torah and Early Prophets. The term homiletic nature is used because the motif has been interpreted in such an extreme way that it extends the original meaning almost beyond recognition. Amalek is no longer adduced as a specific historic tribe that plots against the Jewish people. Amalek is the connotation of evil that springs from an adherence to instinctual drives and a passion for power for its own sake. When these drives and passions overrun the bounds of moral consideration—they represent Amalek anew, and even when the Jewish people do not oppose them, they become the first victim. If this is so then the story of *Megillat Esther* is indeed the story of combating Amalek; that is, the Jewish people's trial in each generation so long as they are in exile.

RESPONSE TO EXILE

Proceeding on what has been said, it is evident that the Festival of Purim is an exemplum of the people's life in exile. It is intended to mirror a major aspect of the exile, a reflection of the Jewish people's relationship with the foreign environment that surrounds it. So much is this the case that the people recognizes a selfhood that is undergoing a process of camouflage and suppression, understands the lurking internal and external dangers, and learns to respond in a manner that will prevent disaster. What is the response embodied in the commandments and customs of the holiday?

The first response is recollection and consciousness raising: reading the *megillah* in the setting of a noisy and mirthful public ceremony intended for everyone, including the children, and so engrave the story of exile on the consciousness of the people. There is something paradoxical in this light-hearted mode of remembering such a grave matter, but it is precisely the paradox that exposes the double-faceted irony of the *megillah*, helping to see what a people in exile prefers not to see. And if—after the *megillah* has been read in the synagogue and one is sitting at the festive meal—the Jew is commanded to drink until he cannot distinguish between cursed be Haman and blessed be Mordecai, then there is nothing like the irony of this commandment to remind one that the desire not to know is the essence of exile; yet deliverance requires one to know.

Jews use the customs of Purim to remember while acting out their desire to forget; this is the distancing irony. Among the commandments of the holiday, another response is noted, one that approaches the overt, ethical message of the *megillah*: that of reinforcing the fraternity of the people. The exchange of food and giving gifts to the indigent symbolizes this fraternity. Indeed the charitable act that makes the mutual responsibility of Jews as members of a covenant palpable is the secret of their remarkable cohesion even under circumstances of dispersal. The charitable act maintains the nation; as opposed to the spirit of Amalek, it expresses a moral, spiritual uniqueness that actually exists, not something relegated to a passing thought or mere lip service. It is from this that the great emphasis placed by scholars on charity, particularly in exile, is derived. In the context of charity on Purim, it is worthwhile to recall Maimonides's words that gifts to the poor are the very essence of rejoicing. An amplification of this would be the recognition that the charity that arose at that time was, and is, the symbol of deliverance. It is therefore also the heart of genuine rejoicing on the holiday.

But the unusual, jovial customs that supposedly envelop the joy of brotherhood cannot be overlooked. Granted that in this case these are folkways that burst from below, breaking into the realm of aristocratic mitzvot, whereas generally it is the mitzvah that gives shape and limits to popular custom. Well, then, why were popular customs, which at least appear to be frivolous, permitted at Purim? Why were customs allowed that, on the surface at least, appear to imitate the non-Jewish environment, particularly customs whose characteristics are antagonistic to the Torah tradition? Drinking "like lords" at the Purim meal seems to be a parody of the feast of Ahasuerus; clowning, Purim skits, burning Haman in effigy, wearing costumes—all look like carnival doings. When they want to underscore the qualitative difference between the behavior of Jews and Gentiles, Jews generally call these the activities of the "goy." If this is so, is this not a license for Jews to behave like *goyim* for a day, tasting the flavor of their holidays?

There is a tendency to answer in the affirmative but before a headlong rush to judgment, it is useful to focus on the covert irony of Purim customs and the nature of the *megillah* that colors them. It is true that Jews dissemble as *goyim* in some of the holiday customs. But even as they are doing so, their probing gaze sees though the partying and they know; such knowledge holds a great deal of incisive self-irony, which, often as not, characterizes the ambivalence of Jewish humor inherent in exile. It is the humor of someone who sees himself through the eyes of another and then re-examines the other person who is observing him through gentile eyes. Irony limits the daring of a number of Purim customs and serves as a dam that channels them into a way of life of Torah and commandments. Consider the situation in which a person knows that he is commanded to get drunk, that he may not shrink from that limit but also that he may not cross it—can he truly become intoxicated? The entire time he is drinking he is required to examine himself to determine whether he has reached the point where he cannot distinguish between cursing Haman and blessing Mordecai, which means that when he gets to such a point he still knows, so to speak, what it is that he no longer knows. This is the formulation of a *halakhic* norm, and irony pokes out from it as though restraining the commandment from itself, by itself. A commandment of commission rolled up in a prohibition: become inebriated soberly! Ironic distancing is retained as an internal perspective of the ego that observes itself even as it alters its external behavior. The same ironic distancing appears to be functioning in other Purim customs, a demonstration that even what seems to be a departure from Torah morality is in effect a binding requirement.

There is a story in the Gemara about two great scholars whose behavior at Purim can illustrate and explicate what has been discussed above. "Raba said, 'A man is obliged to drink at Purim until he cannot distinguish between cursed be Haman and blessed be Mordecai.' Raba and Rabi Zirah sat down to a Purim *seudah*. Raba stood up and murdered Rabi Zirah. The next day, seeking mercy, he brought him back to life. On the following Purim Raba said, 'Come let us celebrate a Purim feast together.' Rabi Zirah responded, 'Miracles do not happen all the time'" (Tractate Megillah, Chap. 7, p. 2).

This legend, which could be a typical Purim story, resembles the *megillah*. Should one wish, it may be seen as a fabrication, or one could say that it is the way Torah scholars laugh at themselves. Certainly it carries a serious barb. It is a tale intended as a caustic illustration of latent instincts in some Torah scholars who, envying one another and competing for honors, have murderous feelings (heaven forfend!) toward one another. Drinking like lords on Purim bares such feelings, at least to the extent that they can be expressed as a comic story. Without doubt the story shows the hidden danger in such outbursts as part of a way of life that is generally demanding to the point of repressing even fantasies of violence. But one could also say that the story itself is the overstatement of danger that serves to articulate the ironic distancing that holds it in check. One can understand then why the Gemara does not employ this story as a rationale against the *halakhah* attributed to the great *amorah*,

Raba. On the contrary, it is evidence that the *halakhah* actually was in force and that it continued to be observed.

Therefore one can claim that the story demonstrates—directly or by inference—that the reason for the strange commandment to become inebriated is to move Jews, particularly Torah scholars who regard themselves as observant and loyal to the Torah, to understand what is latent and suppressed in the depths of their psyche. Of course every Jew must know that the evil inclination constantly skulks in the depths of his soul. But a theory is neither as strong nor as potent as experiencing things consciously. The Purim story teaches that the drunkenness of Purim carries the potential of experience. Since this is so, it is proper to set limits in a way that will prevent the mitzvah of tipsiness to become one of drunkenness that is attended by debauchery for its own sake. What is the limit of *Ad lo yada*—until one cannot distinguish? Maimonides has a simple answer: until one falls asleep. Anyone who is fast asleep can no longer make distinctions and is not likely to continue drinking. Other commentators interpreted *ad* as "prior." In other words, one should stop drinking close to the point where one loses discretion. The most far-reaching commentary is "until one's reading of the *megillah* is muddled." In any case, everyone agrees that one should not actually become drunk. Rabbi HaMeiri sums it up, "At any rate, we are not commanded to become intoxicated and degrade ourselves through rejoicing for we were not commanded to folly but to pleasurable joy by which one approaches a love of God and gratitude for the miracles He performed for us."

This singular and regulated departure from usual practice fills a vital role precisely for those individuals who generally demand of themselves that they severely control their instinctual drives. The didactic tenet that holds that "sinful thoughts are worse than the sin itself" necessarily brings a repression of desires and instinctual drives that of course rumble constantly in the secret recesses of the individual. As observed from the story in the Gemara, the Purim reversal enables a simulation in which repressed appetites are satisfied, and through it a person uncovers aspects of himself he generally does not admit to. The didactic-ethical purpose of such self-knowledge is apparent: from this standpoint an ex post facto, paradoxical comparison is created between the festival of Purim and the day that ostensibly is its polar opposite, Yom Kippur. Nonetheless, this is presumably not the primary and original aim of the festival. In effect we have the exploitation of a wonderful opportunity for the acting out of behavior toward which the Torah way of life does not incline. One might say that a profound, popular insight seized upon a narrow crack that became available, and the leadership in its wisdom approved of it in a sort of wily sanctity. This is the popular fascination of Purim, the enchantment of forbidden fruit that is suddenly permitted, and the attraction of a catharsis that purifies the soul's dross.

What was the initial intention of Purim customs? The answer must be sought in the *megillah*, the underpinning of the holiday. By analyzing the narrative of the *megillah*, a characteristic diaspora dichotomy is revealed between loyalty to the authentic content of the nation's life and between the blandishments of a foreign culture with the satisfactions that it offers. The Jewish public maneuvers between the consciousness of being a chosen people isolated from the pagan environment, and a covetousness for the trappings of that very environment. Even when Jews do not consciously wish to assimilate, they are unavoidably involved in a process of losing their independent mien, and it is an almost unwarranted assumption to presume that sinful, wishful thinking is unknown among the pious and the righteous. It is the burning desire to vault the fence in order to taste the forbidden life. The unusual commandments and customs of the Purim festival fuel this hidden desire, driving it toward full satisfaction while fashioning an ironic reaction. By celebrating their victory in the manner that the pagan environment celebrates its victories, Jews mirror the great danger from which they were saved.

In other words, the customs of the Purim festival contain an ironic actualization of the meaning of diasporic existence. The nation perceives itself through these customs as occupied in an assimilatory process and recognizes the repressed desire to engage in the life of the environment, mimicking even practices that it consciously holds in contempt.

Several aspects of Purim as the holiday of exile have been stressed: the *megillah* as an interpretation of the essence of exile and its dangers; an exposition of the miraculous, supernatural nature of survival in exile; an illustration of the internal quality that enables such a miraculous survival—the mutual responsibility Jews have as members of a covenant; the gravitational pull of the assimilating social context and an awareness of the desire to experience it. Finally, yet another motif is noted, which encompasses the whole: Purim expresses a sense of helplessness in leaving the diasporic situation, if only in the fact that the holiday's hilarity takes that situation for granted as an ongoing condition that is not likely to change. In this sense, the difference between Purim and other Jewish holidays stands out. Rosh HaShanah and Yom Kippur strongly emphasize the vision of the nation's future redemption in its own land—certainly the three pilgrimage holidays underscore the idea; whereas the customs particular to Purim disregard a vision of redemption and an ingathering of the exiles. On Purim, it is as though the exile declares the miracle of its salvation, as though there is no further need to be saved from exile. Indeed there is an oblique allusion to this.

On the festival of Purim one does not recite the *hallel* prayer even though a miracle occurred. This sets up an equation between the fact that God's name is not mentioned in the *megillah* while His providence is seen in the outcome of the "lot" and the mercy of a foolish king, and between the fact that the vision of redemption is not spelled out. Is this a continuation of the same *hester panim?* Is this the extension of the same irony? Was a people who could rise to vanquish its enemies—when permitted to do so by the king—really incapable of doing anything to redeem itself from exile? When allowed to return to their land by King Cyrus, did the great majority of the Jewish people exploit that opportunity? Did their self-view as incapable of changing the situation bear witness to a destiny of circumstance; or is it that a weakness of will, coupled with the gravitational pull of exile, served as an excuse for hiding behind the *pur?*

Jubilation over the miracle of survival in exile is readily understood as a *hester panim*—the people averting their gaze from redemption. The averted gaze is the innermost root of exile; it is as well the factor which shapes its existence. However, it must be conceded that the people did not interpret the holiday this way. Throughout the long history of exile, the nation tended to accept the reality of exile as a kind of lot that had been cast, a destiny that they were powerless to change. Nonetheless, there is something that is not ironic in the bewitched rejoicing of the Purim festival. Despite all that has been said above the festival appears as the rejoicing of a people in the grips of a hibernation that paralyzes its national will; it dreams of a temporary salvation at the brink of the abyss, imagining, as a dream within a dream, that the temporary can be transposed into eternity. The consciousness of self as it is reflected in Purim is a consciousness of the end of an ironic wakefulness and the beginning of a bewitched slumber, neither awake nor asleep. Will the nation awake to full reality? Will it regain its will? And on what is all this contingent? Is it on a tidal wave of hatred or perhaps on the greatest wonder of all, the awakening of a will from within itself.

MAKE-BELIEVE ASSIMILATION

The Purim festival as it is celebrated in the modern state of Israel is ostensibly the articulation of a people who wishes to be free of its exile, who returns finally to its own land after many generations of life in exile. Like Hanukkah, this holiday has also easily been incorporated into the atmosphere of the secular public. Indeed, the festival's traditional forms were responsive almost without change to the expectations of a secular public. Here is a holiday replete with joyful entertainment, that jettisons the weighty problems of everyday life, discovers generous friendship and an abundance of joie de vivre, and above all grants each individual the freedom of his imagination to masquerade as any figure he wishes to be. It is true that the secular Israeli version of the Purim festival changed traditional forms by shifting the center of gravity from the synagogue to the public hall and the street, and from reading the *megillah* to a party, a festive meal, a costume parade, and skits. It is also true that the *megillah* has not been entirely forgotten, its memory retained by dressing in the costumes of some of its characters, by staging comic plays in which motifs from the *megillah* story are integrated, and by joyous folk song. In its Israeli version, the Purim festival has gradually taken on a carnival character.

This change in the forms of the holiday is not accidental. The changes are a conscious articulation of the Jewish people's feeling as it comes back to its land to rebuild it as a homeland, the directed expression of a monumental aspiration to return to the life of a natural people. Thus the joyous Purim festival became an interlude in which the Jewish public— reconstructing itself in its own land—could find an outlet from the suffering and anxiety of internal and external struggles that attended it. The great tensions that built up were released through joy and humor. And a young generation, experiencing a potent joy of life as it took root in its old–new land, was free to declare its feelings; the genuine and direct expression of a sense of redemption: a return to the natural and proper state for the nation as well as for the individual Jew. As a consequence, the ironic distancing so characteristic of the traditional customs of the holiday were somewhat obscured; what was retained were the hallmarks of a folk holiday that reflected the historic memory and hopes of the Jewish people. A descent into uncontrolled frivolity was also preserved. The return to a fully natural life was still very much a vision to be attained. The serious meaning of the holiday was reflected in content and forms, and rejoicing was colored by the notion that joy was a mitzvah.

In recent years there is yet another change, another shifting of emphasis. The national historic context has been overshadowed by an unrestrained expression of the aspiration to normalization, which has finally been realized. What does normalization mean? It is, of course, the desire for a normal life, like that of everyone else, which permeated the secular Zionist movement. In certain parts of the Zionist movement, the expression to be like all other nations applied not only to the existential conditions and self-determination of the Jewish people, but also to imitating the normal, cultural forms of other peoples. When Purim is cast in the mode of a fun carnival, it becomes an ideal expression for this ambition. The Purim masquerade enabled the people to disguise itself as any other nation; thus Purim became the vehicle for acting out a latent desire, perhaps even an overt desire, to assimilate just when the nation returned to its own land. Of course assimilation is evident not only when historical content is erased, or in the of jettisoning traditional forms, but also—perhaps most notably—when the internal reserve that guards the boundary between sobriety and inebriation is removed. As the ironic dimension retreated and was lost, a carnival atmosphere for its own sake was to be expected. Is this not a paradoxical inversion of the *megillah's* irony? Precisely in its homeland, the Jewish people allows itself utterly to give up its uniqueness and finds a sense of redemption in becoming like all other nations in its celebrations.

If this is so, then the special role and the meaning of Purim as an exilic holiday, even in the State of Israel, has not come to an end. This is not only because most Jews still live in exile, nor because many of the Jews living in Israel dream about exile and emigrate. Residing in Israel cannot, by itself, protect one against the deeply rooted predisposition to emigrate. On the contrary, there is a kind of *galut* mentality that is possible in Eretz Israel alone: the desire to assimilate as a nation among the nations not as the result of erosion and seduction, but rather as an articulation of a well-defined and institutionalized national will. This examination of the *megillah* has already indicated that exile was inherent in the sin that King Saul and the people transgressed while still in their own land: their refusal to pursue the war against "Amalek" to its decisive end; and we have previously interpreted the symbolic significance of Amalek and the affirmative use of the war against it: maintaining the selfhood and moral uniqueness of the people.

The Purim festival is a reminder that exile is a constant option and a constant danger that lies in wait. It must be fought in Eretz Israel too because the seduction that paralyzes the will to selfhood operates in Israel as well. But for Purim to fill this role, the traditional, internal reserve that differentiates between assimilation in earnest and a make-believe assimilation must remain in force. In Israel, as well as in the diaspora, the danger point is the point of forgetting identity beyond sober irony—Purim as a carnival rather than a holiday of assimilation. As justified as some of the changes may be that adapt the holiday to the experience of a people returning to live a normal, national life, the ironic sobriety must still be preserved as an internal barrier at a time of frivolity and levity. This is what will retain the original sense of the wondrous holiday.

NINE

PASSOVER:
EDUCATION TO A LIFE OF FREEDOM

SPRING HOLIDAY OF REDEMPTION

With the celebration of Passover—the Festival of Spring—the Jewish
yearly cycle begins for a second time in the month of Nissan. The first
beginning of the cycle is reckoned from Creation, the second from the
founding of the people as a nation. Passover commemorates the event in
which the Children of Israel united and embarked on their road as one
people with a common goal—the exodus from Egypt. Despite the
holiday's pronounced historical content, however, Passover is also an
outstanding festival of nature, a fact well sustained in its early ritual
patterns: the Passover sacrifice, the prohibition on eating *hametz*, the
eating of matzah, and the harvesting of the first barley. Scholars of ancient
Israel conjecture that two traditions common to the peoples of the area
merged in biblical times—a shepherds' festival associated with the birth
of the first lambs, and a farmers' festival linked to the first reaping of grain
crops. Though the early Passover rituals are the same rites common to
both the tribes of Israel and the neighboring peoples, these rituals
acquired a national and a historic interpretation in the Torah. Neither the
Book of Exodus nor the Oral Tradition, however, did away with the

meaning of the festival as a Festival of Nature. Passover is the Festival of Spring, the time of the first reaping of barley, and the Oral Tradition emphasized this quality by choosing the "Song of Songs" as the scroll to be read during the holiday. Beyond the symbolic interpretation of the scroll as an expression of the union between *Knesset Yisrael* and her lover-Lord, it is after all, a song of youth and of spring.

In any event, it is clear that the rituals that constitute the pre-existing and renewed core of the holiday are also the rituals that constitute the structural axis of the exodus story, which Jews are charged with "telling" to their children and grandchildren on Passover. On the last night before the departure, the Children of Israel were ordered to gather in their homes with their families, in numbers sufficient to eat goat yearlings, to slaughter the yearlings, and to mark a sign with the blood on the doorposts of their homes so that the Angel of Death, who on that night was to strike every firstborn in Egypt, would pass over their houses. They were ordered to eat the roasted goat meat together, leaving nothing until morning; thus they would be prepared and ready to leave at daybreak. In effect, this is the event that the night of Passover—the night of the seder—marks. Each year, on the same night, the Jewish people gather together with their families. While the Temple stood, the Passover offering was sacrificed and eaten in the assembly, and the story of the exodus retold. Since the destruction of the Temple, Jews gather round the table for a meal fraught with symbols and signs of remembrance, and tell of the exodus from Egypt. In other words, each year the Children of Israel *reconstruct* the night before the departure; and the tale is both the background that explains the occasion, and the source of the *Haggadah* being retold.

Another ritual motif connected with the biblical account of the Exodus, though not linked to Passover night, is the dedication of the first-born son. The commandment marks the rescue of Israel's first-born sons on the night of the affliction. Having been saved by God, the first-born were dedicated to Him and subsequently designated for the service of God. This priestly role was later assigned to *Cohanim* from the tribe of Levi, after which first-born sons were redeemed by *Cohanim*. Finally, mention should be made of the ritual prohibition on eating *hametz* and the injunction to eat matzah. The biblical story deals with these commandments by explaining that the dough that had been prepared did not have sufficient time to rise because of the hasty departure from Egypt, so the unleavened dough was baked as matzah.

It is quite obvious that the biblical story accords historical significance to these rituals. But the relationship between the story and the ritual flows in one direction only. The story is molded for the purpose of the ritual, and its early meaning became a kind of pattern that preceded the historical meaning. In this context, one must first point out the parallel delicately alluded to between the natural/mythological motif of the renewal of the life cycle at the arrival of spring, and the historical/narrative motif of the exodus. This is pure poetic metaphor, but these metaphors enrich the holiday and convey a great deal of its charm. The story of spring is the story of seeds buried in the ground, seemingly disintegrated and lost, which suddenly burst forth with a powerful life force. With time, multiple seeds will ripen from each seed. The story of the exodus is the story of the "few in number," the sons of Jacob, who went down to Egypt, were enslaved there and nearly lost, but "the more they were afflicted, the more they multiplied and grew." When spring arrives they burst forth and depart to freedom. This delicate parallel between the myth and the historical narrative, designed as a legend for the purpose of ritual, was enriched by tradition. The reading of "Song of Songs" on Passover added another parallel between spring as a ripening of life forces in young people and the exodus story; the *midrash* literature connected with the exodus also served to open lines of analogy in many ways, enriching the holiday with creativity that is varied, overflowing, and nearly limitless.

A second matter that requires examination in this context is that of structuring the exodus story according to the gradual unfolding of the ten plagues, which culminated in the Plague of the First-born. Why did redemption come about only after this terrible plague, and why was this particular plague chosen as the "crowning glory"? Scholars of antiquity would claim that the historical tale crystallized around an existing ritual connected with protection against a "reaper" that threatened the first-born, that the tale came into being only in order to replace a typical pagan connotation with a historical one, which would conform to the Torah's point of view. It is an explanation that appears quite convincing, but the purpose of structuring the story around the ritual could not be merely a mechanical replacement of the occult/pagan meaning with a symbolic historical one. The Plague of the First-born required correlation within the framework of the exodus story, and in the moral/theological meaning that the biblical story confers it should be understood that for the God of Israel, the people of Israel are as the first-born son. The Egyptians wished to torture and destroy the first-born, the appointed son, and enslaved him with hard labor and harsh decrees. The Plague of the First-born is, therefore, full and just retribution according to the principle of "measure for measure." The rescue of Israel's first-born sons contains something of an act of dedication. By saving them, the first-born become consecrated to God; by analogy the first-born people of Israel, by means of their rescue, are consecrated to be their God's prize and treasure, "a kingdom of *Cohanim* and a holy nation."

A third development results from this, fashioning the holiday's historical character as a symbol that surrounds the core of its ritual: Passover is a holiday directed at the children. The entire people of Israel departed from Egypt, but the main survivors are not the adults who represent the present in the life of the people, but the children who represent its future. Passover illustrates the rescue of those who carry the future with them, and it is toward them that the holiday is indeed directed. Their redemption, as carriers of the people's future existence, is passed on from generation to generation in a bond rewoven every year. The parents' first role was to save the sons by gathering them together for the Passover sacrifice on the eve of departure. They fulfill the very same role when they carry out Passover's primary commandment, "And thou shalt tell thy son in that day, saying, It is because of that which the Lord did for me when I came forth out of Egypt" (Exodus 13:8). In other words, the *Haggadah*, the bequeathing of the story from generation to generation, is the act of connecting the generations. The story creates the continuity, maintains and strengthens it, and thereby performs the act of redemption itself—the link, the unity—of that which is bequeathed from generation to generation.

Focusing the story of the exodus on the Plague of the First-born and the rescue of Israel's first-born infuses an early ritual motif into the center of the historical narrative. It becomes the symbol of the event whose memory unites the people and determines its path.

SLAVERY AND FREEDOM

In terms of its place in the holiday, and the contribution it makes to the exposition of the holiday's ideas, the story that appears in the Book of Exodus bears examination. It is significant that the holiday rituals, as they formed in the Oral Tradition, do not include a continuous reading of the entire biblical story. The *Haggadah* presents some verses and interprets them, but it does not offer the full biblical version of the story. The chapters that are intended for reading on the holiday during the Torah service in the synagogue revolve around the commandments regarding Passover. As the commandments are read, parts of the story are also retold, but the reading does not encompass the entire story. Not until the seventh day of Passover is the last part of the account read continuously from "And it came to pass, when Pharaoh had let the people go" (Exodus 13:17), through the story of the sweetening of the waters of Marah. The "Song of the Sea" is the principal part of the reading. This is clear from the *Haftarah*, which places it in apposition to David's song of victory over his enemies (Samuel II, 22:1–11). And from this emphasis it is also clear that poetry holds a special position. The poems are not a regular part of the story; they are rather a festive elevation of the story to a plane of "timelessness," thereby becoming a kind of peg that connects the story and the ritual.

In other words, the ritual is joined to the story by the commandments and by the poetry that is absorbed into the ritual. The poetry is a kind of prayer, an expression of thanks for the redemption, not simply a narration. Consequently, the "Song of the Sea" gained a prominent place in the daily morning prayers; on Passover it is accorded an even more celebrated and central position because this is its express time. What may be understood from all this is that the holiday ceremonies deliberately refrain from presenting the entire story as it is formulated in the Torah. The ceremonies draw elements of commandment, symbol, poetry, and, naturally, the story from the Bible, but not by *reconstructing* their own version.

What does this mean? A study of the *Haggadah* is useful in dealing with the question. Despite everything mentioned above, the story in the Book of Exodus does hold a central place in the holiday and its rituals. Though not read in its entirety, the story is quoted and it is related to from various aspects, and it is taken for granted that all those seated at the seder table have heard it and learned it thoroughly. Certainly anyone who had not studied the story would understand very little from what is written in the *Haggadah*, and if required to add anything of his or her own to the conversation about the exodus from Egypt, would not be able to pass muster. Since this is so, a study of the concepts of the Passover holiday may begin with an examination of the world view expressed in the biblical narrative. How is slavery interpreted? How is freedom interpreted? How is the destiny of a people who began its journey with this event viewed?

The story of the Children of Israel's descent to Egypt and their fate there is the background to the explanation of slavery. The Children of Israel went down to Egypt of their own free will, as free men, to save themselves from famine. They were lured to Egypt by Joseph, one of their own. Joseph's rise to power in Egypt opens an avenue of rescue for them. Later a new king, "who knew not Joseph," arose and enslaved the Children of Israel. But close examination of the story reveals that the king who did not know Joseph merely brought the process that Joseph had started to its conclusion. Joseph was the one who established conditions of enslavement by exploiting to the fullest Egypt's attributes as the cradle of a mighty civilization.

Egypt is a typical river civilization. Like Mesopotamia, it enjoys the conditions for establishing a great civilization. The Nile River, traversing the land, ensures prosperity in a manner that seems to give the inhabitants a sense of assurance; they hold the basic conditions for their survival in their hands. Such river countries attract peoples; great civilizations develop there since, after all, great civilizations are the fruit of men's labor to achieve control over the conditions of existence and thus be spared fear of the future. A review of the stories in the Book of Genesis confirms that the Bible presents this aspiration as an element of pagan life. Paganism is a belief in the internal powers of nature, powers that man would like to control, or at least bend in his favor, so as to safeguard himself from the anxiety involved in a human existence that is not satisfied with what nature itself gives to man. But there is a problem here: as human civilization develops, there is a commensurate rise in the requirements that enable the actual viability of that civilization which is striving to ensure man's existence and welfare. As a result, fear of the future is not nullified; on the contrary, it grows stronger, and often what seemed secure and in man's control is revealed as illusory. In river countries, as well, drought strikes.

How does pagan culture deal with such adversity? Pagan ritual is, perhaps, part of the solution. The forces of nature upon which man's existence hangs, his welfare and future—these are the very gods. The Nile is one of the gods of Egypt, and its worship is meant to ensure, through magic means of coercion, that the gods will do their part for man's good. The story of Joseph, however, offers another way, possibly based on a different, non-pagan point of view; but at that time, under those circumstances, it leads idolatry to a conclusion that touches not only upon what lies between man and nature, but also upon what lies between man and man. Joseph's proposal to Pharaoh on how to safeguard the nation against famine is rational; it is not based on pagan magic. It is a plan that rejects the fateful terror that lies over Pharaoh from his dream. This may be the reason that Pharaoh and his magicians were unable (did not want?) to interpret a dream that seems so transparent. Grounded in their pagan point of view, they did not know how to protect themselves from the future implied in it.

Not so Joseph. His belief that God spoke in the dream not only enabled him to interpret the dream, but also to offer a way by which catastrophe could be avoided. Though drought cannot be controlled, its consequences can be averted. Thus Joseph, appointed to rule in Pharaoh's name, builds granaries and stores grain. During the famine years he distributes to the needy from the bounty that has been collected during the good years. So far so good; from this point on he must make a choice. The bounty could be distributed to the needy according to their need until the drought years pass, but Joseph does not distribute food—he sells it. When the people's money runs out, they pay with their property, their cattle, and their land. When the years of famine end, all the lands in Egypt, except for those that belonged to the priests, are the property of Pharaoh, and all the inhabitants of Egypt, except the priests, are his slaves. The Egyptians, including Joseph's brothers, are grateful for his enterprise. They do not remember that they themselves grew the grain stored in the granaries, and that they actually built those same granaries. They forego their freedom in order to guarantee future security. It is in this manner that the pagan way of life achieves its end. What began as a desire to control the natural conditions of existence ends in the ruling class taking control of all the population. Egypt is turned into a house of bondage, and when a new king "who knew not Joseph" comes to power, the regime that Joseph instituted becomes binding on the Children of Israel as well.

Two important things may be learned from this complex affair. First, the unavoidable outcome of a way of life based on the aspiration to control the sources of existence is a regime of slavery. The desire to control nature culminates in the control of the same people whose labor produces from nature more than nature gives of itself. Accordingly, it is elementary: to control nature, one who aspires to rule must control the laborers and capitalize on their enterprise. Thus Pharaoh became the *god* of Egypt as an absolute ruler over a kingdom of slaves. Soon, however, it becomes clear that he who rules a kingdom of slaves is himself not a free man. He is enslaved by the craving to rule and by his own image. Second, like Abraham who began his path by abandoning a pagan culture for freedom and its dangers, so the people of Israel began their journey as a people at the heart of a pagan culture whose regime had taken its own principles to their logical conclusion. In other words, the exodus from Egyptian slavery was intended to establish a different culture, based on a different principle. Not a culture of slavery, but a culture of freedom.

What, then, is freedom? How is it different, in effect, from the principle of slavery? If the exodus from Egypt was meant to establish a different culture, then the story of the exodus will interpret the nature of freedom.

A LIFE PLAN FOR FREEDOM

The exodus from slavery to freedom began when the state of slavery reached a degree of suffering that was unbearable. Pharaoh's edict to slaughter "every son" born to Israel was the climax as well as the most difficult ordeal that the Children of Israel experienced. The effort to resist the terrible decree despite the danger involved is the onset of freedom. Symbolically, Moses' birth is related to it—his rescue, rearing, and the return to his people as leader, law-giver, and conductor to freedom. What does the resistance to the decree of annihilation, hopeless as it seems, testify to? To the faith that survived despite all that had happened. Without faith people do not have children under such circumstances; without faith the child would not have been hidden and sent upon the water. In fact, Yocheved entrusts the child to God after doing everything in her power to save him. It is God who saves Moses, but it is significant that the medium of his rescue is a spark of humanity created "in God's image" not extinguished even in the house of Pharaoh, the quintessence of the despotic regime. Pharaoh's daughter takes pity on the child, and rescues and raises him. Consequently the reality that surrounds him as he matures is not one of enslavement, like that of his brothers, but the reality of a *free* man in the accepted sense of the word. He is accustomed to the ways of government from within the center of power itself. It is from here that he must go out to his brothers to become acquainted with the ways of slavery, to understand the condition of slavery not only as the relationship between enslaver and enslaved, but also as the mentality of those who are enslaved.

That, after all, is the twofold lesson of his first two encounters with slavery—the Egyptian who beats the slave, immediately followed by the two Hebrew slaves who are fighting, and the accusation hurled in his face after killing the Egyptian. He learns that slavery is not only the domain of evil and violent men who dominate those who are vulnerable; it is also the lost sense of justice in the heart of the weak, for the weak man—finding himself in an advantageous position—imitates the actions of the tyrant. Moses, born and rescued due to a remnant of faith preserved in his forefathers' hearts and by virtue of a vestige of humanity that remained at the heart of the regime, learns that slavery has myriad different faces that are, nevertheless, similar to each other within enslavers and enslaved. When his period of education ends and he returns to take his place as the leader of the people, he is aware that his role will not end with dislodging the people from under the yoke of bondage. In fact, only then does his duty and obligation begin to educate the people to a life of freedom, to establish an agenda for life; that is, to establish an entire culture that is different from the culture of slavery—a life plan for freedom.

Moses' appearance before his people and Pharaoh, the ten plagues brought upon Egypt, Pharaoh's refusal and final surrender, the affair of the prideful departure, Pharaoh's change of mind and pursuit of the Children of Israel, the parting of the sea and drowning of Pharaoh's army before Israel's eyes—from beginning to end the narrative does not appear to scientific researchers of history as a historical story. Scientists may say that there could be a *seed* of historical verity in the wondrous story. The Children of Israel were slaves in Egypt and, on a background of unclear political circumstances, they succeeded in revolting and escaping; or perhaps they were expelled by Pharaoh and left to wander in the desert? The historical facts are undoubtedly different than those described in the Book of Exodus. A researcher is likely to present this argument and, as far as he is concerned, he may be correct.

But the Book of Exodus is engaging as Passover's constitutive story, and as such the search must be for its underlying truth; that is, the meaning that it imparts to the history of the people of Israel. Nor does it apply only to the founding event of Jewish peoplehood, its importance is central to the history of the people of Israel from then on through every generation that has celebrated Passover as an act of testimony. In other words, the exodus story must be treated as the story of Genesis was in the attempt to understand Sabbath and Rosh HaShanah. This is the beginning of a historical story, a beginning that is not *historical* in the scientific sense. It can be said that the biblical narrator does not suppose that he is relating events as they happened; he has other, more important intentions. He is trying to uncover the significance of the events that took place for all time, not solely for that period.

The exodus story is the pattern upon which everything that occurs in the winding history of the Jewish people should be interpreted. As the story of the Creation testifies to Nature as it must invariably be, so the story in the Book of Exodus testifies to the history of the people of Israel as it invariably is. For this purpose, the event was fashioned from historical materials in such a way that it is carried in the memory of the people as a pre-eminent monument that rises above the inclines and declines of the historical course. In every age, in every situation, the people can look to this landmark and find their way by it. Indeed, with this as the objective, the story could be built around the elements of early ritual described earlier, reinterpreting them. Instead of a pagan myth describing the cycle of life in nature, there is a mythos that embodies a historical enterprise.

When Moses contends with Pharaoh, he does so as a prophet. A messenger of his God, he opposes a king who represents a pagan system upon which his kingdom is based. It is a radical confrontation between the biblical sense of faith and pagan belief. Idea opposes idea, knowledge opposes knowledge, strength opposes strength. It is important to note that idolatry is not described as a worthless affair, lacking truth or dignity of its own. On the contrary, the victory over Pharaoh is no small matter. The gradual unfolding of the story reveals the power of the defeated side and the consistency of its system. Only when the entire system is exposed and its power—not lacking in splendor—is fully exhausted, is it crushed by a greater power.

Naturally, such a description expresses an educational propensity. People about to embark on the path of freedom must know the source of the power that enslaved them because only by knowing its source can they understand its limits and find the courage to oppose it and free themselves. Idolatry is not an illusion or a mere fallacy; its real source of power is a truth of sorts. On a personal level, the confrontation is expressed in the encounter between the prophet's daring and the king's intransigence. Moses' audacity is remarkable: alone he confronts the powerful king and his ministers, without fear for his life; it is a testimony to the strength of his faith. But one should not make light of the will power that is revealed in the king's resolve when he is faced with the plagues; he does not yield until, finally, he breaks. Nor should the Egyptian government be underestimated. It is an effective system, and the science of their wise men accords them a certain measure of control over the forces of nature. This is the basis of the government's power. Those who are enslaved know it from experience and they are conditioned to viewing the regime as a power that cannot be overcome. As long as they see the regime in this light, they will never be free of it.

Pharaoh represents the idea of dominion; he represents human striving for absolute sovereignty. In its extreme form this striving reaches self-deification, and Pharaoh indeed presumes to be a god. As a god, he does not recognize the God of the Hebrews whose name indicates that

He is the sovereign of a world that He created. "Who is the Lord, that I should obey Him to let Israel go? I know not the Lord, neither will I let Israel go" (Exodus 5:2). In fact, at that point, he really does not yet know the Lord; in other words, Pharaoh has not yet experienced the supernatural power of the God of the Hebrews. But even after he is struck by plague after plague and *knows* the Lord, he still does not yield. On the contrary, the overt challenge presented by Moses forces him to refuse, to stubbornly persist because Moses pronounces his demand as a command to the king that he recognize the true Sovereign and deny his own sovereignty, the underlying tenet of his kingdom. Step by step, Pharaoh is pressed into overcoming what is humane in himself, ignoring the limits of his ability, playing the sovereign who does not give in to a superior authority. This presumption is the trap that Moses lays at his feet, and he is caught in it to his own undoing. Initially his scribes say to him, "This is the finger of God" (Exodus 8:15), but precisely because it is the finger of God he does not recoil; he must prove that his will is greater. His prestige as king is at stake. To capitulate would be an admission that his reign is based on a false presumption.

From this point on the story continues as a classic tragedy, though it is described from the perspective of a believer who does not share the tragic hero's assessment of reality. Nonetheless, the believer understands very well how the hero assesses the situation, and how he must behave as long as he adheres to his assessment. If one looks at matters through Pharaoh's eyes, then he is a godly king who meets up with blind fate and battles his destiny to prove his godly sovereignty. From Moses' point of view this is a profound error. Pharaoh imputes to himself a sovereignty that he does not possess and thereby denies himself the same measure of freedom possessed by a man who knows that he is but man. Pharaoh could choose the correct way; he could do what God commands him to do, find his freedom, and break out of the cycle of his *fate*. But to do that he would have to admit that he is a mere mortal with limited powers. Having become enslaved by the idea of sovereignty, this is the very notion that he is not willing to concede. In other words, what seems to be freedom to Pharaoh, Moses regards as enslavement that turns man into a victim of his *fate*, and what is truly fatal is man's persistence in not acknowledging his mortal limits.

Yet Pharaoh's humanity does not disappear at once. From time to time it tragically and ridiculously reappears from the depth of his suffering. When a plague strikes, Pharaoh cries out in pain and shows a willingness to yield, yet when the plague is removed he recants. He appears to admit that he is not a god, but when he comes back to *himself* he denies it. He has his reasons. Even after the plague is withdrawn such an admission would undermine the basic assumption of his kingdom and he cannot allow this. It could be said that the pagan system of the Egyptian kingdom is the fate of the king; this, paradoxically, is the reason he cannot recant though he sees his kingdom going down in ruins. Even at the cost of its destruction, he insists on its principle. "And Pharaoh's servants said unto him, How long shall this man be a snare unto us? Let the men go, that they may serve the Lord their God: knowest thou not yet that Egypt is destroyed?" (Ibid. 10:7). Pharaoh's slaves now see the correct choice their ruler could make.

But the king—even if he sees it as they do—cannot yield. Particularly at this moment the quality of humanity is totally closed to him. Is his behavior incomprehensible? It is all too human. At this stage, it is understandable that admission would be a total surrender of his prestige. At an earlier stage he could have acknowledged a superior authority without entirely foregoing his independence as a ruler; such an admission made on the verge of total collapse would simply be that of a loser. His slaves, who beg him to yield, would be the first to see him that way. Perhaps at that moment Moses would have viewed the king's capitulation differently. In his eyes, Pharaoh's surrender to save Egypt would be a manifestation of true human courage, but it would be the courage of a believer. Certainly Pharaoh cannot envision himself as Moses does. He perceives himself as his slaves do; he is therefore pressed to save his prestige even at the cost of his kingdom. He drives Moses away so that he need not constantly see before him the escape route he cannot take except at the price of admitting failure. He continues to maintain his position.

Only when calamity strikes that which he holds dearer than anything else, his son, does Pharaoh react from the last depths of his buried humanity, and relent. He lets the people go. His power is broken. But submission at this stage does not express a change in the king's way of thinking for immediately after the Children of Israel have gone, Pharaoh rises up to deny the significance of his surrender, leading his army in a chase after them. The story does not end with a change in the pagan view of Pharaoh and his people, but with their death by drowning in the Red Sea. Incapable of internal change, established paganism is destroyed when it meets with a superior power.

This is the drama that illustrates the structural inevitability in the notion of pagan sovereignty. Based on man's enslavement to his impulses, initially it appears to be a declaration of independence; shortly, however, it runs up against the limits of human ability and identifies these limits as fate. Thus the ruler who confronts his fate cannot see an escape alternative open to him, which would be expressed in the ability to yield. As the biblical interpretation views it, Pharaoh embodies the principle of both the strength and inevitable destruction of paganism.

Moses' role is parallel and opposite to Pharaoh's. In contradistinction to Pharaoh, Moses presents himself as human in everything he does. He does not presume to have superhuman attributes. He does not presume to rule but presents a different power to Pharaoh, a triumphant power—the spiritual power of a believer. The audacity to stand—again and again—before Pharaoh and his advisors, vulnerable and exposed, and state his case in unbending persistence despite the king's growing wrath—this boldness is a supreme manifestation of faith. In a certain sense this bold exploit is Moses' most noble deed. By standing before Pharaoh he frees his people from slavery. If Pharaoh knew not God beforehand, and if the people had forgotten His greatness, then both Pharaoh and the people now learn of the Lord, not only from the plagues but from the testimony given by Moses through his incredible daring.

Such courage is based on the fact that God sent him and is with him. This certainty comes out of Moses' belief, belief in its primary biblical meaning. God rules the world with justice. According to that justice, the Children of Israel, enslaved and tortured through no fault of their own, are worthy of salvation. But justice is not revealed in the actions of men if they do not prepare themselves for it. Faith, which expresses itself in a readiness to act assured of the moral justice of the action, is an internal condition for the revelation of God's leadership and providence through justice. This is Moses' charge. Having overcome hesitation and accepted the responsibility upon himself, he goes out to the people to rekindle their dying faith. How? By the example of faith. When he accepts the role at the scene of the burning bush, a surprising certainty is revealed within him. If his first steps are still hesitant, it stems from the realization of the additional suffering his intervention with Pharaoh will cause his people. He is not afraid for himself.

The danger that Moses faced was real. Killing him would surely be the first thought to cross the mind of a ruler such as Pharaoh, and his words toward the end of the story indicate that the thought had crossed his mind. At the height of his despair Pharaoh says what he had refrained from saying till then, "Get thee from me, take heed to thyself, see my face no more; for in the day thou seest my face thou shalt die" (Ibid. 10:28).

Moses' answer is a display of his confidence, "Thou hast spoken well; I will see thy face no more" (Ibid. 10:29). This is not the acceptance of a decree but a simple statement of fact. Moses knows that there is no longer any need to see Pharaoh. If the king has dared to say what he had refrained from saying all along, then he is on the verge of breaking. His fate is sealed. The truth of this becomes clear in an understanding of why Pharaoh held back from injuring Moses. Had he been stripped of his ability to do so? The biblical story does not say that; certainly Moses did not present himself to Pharaoh as having supernatural powers.

Following Moses' words, unnatural events do take place, but Moses explicitly avoids giving the impression that he is causing them. He only announces their occurrence and subsequently calls for their cancellation; there is nothing superhuman in him. He remains a vulnerable man who is well within immediate reach of the ruler. Actually, killing Moses is the easiest thing that Pharaoh could do. Why does he hold back? The only possible answer is an emotional one. Pharaoh recoils from the human power revealed in Moses, from the spirited confidence and the unwavering courage that demonstrates Moses' solid faith. Pharaoh senses that Moses knows something that is not known to him. There is a riddle in Moses, a riddle of spiritual power in the face of which Pharaoh feels impotent. The challenge that Moses presents incites Pharaoh to prove that he, and not the God of the Hebrews, is ruler in his kingdom.

Hence, unknowingly, he virtually makes Moses his judge. And during Moses' first appearance before Pharaoh and his scribes, Pharaoh becomes entangled in the surprising contest. All the events now occur as a kind of argument between Pharaoh and Moses, in the presence of the scribes and the people of Egypt, over the question of who the sovereign is—the God of the Hebrews or Pharaoh? Pharaoh needs Moses to prove that he is the winner; if he kills Moses, what does he gain? Moses is not proposing himself as sovereign or as one who is invulnerable, only as a man whose faith cannot be thwarted. Undermining this faith would be Pharaoh's victory before his scribes and his people; killing Moses would be an admission of his failure and Moses' victory because, even in death, Moses would have demonstrated the strength of his belief. And this is confirmed by a close examination of Pharaoh's last words. There is no point in making threats since from the beginning Moses knew the sort of danger he was getting himself into. What is actually expressed in Pharaoh's threats is his fear that he might not resist his urge to kill Moses, thereby confirming his weakness as a man who can no longer control his actions.

Moses understands that the threat represents the threshold of breakdown. Pharaoh will not hold out much longer.

Perhaps Pharaoh's dread of harming the captive Moses is the greatest wonder of all those that occur in the story of the exodus though, from another aspect, it is not so much a wonder as the manifestation of a complex human trait. This is the story's delicate center of gravity: the ongoing struggle in the heart of man who stands at the crossroads between faith and a presumption to control his own destiny. The story intends to prove that in this struggle the moral power of the believer overcomes the sovereign power whose anchor is in nature. This is the significance of the overt miracles revealed in the narrative. The unnatural events, such as the advent and cessation of plagues at the times indicated by Moses and Aaron, and the parting of the Red Sea before the Children of Israel, are proof that God who executes justice overcomes the powers of nature that are the gods of Egypt.

Egypt depends on the Nile, which is the source of her wealth and power, yet the plagues change the river into a source of pestilence; its waters turn into blood and spew forth frogs; the earth of Egypt gives forth lice; the sun, moon, and stars darken; the desert winds bring locusts, the rain descends as a curse of hail and not as a blessing—all the powers that Egypt worships as gods bring affliction instead of blessing. It is a validation that the power to do good or evil neither originated with the gods nor was it ever in their possession. God the Creator rules them, and by His will they perform, both for bad and for good; that is, as punishment for sins and as reward for good deeds. The covert wisdom of Egyptian scribes presumes to control the powers of nature. They "do with their enchantments." The biblical story does not deny a certain measure of human control over the forces of nature but it mocks this ability when it presumes to be something more. The scribes of Egypt have no control over their "wonders." Instead of preventing the plague, they augment it. The conclusion is simply that the scribes have no control over their actions; on the contrary, the actions control them. Not so the miracles that occur on Moses' testimony. (Again, Moses is painstaking not to ascribe them to himself. His task is only to testify and point to God as the Source of everything that is happening.) These miracles signify total control, the ability to bend everything that happens in nature to moral purposes. Accordingly, the moral law stands above natural forces.

So truth prevails over pagan falsehood; the triumph of this truth and its place in the consciousness of the people are prerequisites for their departure to freedom. Only if the Children of Israel believe this, if they trust what morally ought to be—which God assures—and do not recoil from the frightening power rooted in nature, only then will they be free. Moses knows well what is waiting for him along the road. The people, who have been freed by God's manifest victory over Pharaoh, have not yet internalized the truth embodied in the victory. Slavery as an inner emotional reality is still unduly prevalent. They cannot be free until they are no longer shackled, and the process of freeing themselves is a long one, replete with failures. The process continued in the desert, during the period of settling the land, during the period of the monarchy, and through the exiles that followed. It continues "in every generation" to this day. This is the enduring value of the story, the value of Passover as a renewing enterprise that educates the Jewish people toward its future in the light of past memory.

THE *HAGGADAH*—LIFE DRAMATIZING ITSELF

From the biblical story that rises monument-like above the history of the people, we return to the way in which the recurring holiday reflects the primary and singular memory. The holiday rituals do not reconstruct the story of the Exodus as it is narrated in the Bible. If there is a seed of *reconstruction* then it lies in reconstructing the ritual setting of the night before departure. On this night, Jews assemble to once again experience the ancient event. Here there is indeed the setting for re-experiencing, or reconstructing; that is, there is a ritual, which is a play of sorts that casts all the participants in particular roles. Examined from this point of view, one could say that the *Haggadah* is a literary work that belongs to the genre of drama. It is also obvious that this is a unique kind of drama, different from classical drama and its developments.

A literary and experiential phenomenon presents itself, which raises an interesting problem. Ancient and traditional Jewish literatures never developed the poetic form of drama, nor did they absorb it from their surroundings. There are drama-like chapters in some works (such as the Book of Job in the Bible), but drama as a literary form, not to mention the enacted drama, never found a place in Jewish literature. Even in the modern era this genre has been late developing, and original Hebrew drama does not compete with translated plays from foreign literatures. What is the meaning of this phenomenon? Historical research is important here because it sheds light on a fundamental difference in the formation of Hebrew holidays as compared to earlier pagan nature festivals.

The drama is a literary form that developed under the inspiration of the pagan myth and first functioned within the framework of pagan ritual. The Torah, both written and oral, fought all forms of pagan ritual so that drama was forbidden as being part of paganism. This prohibition was valid as long as there was a direct link between the drama and its enactment, and the pagan myth and its ensuing rituals. It was still valid when Christianity embraced the dramatic play, once again as part of its ritual or as an ennoblement of its ritual. Only when *secular* drama began to form, at the beginning of the Renaissance, could the Jews employ this literary style. But still further investigation is needed regarding the connection between myth and pagan ritual—especially in ancient Greece—and drama. Is it an accidental historic fact, or is it an intrinsic link? Naturally one can find drama that is not directly connected with either myth or ritual but paganism's reliance on drama, which gives concrete form to the myth lying at its core, is fundamental.

Pagan ritual seeks to demonstrate to its followers the direct presence of its gods; it strives to have pagan worshippers participate in the story and deeds of the gods. A narrative couched in the past tense is not enough. Myth is renewed within the life cycle of nature, reflecting reality that reoccurs again and again. Like nature, the interpreting myth is always relevant, and this relevance requires demonstration. Pagan ritual therefore has need of all the arts that fashion reality through mimesis: painting, sculpture, music, dance, and above all drama—integrating them all— since in drama the myth *seemingly* happens in real life. The drama presents the myth as a concrete reality and the worshipper can participate in what occurs and feel how his worship affects the reality that surrounds him. This fundamental connection between drama and pagan ritual is the reason that drama was rejected by Jewish ritual; all of which make it clear why the epic of the Book of Exodus was not transformed from a story in past tense to a play in the present tense. If the Children of Israel had enacted the story of the exodus from Egypt and reconstructed it as a play, as the Christians do with the story of Christmas, they would have abrogated the historic interpretation that was given to a nature festival, and in this form brought it back to a pagan perception.

The Jewish faith, however, also has rituals. These were deliberately purified of any pagan element, and none of them contain anything similar to the dramatic reconstruction of a myth. Yet ritual is an occasion for the direct expression of experience through symbols and such expression is a play of sorts. There is no ritual without an element of acting, and there is no acting without an element of drama. This was apparent in the performance of ritual sacrifice, which is a chain of symbolic acts that demonstrate man's bearing toward God, and an inducement to God to relate to man. The same is true of the prayers that accompanied the sacrifices and subsequently were offered in their stead. How did Jewish ritual sacrifices and prayers differ from pagan ritual in terms of form? The answer, which comes out of the comparison, is the key to understanding another kind of drama, fundamentally different from classical drama and its theatrical development to this day; a drama of which the Passover seder is the most complete and well-developed representative.

The rituals of sacrifice—even more the prayers—do not wrest man away from the concrete level of his life, do not transfer him into a fictional reality fashioned by means of idyllic imitation. The Jewish worshipper remains on the plane of his real life. He stands inside the sphere of daily experience and raises his eyes to heaven. From the plane of human life, he strains to relate to the spiritual sphere above him but he does not *dramatize* the sphere in order to bring it down to himself. This becomes obvious when the typical atmosphere of a synagogue is compared with that of a church. A synagogue may be ornate, uplifting, or inspiring but it does not create an architectural environment that is unconnected to ordinary human surroundings, and it does not devise a level of total reality that is fashioned through imitation by art. The *play* in the Passover seder is different from classical drama in the same manner. It does not take place on a stage, and it contains no imitation or reconstruction. It does not remove its participants from the usual context of their personality, time, or location. It could be said that it is a play that is not a real play but is life dramatizing itself.

"IN EVERY GENERATION . . ."

The Passover *Haggadah* was not written all at once. It *accumulated* over many generations and, even though it was canonized at certain stages through copying and then in print, it has been open to additions and changes in various localities and religious movements. Yet the *Haggadah* maintains a *halakhic* framework, which strives to unify while at the same time interpreting the commandments regarding Passover in the Torah. Moreover, though it does encourage and guide the augmented story through its style and direction of thought, the *Haggadah* is not intended for reading as a given since "whoever dwells at length on retelling the story of the exodus is praiseworthy." The *Haggadah* is a formulated text that organizes the liberty given to those who participate in its framework; in this sense it would be correct to regard it as a *play* intended to be enacted. Who are the *actors?* Family members and guests who gather at the table. Each one of them takes on the role intended for him according to his personal station among those assembled. The father has the role of the father. The mother, the role of the mother; the sons, the part of the sons; and the guests, that of the guests. Together they also form the *chorus* that intervenes in the enacted *plot* at appropriate moments. The text does not have an exact division of readings according to roles except for the part of the father as head of the seder, and the role of the sons at the beginning. The parts are allocated on the strength of custom in the community or congregation, habit in families, and the initiative of individuals who know how to integrate their innovations without disrupting custom and habit. In any event, the *Haggadah* itself and its accompanying tradition contain minimal but sufficient instructions, and a family that functions with a mutual will may produce a laudable presentation. It is certainly not a play in the classical meaning.

First of all, it is not a play that is created by *imitating* a plane of reality separate from the daily life of the *actors*. Consider first the content. As opposed to classical drama, the content is not a reconstruction of myth; it is drawn from history. And though in the Bible this history has crystallized into a mythos, the *Haggadah* does not present the historical mythos; it does not even retell it. It tells *of* it; that is, the people who have gathered tell of an event that occurred in order to understand the meaning that it has for their lives. During the seder the past is not rehearsed as though it was occurring at the moment. Those seated at the table are in their authentic present. This is true of the physical backdrop (no changes are made in the house) and of the actions that embody the experience of the exodus: blessing the wine, eating the matzah, bitter herbs, roasted shank bone, etc., the meal, and the singing. The *Haggadah* declares, "In every generation each person must regard himself as though he personally left Egypt." Every participant in the seder must view himself as though he is leaving Egypt in his own present. He is not acting out the event that took place but interpreting the events of his own time according to this event. The experience of time in the drama is therefore completely realistic. The participants remember the past, imagine the hoped-for future, and live the present in between memory and hope with great intensity. What is enacted is a festive elevation of the present by a festive elevation of the past, which enables the remembers/hopers to understand and know.

The same is true of the attitude of the *actors* toward their roles. The role and the social image of its performer are identical. People do not change their appearance, they do not dress in costume, and they do not display an ideal character of themselves. Though they make an effort to appear at their best, it is a festive elevation, nothing more. An important point must be emphasized: the seder does not strive for artistic perfection. It could even be said that striving for artistic perfection in executing the readings and singing would ruin the effect. At the seder one ought not demonstrate a stage personality that is in perfect control of its performance. The *art* of the participant at the seder is the art of joyous, direct speech that is demonstrative of his usual personality. In what is said as well, he must strive for an interpretation in which he is shown at his best but without bedecking himself with sayings of others that could not have come from his own heart.

TOGETHERNESS AS A DEMONSTRATION OF FREEDOM

Does the seder play have a story or a plot line? It is difficult to answer the question if the concept of plot is still that of an ordinary play. There is no real story. However, there is a plot in the sense of a chain of situations that develop out of each other, whose purpose is the experiencing of the exodus as a contemporary event. The situations are as follows: the gathering of participants at the table; the blessing of the wine and pointing out the symbols of the exodus that lie on the table in front of everyone; the son's questions suggested by the sight of the special symbols for "this night's" meal; the father's response; the involvement of those attending who are drawn after the father, and the story of the exodus from Egypt; the meal; the blessing and singing of the *hallel*; and, finally, planned game songs connected to the exodus in a folk spirit of childlike fun. In other words, the ending is not a dramatic climax but a gradual relaxation that brings those attending back to the prosaic and usual circumstances of a meal from the festive ritual elevation that reached its peak with the recitation of the prayers of praise for miracles. The exodus from Egypt continues to be experienced throughout all these situations. It must be remembered that this is a *reconstruction* of the last night of bondage, already on the threshold of redemption. Therefore at the seder those who are present actually undergo an experience of threshold—the memory of slavery as something that was, the hope of redemption as something that will be. One's gaze is transferred from the past to the future in order to experience the present of those who have been redeemed. This is the story of this night.

The midpoint, the present that is forming between the story that confronts it from the past and the hope that gazes out to the future, is the meal. It is as well the central ritual that is reminiscent of the Passover offering. How does a simple meal becomes a rite that contains elements of a play? How does the meal become the symbolic experiencing of an intended meaning? The fact that the meal is not only the exercise of eating but a disciplined and significant act is first and foremost expressed in the manner in which one sits at the table. It is not accidental; it is a special, well-staged manner of sitting—a reclining. There is nuance in the matter: he who reclines is not performing an instinctive or habitual action; he must pay attention to his mode of sitting. So he is already performing for himself and for those who are assembled with him, and the performance is accompanied by an explanation. Staged sitting in a certain manner has a reason and a purpose. Reclining is the distinctive way that free men sat, a way that demonstrated trusting equanimity, prosperity, and enlightenment among relatives and friends, equal in their honor and status as free men.

In order to understand the meaning of reclining, mention should be made of the source from which it was drawn. In its outward form, the seder meal imitates the feasts of the Hellenic aristocracy during the Second Commonwealth. This was the dining style of free men who knew their status and wished to broadcast it to others. When they sit down to the Passover meal, the Jewish people as well demonstrate their status as "sons of kings" who sit together, equal in their honor. With this bearing they demonstrate their freedom, and experience it. However, if this is an intended imitation whose aim is to emphasize meaning, then the meal itself interprets freedom in the traditional way. People who eat together experience a deep feeling of unity. The common meal establishes fraternity, it symbolizes the natural unity of a family. In the story of exodus one finds that assembling into a family gathering embodies the burgeoning feeling of freedom. The terror stalking outside is gone; the Jews can be with and for themselves, can provide each other with the feeling of confident protection that enables the individual to grow and find his destiny. The experience of freedom is therefore the experience of togetherness, that same experience that a wise woman from

Shunam expressed to the prophet Elisha in the words "I dwell among mine own people" (Kings II, 4:13). The meal embodies genuine freedom in the feeling of togetherness, independence, security, and mutual protection that the family gives its members. Brothers sitting together in conscious awareness of the value of togetherness is a demonstration of freedom.

FREEDOM IN LEARNING

Reclining around the table and dining together is indeed the framework of the entire seder. From the start, activity is directed toward the meal; and therefore the gathering opens with the blessing over the wine, washing the hands, and splitting the matzah to emphasize the *bread of affliction* that symbolizes the evening's significance. Before the meal is actually served, however, the participants turn their gaze to the past and pull it toward the present. The activity begins in a particular way with a drama and continues in the special manner of a story that is also a play of sorts. The story of the exodus unfolds as the symbols displayed on the table are pointed out and their intention noted—first the matzah, then the rest of the symbols. In this fashion the story of the exodus from Egypt is linked to the nature and purpose of the symbols; as it is written in the *Haggadah*, "Rabbi Gamliel would say, 'Whoever has not said these three things at Passover has not fulfilled his duty. What are they? Passover, matzah, and bitter herbs.'" So by means of the symbols that lie on the table, the past is noted and pulled into the future. The act of pointing to the symbols and announcing their purpose joins with the conscious experiencing of freedom during the meal. On this evening no activity is left to chance. Every act, and its meaning, is deliberately intended. Here then is another interpretation of freedom: action that expresses the doer's intent, action that has significance and is not a result of coercion or of life's circumstances. Freedom, in its internal sense, is choice out of intention and action with purpose. When the participants inform each other of the purpose of their sitting together and the purpose of all their actions at that hour, free men are demonstrating their freedom.

After the symbols are pointed out and interpreted, the story of the exodus continues. The fact that the story is linked to the symbols that are now lying in front of the reclining diners explains what was stated earlier: the *Haggadah* does not reconstruct the story of the exodus from Egypt, it does not present it as though it were happening now. What is happening now belongs to the real present, and the past is pulled toward the real present as its interpretation. The story of the exodus is not recounted; it is the departure from Egypt that is dealt with. In other words, present circumstances are learned about from the ancient story. The conclusions drawn orient the present in light of the ancient story toward the future to which the story alludes and toward which it orients. If there is an element of drama in the story, it is the drama dialogue. It is not a spontaneous discussion, even though the element of spontaneity enlivens it; rather, it is carried out in a certain style and according to a certain pattern. In its style and pattern, it maintains the link of continuity between the past and the present. In this way, tradition is revealed in its role of bridging the link.

How should the *Haggadah* be recited? One can read it paragraph after paragraph like an actor who repeats a text written for him. This is not the *Haggadah*'s intention. Indeed, the *Haggadah* is nothing so much as it is a form of study. Those who simply repeat are not discussing, they are reciting, and such speech does not have the same degree of vitality as is possible in dialogue. Only if the reader adheres to the model in order to imitate it and present his renewing thoughts on the basis of its pattern, only then will he enliven the monologue and develop a lively conversation. This is a personal, guided dialogue. Anchored in tradition, it creates space for free expression within the tradition so that the individual can present his knowledge, talent, judgment, and experience. Hence the unfinished character of the *Haggadah*. It is a creation that is intended to grow, to change, to renew itself, and to be added to. Every generation finds its own version according to its way; each individual at every seder interprets it according to his particular times. Once again there is the experiencing of freedom, this time freedom in learning, a continuing openness to innovation, change, and growth not by withdrawal from the continuum of the past, but within it as a vital continuity.

MIDRASH AND DIALOGUE

We come now to an examination of the detailed structure of the dialogue, beginning with its form, which is of a typical *midrash* that incorporates the idea of continuity and renewal by drawing the past toward the future. *Midrash* means the study of texts; that is, an interpretation that searches for what lies beyond the apparent, immediate meaning of a text; additional content, an *innovation* that serves as an illuminating lesson that will provide answers to contemporary questions. The *midrash* assumes that the truth to which the text testifies is not relevant only for the past. There is eternal truth, but in every generation it has new aspects that relate to new conditions and questions. The seeker is therefore searching the text for the truth as it relates to him and his generation. In this fashion he draws what was discovered in the past, along with its forms of expression, down to his own time creating a literary–stylistic bridge between eras. From the very first statements uttered at the seder, the participants enter a *midrash* dialogue. The *Haggadah* begins, after the ritual opening of the meal, with the dramatization of the commandment on which it is based. The action of the *midrash* is immediately recognizable. The commandment from the Torah is "to tell" the sons; that is, to tell them the story of the exodus from Egypt and transmit it from generation to generation. Close examination of this commandment, which the Torah repeats four times with slight variations, shows that the Torah expects the sons to ask their parents questions that relate to the Passover commandments, and the *Haggadah's* bidding is fulfilled by answering these questions. The *Haggadah* opens with a ritual enactment of the question and answer, a custom in which there is a conspicuous element of drama. The young children learn their parts, and at the right moment they play themselves in the role of the asking child. The father also takes on a role. He plays the part of the father who responds according to a set formula. The contemporary ritual is thereby fastened onto the ancient pattern, enlivening it. The child learns to ask about the things that seemingly surprise him regarding the dining customs of this special night. What is the meaning of these changes? *"Mah nishtanah halailah hazeh mikol haleilot?"*

What is the father's answer? Scrutinizing closely, the observer learns how, by way of the conventional pattern, one enters into a dialogue that is continuously being renewed by the ongoing *midrash*: "We were slaves unto Pharaoh in Egypt and God took us out with a strong hand and an outstretched arm, and had not God, Blessed be He, taken our forefathers out of Egypt, then we and our children would still be slaves unto Pharaoh in Egypt. So that even if we were all wise, all venerable, and all learned in the Torah, it would be incumbent upon us to recite the exodus from Egypt, and whoever deals at length with the exodus from Egypt is praiseworthy." Is this the answer to the child's four questions? It would appear so. The father explains to the child that all the special customs on this night—eating matzah and bitter herbs, dipping twice, and reclining while sitting—are connected with the celebrated event of the exodus from Egypt, that we follow these customs that remind us of the event because it touches upon our lives today as well. If our forefathers had not left Egypt, we too would be slaves. Therefore, at that hour we gained our freedom as well. But a study of the particulars of the four questions shows that the answer avoids the main issue.

What is the meaning of these customs? How are they connected with the exodus from Egypt? The reply above does not provide a direct answer. What is the main purpose of the dialogue? The father reminds the participants that the ancient event touches everyone, obligating all those present to retell the story of the exodus, and to do it as well as it can be done. In other words, instead of direct answers to the questions, the father suggests that the participants begin with the *midrash*, which is the dialogue about the exodus. What knowledge can be gained from closely examining the meaning of these customs, which, after all, is the essence of the commandment? When the first part of the *Haggadah* ends, the children have received full and detailed answers to all their questions. But along with these answers to their explicit questions there are many other answers to additional queries, and still other, deeper questions may have arisen, which require discussion not only of the texts that the *Haggadah* is studying, but also of the *midrashim* of the *Haggadah*. The opening, therefore, is not a closed *scene* in a ritual enactment; it is open. The first discussion stimulates the continuation of the *midrashic* conversation and directs it.

Directing the homiletic conversation and assigning the participants to their roles is truly the concern of those homilies that follow the father's answer. The affair of the Sages who were seated in B'nai Brak is intended to show the extent of "dealing with the exodus at length," and Rabbi Elazar Ben Azaria's words from the text teach the great importance of remembering the exodus. This memory should accompany a Jew all his life. This memory is the guarantee that the hope of redemption in the days of the Messiah will come true. But the main guidelines for the continuation of the homiletic dialogue in the ritual drama that embodies the intended association between the participants can be found in the wonderful *midrash*, "Blessed is God, blessed is He Who gave the Torah to His people, Israel, blessed is He. The Torah spoke of four sons." This ceremonious opening of the *midrash* indicates its special importance. This is a discussion of the manner in which the Torah is transmitted from generation to generation in the story of the exodus from Egypt. How is the Torah transmitted time and again? The *midrash* uncovers new insights in the Torah during the lively dialogue between fathers and sons.

This is a typical *midrash*. It is based on the fact that the commandment to "tell" the sons is mentioned in the Torah four times with slight variations. The first time in the Book of Exodus (12:26–27), "And it shall come to pass, when your children shall say unto you, What mean ye by this service? That ye shall say, It is the sacrifice of the Lord's passover." The second time in the Book of Exodus (13:8), "And thou shalt show thy son in that day, saying, This is done because of that which the Lord did unto me when I came forth out of Egypt." The third time, again in the Book of Exodus (13:14), "And it shall be when thy son asketh thee in time to come, saying, What is this? that thou shalt say unto him, By strength of hand the Lord brought us out from Egypt, from the house of bondage." And finally in the Book of Deuteronomy (6:20–21), "And when thy son asketh thee in time to come, saying, What mean the testimonies, and the statutes, and the judgments, which the Lord our God hath commanded you? Then thou shalt say unto thy son, We were Pharaoh's bondsmen in Egypt." One of the principles of midrash is that the Torah does not repeat itself in order to say the same thing. If something is said four times, then each time it is mentioned something special is being said, which requires investigation and study. This is the formal, literary starting point of the midrash, clearly well focused since it is directly connected to the opening statements: the sons ask, the father responds in the version from the Book of Deuteronomy; the midrash on the four sons is then presented to interpret the scene and direct its continuation.

The midrashic solution to the question of why the commandment is repeated four times is "The Torah speaks of four sons" and, to the extent that it is possible, a distinction between the sons according to the character of each is made according to the text. Most conspicuous is the identity of the one who does not know how to ask. The version in the Book of Exodus 13:8 does not indicate a previous question, but calls for an initiative on the part of the father. "And thou shalt show thy son in that day, saying." The other versions mention a previous awakening to ask a question on the part of the sons, and the differences among the wise son, the wicked one, and the simple one are fashioned according to the shape of the question. It is clear that the typology "the wise, the wicked, the simple, and the one who knows not how to ask" presents a thought pattern that has its own internal logic.

The wise son, who studies the texts, documents a well-formulated position in the tradition of the Torah concerning the education of sons. The first general assumption, which is at the basis of this point of view, is formulated in the sentence, "The Torah speaks of four sons." The process of education must be appropriate to the character and spiritual qualities of each son. An educational dialogue whose aim is to instill historic memory and the commandments connected with it should not be a uniform formula, but a plan aimed at each son according to his abilities—his age, character, and spiritual inclinations. It is preferable to wait until the son himself asks—the result of an earlier awakening—thereby expressing the desire and willingness to listen. In this way, not only is motivation to learn insured but so is proper guidance since the question reveals to the intelligent respondent what the questioner's spiritual position is, and what answer would be suitable.

However, what is said about "the one who knows not how to ask" applies to some extent to all the sons: "You ask for him." The expectation that the sons will take the initiative in asking does not mean passivity on the part of the father/educator. He must initiate a situation that will raise the question, and if the son still does not know what to ask—"ask for him." How? By explicitly pointing out the action that should have stimulated him to ask the questions himself. (The *opening* question is in the text: "*This* is done because of that which the Lord did unto me." *This* refers to the symbols of the Passover meal laid out before the participants.) To summarize: the commandment to "tell" is imposed on the father/educator. He must initiate a situation that makes possible the proper fulfillment of the commandment, for this the son's previous awakening is valuable. Willingness to listen is a condition for discussion, and it guides the form, level, and content of the answer.

What can be learned from the distinction among the wise son, the wicked one, and the simple one? Clearly the *midrash* does not claim that the three types are identical, though there is a basis for the interpretation that asserts that every child in Israel goes through all four stages while growing up. First he does not know how to ask, then he is simple, then he is wicked and tries to emphasize his individuality and rebels against the authority of his parents and teachers, and finally—only at the end—is he wise. In any event, it is obvious that the *midrash* points to the wise son as being the ideal figure, and it is plain that the ideal of the wise son is measured in comparison to the other figures. In examining what differentiates the wise son from the others, it becomes clear that his figure is created not only by the difference between him and them, but also by a combination of their positive qualities. The simple son's negative quality is his lack of discernment and curiosity. His question—"What is this?"—is general and undefined.

Therefore, in order to draw his attention to the event's special quality, the answer he is given points to the most impressive general element in the story of the exodus, "With a strong hand God took us out of Egypt and the house of bondage." "A strong hand"—the great wonders unique to the exodus told in a straightforward, overt manner that the simple son can comprehend. But what awakens discerning,- curious thought? A critical attitude, one based on a certain reservation within the individual, an insistence on his independence and *sovereignty* against the authority of teachers and parents. Such a statement immediately underscores the simple son's positive quality. He trusts, he tends to accept lovingly what his parents and teachers tell him. It is an important, elemental quality. The educational point of view represented in the *midrash* under discussion maintains that it is not criticism that is the starting point of learning but the trust that a person places in the people who are responsible for his education. On the basis of that trust, discerning curious thought must be developed, thought that contains an element of critical independence, which is the most prominent feature in the make-up of the wicked son.

As opposed to the simple son, the wicked one emphasizes his individuality. This is how the *midrash* interprets the question: "What is the meaning of this service for you?" For you, but not for him. He places himself outside the pale; in other words, he repudiates the teaching authority that is trying to reach him through his parents and teachers. The wicked son's negative trait is that he undermines the elemental trust of the simple son. One should not, however, ignore the positive quality linked to it: his question is discerning. The reservation in it involves attention to special, unusual details in the order of the day's service.

The perfection in the ideal figure of the wise son is his combination of the positive traits of both the simple and the wicked sons. He trusts his parents and teachers. They are the ones that God taught all that he needs to know. Yet he emphasizes his individuality and asks discerning questions that will advance his knowledge and understanding. Unlike the simple son, he asks detailed, perceptive, and explicit questions: "What does the wise son say? He asks, 'What are the testimonies, statutes, and judgments which the Lord our God commanded you?'" Unlike the wicked son, he does not ask the questions in order to rebuff duties, but to receive answers. A practical question is one in which the criticism is anchored in previous trust that puts unquestioning value and importance on the matter being studied. It would therefore be correct to say that the combination of the positive qualities in the simple and wicked sons—found in the personality of the wise son—is also a corrective for their negative qualities. The trust is no longer spiritually passive; it is an active deliberate spiritual position. The inquisitive criticism is no longer destructive rebelliousness but becomes true spiritual study. The answers given in the *midrash* to both the wicked son and the wise one comprise this assessment.

The answer to the wicked son is meant to instruct him about the destructive nature of his resistance to the authority of a tradition that is directed toward him with love. He does not ask in order to get a straightforward answer but to highlight his critical individuality. The results are destructive from his point of view as well. One who puts himself beyond the pale remains lonely and does not get the essential attention by means of which society rescues the individual from his loneliness. In this way the wicked son is informed about the damaging implications of his position, true both for society and for the individual who places himself outside the pale.

The answer to the wise son is intended to enfold him into the very midst of the Torah discussion, which molds him within the community of Israel. Close examination shows that the answer to the wise son includes a great deal more than what is said in the Torah: "Then you should instruct him in all the laws of the Passover, also that after the *afikomen* no desert must be added." This does not appear in the Torah. It is taught in the Oral Law, which grows and is added to by each generation of Sages, those who have the same combination of qualities recognized in the figure of the wise son: trust and discipline, on the one hand; willingness and ability for independent revitalizing understanding, on the other. Looking at the educational guidelines expressed in this *midrash*, one recognizes the central role it has in fashioning the ritual/educational presentation on seder night. It is instruction through example of how two sides, destined to participate together in the story of the exodus, should ideally behave. The parents and the members of the older generation who are commanded to teach and transmit, and the sons who are enjoined to learn. The combination of continuity and innovation that creates the living tradition is embodied in the *midrash* itself in its form and content, and is given as a paradigm for the lively dialogue that will develop afterward.

Finally it may be added that the *midrash* about the four sons contains within it an educational viewpoint that was accepted among the Jewish people during a certain period. The Sages who fashioned the image of the *Haggadah* for generations to come stamped it with the mark of their educational and moral/religious outlook. Indeed, from this *midrash* one can understand not only the character of the *Haggadah* but also the thought patterns of the legends and the Oral Tradition during the period of the *Tanaim and Amoraim*. This was their understanding of how the heritage of the Torah should be transmitted as a living, developing legacy. There is clearly a great difference between their educational outlook and study methods, and the viewpoint and study of prophets from the First Commonwealth period. In general, it appears that during the Bible period, Passover was experienced differently than what has been fashioned in the *Haggadah*. The styles of both the narrative and study were different. The dialogue found in the *Haggadah* is, in any event, typical dialogue of the Sages who returned to the Torah out of the Oral Law, which was transmitted and created by them. Can contemporary dialogue imitate theirs? Can it continue with the same style, form, and conceptual content? It is doubtful whether this is the lesson that comes out of this *midrash*. On the contrary, the instruction is to engage in dialogue according to our own fashion, as long as continuity is preserved. The *midrash* in the *Haggadah* is the starting point. If, for example, it is understood as it was interpreted above, one proceeds through interpretation to a way of study that is acceptable in the contemporary period. As the Sages pulled the Bible toward themselves and drew from it according to their fashion, so both the Bible and the *midrash* are pulled forward, and the tradition renewed and sustained in a continuing story from generation to generation.

REDEMPTION BY THE GRACE OF GOD

The *midrash* on the four sons introduces the *seder* participants to the framework of the story and guides them through it. The actual story is told by the *midrash* that follows. A long *midrash*, it follows the establishment of the people from "Get thee out of thy country" till the descent to Egypt, and from the enslavement in Egypt and the stories of miracles and wonders till the exodus from Egypt and the parting of the Red Sea. Again, the *Haggadah* neither presents the story as it appears in the Bible nor does it not give it in full. Its circumscribed role is one of study, tracing the main conceptual motifs according to the Sages. In other words, this is an inquiry that draws lessons from ancient events—as seen by the Sages in their time—in answer to questions raised under contemporary circumstances.

What ideas in the biblical story did the *midrash* consider appropriate to emphasize? From the start of the *midrash* through its conclusion, the first notion that stands out is that the act of redemption was God's grace to His people, by grace and not by right. "In the beginning our ancestors were idol worshippers but now God has brought us closer to His service." The sentence is important not only because it opens the *midrash*, but because it joins together the entire cycle of time from the very beginning of the nation's existence, through the exodus from Egypt, to the period when the Sages sat and recounted the story of the exodus. The "now" in the sentence is the now of those who tell of the Egyptian exodus. It is present time, but it is a present that has continued from the time of the exodus. In what sense? In that sense of "bringing us closer to His service." This is the enduring legacy of the migration from slavery to freedom, given to the forefathers by grace and not by right since, after all, they worshipped idols. From here on the *midrash* lists the graces of God who kept His promise to the people of Israel and saved them from their enemies: "For it [the promise] stood our forefathers and us in good stead." Thus the *midrash* reconnects the early past with the present of those sitting at the *seder* table: "Not only was there one enemy who would have destroyed us, in every generation there are those who would destroy us but the Lord, blessed be He, saves us." The *midrash* story, even when it relates the terrible enslavement in Egypt, places the emphasis on God's grace, which was never withdrawn. Israel multiplied in captivity; through its suffering, Israel matured to become a people; from the depth of their enslavement they prepared for their union. "And I said to you in your blood shall you live, And I said to you in your blood shall you live." God Himself descends to rescue the people. This is complete grace, an expression of unconditional love.

The second idea, connected as it is to the first one, has already been mentioned but needs to be highlighted on its own: grace is also revealed in the suffering and torture of exile; in other words, not only salvation testifies to God's love for his people. Even in the depth of suffering and the agony of exile, one can find signs of grace; and, though a superficial examination of the circumstances of their life may seem to deny it, the people of Israel are never abandoned to their fate. This is the second conclusion that the Sages come to from the story of the Egyptian exodus.

The third lesson touches on a realization of the greatness of salvation that accompanied the signs and wonders. The *midrash* deliberates on the miracles at length. First it emphasizes that these signs and wonders testify to the fact that God Himself brought his people out of Egypt. No mediating power separated Him from His actions. "I and not an angel . . . I and not a seraph . . . I and not a messenger . . . I am the Lord, I and no other." Immediately afterward there is evidence that the plagues are a direct manifestation of His mighty hand, His outstretched arm, and monumental sureness, but subsequently there follows an amusing *midrashic* game concerning the number of plagues that came down on

Egypt. The sum grows until finally the ten plagues turn into fifty, with two hundred plagues on the sea.

It is not difficult to identify the emotional motivation expressed in this fancifulness. It is an elemental emotion, perhaps childish. If parallels are sought between it and the answer to the simple son's question ("With a mighty hand God took us out of Egypt from a house of bondage"), it is clear that these matters are intended mainly for children who respond to a righteous feeling of vengeance and are happy at its fulfillment. The degree of punishment suffered by Egypt should correspond to their cruel and wicked acts toward Israel, and when this expectation is answered, children ̃experience the palpable taste of redemption. God, as a father who defends his children, provides His people with protection, smotes their enemies as they deserve, and brings the people to freedom. The multiplying number of plagues excites the imagination of the listener, illustrating the wondrous dimensions of what occurred and its experiential significance. Joining the game of counting the plagues, one enters the very essence of heightened emotion at the moment of victory; it is then that the past materializes in the present.

Written during a period of national anxiety and enslavement, it is not difficult to infer which questions the writer sought answers to in his *midrash*. It is replete with the expectation of a great revenge and the hope that God who "hides His face" from the House of Israel will once again reveal Himself directly, not through a messenger, and will do what— under *natural* circumstances—seems unlikely. A strong desire is expressed to find a foothold for the hope, and it is found in the ongoing promise. But it seems it would be impossible to believe in the promise unless the *midrash* writer could say that now, in the midst of their suffering and enslavement, the people of Israel see themselves as though they themselves left Egypt; that is, something of the ancient salvation has not been lost. God's grace continues to accompany His people, even in captivity and exile. The opening idea of the *midrash* is that salvation is granted not by right but by grace—an expression of unconditional love. God loves His people and His grace is not lacking even when His people are suffering. The *midrash* writer experiences the manifestation of grace first and foremost because "God brought us closer to His service." The Lord is close to His people. The feeling of closeness is itself a feeling of salvation—to be with God, to feel His love.

Examining the matter, one finds this is also the feeling behind the childish glee in counting plagues. It is not only that God Himself acted without an intermediary but also the secure feeling of protection that extended over the people during the act of revenge. Only a lover revenges his loved one's agony in such a way. How is God's closeness preserved in this hour? Through worship; in keeping His commandments. In the sense of what was gained then, when the seder participants fulfill God's commandments and tell of the story of the exodus, they actually feel that they are close to God, gathered before Him on this night. The feeling in the present, therefore, strengthens the certainty that what occurred in the past is a sign of the future. The current enslavement, too, will pass, and the people will be redeemed.

The hymn that immediately follows the *midrash* summarizes it, carries on its main motif in a more concentrated, structured manner, and introduces the participants to the dramatic course of a redemptive experience. "How many ascents the Almighty has performed for us." Joining as one, the participants sing the hymn and are together as the hymn's use of the construction "we" articulates the inclusion of the individual into the community, and the inclusion of a particular community into all the generations of Israel. The poetic structure allows for common recital in what is, after all, a union of sorts to create a common pathway symbolized by the hymn's story line. "How many ascents the Almighty has performed for us." Reciting these lines, the participant rises with his people in these degrees of grace. Symbolically, the experience itself takes place during the singing. But what is the actual experience? Even as the *Haggadah* does not enact the story of the exodus from Egypt, neither does the hymn. It is satisfied with mentioning the main stages of the story: the departure, the plagues, the Egyptian exploitation, the parting of the Red Sea, the fulfillment of the people's needs in the desert, the manna, the Sabbath, the giving of the Torah, the entry into the Land of Israel. The singing enables a mutual sense of entering into a process of remembrance that portrays the mounting emotional experience in the exodus from enslavement.

Two elements comprise the structure of emotion in the departure for freedom. First, there is a delineation that brings to the foreground the enormity of the events. The hymn recounts the blessings one by one and thereby creates an explicit feeling of surfeit, which is the essence of grace. Second, there is a grading that leads upward in levels of importance, all the while emphasizing that it would be more than sufficient had there been only the first blessing alone. Everything that was given beyond freedom from enslavement is more than could have been expected. However so much was given after the first gift—not only in quantity but also in degree of importance. There is here, therefore, the emotional simulation of a common upward movement toward an apex of joy, every stage of which marks a feeling of grace and trust in the Benefactor.

What is the summit at the top of the mountain? The hymn ends with the building of the Temple "to atone for our sins." More than the final act, it is the value that imparts meaning to the entire path: "God has brought us closer to His service." In other words, redemption is the ability to live with God in His temple, or in the words of the Book of Psalms, "But it is good for me to draw near to God." Placing the hymn back in its time and place, one sees that the hymn's climax is the climax of the seder. The participants are fulfilling God's commandments by worshipping Him. Now they are experiencing His presence. Now they are redeemed. In this sense each person in every generation sees himself "as though he personally left Egypt." But not in this sense alone.

PAST AND FUTURE

The text that follows the hymn completes the cycle, closing the first part of the seder drama. The ending brings the participants back to the opening. The story began with the questions of the son, seemingly stimulated by the sight of the Passover symbols displayed on the table. The father did not answer the first question completely but expanded on what arose from the question in order to spark the story of the exodus. Answers to the direct questions have not yet been given. The father answers these questions as part of the Passover ritual at the onset of the meal, the main part of the festive occasion. He points to the symbol of the Passover sacrifice, to the matzah and the bitter herbs, and interprets their symbolic meaning and the memories related to them. In this way the context that imparts meaning to their common meal is brought to the consciousness of the participants, and the father ends with the words meant to direct the participants' enactment of themselves when the meal begins: "In every generation." It would appear that this unadorned, direct sentence and the symbols lying on the table acquire their full meaning only on the background of everything related to the exodus story. They are there not only as a remembrance of past events, but also so that their meaning is experienced in the present.

Before they start the meal, the participants sing the first part of the *hallel* psalms, a group of hymns from the Book of Psalms (113–118) that, by the time of the Talmudic sages, was intended for recitation to mark days on which miracles of redemption occurred. The theme of these psalms is praise of God for His leadership and forthright rule over the entire universe, the peoples of the world—especially the people of Israel—the fate of individuals, and the recitation of blessings and thanks for the favors bestowed upon His people. In singing the *hallel* as an acknowledgment of redemption, each generation again personally experiences the outcome of past events. The song pulses with a feeling of salvation.

In the context of discussing the structure of the *Haggadah*, it should be noted that the *hallel* hymns are divided into two sections. Two psalms are sung before the meal, "Praise, O ye servants of the Lord," which exalts God as ruling over all His people yet watching over each individual: "Who is like unto the Lord our God, who dwelleth on high, Who humbleth Himself to behold the things that are in heaven, and in the earth! He raiseth up the poor out of the dust and lifteth the needy out of the dunghill." The second, "When Israel went out of Egypt," touches especially on the miracle of redemption. This is the combination of a national experience of salvation that occurred in the past and a direct progression from the first part of the *Haggadah*. Not so the second part of the *hallel*, recited after the blessing over the food. In these psalms the gaze is turned toward the present and the future, though on the basis of what occurred in the past. In other words, these psalms give expression to the hope that becomes a certainty until, finally, thanks are given for the future as they are for the past.

It can easily be seen that in the first part of the *hallel* preceding the meal, a continuous turnabout is created. The gaze that was directed toward the past and pulled into the future begins to point directly to the present, and from the present it turns to the future. Even at the height of joy based on the element of grace and salvation that exists in the people because God brought them closer to His worship, one cannot ignore the proximity of a historical present that is far from redemption. Do the people of Israel need a new miracle of salvation that will take them from slavery to freedom? If the *Haggadah* did not contain any expression of a present actuality through the actuality of the past, there would be no place for the true expression of the participants' feelings in their own time. And indeed, after the meal and the blessing there is an obvious turn in the *Haggadah* toward the present within the context of a hoped-for future.

The turn toward the present occurs under dramatic circumstances. The participants pour Elijah's cup (the fifth cup of wine, which however is not drunk); they open the door to the night outside, stand and say: "Pour forth Thy wrath upon the peoples who do not know Thee, and upon the kingdoms which have not called upon Thy name. For they have consumed Jacob and laid his pleasant dwellings waste. Pour forth Thy fury upon them, and may Thy raging wrath overtake them. Pursue them in wrath, and destroy them utterly from under the heavèns of the Lord." This part of the seder has a double meaning. On the one hand, it carries the participants back to the primal happening on the night of the Plague of the First-born, on the verge of departure. It was a night of great revenge in which God's wrath came down upon the enemy that "devoured Jacob." It was also the night of the beginning of the redemption. Though the people were still in Egypt, the dreadful fear of their enslavers was gone. Openly they gathered together and prepared to leave. It is this feeling that is symbolized by opening the door to the outside and reciting, out loud, the expectation of revenge. Calling on Elijah is an indication of future redemption, since Elijah is its herald. However it is clear that, at one level, we are no longer speaking of that primal night, but of this night, a night of second and third exile. The terrible things said at this time describe the current exile, the contemporary enslavement, the yearning for revenge on enemies who now seek Israel's blood. This is a position taken within contemporary history, but out of the hope for a future redemption that becomes a certainty while being recited. Shaking off fear is the beginning of freedom that points to the future. In reference to this future, whose joy of salvation is already felt, the participants recite and sing the second part of the *hallel*.

In this second part of the *hallel*, the psalms describe the feelings of the persecuted, just man who trusts in God, the suffering and pain that is the lot of the faithful, the oppressed people who have kept their faith in the Lord. Here again there is a sense of the present by the participants in the seder. But the descriptions of suffering are not tendered to express despair. On the contrary, the prayers to God for justice and salvation turn into a certainty that presages a future redemption as though it were a reality that could be concretely known. In opposition to the fierce suffering there rises the great joy of those who are delivered by God, "I will praise Thee: for Thou hast heard me, and art become my salvation. The stone which the builders rejected is become the cornerstone. This is the Lord's doing; it is marvelous in our eyes. This is the day which the Lord hath made; we will rejoice and be glad in it." The confrontation between the future and the present now appears to be a thing of the past; in the second part, it is the confrontation between depths of suffering and the great salvation that characterizes all the psalms of the *hallel*. The *Haggadah* ends with praise and thanks not for salvation in the past but for a future redemption, and with the wish that is uttered as an unalterable truth, "Next year in a rebuilt Jerusalem."

To recapitulate: in both the light of memory and the light of hope, the exodus story in the *Haggadah* presents the participants in their own time and place as though they themselves left Egypt. In the light of memory, the *Haggadah* pulls the past toward the present and discovers a verity of salvation even in the harsh reality of an exiled, suffering people. The participants experience their freedom by sitting together as free men, among their people, to tell of what occurred and to worship God who saved them. In the light of hope, the *Haggadah* pulls the present into the future and finds a certainty of salvation for the depths of suffering that still exists. In this way the memory of the past is perceived as a guarantee of the hoped-for redemption in the future.

ENDING IN JOYFUL SONG

The end of the *Haggadah*—continuous singing from the grace over the meal through the closing of the seder with the "Next Year" wish—is an ascension to a climax of exhilaration. Yet a drama of this sort—which is not acted on stage in front of an audience but is one in which the participants enact their own reality—cannot end in a climax after which the participants seemingly plummet to the level of daily life. Even at the zenith there ought not be a quasi-artistic detachment between the reality of life and the experience that is formed by an imitation of it. Indeed such distancing does not occur during the seder. The regular daily life of home and family is in no way constrained; there is no attempt to hide it with scenery or acting. The dialogue and singing do not block the spontaneity that exists in the relationship between people who know each other well. If the festive singing pulls toward an intensification of emotions that is much higher than the usual level, then it is necessary that a return to the plane of ordinary life be a gradual one. And though neither fundamental or obligatory, this is the role played by the final part of the *Haggadah*. This segment is a kind of late addendum, seen by many as common folklore custom. Its addition to the printed *Haggadah*, however, not only made it an inseparable part of the seder's totality, but gave validity to the feeling that it is essential and that its omission would leave behind a confusing emptiness.

Though the seder cannot end in the manner of an artistic play—by expressing appreciation for the performance and leaving the theater—it also cannot end with the poetry of the *Haggadah* and proceed immediately to the prose of day-to-day relationships. There is a need for a moderating passage that continues the previous emotional and spiritual activity but modulates it, and in this way returns the participants to their ordinary interpersonal relationships. The last part of the *Haggadah* seems most suited to fill this purpose. Here are a collection of folk hymns, "Thus It Was At Midnight," "Adir Hu," "Echad Mi Yodeah?", "Had Gadya," and others. In terms of content, all the songs deal with motifs from the *Haggadah*, particularly the theme of God's concern for His people throughout their history. But now merriment takes the place of serious-ness. The element of fun is varied, from riddles that challenge the participants to solve them or demonstrate their knowledge of the sources, to folk chants that characterize all the tunes of "Had Gadya." While the children are excited, generally a relaxed atmosphere of levity is created, one of contentment and satisfaction. In this mood the participants retire from the seder table to rest or pursue the holiday's next activities.

EDUCATION AS THE AXIS OF THE *HAGGADAH*

This discussion of the substance of the Passover holiday has revolved around the idea of freedom as expressed both in the biblical story and in the *Haggadah*. The special literary character of the *Haggadah* has been revealed as a *play* in which the idea of freedom is developed, not only through story and study, but through experience that integrates story and study in a *plot* that passes through a series of situations; this *plot* is guided by rather specific instructions though considerable room is left for innovation and spontaneity. The meaning of this special literary form will be examined subsequently not only in terms of its place in the Passover holiday but also its place in the framework of Jewish traditional life.

To summarize what was mentioned above about the *Haggadah* as a drama intended for enactment: first, the difference was discerned between a play in its customary theatrical meaning and the seder presentation. Not all the characteristics of a theatrical play are found in the seder drama—there is no differentiation between audience and stage, no scenery, no precise script to be repeated word for word, no reconstruction of a plot as though what happened in the past is actually occurring at the moment of presentation, and no striving for a perfect performance. The seder participants act themselves as themselves. They present their personalities as they are in their family roles, in their own time and place.

They do not create an *ideal* fictive reality nor do they reconstruct an event that took place in the past. The *plot* that continues in their own time is the form through which they experience the early event as an occurrence whose meaning radiates from the past to their own time, and they interpret that time as it is. In this manner, they experience together an hour of trusting expectation in redemption and freedom from slavery. In their behavior with and toward each other they personify and interpret freedom as a willing response to commandments, as the conscious bequeathing of a tradition that maintains a people and guides it to its destiny, as a gathering of brothers under the beneficence of closeness in expectation of redemption. In this manner they know freedom not only as an uplifting idea but as a lived experience. This is, therefore, a singular play form that develops out of a perception of ritual that is unique to the Bible.

This last sentence should be examined more closely. Earlier in the discussion about the *Haggadah* as a literary form the claim was made that traditional Jewish literature did not develop drama of its own accord, that this form was rejected when it was introduced by Hellenistic culture. This rejection resulted not only from the apparent link between classical Greek drama and myth, and pagan worship, but also because the Sages sensed in the essence of this form—which establishes a perfect image—the indispensable sense of the pagan world's reality. Yet the Sages did not refrain from acceding to a great many influences from Greek culture as many of the details in the seder indicate. The style of reclining, after all, is the reclining style of Greek free men at their meals. Would it be far off course to suggest regarding the entire seder night as the reinterpretation of an element of ritual drama by a brilliant adaptation and internalization of this element into a traditional viewpoint and way of life; not the creation of an imaginary reality alongside something tangible or something above it, but an artistic fashioning of the actual way of life?

The *Haggadah* is a special and unique composition in Jewish liturgy. However, as a play-like form of family or community behavior it is neither unique nor unusual. Traditional worship in the synagogue forms a rich internal background to the *Haggadah*. Several examples were discussed in previous chapters—reading the Torah on the Sabbath and holidays, "Kol Nidrei" and the confessional prayers on Yom Kippur, the *hakafot* on Sukkot and Shmini Atzeret, and many others. The general trend in the *halakhah* is to establish a detailed way of life for the individual within his family and community, primarily in matters of home and synagogue. In these two focal areas the commandments are guidelines for a delineated life-style that imparts an intentioned meaning to every act. Therefore, it would not be an exaggeration to describe the *halakhah* as a kind of art that endeavors to fashion its forms into the process of how people live their lives. The *halakhah* does indeed rise to a level of symbolic self-identification on the Sabbath and the holidays as it attempts to achieve perfection using the significance of symbols to fashion the behavior of ordinary society. In this sense, the scope and richness of the *Haggadah* is simply the most complete and impressive example of a phenomenon that characterizes all the holidays.

Assuming the above is true, the following conclusion can be drawn. If there is an art in the *halakhah* that unifies the holidays of the Jewish people and the prayers that fill the holidays with content, then it is the art of education. Educational artistry presents models of required behavior that individuals and communities adapt for themselves to give their lives direction, to raise the consciousness of the meaning and purpose toward which tradition educates. Holiday climax situations are filled to bursting and complete, experienced for their own sake, thereby renewing the consciousness of direction that the *halakhah* strives to impart to the individual and the community in its daily life.

The Passover *Haggadah* is an outstanding educational drama. If it has an artistically fashioned plot, then it is the dramatization of an educational activity that is fully conscious of its role. The *Haggadah* not only unifies and directs the educational process, it also inspires the knowledge that it is important to educate and considers the correct ways of engaging in the educational process. In other words, the *Haggadah* educates the educators to be educators. It motivates them to educate and be educated, and teaches them how to play these roles properly. In this way education achieves the status of an activity in its own right, embodying the highest values in its very existence. To be a parent means to be an educator, to be a son means to be educated, and both roles are replete with self-education. What meaning does education have as an activity in its own right? In the context of Passover this question appears to have an answer that is both elementary and obvious: without education there is no people; without education there is no continuity of tradition; without education there is no ongoing road toward a goal; without education there is no humanity. Without education there is no freedom, because freedom is the manifestation of human will directed by values. In this sense education is a role that has its own meaning. It is a commandment that forms a basis for the creation of a sphere of human existence. Perhaps this explains why the *Haggadah*, in particular, attained the most complete formal design in Jewish liturgy. Raising the consciousness of education's importance created the need to dramatize the educational procedure itself within the scope of a uniform and complete framework.

Why was Passover, in particular, chosen to emphasize the importance of the educational process? The question has a simple *halakhic* answer— Jews were commanded by the Torah to engage in education on Passover. "And you shall instruct your son," is said on Passover. An explicit reason was also found in the Torah. The first to be saved on Passover were the sons, and the holiday is celebrated pre-eminently for their sake. This, however, is still within the range of a formal reply, though the substantive answer is inherent in it. Passover is intended to be a reminder of the event in which the nation was established and the people were granted independent life. The educational role transmits this memory and embodies within itself the continuity of the people's existence and self-awareness that is their freedom. Therefore, if on Passover we are commanded not only to think about the idea of freedom but to live it as a renewing event in the life of the nation as long as the people exist and are faithful to their destiny, then education is the basis on which to begin. Thus we come to education as the conceptual and literary axis of the *Haggadah* drama and all the other meanings imparted to the idea of freedom are based on it.

TEN

THE CONFRONTATION WITH SUFFERING (HOLOCAUST MEMORIAL DAY AND TISHA B'AV)

THE PROBLEM OF SUFFERING

During the fifty-day harvest period between Passover and Shavuot, the practice of counting the omer creates an unbroken link between these two pilgrimage festivals. It would seem therefore appropriate to discuss Shavuot at this juncture. Yet it is precisely during this period that a number of memorial days make their appearance. Because they are a departure in both content and form from earlier holidays that were shaped by the Sages, these days—which mark the Jewish historical experience in the modern era—present a discontinuity. The problematics of adapting contemporary holidays to the pattern of traditional holidays became evident earlier in discussions on Purim and Hanukkah. A different adaptation to the flow of history and, one might say, a different consciousness of orientation in time is required for Memorial Day for Holocaust Martyrs and Heroes, and Memorial Day for Fallen Soldiers that precedes Israel Independence Day. (Jerusalem Day might be added despite the fact that it has not yet acquired a distinctive pattern.)

This new dimension in the Jewish people's perception of time bears looking into. To understand what the older tradition (that embraced the year as an unbroken round) has in common with subsequent segments

superimposed on it, a comparison is needed between contemporary
memorial days and older special days that have a thematic resemblance to
them. To that end Holocaust Day is examined through a comparison to
Tisha B'Av (particularly apt because of a controversial proposal to combine
the two days), and Independence Day in relation to Hanukkah and
Passover, holidays that also speak of the aspiration to national independence. Using this approach, Tisha B'Av has been moved from its place in
the yearly cycle to begin the discussion. But one can also support
beginning with Tisha B'Av from the standpoint of tradition because the
destruction of the Temple is first commemorated on the tenth day of
Tevet, earlier in the calendar than either Purim or Passover.

What then is the experiential and theoretical theme unique to such
national days of mourning as the Tenth of Tevet, Tisha B'Av, and
Holocaust Day? Ostensibly they imply a motif of national calamities that
parallels the themes of miracles and redemptions throughout Jewish
history marked on such holidays as Sukkot, Hanukkah, Purim, and
Passover. Since historical consciousness is central to the cultural structure
of the Jewish people, the problem of repeated failure as a constant shadow
is undoubtedly an existential as well as a spiritual/religious dilemma of the
first magnitude. In light of their self-image as the chosen people, how do
Jews understand devastations such as the destruction of a Temple; loss of
a homeland; the anguish of wandering, pogroms, and exterminations?
Close examination of the question finds this paradox at the core of
holidays that recall miracles and redemptions. No less than the miracle of
redemption, enslavement—both as memory and actual experience—is a
central motif in the Passover Haggadah. The same applies to Hanukkah
and Purim. The notion of martyrdom is part and parcel of the traditional
Hanukkah celebration as is the motif of exile and its danger at Purim.
Consequently, through the content and form of these holidays, the
philosophical and existential answers advanced by the Sages to the
question of failures in the history of the chosen people are alluded to quite
broadly. It is true that the particular motif of national days of mourning is
associated with the problem of failure and the problem of God who averts
His face from his people, but the emphasis is on mourning as an
existential experience. If there is a central dilemma in this, it is both moral
and religious; it is the problem of suffering—the problem of human
suffering in general, the specific problem of the righteous person's
suffering, and the particular suffering of the Jewish people because of its
purpose and goal.

SUFFERING AS A TEST OF FAITH

To understand this subject one must first confront the moral roots of the phenomenon of human suffering as conceived of in biblical and homiletic literature. Morality is a qualitative component in the phenomenon of suffering; from this aspect man alone is seen as having a volitional, conscious affinity to morality. In the biblical and midrashic construct, man is a suffering creature, a judgment that stems essentially from his faith. Of course, suffering first and foremost afflicts man's physical existence: deprivation of physical needs; pain which comes from physical injury; illness, which impairs the body's functioning; and death, which utterly destroys the body. These are tangible modes of suffering. In all these ways man suffers like all animals, perhaps even plants. But there is one essential trait in which man is alone as a suffering creature. By virtue of his consciousness of self, which attends pain and fear of death, the pain and death are accompanied by an awareness of pain and an awareness of death. They are also accompanied by an awareness of the threat to "ego" and "self" inherent in pain for the person who possesses consciousness. This threat to the singular, core personality of an individual upsets the innocent certainty so essential to the consciousness of his ego, and to the absolute value and absolute validity of his existence.

It is this dimension that defines suffering as a human phenomena, and it is here that the moral problem inherent in suffering is exposed. As a physical reaction, pain is simply a physical fact possessing certain physical causes; as such it raises no moral quandaries. The dilemma arises only if pain is seen as having a purposeful meaning; that is, as a phenomena that expresses the volitional relationship of someone who possesses will and consciousness toward someone else with a will and consciousness. It is here that the question arises, why? It is here that the hurt person in his initial innocence, conscious of his pain and aware that pain endangers his awareness of self, asks this question. And it is this question that raises pain to the plane of suffering. When the individual regards himself as an "ego" possessed of will and consciousness, he projects this same feeling onto the environment that raised the consciousness of ego within him, and he is likely to regard the environment's *attitude* to him as intentional and willed. Should support disappear, innocence cease, the provision of his needs end, and an element of pain appear, he will, at the outset, regard these circumstances as treatment directed against him. Out of the utter naivete with which he takes himself for granted, he asks, why? Why should anyone wish him harm? What explanation is there for the pain that threatens him?

Man's tears, his cries of pain, are not merely an indication that he feels pain. They are also a protest. The more childlike is his experience of the environment, that is, his inability to differentiate among various kinds of suffering and how to prevent many of them, the more sweeping and absolute his protest will be. Indeed, in the deepest core of his being, the adult remains forever a child who takes his existence for granted so that, in principle, any threat to his person is unjustified. He reacts with tears, outcries, fury. He protests vigorously against the pain and as long as he remains without a comforting answer to the question, "why?"—in the consciousness of the sufferer the dimension of moral outrage takes a greater toll than the measure of physical injury.

Thus the description of the initial reaction to pain is also the answer of the child within the adult. Nonetheless, adulthood is informed by the fruits of repeated experience. The child learns to distinguish between the unwilled hurt of natural forces and injuries inflicted by people, between unconscious injuries and intentional hurts, between reciprocal deeds and intentional malice. Though not all pain elicits the same degree of suffering of the kind bound up with moral protest, a sense of hurt does seep through to the deepest recesses of the individual, a protest at the hurt itself as opposed to all concrete experience of pain. If he believes that his very existence is not *accidental* but a given, that there is something teleological that explains his existence as he is as well as the conditions for his existence, then the question of pain, disease, and death as man's fate arises as a moral question. Of course a more far-reaching thought is possible. The maturing person will tell himself that his surroundings, and his existence as a given within those surroundings, do not infer any purpose. These are simply physical facts which should be accepted at face value. If this is the case, the question "Why?" is ludicrous. Even when one person injures another, it should be attributed to the functioning of natural impulses and nothing more. If a person wishes to avoid pain he must try, in so far as possible, to control the forces surrounding him and the factors necessary for his existence and welfare. If he understands his environment and the laws that govern it and his activity, he can avoid a major portion of things that cause pain. Of course he cannot overcome all of them, but he must keep trying and should avoid attributing morality to elements of suffering. In this way, he at least saves himself moral suffering since the injuries are not, after all, directed at him. He is merely an accidental object of a natural process.

The important question is whether man can overcome a response of moral protest that wells up from his self-consciousness as a creature possessed of will and intent, having a uniquely autonomous focus. Even a decision not to grant pain moral significance is a decision that has moral ramifications. No one is indifferent to his own suffering so that if one denies the moral significance of pain, in effect it is denied others as well. In other words, for the sake of his own consummate benefit, an individual denies the moral obligation he has vis-à-vis his surroundings because he sees that such recognition cannot deliver him from suffering. Nonetheless, there is a moral consequence to a psychological stance that repudiates suffering's moral meaning; thus a person who maintains such a stance—according to the biblical view this is basically a pagan approach—is a creature who suffers in the moral sense. In any case, it would be considered an attempt to solve the problem through denial. This is not the position of someone who, in the biblical view, is a believer. If belief calls for reliance on a moral orientation that explains the existence of both the world and mankind, and if man is required to do that which is good so that he may benefit, then the moral problem inherent in suffering is that of a primary and most severe trial of faith as the broadest approach to reality.

Recall Job, the pre-eminent figure in biblical literature who symbolizes this. Job is a figure who believes in his suffering, a suffering expressed in terrible physical pain. Yet, as one after another these ills befall him, and he feels surprise at the pain, he does not utter a cry of protest. The sufferer's protest arises only when, out of his pain, the moral question is illuminated; it is this which gives him no rest—"Why?" It is the "Why?" of a man who knows that at the very core of his unique existence he is blameless; this suffering transcends pain. Job was a wholehearted and upright man, a man who feared God and shunned evil. All his days, he strove to do only that which was good and to atone even for the sins of those near him in order to forestall any evil design. In the depths of his soul, he knows he is not to blame; therefore, he cannot understand why all this pain has befallen him. The fact that despite all his deeds, he experiences ferocious pain is the worst agony he suffers. He confronts his Creator with the kind of revolt that only a believer can achieve. He insists on knowing why. As long as he does not receive a comforting answer— and for anyone who believes in his own virtue, comfort is the only answer to the question—he cannot be a believer. Out of the depths of his anguish he learns that only as a believer is his question a question, and only a believer can receive an answer. So we come to the heart of the problem.

DISCOVERING RENEWAL IN PAIN

The answer Job hears out of the whirlwind in effect casts him as someone who asks everyman's question, from the standpoint of being a creature of nature. Job was a wholehearted and upright man, but can everyone be considered wholehearted and upright? Not by the criteria of other men. From the Book of Job it is clear that neither did his companions regard him in this light—not his own companions; all the less so by strangers. It is in his own eyes, as in God's, that he is wholehearted and upright. This is what makes it possible to say wholehearted and upright about all men. Within the recesses of his heart, every man knows that he is blameless; a priori he is wholehearted. Thus he was created, a creature of his Creator. Regarding man's suffering, it is neither the malice of others nor their intentional acts that injures man. He is the victim of natural forces, or of unbridled human drives that at times are part and parcel of unrestrained natural forces: storm, robbery, illness. It is true that everything descends on Job at once, but this can be regarded as a literary exaggeration. Job suffers the pain that befalls human beings by virtue of their being human, transient beings in a human body. These are the circumstances of life—loss of property, death of family, illness, misunderstandings by friends and colleagues. Job voices his protest at having been predestined to all these by the very fact of his having been created, even though he is blameless from conception. What answer does he get?

The first answer comes from his companions. It is an answer one could presumably have expected from believers: you have sinned before God and suffering is your punishment. Man is a sinful creature. Is there any upright person who does not transgress? In God's view, can anyone be wholehearted and upright? Apparently there is some truth in the words of the companions. Guilt is a constant that accompanies man's weakness. Sin is unavoidable, and when suffering descends on man, he can regard it as suffering for his sin. Still, Job does not accept the conventional answer of the believers, and indeed, at the end of the debate God justifies Job's refusal when He says to the companions, "For you have not spoken the thing that is right about Me as My servant Job has." And He blames them in the same measure that they blamed Job. Theirs is a moral fault—they did not stand by Job in his sorrow as companions should. Does Job know that there is no one in the world who is fully upright, who does not sin? Is it pride that is heard in his protest? God's confirmation that Job spoke "correctly" about Him testifies to the fact that the protest is not a cry of pride but of pain—genuine pain. At such a time, the suffering person is blameless; the blame for sins that derive from human weakness cannot serve as an answer to his question. To speak of blame in a time of anguish is to mislead; to turn a blind eye to another's suffering, instead of empathizing. Had the companions experienced suffering with Job, they would have had pity. If they had had pity, they would not have spoken of guilt; instead they would have found words or deeds that could offer comfort.

And that is what Job expects from his companions, not excuses that he himself knows. He seeks a consoling answer, an answer that eases pain and reinstates the sufferer into the circle of life so that—beyond the pain—he can feel the sure force of life, the reassuring sensation of life that pulsates within him. Job is not seeking either theological or moral rationalizations. He wants a return to the sense of life's worthwhileness that has been taken from him, the worthwhileness of existence. In its absence he finds death preferable to life. If good is the prevailing thrust of creation, in the midst of his terrible suffering he wants to feel that good. Instead of this, Job's companions extend words that reek of obtuseness. They add suffering to suffering.

Does Job ever get a consoling answer? From the narrative's ending we learn that he actually does. In a straightforward manner, the consoling answer is found as God reinstates everything that had been taken from Job—property, sons, health. Can this be considered consolation for the terrible suffering? Here, too, it seems warranted to regard such an ending as a literary device that alludes to something else. After the suffering, Job returns to the circle of life and discovers the wondrous power of renewal that it holds. Perhaps it is this discovery that is the real consoling truth that transcends suffering. How can that be? The answer requires a further examination of the Book of Job. A different answer is sounded much earlier in Job's words as in a forceful outburst, seemingly at the height of his suffering, he says the following remarkable words.

> Oh that my words were now written!
> Oh that they were inscribed in a book!
> That with an iron pen and lead
> They were graven in the rock forever!
> But as for me, I know that my Redeemer liveth,

And that He will witness at the last upon the dust;
And when after my skin is destroyed,
Then without my flesh shall I see God;
Whom I, even I, shall see for myself,
And mine eyes shall behold, and not another's.

                                              Job 19:23–27

When these words are correctly understood, one discovers the consoling truth found in faith itself. In the midst of suffering, Job suddenly
knows that God is with him, yet there is neither an explanation nor
rationalization of suffering. Perhaps it is knowledge acquired through
suffering, after it has been experienced. In this sense, belief itself answers
the doubt in the heart of the believer. Is there any substance to this
answer? Is it sufficient that faith does indeed strengthen man's ability to
withstand the pain which put belief in question? What will sustain faith?
On what is it based? Even when he finds the truth within himself, Job is
not placated. He reaches the height of overcoming doubt only to
plummet once again into his cycle of uncertainty. Tranquility and solace
is found only after the ultimate answer where the respondent is God
Himself.

As the narrative takes shape, still another aspect claims the reader's
attention. Beyond the words enunciated in the peroration that closes the
book, the significant fact is that God Himself is the ultimate respondent.
And that which Job had envisioned much earlier is realized in this fact:
"But as for me I know that my Redeemer liveth . . . And that he will
witness at the last upon the dust." God hears and responds, He is thus
revealed to Job which is something of a consoling truth. The essence of
the truth, however, is interpreted only when God's words are perceived as
the revelation of God's attitude toward man. Once again God does not
give a direct answer to Job's questions. Does not Job already know that
God created the world and rules it and that the spectacles of Nature are
marvelous? Can this be the answer to the moral injustice of human
suffering? At best, what is posited is that because of his intellectual
limitations, man does not fully understand God's intentions and wondrous
deeds; when such a claim is offered in the context of a theological debate,
it is certainly far from a consoling truth. It does not remove the
substantive sense of injustice experienced by the sufferer.

Then what is the answer? Apparently only the fact that it is God who
utters it explains its content. Job is told, or more precisely he is made to
perceive, that the wonders of Nature are God's presence around him and

near him. The wonders of Nature are the word of God; they are a concretization of His beneficent will, and His love, which sustains the world; that Job's suffering is part of the cycle of these forces, which sustain the universe. You do not understand Him just as you do not understand these forces that overwhelm you. But you should sense them around you and within you. They are mightier than suffering. They renew life and even now they return you to life through suffering. No, these thoughts are not intended to make excuses for suffering, and because of this Job's rebellion is understandable. His incisive question is in place. It is unavoidable. Job spoke appropriately. As a sufferer he could not have felt differently, so that even if he overcame his rebellion, the rebellion would have moiled in the recesses of his mind. It is better for Job to confront directly the core of suffering—the sense of moral injustice inherent in pain—because it is precisely through this confrontation that he will again feel the consoling truth that surpasses him, rejuvenates his powers, and, despite all, reinstates him into life and its affirmation.

Once he feels God's love streaming toward him through these powers, he will also feel renewed belief and experience it as a great will to live. Then he can accept the answer that appears as something beyond a simplistic, tangible experience: man will not be able to understand the fact of suffering, in and of itself, unless he sees creation as a totality—as God sees it—embraced in the cycle of perpetually renewed creation. Therefore, despite affliction, man ought to believe that God's love sustains the world and sustains man within it; indeed, this is how things ought to be even though they are more sublime than our understanding permits.

Job's travail, it should be remembered, is described at the beginning of the book as a "trial." God, as it were, tries Job to see if his belief will withstand the trial of suffering. By story's end one finds that Job endured the test precisely because he spoke fittingly, not holding his tongue to obscure his revolt. It would seem that in understanding the final soliloquy of the book as the word of God, the meaning of suffering is indeed interpreted as a trial. This is not a theological rationalization that counters the moral problem even before it arises. The moral problem is, after all, a trial one has to endure. Anyone who does not question it, more correctly anyone who does not hurt because of it, has not been tried because he has not engaged the moral problem. But the person who has experienced suffering and rebelled against it in a believing protest, ultimately discovers—by means of the pain—God's abundant love, which renews the cycle of life and embraces each and every individual in it. Only then does he understand suffering as a trial from which he will emerge stronger

than he was, more profound than he had been in his own view and in the
Creator's view of him.

PROTESTING INJUSTICE

These elements in the book of Job are the theological underpinning to the
episodes of suffering in the life cycle of man as a created being. Primarily
this is true for bereavement. When man faces the death of loved ones, he
does so as a Job. Even when, in the prescribed wisdom, he voices the
noble truism that only at the end of his mourning might he reach the
wisdom of its truth.

> Naked came I out of my mother's womb,
> And naked shall I return thither;
> The Lord gave and Lord hath taken away;
> Blessed be the name of the Lord.
>
> Job 1:21

He rises up in protest, and in the outcry bursting from his heart one
hears the scream of protest. Thus Job also cries out.

> Wherefore is light given to him that is in misery,
> And life unto the bitter in soul—
> Who long for death, but it commeth not;
> And dig for it more than for hidden treasures;
> Who rejoice unto exaltation,
> And are glad when they can find the grave?—
> To a man whose way is hidden,
> And whom God hath hedged in?
> For my sighing commeth instead of my food,
> And my roarings are poured out like water.
> For the thing which I did fear is come upon me,
> And that which I was afraid of hath overtaken me.
> I was not at ease, neither was I quiet, neither had I rest;
> But trouble came.
>
> Job 3:20—26

Customs of bereavement shape response. The mourner reacts as Job;
the customs of bereavement are not aimed at silencing his cry or the
protest in which it is suffused. Let the mourner speak truly and give vent

to his lack of acquiescence. The relatives and companions who come to him, come to comfort. Their concern is not to justify the decree or to point out sins that ostensibly are the grounds for suffering. Their role is to lend a loving ear, and if they are capable of comforting speech or consoling deeds, they should speak and do. But their duty is primarily to be present because the presence of those who care gives solace. They affirm that in the encompassing life there is supportive strength that can sustain man, pluck him from the abyss of his suffering, and return him to the circle of the living. The customs of mourning purposely interrupt the ordinary cycle of life. Thus the mourner is able to express the feeling of protest that is roiling within him. What has befallen him prevents his immediate return to the ordinary course of life; it would be improper— worse, immoral. The protest that is expressed in the suspension of life's regular pattern is seen as the appropriate way to return to life, as a resignation to suffering without forgetting or obscuring what has happened. In this way human protest at suffering is brought fully into a life of faith: it is a trial to which man is subjected; withstanding it, he is enabled to emerge strengthened in his belief.

The suffering that man encounters by virtue of his being a creature of nature, short-lived and vulnerable to pain and disease, is the existential background for every kind of suffering that befalls man, including that caused by the wickedness of others. If man were not a creature exposed to suffering because of his nature, he would not be vulnerable to the evil of wrongdoers.

It is clear, however, that the suffering a Jew undergoes on national days of mourning is not the same as that which is dealt with in the figure of Job. The tenth of the month of Tevet, the seventeenth of Tammuz, and the ninth of Av are days of lament filled with mourning customs. They are a direct expression of the feeling that, in the destruction of Jerusalem and the Temple, the Jewish people lost something exceedingly precious, something whose loss rattles the normal flow of life to a point that is irreconcilable, just as the death of dear ones deprives a man of something real in his life. But this is not natural injury; it is the wicked and evil action of foreign peoples and enemy nations, expressly against a unique people intended as the chosen of the One God, Creator of the universe and its Master. A new context is created here in which the questions of suffering, and of blame connected to suffering, are raised for further examination. What is the extent of man's responsibility for the injustice, wickedness, and evil-doing that permeate his society? What is the extent of responsibility for injustice, wickedness, and evil that pervade the relations among nations?

The question of the individual who suffers social harm should presumably be discussed first. This is the suffering of the poor, which finds fullness of expression in Psalms. The poor man is a victim of the injustice that pervades society; he is as well the victim of wickedness and ill will of individuals who could, but do not, help and those who persecute him because of hatred. This fact gives rise to another point. The needy and afflicted of Psalms is also the righteous person—the tzaddik—whose suffering stems from his desire to do what is right in God's eyes and to avoid evil. His abstention from evil-doing deprives him of the success that an unjust society awards to those who are willing to take anything they can by force. His desire to act righteously puts him on a collision course with evildoers in whose way he stands. So his righteousness becomes the cause of his suffering. The destitute are the righteous persecuted for their righteousness and loyalty to God's commandments.

If, indeed, the core of suffering is the moral injury that is inherent in pain, then this is a suffering that exceeds Job's. Job does not protest that he is persecuted because of his righteousness. Nor does he remonstrate that someone overtly and intentionally caused him suffering. He declares that he is persecuted despite his righteousness; which is to say that his righteousness did not save him from his terrible fate. He rails against the fact that "The earth is given into the hand of the wicked." In contradistinction, the needy person in Psalms is embittered and pained that he suffers because of his virtuousness. From a moral standpoint this suffering seems unbearable.

It is indeed unbearable, but at the same time it raises a moral and experiential element that is missing in Job. The afflicted chose the path of righteousness, chose to do God's will, not only to escape the punishing agony meted out by man as well as God, but also as a fulfillment of life's true aim. He undertook to make God's will publicly manifest. For this he suffers. Certainly this does not mean that he can, or should, acquiesce to the injustice done to him. In any case, his suffering expresses a struggle in the name of a way of life that has been freely chosen. It is the only path open to him if he is intent on achieving his life's goal; therefore, inherent in the unbearable suffering a new source of moral strength is revealed, which, nonetheless, enables him to bear that which is unbearable. What is that moral strength? It is first of all the firm belief of the poor man, a belief not found in Job's words, that in his suffering, too, he advances along the path of the true good; whereas the path of his persecutors, despite their apparent success, is evil. The evil they do is not restricted to others but is done to themselves as well. This resolute consciousness is expressed in the first psalm, which serves as the introduction to the Book of Psalms.

> Happy is the man that hath not walked in the counsel of the wicked,
> Nor stood in the way of sinners,
> Nor sat in the seat of the scornful.
> But his delight is in the law of the Lord;
> And in His law doth he meditate day and night.
> And he shall be like a tree planted by streams of water,
> That bringeth forth its fruit in its season,
> And whose leaf doth not wither;
> And in whatsoever he doeth he shall prosper.
> Not so the wicked;
> But they are like the chaff which the wind driveth away.
> Therefore the wicked shall not stand in the judgment,
> Nor sinners in the congregation of the righteous;
> For the Lord regardeth the way of the righteous;
> But the way of the wicked shall perish.

This short psalm begins with a vigorous negation of the counsel of the wicked, in an intentional confrontation with conventional opinion. Ordinary people have only the evidence of their eyes; they see that the wicked ostensibly prosper as they consume the bounty of the land, whereas the righteous suffer. The negative formulation of the psalm's opening line is intended to stress that things are not as most suppose; instead, happy is he who goes in the opposite way; it is precisely he who deserves to be called "successful." Undoubtedly this cannot be said unless one has a different value system. The psalmist does not have the same view of what is desirable as do the wicked. The psalmist is concerned with an altogether different matter. What is the real difference between the way of the righteous and that of the wicked? Not that they do not achieve their desire; merely that what they desire is unsuitable because it holds no lasting value. Everything they acquire is transient. Their deeds bear no fruit and bring no lasting attainment to the world. Therefore, their way is null and void. They leave nothing to be remembered. This is not true of the righteous. They succeed because their deeds have a lasting value and they bear fruit. Their deeds are preserved from generation to generation. This is the meaning of the profound philosophical verse, which is the coda of the psalm.

> For the Lord regardeth the way of the righteous;
> But the way of the wicked shall perish.

Whatever God knows, exists for eternity. Whatever does not hold permanent value is null and void, and God does not recognize it. Therefore even when they suffer, the righteous ought to be called "successful," whereas the wicked, even as they prosper, deserve to be called hopelessly lost.

It must be admitted that this psalm says nothing about the suffering of the righteous though their suffering is heard repeatedly in subsequent psalms. But the sense of confidence and assurance that emanates from the first psalm serve the faithful as a constant underpinning for even their most painful outcries. The wretched sufferer knows with absolute certainty that in his suffering, too, he stands before God, and God discerns his path. Therefore, the gates of prayer stand open. Even when he feels that God is distant and that he is abandoned to his enemies, he implores God directly and trusts that his cry will be heard. Does he protest or resent his suffering? Both. But even when he protests it appears that he does not lack a certain knowledge of which Job is bereft to the point of despair. Job does not know the cause of his suffering whereas the woeful man in Psalms knows very well. He knows, first of all, that it is not God who is the cause of his suffering. Anything man knows directly and explicitly as God's doing is only good and never bad.

> The heavens declare the glory of God,
> And the firmament showeth His handiwork;
> Day unto day uttereth speech,
> And night unto night revealeth knowledge.

And just as the heavens elucidate His glory, the Torah expounds His justice.

> The law of the Lord is perfect, restoring the soul;
> The testimony of the Lord is sure, making wise the simple.
> The precepts of the Lord are right, rejoicing the heart;
> The commandment of the Lord is pure, enlightening the eyes.
> The fear of the Lord is clean, enduring forever;
> The ordinances of the Lord are true, they are righteous altogether.
>
> Psalm 19

If this is so, where does evil come from? Clearly from man. The righteous who suffer are victims of the evil intent of the wicked who act against God's will. Consequently the righteous man—the *tzaddik*—sustains his suffering not only before God but together with God. He fights God's battle so that His will shall prevail.

Does this mean that the righteous person does not expect God's help in his struggle? Certainly he expects it. He even remonstrates and protests when salvation is slow in coming. The Psalms are full of yearning, pleading, and impatient demands for God to finally intervene, revealing to all who it is that goes in the way of truth.

> How long, oh Lord, wilt Thou forget me forever?
> How long wilt Thou hid Thy face from me?
> How long shall I take counsel in my soul?
> Having sorrow in my heart by day?
> How long shall my enemy be exalted over me?
>
> Psalm 13

> My God, my God, why has Thou forsaken me,
> And art far from my help at the words of my cry?
> Oh my God, I call by day but Thou answerest not;
> And at night, and there is no surcease for me.
>
> Psalm 22

If this holds true for the suffering individual, it is all the more true for the suffering nation.

> Why, oh God, hast Thou cast us off forever?
> Why doth Thine anger smoke against the flock of Thy pasture?
> Remember Thy congregation, which Thou hast gotten of old,
> Which Thou hast redeemed to be the tribe of Thine inheritance;
> And Mt. Zion, wherein Thou has dwelt.
>
> Psalm 74

> Or: Oh God, keep not Thou silence;
>   Hold not Thy peace, and be not still, oh God.
>   For, lo, Thine enemies are in an uproar;
>   And they that hate Thee have lifted up the head.
>   They hold crafty converse against Thy people,
>   And take counsel against Thy treasured ones.
>
> Psalm 83

And many more instances in this vein.

Still, the righteous man knows why he is persecuted and does not regard God as the adversary who caused his suffering. The question burning in his heart is different: Why does God permit the wicked to hold sway? Why does He not intervene to save those loyal to His covenant? But sharp as these questions may be, the persecuted righteous person never regrets the path he has chosen. Even when he is downcast to the point of despair, he remains faithful to that path. Nonetheless, the question is asked, and it calls for an answer.

With respect to Job, a consoling answer is required. Does also this apply to the righteous man who suffers because of his righteousness? One would assume that he too needs solace. But it is a consolation arrived at by an altogether different route. Job cries out, protesting; yet his outcry does not deliver him from pain. Only a hand extended to him from without—the hand of relatives and companions, or the comforting hand of God, which returns the sufferer to the previous goodly routine of his daily life; only these things can comfort. In contradistinction, the tzaddik who chooses a path that brings suffering upon him, answers himself even before he hears the words of comfort, and his answer not only scrutinizes the riddle of God's stewardship but is an active, emotional, and practical reaction to suffering. Through this answer the righteous person seeks an actual disentanglement from distress. He gives shape to his feelings even as he tries to change his surroundings. Aware of his distress, it would appear that the ability to respond actively to it is the basis of his self-assurance.

In stead of "answer" and "active response" it would be more accurate to say, "answers" and "active responses." In Psalms, one finds at least two such answers/responses. They do not run counter to one another; rather, they offer an option between two ways of concretizing the same world view. Consequently one finds these two answers close to one another in the text, sometimes in the same psalm. The first answer raises anew the motif of sin and guilt. Protesting against existential suffering, which stems from man's vulnerability to poverty, pain, sickness, and death, Job cannot regard himself as guilty. Or more precisely, even if something within him is sinful, that sin cannot explain his suffering because suffering derives from a condition that preceded any possible guilt. Nonetheless, it could be that the explanation for man's sins is the suffering that stems from his natural vulnerability. At the root of its existence, the *ego* is *innocent*. But, when the righteous person denounces suffering whose origin is in the ill will and evil-doing of human beings, can he allow himself the luxury of not being judged by the same yardstick he applies to his persecutors? Can he regard himself in this context as *innocent*? Is he free of evil-doing and ill will? Does he bear no responsibility for the injustice found in his society? Certainly if we compare his deeds to the misdeeds of his enemies, he is righteous and his suffering is unjust. But if the judgment is made by God's absolute standard, even the righteous man is not found blameless. And the righteous man, precisely because he is righteous, knows this. Therefore his initial answer/reaction is an acknowledgment of the rightness of divine judgment that has been meted out to him, and a mighty effort to atone for his sins:

> Oh Lord, rebuke me not in Thine anger;
> Neither chasten me in Thy wrath.
> For Thine arrows are gone into me,
> And Thy hand is come down upon me.
> Their is no soundness in my flesh because of Thine indignation.
> Neither is there any health in my bones because of my sin.
> For mine iniquities are gone over my head;
> As a heavy burden they are too heavy for me.
>
> Psalm 38

This insight applies to an accounting of the nation's behavior:

> We have sinned with our fathers,
> We have done iniquitously, we dealt wickedly.
> Our fathers in Egypt gave no heed unto Thy wonders;
> They remembered not the multitude of Thy mercies;
> But were rebellious at the sea, even at the Red Sea.
>
> Psalm 106

Therefore the righteous person assumes the burden for his share of guilt. His sins justify his suffering, even when he is guilty by association with his surroundings. This ought not be considered a passive, acquiescent response to suffering. On the contrary, confession is an act of atonement. Prayer is an inner effort to be cleansed of sin. By taking on his guilt, the *tzaddik* becomes worthy of salvation. In fact the endings of psalms such as those that have been quoted here, frequently sound a note of certainty that redemption will indeed come and not tarry. The second answer/reaction is anger against evil-doing. The righteous person feels that he cannot bear injustices, which run counter to the desirable and worthy order of things. How can the world exist if such actions take place

within it? How can God remain silent? The *tzaddik* remonstrates and calls
for vengeance.

> Lord, Thou God to whom all vengeance belongeth,
> Thou God to whom vengeance belongeth, shine forth.
> Lift up Thyself, Thou Judge of the earth;
> Render to the proud their recompense.
> Lord how long shall the wicked,
> How long shall the wicked exalt?
> They gush out, they speak arrogancy;
> All the workers of iniquity bear themselves loftily.
> They crush Thy people, Oh Lord,
> And afflict Thy heritage.
> They slay the widow and the stranger,
> And murder the fatherless.
> And they say: "The Lord will not see,
> Neither will the God of Jacob give heed."
>
> Psalm 94

Ostensibly such an outlook purges the sense of guilt. The righteous
person does not see himself as party to sinfulness. This protest transcends
personal suffering. It is not merely his own suffering that the *tzaddik*
protests, but that of all who are afflicted. The very fact that injustice exists
under the sun incites his anger. Therefore this is not his personal
accounting. It is an account of the world and, by extension if one wishes,
God's accounting. It is because of this that the *tzaddik* feels that he can
denounce and castigate, that by doing so he stands actively at God's side.
This is not a passive reaction. The righteous person disengages himself
from his personal distress by making God's war his own. Once again, one
is not surprised if here too, at the end of the protest, there is an absolute
certainty that God's vengeance will come about swiftly. Justice will be
done, will be seen to be done, and the suffering righteous will be
redeemed.

This certainty, both at the end of the confession and at the end of the
protest, is the very heart of the consoling answer that is advanced in
Psalms to the question of the suffering of the poor. The fact that in the
entire Book of Psalms there is no expression of ultimate despair is
surprising and instructive. Even the sharpest expressions of dejection, the
sense of a distancing of God, are but the prelude to an enormous,
overflowing sense of assurance. The *tzaddik* not only believes, he is certain
that salvation is nigh, and he sounds his thanksgiving even before it

arrives. Today one wonders, what was the secret of such certainty? What was its basis when it appears to have been so contrary to the reality in which the righteous person lived? Is the power of a constant outlook so strong? The religious/moral outlook that is found in the first psalm is surely the underpinning for the righteous man's assurance. He knows, even in his suffering, that his way is the way God desires; therefore it subsumes the true good. The steadfast certainty that justice will be seen is a product of the willed effort that works itself out in societal and psychological behavior. The righteous person acts so that justice should be done. And, despite all that has been said about the evil-doing of the wicked and their power, the righteous person does not feel totally impotent or that his actions have no consequence. In his prayer he feels God with him; God's love touches him and is the certainty of his salvation.

> Only for God wait thou in stillness, my soul;
> For from Him commeth my hope.
> He only is my rock and my salvation,
> My high tower I shall not be moved.
> Upon God resteth my salvation and my glory;
> The rock of my strength, and my refuge, is in God.
> Trust in Him at all times, ye people;
> Pour out your heart before Him;
> God is a refuge for us.   Selah.
> Men of low degree are vanity, and men of high degree are a lie;
> If they be laid in the balances, they are together lighter than vanity.
> Trust not in oppression,
> And put no vain hope in robbery;
> And riches increase, set not your heart thereon.
> God hath spoken once,
> Twice have I heard this:
> That strength belongeth unto God;
> Also unto Thee, oh Lord, belongeth mercy;
> For Thou renderest to every man according to his work.
>
>   Psalm 62

Realizing the overpowering presence of God turns the environing evil into vanity. Anyone who grasps this truth knows that what appears to be so solid, so forceful in the rule of the wicked of the earth is a transient chimera. So the righteous person feels that he has already been saved, even as he prays. God's redeeming might stands revealed to him. This applies as well to prayers of anger and protest. The source of the certainty that a day of vengeance is approaching stems from the sense that it is not possible for the wicked to be victorious because, from Creation onward, they negated the order of the world. In the very depth of suffering, one crosses the solid threshold of faith.

The emotions that well up on days of national mourning for the destruction of Jerusalem and the Temple are drawn from these two answers/reactions. The feeling of serious guilt, on the one hand, and the feeling of angry resentment at injustice, on the other, lead those who mourn the destruction of Zion to the assurance of redemption.

DIVINE JUSTICE

The principal work of the Bible dealing with Tisha B'Av—the Fast of the Ninth Day of the Month of Av—is the Scroll of Lamentations, *Eikhah*. This extended lament is a heartrending cry over the destruction of the nation, of Jerusalem, and of the First Temple. What is a lament? First and foremost it is the painful moan of a mourner when consciousness of the magnitude of the disaster bursts through the veil of initial shock. Again and again the mourner rehearses what happened. He tells it to himself while conjuring it up in greatest detail. Each memory occasions a renewed gush of tears, tears that perhaps were suppressed as the event took place. Now too it seems that he cannot comprehend what happened. As a dirge, he repeats the question, *"eikhah?"*—how? How could such events possibly have occurred? How could people conceivably have acted in such a way? How can one possibly comprehend such pain? Yet the very refusal to believe is in itself an initial comprehension of the facts. Even as one recoils, reality penetrates the conscious. Cruel and painful as it may be, the process is all the more necessary. It must not be held in check. The mourner must comprehend actuality. If he is to return to the cycle of life and function in the new reality that comes after the tragedy, he must relive what has happened to him rather that hide behind denial. Otherwise, he will remain in a constant illusory hallucination, and knowingly brought about, illusory hallucination as an escape is the beginning of madness. From this standpoint, the cruel process of comprehension is a return to life.

The lamentation, *Eikhah*, which tradition accords to the prophet Jeremiah who witnessed the destruction of the Temple, continues to fulfill its primary role, though it is an "ancient" anguish, a pain as old as the two-thousand-year exile. By prostrating themselves on the ground, sitting as mourners while reading the Scroll of Lamentations on the eve of Tisha B'Av, the Jewish people inculcates the actuality and magnitude of the tragedy into its consciousness. Although the mourning has become institutionalized, something of its initial pain has a continuous presence and as new tragedies befall the nation, these are integrated into the generations—long lament. Despite the two-thousand-year exile, until the re-establishment of the State of Israel, the land remained desolate, Jerusalem the province of strangers, and to this day the Temple is unreconstructed. Therefore throughout the long generations, the Jewish people were not unlike a mourner maintaining a death watch over the corpse of a dear one, the lament serving to jar his consciousness lest the vital truth slip away from memory—he lives in exile.

The essential meaning of exile is a nation destroyed, murdered, and massacred, helpless to defend itself, suffering derision and degradation, uprooted from its homeland, ruled by despots; above all else, exile is the condition in which God abandoned His people to their own fate. The Temple symbolized the direct link between God and His people. As long as it stood, God dwelled among His people, granting them protection and guidance. The destruction of the Temple meant that Providence had absented itself. It is true that even in exile the Jewish people felt it had avenues of direct contact with God. In the synagogue and the house of learning—those "miniaturized temples" that the people retained—they were able to achieve a sense of closeness to their Creator by prayer, study of the Torah, and performance of the mitzvot. Hence the occasional comfort that God did not completely abandon His people. Sometimes there were events that the people regarded as *providential*, perhaps heralding salvation. The Festival of Purim was most expressive of this sentiment. But if the fate of the people as a whole is observed from the standpoint of nationhood, it is evident that even in the most benign exiles honor is lost, the divine presence banished. What happens in exile, for better or for worse, is an outcome of the initiatives of non-Jews who rule, so that from this standpoint nothing is left but the burning hope that the people will be redeemed in the future. On Tisha B'Av, the lament reminds the Jewish people of the earliest meaning of its fate, a fate that lasted so many generations. Exile is a life of dispersion, persecution, pillage, and enslavement far from one's land, far from one's city, bereft of the Temple that symbolized God's indwelling presence.

Yet the *Lamentations* scroll is not simply a mourner's dirge. A tonality is heard in it that is not found in the words of Job mourning on his mound

of dust and ashes. It is in *Lamentations* that a detailed explanation is found
of the tragedy that befell the nation. In a single-minded way, without any
reservations, the great lament attributes the disaster to the guilt of the
people. And with the details of the tragedy, the lament spells out the
moral and religious transgressions of the people. Robbery, oppression,
mendacity, prostitution, and paganism. The people have abrogated the
covenant sealed at Sinai. Repeatedly, through the prophets, God warned
His people but to no avail. The people did not abandon their evil ways,
and punishment was exacted *measure for measure*. Therefore, more than it
recounts the tragedy, the wailing of lamentations recites the guilt that
preceded it. "How" then can it be believed that the people whom God had
led while performing all His promises in the covenant could so grievously
betray the covenant? Now that they are punished, the people cannot
understand its own behavior. It prostrates itself beneath the burden of
guilt. What is the meaning of this profound gesture, which understands
mourning as guilt? Perhaps this, too, could be the initial step on a return
to the cycle of life in a reality created after tragedy? Indeed such is the
case.

The lament becomes a sort of confessional prayer, resembling in its
themes the confessional of Yom Kippur. The people undertake the burden
of guilt and justifies the judgment. It is the beginning of repentance. Who
knows, perhaps God will forgive the people's sins and rescind the decree?
Out of the depths of suffering and repentance, the hope for redemption
seeps through. In the historic reality during which the *Lamentations* scroll
was written, a prophet like Jeremiah could justify the decree. For a
modern person there is possibly something surprising in this. In any case,
the fact is that Jeremiah, in other prophecies as well, felt no lack of
symmetry between the extent of the sin and the extent of the punishment.
Jeremiah's prophecies and the lamentations of *Eikhah* evidence genuine
pain at the destruction of a people but they do not protest the punishment. The protest is inherent in the outcry of pain—there is never an
outcry of pain without some protest—directed at the people, particularly
at its corrupt leaders. He regards the punishment as just and necessary, a
lawful punishment. This is an unquestioning faith and inherent in it is a
great hope—trust in God's justice. Should the people repent because of
the punishment, its terrible suffering will be its atonement, and after the
wrath compassion will come forth: "Turn Thou us unto Thee, Oh Lord,
and we shall be turned; Renew our days as of old" (Lamentations 5:21).

This is the first reaction to the suffering of destruction and exile, and it shapes the character of Tisha B'Av. Still it is not the only response. The emotional and philosophic response of the Sages to the destruction of the Second Temple was more complex and finds its expression in their attitude to the destruction of the First Temple. In several profound midrashim about the *Eikhah* scroll, Jeremiah's lament—permeated as it is with feelings of guilt—is placed in apposition to the mourning of the nation's patriarchs, Abraham, Isaac, and Jacob; and the mourning of the matriarchs, Sarah, Rivka, Rachel, and Leah; as well as the mourning of Moses. In contradistinction to Jeremiah, they defend the people and refuse to justify the decree.

True, the Jews have sinned. But balancing the sins, the Sages point to the virtues of the patriarchs, indeed the virtues of the entire people; this is the only nation that undertook to fulfill God's commandments. The emotional and theoretical peak of these homilies is found in a description of Abraham's apparent mourning over the destruction of his people. It is a modality for expressing a Job-like protest against the terrible punishment without letting it appear to be a revolt against God when the attribute of divine justice itself appears to exceed justice. When suffering is at its extreme, it cannot appear to be just. The sufferer is no longer a sinner. Moreover is it sin alone that is weighed on the day of judgment? The question emerges even more sharply in the words of the Sages concerning the destruction of the Second Temple. Repeatedly they ask, why was the Temple destroyed? Or, why was Betar destroyed? And they, too, indicate a number of sins that were the cause of the punishment, allegedly *measure for measure*. Yet the question itself seems to bear witness to the fact that the justice meted out did not appear clear to them, and that something remained problematic even after their own answers. The people sinned. The people broke the covenant.

Nonetheless there seems to be a disproportionate severity in the measure of divine justice. Why is God so severe regarding His people's sins when He seems to disregard the greater sins of enemy nations? Despite all their sins, why were the Jewish people not credited as the only nation that undertook God's Torah? One hears a complaint in these questions not unlike the complaints heard in Psalms. In this way, the people resembles an oppressed, pious person who does not overlook his sins but nonetheless knows his own merits, knows that he is persecuted not only in spite of these merits but also because of them. It is the complaint heard when one laments the suffering on Tisha B'Av.

Are these two responses contradictory? There is certainly a tension between them but in the unusual atmosphere of Tisha B'Av, the two responses combine and are integrated. The theme that unites them is the certainty that redemption will come. Recognition of their guilt brings redemption closer through repentance, which transforms suffering into atonement. Awareness of their merit inspires the certainty of God's merciful attribute. The Jewish people deserves redemption; suffering is meant only to prepare for it. In the throes of suffering, one senses the nearness of salvation and consolation. The Sages said, "The Messiah was born on the day the Temple was destroyed." From the time the Temple was destroyed until the beginning of the Modern Era, wise men found allusions to an imminent redemption expressly in prophecies of destruction. When suffering can no longer be withstood, it augers the birthpangs of the Messiah. Notice that the depth of devotion in the Tisha B'Av prayers and all its practices are intended to bring redemption closer, and when one devotes oneself fervently to bringing redemption closer, one actually feels its nearness.

It would appear that not only those who justify the decree, as Jeremiah did in his lament, but others, spurred by the injustice of a suffering restricted to the only people who accepted the Torah, feel certain that suffering does not weaken their belief that God guides the Jewish people on its path among the nations. In itself, a repudiation of suffering reveals an acceptance of the decree. Even if the decree meted out to the people is not fully comprehended, even if the reason for suffering remains unavailable until the end of days, one thing is known—the God who participates in His people's sorrow did not abandon them. There is a reason for suffering and its end is near. This is the comforting answer that transforms the unbearable to the sustainable by virtue of an active psychological process. Tisha B'Av concretizes the exilic condition as a state of being on the threshold: the threshold of fortitude to suffer and the threshold of the certainty of redemption. As with the trial described in the earlier discussion on Purim—the consciousness that God accompanies his people even when they are in exile, watches over them, and redeems them—Tisha B'Av expresses a capability to adapt to the situation that developed after the destruction despite the consciousness that this is a fundamentally unbearable state.

Paradoxically, internalizing the perception that a situation is unbearable becomes a kind of tense adaptation to that state. Of course this is dependent on not seeing it as a long-term situation. Even the unbearable can be borne when regarded as the threshold to a hoped-for change, pointing with certainty not only to the termination but also to the compensation for suffering. At Tisha B'Av, the sense of being on the verge of redemption balances Purim's bewitching seduction in which exile keeps the people in its beguiling coils. As long as it was possible to live in the midst of this double tension, it was possible to maintain a wanderer's tent as the people's home in exile.

HATRED OF JEWS: FROM THE
SECOND COMMONWEALTH TO THE MODERN ERA

Does Holocaust Memorial Day for Martyrs and Heroes blend into the same cycle of ideational and emotional themes? Can the Jewish people contend with the suffering it witnessed in the Holocaust in the same way? There are those who think so. It is only if one assumes that the meaning of the Holocaust is similar to the meaning of the destruction of the Temple, and subsequent persecutions, and that it can be dealt with in the same traditional manner, that one could propose that Holocaust Day and Tisha B'Av be combined. Indeed this is the way that past generations coped with persecutions that the Jewish people encountered in exile. Nonetheless, most Jews appear to reject this notion. So long as people are alive who personally experienced the Holocaust, or who lost dear ones in the Holocaust, there will certainly be opposition to the idea of combining the days because of the psychological need to specifically and separately commemorate the cataclysm and to remember those who were consumed by it. A large part of the public seems to regard the Holocaust as unlike either the destruction or persecutions. The Holocaust marks the entry of the Jewish people into a different period because the conditions and the spiritual problems involved its existence have changed. The suffering of the Holocaust raises something that did not exist before, which is no longer possible to confront in accustomed ways.

Historical accuracy requires noting that the consciousness of change occurred among Jews long before the Holocaust. The Holocaust was plainly the nadir in a process that began much earlier but it was through the Holocaust that the process as a whole acquired a conclusive definition. The perception of a "New Era" was felt as early as the Renaissance, when a growing sense of change in the circumstances of the Jewish people's existence broke upon Jewish consciousness. This consciousness of change eventually took hold within two large movements, which, to this day, remain adversarial: the movement that called for emancipation and the complete integration of Jews in the country in which they resided; and the movement that called for the return to Zion through an independent initiative.

One view no longer regarded exile as an involuntary captivity; what had originally been perceived as a tragedy was really a positive turn in Jewish history. The people had been uprooted from its own land, its city and sanctuary, so that it could fulfill its calling as a universal people. In diametric opposition, the evaluation was that the Jewish people stood on the brink of total disintegration in exile, that it had no hope outside of a return to *normal* national life in its own land. In any case, both these approaches shared the view that the historical reality that came into being following the destruction of the Second Temple had changed radically. The period of exile had terminated; a new way would have to be sought to deal with the unique suffering of the Jewish people, which, everyone agreed, continued. The approach that posited emancipation pointed toward integration into modern, Western, secular society and culture. Zionism pointed toward the road of national independence.

Each of these approaches clearly departs from the modalities of confronting Jewish suffering found in relation to Purim and Tisha B'Av. Two principal assumptions at the foundation of the traditional mode were undermined by the historical experience of the Jewish people in modern times. The first was that the suffering of the Jewish people stems from its sins. The second was that radical suffering heralds a near redemption that is not generated by the powers of the people themselves but by supra-natural divine intervention. Ultra-Orthodoxy does indeed continue to hold these assumptions, but the majority of the Jewish people have discarded them, and when belief is examined—not only in its declarative mode but according to actual response—it is found that even ultra-Orthodoxy has come a long way from the simple belief that sin is the cause of suffering and repentance is a sure guarantee of redemption. Only people so fanatic that they have lost all moral sensitivity claim that the Holocaust should be regarded either as punishment for sins or birthpangs of the Messiah. The traditional theological justification could not be maintained even as a paradoxical protest against God. Anyone who maintained his faith either despite the Holocaust, or because of it, could do so only by virtue of an unshakable certainty that it was not an act of God but an act of man. If this is so, does the believer retain his faith in a divine providence that directs the Jewish people among the nations? Can he leave the fate of the Jewish people in God's hands? Will suffering be regarded as an assurance that redemption indeed comes through supra-natural intervention?

Such questions reveal a change in the consciousness of the Jewish people in modern times. Serving as a focus for these questions, Holocaust Day is emblematic of the entry into a new historical period, in the same way as Tisha B'Av symbolizes the beginning of the exilic period. Again, the process began much earlier; it did not spring forth suddenly but found its way through the winding awareness of a new network of relationships between the Jewish people and the nations among which it lived. Most Jews gradually realized that their earlier perception of the Jewish people's position among the nations, and their understanding of the relationship between the Jewish people and its God, no longer held. That approach no longer had a convincing grip on reality and therefore could not guide the people in its struggle to exist or fulfill its mission. There is an instructive parallel here between what occurred in the Modern Era and what occurred in the period between the First and Second Commonwealth. The break that came in the Modern Era was more radical and more extreme; it called for a renewed examination of the mechanism by which the people confront the phenomenon of national suffering.

Lamentations describes the destruction of the Temple as a just punishment for the sins of the people. The Sages believed that though the destruction was a punishment for sin, they were no longer convinced of the justice of the punishment when comparing the actions and fate of the Jewish people to the fate of their persecutors. What explained this transformation in the Jewish people's consciousness of its situation? Was it a heightened moral sensitivity, or did something change in their assessment of circumstances? There is no reason to think that Jeremiah's sensitivity to the nation's suffering was one whit less than was the sensitivity of the Sages, and an examination of their utterances discloses that unlike their attitude to Isaiah, the Sages regarded Jeremiah uncritically. Jeremiah's grief over the destruction is incomparably profound and burning. If this is so, why did he justify the cruel decree?

The explanation probably stems from a realistic evaluation of historic circumstances. Jeremiah became convinced of a direct causal link between the nation's sins and its dreadful fate. That link was the basis for the warnings and chastisements he sounded while there was still time. Years prior to the destruction he prophesied about the moral disintegration that divided the nation and withered its strength. Years prior to the destruction he prophesied that the passions of the kings of Judea—like those of the kings of Israel before them—to be directly involved in, indeed, instigate, conflicts among surrounding nations would embroil the Judean state in campaigns beyond its strength. He was certain that if the nation kept its moral vigor, if it remained faithful to the covenant with God, and if the kings were loyal to their role as shepherds of the people rather than pursuing pagan lusts for domination, the tragedy would be averted and the Jewish people would continue to live in its land. It is this practical appraisal of the historic situation in *Lamentations* that serves as the basis for justifying the decree. The nation's sins were the cause of the calamity; consequently the cruel punishment is just.

Observing the historic situation on the eve of the destruction of the Second Temple, Jeremiah's conclusions no longer seemed to apply, though internal schisms did undermine the power to withstand external pressure and there was some basis to the belief that sin was among the causes for the downfall. But the majority of the people accepted the leadership of the Sages, and remained faithful to the Torah. This was a *merit* that could not be overlooked in a moral stock-taking of the nation. Can it be claimed that if the nation had not been sinful, the Hellenic and Roman conquests and the rebellions against them—rebellions that broke out because the conquerors grievously challenged what was most sacred to Jews—could have been prevented? The Sages had an accurate assessment of Roman rule and knew well that it was actuated by pagan impulses, that the confrontation between the Jewish people and its occupiers was a conflict between two opposing world views that could never co-exist.

The military superiority of the Roman rulers was clear. Only those who believed wholeheartedly in God's supra-natural leadership dared to rebel against the will of the empire. To anyone who weighed the real strength of one against the other, the outcome was clear from the beginning; it is therefore difficult to place the entire blame for the destruction on sinfulness. The unavoidable question was why did not God save his faithful in their war against the malicious conqueror who wanted to divert the Jews from the ways of the Torah? So it is not sin alone that explains the destruction. There is an explanation that goes beyond sin, and it is apparently lodged in the developing confrontation between a nation faithful to the Torah and a paganism eager to rule the world.

The assessment that sinfulness was not the sole explanation for the suffering of exile, that the primary reason stems from a spiritual encounter between the Jewish people and the nations surrounding it was reinforced after the destruction of the Second Commonwealth, and this formulation became clear when Jews came under the rule of nations that had accepted Christianity and Islam. Now the confrontation had become interreligious, direct, and intimate, and the religious reason for Jewish suffering in exile was manifest and self-explanatory. The religious consciousness held in common by the Jews and their environing nations actively maintained the belief in a divine providence which directs the history of nations. The fate of the Jews was interpreted, both by the Jews and their neighbors, as testifying to God's will. In Christian and Muslim eyes, this was evidence of the sinfulness of a stiff-necked people and it justified persecuting Jews and discriminating against them as a punishment for their sins. Clearly in Jewish eyes there was a different explanation for exile. The sufferings of the Jewish people were seen as a trial or as *Kiddush HaShem*, the sanctification of the Lord.

In order to understand the shift that took place in the transition from the Middle Ages to the Modern Era, this aspect must be examined in greater detail. The issue to be addressed comes up as early as the ironic story of *Megillat Esther*. Against the deteriorating background of hatred of the Jew, a phenomenon that goes unmentioned throughout the First Commonwealth period but which looms ever darker in Jewish history from the period of the Hellenistic conquest onward, one asks the question, what explains such hatred? Why did this hatred swell to such irrational proportions during the period of Israel's dispersion among peoples who prided themselves on having embraced religions that had inherited the Torah?

Admittedly, hatred is a central and reigning motif in relations between neighboring peoples since the dawn of time. Individuals who achieve a stable social arrangement can maintain a reasonable balance between feelings of love and hatred, but relations between peoples tend toward competition more than toward mutuality, common interests, or a balance between national forces, which is the basis for cooperation. Even then competition does not disappear. The presence of the other, the competitor, can be dangerous and threatening, and requires alertness. The feeling of hatred is a primary psychological reaction to the very presence of a competing foreigner. It is easily ignited between neighboring peoples. Of course, hatred toward the Jews too is grounded in this normalcy of relations between peoples, which is what appears to have been the case in the Jewish people's relations with the environing nations during the First Commonwealth period. The wars between the Jews and their neighbors were *normal* wars over national interests, and the Jewish people intervened and merged, in keeping with its military strength, in the complex network of relations between the nations surrounding it. Even the war that ended with the destruction of the country and the Temple did not give vent to a particular hatred by the conquerors vis-à-vis the Jewish people.

This was the behavior of the Assyrians, then the Babylonians, toward all the nations they conquered. First the Kingdom of Israel, then the Kingdom of Judea stood in the way of the imperial interests of the victorious empire. This was the transgression for which they were punished. But there was no indication of a hatred directed particularly at Jews as a people representing a divergent world outlook. Naturally, in keeping with their inclinations, the conquerors believed that their victory was a victory of their gods over the gods of defeated nations. For the Jewish prophets this was a spiritual challenge to which they responded in consonance with their outlook: the Jewish people sinned and God punished them. The pagan empire was nothing but an instrument in God's hands.

As early as Second Commonwealth times, a new phenomenon manifested itself between the Jews and the nations around them. A hatred directed toward Jews in particular—even when they did not rebel against foreign rule—became evident, distinct from the natural enmity that rises among nations because of a conflict of interests. The Jews represent something peculiar that incites to anger, something that departs from the cultural conventions of their neighbors. Their presence is disturbing, discordant, challenging. Nor is there apparently any *rational* proportion between hatred of Jews and their numbers in the population. Moreover, the outbursts against Jews are a departure from the conventional norms of the host people. This was the case in the ancient Greco-Roman world, and the phenomenon was exacerbated during the Middle Ages in the Christian-Islamic world. What explanation is there for this unique hatred? One recalls the concise, dense sentence from *Megillat Esther*: "There is a certain people scattered abroad and dispersed among the peoples in all the provinces of the kingdom, and their laws are diverse from those of every people; neither keep they the kings laws; therefore it profiteth not the king to suffer them" (3:8).

Two elements mentioned here are attributed to Haman the Jew-hater. First, the Jewish people is a nation in exile—dispersed, disunited, living among the other peoples of the empire. It is, by its very dispersion, a pariah. Second, the Jewish people has a *religion*, in other words its own laws. Haman sees this as a manifestation of revolt. Jews faithful to their own laws cannot fulfill the king's laws, laws in conflict with those of the King—for example, not bowing down to rulers with sufficiently vehement obeisance as Haman demanded. The third complaint included in Haman's words was merely ancillary: since the king "profiteth not" from the Jews, he might as well be rid of them, eliminate the obstacle. Such an explanation relates to the uniqueness of the Jewish people on two planes, the national—a people in exile; and the cultural/spiritual—a people who, by their behavior, represent a world outlook that contradicts the accepted world view of the pagan environment in which it lived by its own volition.

An examination of the history of the Jews in exile apparently validates this explication of *Megillat Esther* as concise and trenchant. The inordinate hatred directed at the Jewish people admittedly stems from its being in exile, both from national and cultural/spiritual aspects. They are hated for being scattered and dispersed, and consequently found everywhere, impotently reliant on the regime; they are hated because despite their dispersion and weakness they continue to exist as a unique people, isolated from their surroundings, personifying something opposed to their surroundings. In other words, they are hated for being in exile and hated for having the strength to exist—despite exile—as a separate people that blends into the environment, in some senses; but is aloof from it with an offensive decisiveness, in other senses.

This situation became more highly defined in the Middle Ages. Loyalty to the Torah was the secret of Jewish existence as a scattered people. Nonetheless, though a small and marginal minority throughout Christendom and Islam, the Jews clearly wanted to integrate into the economic life of the majority community in which they lived and wished to remain. Saadia Gaon's well-known pronouncement, "Our people has no peoplehood other than its ordinances," testifies to the truth of this observation. The Torah differentiated the Jews through laws and their way of life; the Torah defined a common content for the life of scattered communities, uniting them into a single people. In this way a brake was put on the natural process of assimilation and an infrastructure created for an independent national culture, faulty and limited in scope but sufficient to nourish the distinct existence of a "certain people."

Still, along with loyalty to the Torah, it is proper to take note here of a political element in the ancient and medieval world by which the host environment enabled the maintenance and existence of separate Jewish communities, and even championed them. Non-Jewish kingdoms were interested in the economic and cultural contributions of Jews. At times there was even a specific interest in bringing Jews closer and appointing them to central roles in the royal court, precisely because they lacked any independent political strength. Their loyalty was entirely reliable. The prevailing modern concept of one law that directly obligates each individual citizen vis-à-vis the central government was not a part of the ancient and medieval world. Accountability to the regime was through

membership in a social strata or locality—towns or rural provinces—
each one comprising a jurisdictional framework of its own. The Jewish
community easily accommodated itself to this arrangement, and its
judicial institutions enjoyed the support of the regime. Under such
circumstances there was a realistic weight to the Jews' feeling that, even
when dispersed and exiled, God had not abandoned them. Jews even
enjoyed economic success and cultural flowering during those periods
when their contribution was so important to their rulers that it overcame
hatred and rejection. Which is to say that loyalty to the Torah worked in
tandem with socio-economic and political circumstances that were
relatively satisfactory, and this enabled the Jews to exist united in their
belief and way of life despite their dispersion, and in isolation from their
environment.

On the other hand, this special separate existence aroused constant
tension and enmity in what was an atypical form of ambivalent relations.
In certain aspects, the Jewish community sought integration into its
environment; in others, it wanted to be completely separate from it. For
its own reasons, the non-Jewish environment was interested and willing to
incorporate Jewish communities; while at the same time there was a
strong tendency to expel Jews, or to place before them the options of
conversion or annihilation. From time to time this propensity broke out
into action: expulsions, pogroms, forced conversion. Even when considerations that called for the co-option of a Jewish community overcame the
disposition to reject it, the enmity did not disappear and segments of the
population who regarded Jews as direct competitors continued to foment
hatred. What explanation is there for this hatred, which was disproportionate to the numerical strength of the Jews? It was leveled principally at
the component that united the Jews and that separated them from their
surroundings: their religion. The sharp confrontation was brought about
precisely by the fact that the host nations subscribed to religions with a
deep historio-cognitive link to Judaism. The refusal of the "mother
religion" to acknowledge its daughters turned the confrontation into a
matter of the utmost importance from the daughters' standpoint; particularly since both Christianity and Islam had pretensions to having
supplanted the parent.

In remaining loyal to the Torah, the Jews challenged the legitimacy of
the religion in their host nations by their very existence. Small and
marginal as the Jewish people was, the significance of its continued
existence and the witness it bore was so crucial and prominent that
Christians and Moslems could not overlook them. To survive the tension

of their rejection, Jews were forced to excel in their economic and cultural contributions, thereby exacerbating the extent of their disproportionate prominence in their foreign surroundings. For extended periods of time, the Jews enjoyed a unique status in such areas such as finance, certain sciences (particularly medicine), and even in the political field. However, this movement from the periphery to the very heart of cultural activity did not grant the Jews, as a national group, any concrete power. Whatever power Jewish individuals had was bestowed on them. One way or another the Jews achieved a degree of prominence that was disproportionate to their numbers. It was this combination of prominence (that presented a challenge), on the one hand, and weakness (that created absolute dependency), on the other, that appears to hold the key to the uncommon situation of the Jewish people. The combination is an ideal focus for hatred.

Had the Jews been less prominent in their surroundings, remaining on the fringes, though it is doubtful they would have had sufficient motivation to persist as a special people, at least they would not have called forth such an intensely emotional opposition. Their very existence would not have been viewed as a threat. Had the Jews continued to live in their own territory, they would not have been a constantly ar.tagonistic presence, nor an irritant to their surroundings. Had they been as strong economically and politically as the opposition they encountered, their environment would have been forced to respect their ability to defend themselves. But the paradoxical blend of prominence at the center of others' lives, and national weakness, incites a special hatred and removes all restraining factors. The Jew became a symbol of all that is ugly, evil, threatening, and dangerous without actually being threatening or dangerous. The fact that he lives behind the partition of a separate way of life facilitates painting him as a demonic figure. Little is known about him as he truly is in his intimate life, yet all manner of faults are attributed to him. Thus, particularly in Christian society, the Jew became the symbol of everything negative, hated, and frightening; despised and disgraced. The less he was able to defend himself, the more he was hated. This is the ultimate expression of a historic paradox: the inner strength that sustained the Jewish people in exile was seen as a hateful challenge, while the essential weakness of an exilic people stoked the fires of hatred because it provided an available victim.

It was not until the beginning of the Modern Era that the foundation of Jewish communal existence in exile was destroyed. In addition to the considerations that had inclined rulers to make a place for the Jews within their domains, it must be added that these were societies guided by religious institutions, or which recognized religion as the supreme spiritual and moral authority. While this focused the confrontation between Judaism, on the one hand, and Christianity and Islam, on the other, it also acted as a common denominator. The position of the religious establishments in Christianity and Islam was that Jews should not be granted equal legal status in their countries. On the contrary, Jews must be stamped with clearly recognizable insignia of inferiority and disgrace. But neither they nor their property should be injured, and they must not be forcibly converted. Generally the higher religious institutions protected Jews from persecution whereas pogroms were initiated by the lower priesthood and popular leaders.

Furthermore, if hatred of the Jews and a desire to expel them was not held in check in one country, Jews had the possibility of going to another country to acquire the protection of another regime that would show some interest in the contributions they could make. Wandering from country to country thus became one of the characteristic forms of exilic existence. Jews adjusted to it, prepared themselves for its possibility, and were ready for it both psychologically and operationally. Finally, it must be remembered that though outbursts of violent hatred against Jews caused serious damage to life and property, they could not escalate to the point of threatening absolute destruction. Technological civilization had not yet invented or developed the necessary tools for implementing the final solution. Any eruption against Jews was necessarily limited in time. Ultimately it flickered out, and the rioters returned to their ordinary routines. It then became possible to rebuild the ruins and renew previous activity.

Examined against a background of the general situation of upheavals and wars among kingdoms, and religious and ethnic groups in that period, the fate of the Jews in exile is discovered to have been extremely grave but still sustainable; therefore no organized effort to change the exilic situation through political, pragmatic means appears to have come forward. The messianic movements that sprang up in every generation doubtlessly gave expression to moments when the people felt that they had reached the limit of their ability to withstand the situation, but they did not depart from the internalized religious/spiritual pattern: repentance, performance of the mitzvot, and devout prayers for the end of days. In effect this means that even the messianic movements were mostly revealed as yet another adaptive technique to exile. It was not until there were radical changes in the economic, social, political, psychological, and spiritual make-up of Jews in the Modern Era that a change in direction took place toward a political initiative for leaving exile by means of the natural power of the Jewish people themselves.

Up to now, the discussion has stressed the reality that underlay both the Jewish self-image, and the religious meaning read into the interaction between Jews and other peoples; both of these elements were concretized in the prototype of the Festival of Purim and the prototype of mourning on Tisha B'Av. Indeed, there was a genuine basis to the feeling that even in exile, when God averts His gaze, the Jewish people is not abandoned to its fate. Similarly there was a genuine basis to the belief that there is some religious meaning to Jewish fate beyond a theology of transgression and punishment. As living proof of the ongoing validity of the Siniatic covenant, the Jewish people were in confrontation with peoples who were initially pagan and subsequently Christian and Moslem.

This fueled the consciousness that history has an internal logic linked to God's direction and His destined sovereignty over all the nations. The assumption that God directs history and determines destinies in accordance with a purpose known to Him was not a subjective interpretation given to history because the Jewish people assumed that nothing was outside His sphere of influence. The assumption was held in common by the Jews and the people among whom they lived. The disagreement between them was about direction and goal. In any case, the Jews understood their fate among the nations as not only having been a punishment for their sinfulness, but also a trial in which they had to bear witness to their faith or, if necessary, die for the Sanctification of God's Name. The understanding was couched in religious terms, the common language between themselves and their host nations, and this belief was a determining factor in the consciousness of those nations, as well as a determining element in the nature of the relations between them and the Jews.

Consequently, the solutions the Jews found to the issue of their suffering derived their strength from this community of discourse, and had a decided influence on the historic reality. In the face of greater suffering, the Jewish people believed in a redemption that would come when they repented and bore witness to the sanctity of God's Name. Redemption did not come. Still the belief in it was an expression of a very real strength that gave definition to the nation's image in its own eyes, and in the eyes of their neighbors. This real strength accomplished, at the very least, the unexplained miracle of the continued existence of the Jews despite the hatred that surrounded them. Admittedly there was less to this miracle than the hoped-for redemption, but it had enough substance to nurture a continued belief in a redemption to come unless their sins prevented it. If this belief had faded and an awareness that exile would be a permanent condition for generations had spread, the people would have been unable to persist in exile.

In the ancient period, and in the Middle Ages, faith in redemption withstood great tests. It did not die, and of course this can be explained by devotion to the Torah and a strong will to exist. One cannot describe the force of will and steadfastness of belief without taking into account actual historical circumstances: the religious consensus the Jews had with their surrounding cultures, that man is subject to God's will and conse-quently God's direction can be discerned in the behavior of human beings. Indeed, in an exile in which one daily senses the genuine feasibility of redemption by supra-natural intervention—"If you heed His voice today"—the Jewish people would have been able to exist for many generations. On Tisha B'Av this truth, which the Jewish people knew from its history, finds striking expression.

JEWISH SURVIVAL—
ONLY BY A RETURN TO THE LAND OF ISRAEL

The ideational, emotional structure on which the religious and moral consensus was based disintegrated in the Modern Era. At the general level, the picture is quite well-known: the appearance of the modern, centralist nation state built on a foundation of a universal law that directly obliges every individual citizen to the government; the development of a secular culture based on an industrial economy, advanced science, and technology; the diminished power of the religious establishment as the directing force in spiritual life. All these changes totally undermined the economic, social, legal, and political bases of the traditional Jewish community. Jews lost their enhanced place in European society, and their former occupations were denied to them. As a result of the need to seek out new sources of livelihood, they had to acquire a modern education and this substituted for, or at least greatly limited, their traditional Jewish education. The Jewish community lost its authority to enforce its legal powers of coercion and essentially became a voluntary organization. Even for those who accepted the jurisdiction of rabbinical institutions, these were limited to concerns of purely ritual and personal status.

Consequently, the rabbinical leadership also lost its competence as an educational leadership. By the logic of a centralized national state based on a single system of law, it was only proper to offer Jews equality of rights as individuals, and sooner or later, democratic governments recognized this claim. But a heavy price was exacted: the surrender of a separate collective existence. Jews could not enjoy civil rights in the nation-states in which they lived if they persisted in regarding themselves as members of a separate national grouping. Many individual Jews were seduced by a path that led to assimilation but it then emerged that the populace of nation-states was disinclined to grant that which was inherent in the legal concepts of the state. The assimilatory movement ran into the obstacle of modern anti-Semitism. At the end of the eighteenth and into the nineteenth century, the Jewish people found itself exposed as a foreign, superfluous entity with an identity that the host society refused to understand and was unwilling to absorb. Their presence was disturbing, their problem was an irritation, and the interest to grant them protection non-existent.

The fact that hatred of the Jews persisted in the new reality, that its social and political manifestations worsened and became more threatening, deserves examination in the context of this discussion. It is true that there was some reason to think that in its humanistic version, secularism would mute the religious confrontations and would suggest universal moral criteria for relating to people that would go beyond divisions of religion and nationality. Several achievements in this area in the democratic countries, particularly the United States, cannot be overlooked. But it transpires that religion did not disappear in one stroke as a factor influencing social and spiritual life. Western culture is still suffused with Christianity, as Arab culture is by Islam. The significance of this is that the mytho-religious background for the image of the Jew as foreign, as someone who represents a satanic opposition to the truths on which the host culture is founded, still has a potent impact.

Yet the modulating force of the religious establishment to hold in check murderous onslaughts against the Jew was greatly weakened. Furthermore, it emerges that relations that were marked by tension and enmity among competing ethnic and religious groups can snowball so that previous sedimentations of hatred take on new forms. Hatred of the Jews on religious grounds was transvalued into hatred on ethnic or political grounds; it acquired a new ideological and racist phraseology whose danger is greater than the traditional hatred was. The efforts of many Jews to find their place in society as individuals, as well as establish themselves in the culture and society of the new era (which is to say their vigorous movement from the social and economic periphery to the center), underscored the fact that they were competitors. The fact that they enjoyed unusual success stood out. In a very short time, Jews made highly notable achievements in some of the most prestigious areas of society and culture as scientists, philosophers, artists, authors, journalists, lawyers, doctors, economists, and even political leaders of the first rank. Despite the efforts of these individuals to blend in and appear as members of the nation in which they lived, their difference did not disappear. Non-Jewish society knew them to be Jewish and related to them as representatives of a most ambitious and competitive minority.

Surprisingly, once again there was a familiar disproportion between the exceptional prominence of Jews at the center of the host people's cultural life, and the weakness of Jews as a separate group whose political resources remained negligible. As individuals, power was refracted to them by the host nation. A new dimension charged with tragic irony accompanied this disproportion. More and more Jews achieved prominence, influence, and status at a time when the unifying national framework of the Jewish people was crumbling and its ability to defend itself as a people was greatly weakened; that is, the weakness of the people grew in direct proportion to the success of its individuals who were doing their utmost to slip away from the fate of their people. At times of trouble when Jews as a body were attacked, Jewish individuals of great prestige could not help. Their discrete strength could not be combined into an aggregate and the Jewish group had no control over them. Another aspect of the awful reality: Jews, as a group, gradually became defined by an external hatred rather than by the positive content its individuals held in common. This is the height of a paradox in which external prominence is yoked to internal weakness. On the eve of the Holocaust in Europe, the Jewish people reached the high point of its prominence and the nadir of its weakness.

There was also a change in the attitude of the authorities toward Jews. As noted, in principle there was a readiness to accept the Jew as an individual with equal rights, and Jews took advantage of the new opportunity to such an extent that when they encountered resistance on the part of European society, they determined to fight for their rights. This is the first time in the history of exile that Jews stood in opposition to the regime. Of course they never had sufficient strength to form their own opposition, a Jewish opposition. As a result, when the expectation that the regime would grant Jews full equality despite social resistance did not materialize, the Jews cast their lot with revolutionary movements. The role of Jews in such movements, particularly in the socialist and communist movements, was much more salient than their proportion in the population. In itself, this fact contained a new cause for tension. But there was a change in governments' assessment regarding the Jews. Previously rulers had depended on their own class strength; they had not permitted the masses to acquire political strength on which the government would be dependent.

In the modern state, however, in both its democratic and totalitarian forms, the central national regime depends on the masses. The wisdom of the government was its shrewdness in manipulating the masses; it is conditional on a responsiveness to the elementary wishes of the masses and the manipulation of their aspirations. From the Jewish standpoint this meant that the government was no longer interested, as it had been in the past, in extending patronage to the Jews and protecting them from the fury of the masses. On the contrary, there were times when the authorities were interested in exploiting that fury against the Jews, or even in inciting it, in order to extract some advantage. The status of the Jews as a highly visible, yet very weak, minority makes of them a most convenient implement for governmental manipulation, and the social ferment that characterizes the modern period creates many situations that tempt governments to use the Jews as a scapegoat.

A fateful fact must be added: modern military organization, modern political and administrative organization, and modern technology placed immense power to kill in the hands of governments. What had been previously unfeasible from a practical aspect now became possible. A ruler, standing at the head of a modern government, could propose a plan such as the *final solution*. All of which serves as a background for the Holocaust. One should not conclude from the background that the Holocaust was "necessary" nor that it may again "necessarily" recur. One can only conclude that the Holocaust was and remains a possibility, that there are forces militating in that direction. In order for such a possibility to become a reality, there must be a ruler who wants it and is capable of pulling the entire governing apparatus after him. This kind of will is in the realm of madness. A rational ruler could exploit hatred of the masses toward Jews, even incite it, but he would not plan a total annihilation if only because it would not be economically viable. Which is why one cannot be surprised that no one foresaw the Holocaust. Before it became a fact, it did not seem reasonable. Only a madman capable of making his madness infectious could have broken through the limits of reason, from political and psychological standpoints.

It is because of this that one so commonly hears that the Holocaust was a "one-time" occurrence and totally *incomprehensible*. But having actually occurred, it is no longer mad to surmise that it can recur. It appears that madness can be inflamed to the proportions of organized mass psychosis; indeed, observing the many incidents of terror and genocide after World War II demonstrates that bursting the dam of reasonable likelihood from both political and psychological considerations is not unknown at all. Granted the Holocaust was madness, but one can say that madness has become quite *normal* in the social and political reality of our time.

In taking stock on Yom HaShoah, as the Jewish people must, it is essential that they remember a simple truth: the Holocaust is a possible jeopardy to the Jewish people. If the people want to exist and preserve their uniqueness, they must be ready to defend themselves; and in exile (or in the Dispersion)—even in the best of exiles—it is impossible to defend oneself against annihilation. Life in exile contains a combination of factors that make a Holocaust possible. On the one hand, it becomes ever more obvious that one cannot arrest the processes of disintegration and assimilation. The Jewish people is losing its separate identity, and the separate circle of its existence, at an accelerated rate exceeding all previous forecasts. Under the best of circumstances continued existence in exile means that the vast majority of Jews will assimilate. In a worst-case scenario, the Jewish people will be exposed, defenseless to a raging holocaust. Because of this, one could say that unlike Tisha B'Av, Yom HaShoah symbolizes the end of the exilic period. The hostel that the Jewish people set up for itself along foreign roads after the destruction of its country, of Jerusalem and its sanctuary, has also been destroyed, and it is irreparable. If the Jewish people wants to survive it must return to its own land and state, and it must do so in accordance with an initiative that is politically, economically, socially, and culturally independent. It must bend all its resources to the realization of the miracle of rebirth.

A CHANGE IN JEWISH SELF-PERCEPTION

From the standpoint of relations between Jews and other nations, and from the standpoint of relations between the Jewish people and its God, there is a transformation in the people's self-perception. Necessarily, the encounter with national suffering takes on new aspects, and the form of mourning of Tisha B'Av does not seem suitable to a phenomenon like the Holocaust, either in scope or context. In the context of Jewish survival in contemporary reality, two prominent interconnected facts require attention. First, in the nations in which Jews live, the force of a religious world outlook has diminished and the powers of the religious establishment as factors that direct, and in large measure shape, the societal behavior and political functioning of the nations has also diminished. This does not mean that the impact of religion has disappeared. The view that many thinkers of the nineteenth and early twentieth centuries subscribed to that religion would totally disappear did not materialize. Nor is there any reason to think that it will.

Religious belief is a vital dimension of a certain type of human being so that one cannot imagine the complete waning of an emotional and cognitive inclination to the supra-natural. It can be said that the major historical religions remain foci of the spiritual values of cultures and peoples, and that many of the disappointments that secular culture occasioned, along with its achievements, even precipitate an occasional revival of religious movements. The historical fact that institutionalized religions do not effect socio-economic activity, political moves, or scientific inquiry and technological development is also clear. From this standpoint, the process of secularization has become so institutionalized that there is no likelihood, at least in the short run, for a change in its status. It is secular leadership that determines the thrust of developments in all of these areas. Neither a religious world view nor religious authority even enters into the judgment of those who decide what will be done. The consequence of this is that contemporary culture evolves on the basis of the sovereign assumptions of human analysis. Human activity here is not accompanied by the involvement of a supra-human element that is mandatory, directive, and orienting.

Furthermore, the real achievements of man in the areas of science and technology are so great and progress so rapid—appearing to be limitless—that man's pretension to direct his own fate appears to have been validated and realized. Indeed, there is great doubt whether man has found a parallel ability to responsibly control his achievements and whether these achievements do not threaten his own existence. In any case, the sense of ruling the forces of nature has almost totally suppressed the feeling of direction that accompanied medieval man in his daily life, the feeling of causes or a supra-naturally willed force involved in his fate. It would appear that in consequence there is also a crisis in the religious consciousness of believers. Even if belief manifests itself in the realm of their emotional experience at prayer and in ritual, they do not feel a divine presence that gives direction to historical social reality.

The link between this combination of factors—the decreased role of religion in culture and the increased influence of autonomous human activity, coupled with the changed status of the Jewish people in modern times—is obvious and distinct. The growth of secularism is the background to processes of emancipation having both positive and negative outcomes. The Jew who awoke to the sweeping revolutions of European society, as a result of which ghetto walls crumbled, saw the energetic, sovereign activity of human potential. He discovered a human society awakening to the possibility of immense revolutionary enterprises through recourse to its own strength, free of divine supervision and unfettered by religious institutions that claimed to represent the divine. It is against these circumstances that a far-reaching spiritual crisis began as early as the end of the Renaissance and burst into the Jewish public sphere along with the conflagration and subsequent downfall of Shabbatean messianism. The traditional believing world outlook, fixed in the Middle Ages by the Kabbalah, no longer adequately describes reality and cannot direct the activity that, in fact, influences and shapes reality.

Suddenly, the believer who directs all his intellectual and emotional powers toward communicating with the spiritual spheres, hoping that by devotion and purpose in his prayers and in the performance of precepts he can change the human condition and the situation of the Jews among the nations, suddenly senses that there is no connection between his efforts and the daily reality in which he lives. Forces other than the ones he imagined actually operate, and anyone seeking to influence reality must learn the nature of these forces in order to intervene and bend them to his own benefit. The believer senses that there is a directing elite in his environment that knows something about the forces of reality that determine man's fate, and that that elite regards his outlook, not only as outmoded and unsuitable to reality, but ludicrous. The more he tries to gain perfection in the traditional manner, the more his position appears weak and ineffective. The material verity that surrounds him becomes more and more tangible. The highest spiritual verity to which he clings becomes ever more nebulous, hazy, and unreal. A terrible sense of isolation attacks the believer as he feels that God averts His gaze from him. God neither reveals Himself nor responds; the believer remains abandoned to his fate, buffeted by palpable forces that are unknown to him yet are endeavoring to take over every sphere of activity vacated by religious creativity.

From the wealth of theoretical and emotional expressions this crisis engendered, the writing of Haim Nachman Bialik may be singled out. Its singular importance to this discussion stems from its unusual intensity and from the fact that it is an unbroken progression of the principal constitutive themes of Judaic sources. "Facing the Bookcase" is an early poem that stands for the transmission of Judaism from generation to generation through the continuity of the Bible, the Mishnah, the Midrash, the Talmuds, the philosophic literature, poetry, prayers of the Middle Ages, and Hasidism. At the same time, the poetry reflects the crisis that occurs in the heart of the believer who encounters the reality of a Jewish fate that no longer allows a believing response—at least not in its previous form—and has yet to formulate a national Jewish ethos that will enable a new response to the suffering of the people.

Bialik's infuriated reaction to the Kishinev massacre, particularly his prophetic poem "In the City of Slaughter," embodies the breakdown of the traditional reaction-pattern to Jewish fate in exile. The fractured myth of his "The Scroll of Fire" depicts the emergence of yet an additional exile, an internal exile, in the religious experience of the Jewish people against the background of sources that formulated classic reaction-patterns to banishment and annihilation. The mytho-poetic element in "The Dead of the Desert" declares a rebellion against the heavens. If even paradoxically, it is the articulation of an ultimate belief that emerges from the vicious cycle of exile; it reintroduces the Jewish people to the nations as a people capable of existing as of right while preserving the uniqueness of its heritage.

In the following discussion the main themes are only briefly noted. "The Scroll of Fire" opens with a stylized literary presentation that describes the destruction of the country, Jerusalem, and the Sanctuary, in keeping with motifs in the legends of the Sages; that is, a God who destroys his own sanctuary and then mourns over the destruction. But departing from the Sages' description, which sustains the notion of suffering as it is acted out at Tisha B'Av, both God's wrath and mourning in "The Scroll of Fire" no longer betoken the unshakable certainty of an inevitable redemption, which will ostensibly come after the worst has happened. Disheartened, God is stooped over the smoldering Temple, in anger and in impotent mourning. There is but one remnant of hope; it is the last ember from the eternal fire that had been kept burning on the altar. An angel rescues the ember, places it for safekeeping on a mountain top in the middle of an island to which the people have been banished—a symbol of exile, an unachievable yearning in this world. The hope becomes more distant, more ephemeral, almost a delusion, able to prolong existence in exile but in no way able to redeem the people from it. A cursed cycle holds the people in its satanic grip. Therefore the next deviation from the interpretation of the Sages is to be expected. The people's feelings of guilt about the transgressions that supposedly caused the exile not only disappear but are transvalued into an opposite guilt. The believer castigates heaven for the guilt of its sin toward him.

> And the heavens are silent
> They know how they wronged us, an abysmal sin
> Silently they shall bear their punishment

Instead of a redemptive hope, the believer's heart overflows with wrath and passionate revenge, which turn into life's highest goal and threaten self-destruction. This, then, is the twofold response of a suffering that has lost its justification: a futile hope of being realized, on the one hand, and a destructive, furious rage, on the other. Both lead the people to *Abaddon*. In the mythic portrayal of "The Scroll of Fire" two "caravans" are annihilated—the caravan of the young women who are misled by a hope from on high, and the caravan of the young men whose avenging passion misdirects them to the river of destruction. The clear-eyed young man, poet and prophet, takes on his mission with a symbolic ascent to the fire hidden on the mountaintop—symbol of hope—and with a desperate leap into *Abaddon*'s abyss of destruction. There was no call from on high. He heard his own heart where hope and rage contested; his mission is understood as a fall from the mythic realm of a struggle between faith and apostasy (the island of banishment) to the historic, realistic realm of exile. In the tragic transition from one realm to the other, which is also a transition from childhood through young manhood to maturity, the great convolutions of soul—his entanglement between belief and apostasy— are laid to rest.

The crisis sinks inward as latent memory gives shape to the life of the individual. A glimmer of belief is saved. Despite suffering, despite suffering and disillusion, it is expressed in a mighty, vital force and a stubborn adherence to truth, though a bitter one. In any case, the exile of a mature person is perceived as a reality totally emptied of God's presence. Even God's nearness found in the words of the Sages and the wise men— the nearness of one who prays, studies, and performs the mitzvot—has now completely disappeared. All that remains is the memory of an intimate experience that once was, which the believer now clutches in an impotent nostalgia: "And he observed the heavens and they were foreign to him, and he looked at the ground and lo it was strange to him." The

same feeling is expressed in the direct personal confession found in the
poem "Facing the Bookcase":

> Again my hand runs through your scrolls
> And my eye roves between the lines
> Seeking blood among the letters,
> Perhaps I shall find there traces of my soul
> And find the first quiver of my way
> In the place of its birth the source of its life,
> Discover the happiness of my youth, my heart is still.

God not only departs from the country, He abandons not only the
sanctuary, but the *shekhinah*—His divine presence—is also removed from
the synagogue and the house of study. It is as though He has left the very
heavens so that only a strange, foreign world remains for the believer.
Only the memory of something not understood carries the believer of
broken faith along the road of life.

> And the youth wandered over the earth
> Like the straying of a star cast off in the void of the universe.
> And he walked naked and barefoot but straight of glance.
> He had nothing but the Great Fire in the depths of his heart
> And the gloom of the dawn in the depths of his eyes.
>
> "Scroll of Fire": VIII

If God has left the world and the Divine Presence is removed from the
heavens, there is no one to set the task. The poet nevertheless feels as
though he has been filled with a message as an emissary. His duty is to
declare the ultimate truth. He must proclaim the breakdown of faith and
the decline of hope. Paradoxically, it is the sole way to survive and cling
mightily to life. Only an echo of the power of a former belief, which
shaped his personality before it was thrown into a directionless, aimless
existence devoid of God, nourishes his vital will. This is the faithful
dedication to the original direction of a person's inner life even after he is
left utterly isolated. Stubbornly he maintains that he testifies to himself,
about himself, as having remained loyal to his truth.

The incongruous mission of a prophet, whom no one sends, assumes
many manifestations in Bialik's work, but their most overt form is in the
poems of wrath closest to the pathos of biblical prophecy. They give vent
to a direct clash with the fate of the Jewish people in exile, a clash with

suffering that appears as a fate devoid of any justification or meaning. Examining Bialik's greatest prophetic opus, "The City of Slaughter," written as a reaction to the Kishinev massacre, one finds that it is actually a poetic essay that might more accurately be described as a reaction to the practiced, traditional response of victims of pogroms. The fact that the Jewish people was still capable of responding to its terrible suffering in the same coin of national mourning as on Tisha B'Av—a feeling of guilt and a plea for forgiveness—is what arouses a furious response in the poet, ousting him, as it were, from God's presence in a self-destroying prophecy. A people who plead for forgiveness for sins that are allegedly the cause of their suffering, transgress as Job's companions did when they spoke improperly to him. Awe in a situation that actually calls for rage appears sacrilegious to the poet because it trivializes the name of God through mendacity. Only a penetrating statement of the truth, be it a truth more bitter than death, can withstand the trial of a faith that has collapsed. Denial appears as the only mode for belief. This is the way in which the poet regards himself as an emissary sent to his people to herald, on God's behalf, the end of belief.

The poem opens as the first encounter with suffering takes place. The poet sees a massacre that conflicts with a primal sense of justice, the experiential core of belief. Such acts contradict the proper order of the world. This world has been created according to the beneficent will of a God who supervises and who directs His world justly. It is inconceivable that such acts should be done without Creation itself reacting, for this is a complete smashing of foundations. But the world tolerates what has happened. The terrible massacre stands alone; the order of the universe is quite apart from it. For the believing poet such apathy to the ordinance of the world in the face of the moral norm that is now in tatters is the greatest atrocity. His response is a reaction to the utter destruction of the primal belief, and the ordeal is subsequently reformulated in each stratum of the enraged response.

> Pause not upon this havoc; go thy way.
> The perfumes will be wafted from the acacia bud
> And half its blossoms will be feathers,
> Whose smell is the smell of blood!
> And, spiting thee, strange incense they will bring—
> Banish thy loathing—all the beauty of the spring,
> The thousand golden arrows of the sun,
> Will flash upon thy curse;

The sevenfold rays of broken glass
Over thy sorrow joyously will pass,
For God called up the slaughter and the spring together—
The slayer slew, the blossom burst, and it was sunny weather!

The sense of injustice serves, first of all, as background for the poet's reaction to the way his professedly believing kinsmen respond to the slaughter. They rehearse the traditional form as though nothing has changed.

And thou wilt come, with those of thine own breed,
Into the synagogue, and on a day of fasting,
To hear the cry of their agony,
Their weeping everlasting...
Are they not real, their bruises?
Why is their prayer false?
Why, in the day of their trials
Approach me with pious ruses,
Afflict me with denials?
Regard them now, in these their woes:
Ululating, lachrymose,
Crying from their throes,
We have sinned! and *Sinned have we!*—
Self-flagellative with confession's whips.
Their hearts, however, do not believe their lips.
Is it, then, possible for shattered limbs to sin?
Wherefore their cries imploring, their supplicating din?
Speak to them, bid them rage!
Let them against Me raise the outraged hand,—
Let them demand!
Demand the retribution for the shamed
Of all the centuries and every age!
Let fists be flung like stone
Against the heavens and the heavenly Throne!

The revolt against heaven becomes the final gesture of belief out of which the terrible truth bursts, couched as God's ultimate message said to the emissary prophet himself.

Forgive, ye shamed of the earth, yours is a pauper-Lord!
Poor was He during your life, and poorer still of late.
When to My door you come to ask for your reward,

I'll open wide: See, I am fallen from My high estate.
I grieve for you, my children. My heart is sad for you.
Your dead were vainly dead; and neither I nor you
Know why you died or wherefore, for whom, nor by what laws;
Your deaths are without reason; your lives are without cause.
What says the Shekhinah? In the clouds it hides
In shame, in agony alone abides;
I, too, at night, will venture on the tombs,
Regard the dead and weigh their secret shame,
But never shed a tear, I swear it in My name.
For great is the anguish, great the shame on the brow;
But which of these is greater, son of man, say thou—
Or keep thy silence, bear witness in My name
To the hour of My sorrow, the moment of My shame,
And when thou dost return
Bring thou the blot of My disgrace upon thy people's head,
And from My suffering do not part,
But set it like a stone within their heart!

These words are straightforward and should be understood on the
manifest level. This is the ultimate response of a believer who demands
justice, who can maintain faith while seeing evil done only by abandoning
his faith because God has allegedly renounced His own divinity. To live
with this truth while confronting the world is the essence of the believer's
mission. If this is so, what action is called for? The question recalls the
analysis of the motif noted earlier regarding the development of Hanukkah's significance; that is, belief as a revolt against heaven bursts forth as
an act of desperation: to strive for national redemption "despite the
heavens and their anger." Hanukkah represents a shift in the people's fate
through a full mobilization of the potential of the people itself. The angry
uprising of the people against its fate could be the force that tips the
balance in a war that a priori appeared to be lost.

Behold us! We will ascend
With the tempest!
Though the Lord has withdrawn His hand from us,
And the Ark stands moveless in its place,
Still we will ascend—alone!
Even under the eye of His Wrath, daring the lightning of His
    countenance,
We will carry with storm the citadels of the hills,
And face to face in combat encounter the armed foe!

Listen!
The storm, too, calls unto us—'Courage and daring!'
To arms! To arms! Let the hills be shattered and the mountains blasted
    into dust,
Or let our lifeless bodies be heaped in countless cairns.
Forward!
On to the hills!

                                        "The Dead of the Wilderness"

SPIRITUAL AND HISTORIC ONGOINGNESS

The poem "The Dead of the Wilderness" symbolizes the theological significance of the revolt against exile inherent in the Zionist movement. In Zionism's "negation of the *galut*" there was not only an intrinsic yearning for redemption but also a revolt against the adaptive techniques to exile of the Jewish people, including messianic adaptation. No longer *Lamentations*, nor a penitent beating of the breast, nor *Kiddush HaShem*, nor even the certainty ostensibly validated by having reached the height of suffering, that the redemption will come from the source of grace and mercy from on high. As the spokesman for Zionism, Bialik's perception of reality swings pendulum-like between a feeling that previous forms of response are no more than fetters by which an angry and unjust God bound His people to the wilderness, and between the feeling that these forms of response are nothing but an illusion; worse—a people consciously lying to itself as it faces a God that is a "pauper-Lord" who demands of His people that they revolt against Him.

One way or another, Zionist consciousness held that there is no purposeful or beneficial progression in Jewish history. Exile is a tragedy and a curse, and the proper response to both the tragedy and the curse is an autonomous initiative by the people. The suitable reaction to Jewish suffering is to confront the human, historical factors that drove the people to its present miserable state. It must mobilize its own resources; it must want to be strong and become strong; it must return to its own land and reconstitute the independent life of a nation. Only by taking the first steps in this direction can the people console themselves for their suffering, can they regain their lost pride.

It would appear that there is no possible counter to the Holocaust without this model, which was consolidated in Zionism. Face to face with the Holocaust, Bialik's words in "The City of Slaughter" are so true that few could deny them. Paying close attention to the meaning of the words, can a Jew respond to the Holocaust by reading chapters of *Lamentations*? Can a Jew justify the Holocaust as a judgment for the people's sins? Many transgressions may be counted before, during, and after the Holocaust but to respond to the Holocaust as Jeremiah did to the destruction in his time, two conditions must be met. First, there must be an apparent—at least partial—cause and effect relation between the people's sins and the punishment that descends upon them. Second, the punishment must be of the same kind as the sin; that is, "measure for measure." Neither of these conditions is met in the Holocaust; even those great moralists of whom there are no lack in Jewry cannot pretend they exist. There is no apparent cause and effect relationship between the sins of the Jewish people and the Holocaust unless one claims that the great transgression was procrastination in escaping anti-Semitic Europe in time. (Could the entire Jewish people have escaped in time?) In any case, one cannot claim that the Jews by their misdeeds caused the evil of an Auschwitz, or the silent reaction of all Europe to Auschwitz. Certainly there is a no apparent "measure for measure" connection between the sins of the people and the "punishment" that was meted out. The transgressions of the Jewish people were the ordinary sins of mankind; serious though they may have been, they did not depart from the actions of civilized people nor did they represent a shattering of the social arrangements of society.

Auschwitz, however, was a manifestation of human malevolence that departs from anything that human beings had previously done. Auschwitz was a human sin for which "satan has not yet conjured up a revenge." Therefore no one can justify the Holocaust as a decree as Jeremiah justified the decree of the destruction. Is it possible to describe the Holocaust as a "trial"? To what could such a trial testify, and in whose eyes? Could one claim that the Jews were persecuted in the Holocaust because of their beliefs? Could one possibly regard the mass deaths of Auschwitz as bearing witness to a religious truth that confounded its deniers? Presumably from the standpoint of a believing Jew, explanations of the Holocaust as a punishment for sin, or as a trial, would be sacrilegious. In the face of the Holocaust, the believer can maintain his faith only if in his heart he is certain that the decree was not promulgated by God, that the Holocaust was executed by man against God's will, and that God was with him at his time of suffering in the Holocaust.

The fortitude to respond in this way to the terrible suffering for sins that were not in any way commensurate with what was allegedly "their punishment," is found in Psalms and in the words of the Sages. A *midrash* of the Sages about God's appearance in the burning bush says, "The Lord said to Moses, 'Don't you sense that I am steeped in sorrow just as the Israelites are steeped in My sorrow? Therefore know, from the place that I speak with you, from among the thorns, it is as though I were a partner in their sorrow'" (*Shemot Rabbah* II). If, in the words of the Sages, this is the case regarding the suffering of the people as they saw it, it is all the more true for a believing Jew today. If, in the recesses of his heart, he was able to preserve belief, he is certain that the acts done during the Holocaust were not in keeping with divine will, but were in opposition to it, and that God was with the murdered and those consumed in the furnaces, with them in their suffering.

Clearly applying this line of reasoning to the Holocaust—that is, the religious paradox of the Sages' words—reaches the limits of internal contradiction. In the Sages' words, God is a partner who participates in His people's sorrow and continues to direct history. Despite this, He has knowingly allowed enemies to oppress His people. When he participates in their sorrow, He wishes to comfort them for a suffering that appears unjust, saying that it was a necessary suffering, and that redemption will surely come soon. The believer who faces the Holocaust recognizes the startling certainty that God could not have saved those who suffered a Holocaust precipitated by a malicious human heart despite the will of heaven. God does not govern the actions of mankind or its historic enterprises. In this sense, He is not an ostensible, but an actual, participant in the sorrows of the Jewish people. That is, the believer recognizes that the Holocaust took place because of the evil in men's hearts and the madness of mankind who appropriated realms that are inappropriate to humanity and did what man is in no case allowed to do. The Holocaust transpired against God's will. Yet God did not prevent it. Man, who had exceeded his bounds, met no resistance. He managed to do as he wished. Had God left the world, abandoning it to the malignancy of men's ambitions? Was God vanquished by the malice of his creatures? Such questions are unanswerable by traditional theology. They undermine the basic assumptions of all classic theology. No wonder then that they fed the theology of the absurd, of the "death of God," just as in Bialik's poetry they furnished a theology of an impoverished God whose dishonor was exposed. But can belief be based on such theologies? Is it not really disbelief disguised in the imagery of a believer's language?

All of which brings us back to the historic development that began long before the Holocaust at the inception of the New Age. Man's increasing control of the forces of nature and his growing certainty that he would achieve sovereignty over the universe has served as background for an erosion in the faith of believers. They now feel that what occurs in the life of the individual, as well as society, no longer benefits from divine supervision. The factors that impact directly on their fate as human beings are not determined in the heavens, but more and more by man. Consequently, viewing Providence as an abstract depiction, people learn not to depend on it. They learn to depend on the science of man and his improving technical tools. Audacious theologians attempt to save the notion of Providence by subsuming it into secular reality. When an optimistic outlook is in the ascent, Providence is identified with the purposefulness of a history ostensibly progressing toward perfection. However, this is already the nullification of a belief in Providence in the moral, biblical sense; divine direction, which metes out justice to individuals and to nations, is abolished. But how does a belief in Providence benefit from even this kind of explanation if it emerges that history does not necessarily have a positive purposefulness, and that man, governing nature, can exploit his control in order to perpetrate a Holocaust?

So it appears that one cannot avoid recognizing man's role in recent history: God's Providence over man's affairs has *retreated* from every front in which man has managed to claim and assert his own leadership. Nothing thwarts man in his efforts to decode nature's secrets; nothing holds him back from exploiting the forces of nature through the perfection of a technology that harnesses those forces in the furtherance of his aspirations. There is nothing that restrains man from doing anything that is technically possible. These are facts that a believer, too, must acknowledge. These are the underlying facts in a secular, humanist world view that challenges the rule of religion over civilization, and these are the facts at the root of the secular Zionist response to the fate of the Jewish people in exile in modern times. Do these facts mandate the total dismantling of a believer's world? It is unavoidable that most people in Western civilization, and even most Jews, affirm such a thought. The faith of the Patriarchs is no longer the foundation on which they base their behavior in daily life; their world outlook holds with either a simplistic atheism or with a skeptical and tortured agnosticism.

Yet a skeptical, tortured agnosticism testifies to their shrinking from a resolute decision to negate belief; parallel to those who embrace atheism one finds people who maintain a simple faith. Even the Holocaust did not enable its survivors to arrive at an identical conclusion. There are atheists. And there are those whose belief has been reinforced. The question must be asked again, what is the fountain head of faith for a generation in which Providence has ostensibly disappeared?

First, some reservations about the generalization in the formulation of the question. It is much too broad. A "withdrawal of Providence" is applicable in the realms of societal, political, and historical events. It does not apply to an individual's most intimate experience in his progression from infancy to maturity, nor does it necessarily apply to what one experiences in the network of intimate relations between man and his immediate surroundings: his family, friends, community. In this area of close interpersonal relationships, believers can—should they wish— maintain a way of life that repeatedly verifies their belief and repeatedly confirms it. Granted that this generation has become adjusted to rapid changes in many areas. There are frequent changes in science, technology, social organization, and political structure, which can occasionally be seen as real progress. Therefore an impression arises that a person's entire world is engaged—or it would be better if it were engaged—in change, or perpetual progress and there is no longer a single area in which man remains fixed and stable. The feelings of many who are enthralled by a headlong rush toward change, which characterizes modernity, is that religion has become outmoded—passé, no longer valid.

But one can easily be convinced that change is not a law that applies to all spheres. The essence of man and of the world has not changed. Even the most advanced science and technology refers to, and partially shapes, a human creature whose abilities and physical, spiritual, mental, and moral characteristics remain as they were; the natural environment has persisted as it was. Belief is inherent in man's primal, unchanging constitution and in the primary relations between man and the natural environment that surrounds him, including his closest relations to those who bore and reared him. In earlier chapters, faith has been described as an elementary stance or as man's rudimentary reaction to his environment, a position that determines his personal development and the web of his relationships with his social surroundings. Such a description stands today, too. Just as the form of his birth and physical growth have not changed, neither has there been change in the educational and socializing processes by which a creature develops into a human being.

The primal experience generates and confirms the expectation of love, and the provision of physical, psychological, and spiritual needs. In the absence of all these, a helpless creature does not develop into a responsible and independent person. In most cases, this means that man's early experience confirms the faith that he places in the natural and human surroundings that support him. Moreover, as he grows up, he must also be trusting despite bitter disappointments that he encounters; this faith in his close environment enables an existence that generally is not entirely disappointing. Indeed, the initial trust without which a responsible and healthy person cannot develop, is the underpinning of the believing gesture. Faith is nurtured by it, and is continually confirmed through it; this holds today as it did in earliest times. It cannot be undermined without completely undermining the personality. Any one who has been raised in a social, familial framework that builds a believing way of life, and a culture of belief on such an infrastructure, finds his reassurance in it. Despite the bitterest experience, such a person will refuse to relinquish belief either in himself or in his surroundings because he has internalized the posture, and he creates it from within himself.

This is apparently the basic explanation of Bialik's poetry. Even confronted by disappointments, the poet remains a man of broken faith but not a nonbeliever. The trust that was shaped as a childhood experience and as an intimate youthful experience is basic. Eliminating it is tantamount to uprooting the roots of personality. On the strength of these insights, it is important to stress that the life experience of a person in modern, secular society neither dislodges nor diminishes the validity of the symbols expressive of a life of belief in the cycle of the year as it has been described to this point. The description of the Sabbath, Rosh HaShanah, Yom Kippur, and the Pilgrimage Festivals depicts a core experience in the life cycle of a believing public. Their rehearsal confirms them and gives testimony to their continued existence for they create a human reality permeated by belief.

Even when attention is directed to modern, historic events where human initiative displaces the notion of a directing divine presence, it is not possible to come to an unambiguous conclusion that totally destroys belief in Providence. While it is true that man finds no obstacle that prevents him from doing anything technically feasible, nor is any moral crime restrained by a metaphysical force, still this does not mean that humanity—seen as a whole—has achieved sovereignty over its fate, and proved its ability to conduct itself as it wishes. When the Holocaust and its background are examined from the perspective of the general human condition, particularly what awaits mankind should the internal processes that enabled the Holocaust continue, a destructiveness appears to which humanity exposes itself by exceeding the frontiers of responsibility. Since the moral force of man has not grown commensurately with his ambitious powers, he increasingly endangers himself with each new achievement of science and technology.

No longer can any human regime predict the results that stem from the enormous achievements of science, nor can it properly consider what—of all that has become possible—should be done, what could bring destruction down on mankind as a whole. Nor can any government devised by man any longer restrain or halt social, cultural, and political processes that appear to be manifestly destructive. Every network that exists between civilization and nature, between peoples and states, between social strata, and even between individuals, is increasingly distorted. Most people in modern time already sense these distortions, endure them, and fear their results. But, they feel helpless in controlling them. They are enslaved to the very processes that mankind's leadership has set loose.

Just as this situation occasions the repudiation of a guiding divine authority, it also engenders a longing that such an authority should indeed be revealed to save humanity from itself. The will to exist is transmuted into the will to believe, because without belief one loses the meaning of existence in the present, and a hoped-for existence in the future. At moments of trying crisis, there are times when the will to believe breeds the renewing force of belief itself. This miracle of renewal was experienced by individuals in the Holocaust. It was the source of their strength to withstand the worst, to survive and return to life. But for most people who grew up and were educated in a civilization that had freed itself from the yoke of heaven it is impossible to see how they can become believers once again, even when the longing to believe is awakened in them. In their eyes, belief is an illusion and no sane person consciously deludes himself. The source of the skeptical, troubled agnosticism that characterizes most people today has its source here.

It is time now to propose the hard answer. It is an answer that consoles, an answer that the believing person gives to the question of injustice whose source is the malevolence of man: belief is not an illusion. It is not based primarily on an expectation that some supra-human force will intervene and restrain people from doing something that is within the realm of possibility. Such action has always been within man's province, and, a priori, man can do what runs counter to that which is good and honest, that which goes beyond the bounds of his moral responsibility. It is mandated in man's substantive liberty. Liberty subsumes the possibility of sin. Punishment is the result of an internal and external distortion caused by sin. In observing assumptions elucidated as early as the Bible, one sees that God does not directly avert the inequities that people cause one another by His intervention, thus preventing an act that man is potentially capable of doing. Natural circumstances are the limitations of man's deeds. To the extent that these circumstances have not been changed by man, they are in accordance with what was set forth in Creation; they can therefore be regarded as divine Providence. Historical experience has shown to what bounds the possibilities of transgression can reach when man makes sweeping interventions in the arrangements of nature, changing their original design.

It is this that accounts for the sensation that God has departed from His world, an outcome of the fact that modern man lives increasingly in circumstances that he has himself designed, having actively intervened in the plan of Creation. Man's enhanced ability to act is necessarily regarded as a more open arena, less limited by a supra-human force. But by the nature of things, the danger is also greater, and the punishment that mankind as a whole suffers—as an organized collective—is commensurate with its proficiency to sin against itself and its surroundings. There is only one way in which God's direct intervention in man's affairs can be seen (stated very clearly in Psalms) and that is through the volitional action of other concerned individuals. Man's moral conscience is the voice of God speaking to him and commanding him. The will of God is revealed through the will of believing people who hear God's message in their heart, as well as in the Torah that was handed down by their ancestors, on which they were brought up and act out in deeds. In other words, the will of believers who stand up against malevolence and evil in order to do what their heart and the Torah teach is God's commandment, returns Providence to a world from which it had departed because of evil-doing.

It must be admitted that from the start it appeared that the task of believers was greater than their capability. They are, a priori, weaker than those whom they oppose, and they lack the resources of their enemies. Is there a measure of hubris that goes beyond the boundaries of human ability in the confrontation with transgression and the social circumstances that enable the mighty to rule? Can man become the vehicle for his Creator? Granted, against the arrogant pride of the evil in men's hearts, what is called for in believers is a no less aspiring zeal. There is no less daring vis-à-vis God than vis-à-vis men in the believer's deeds. When a believer submits his will to his Creator's, his intention is to make his will the will of the Creator. This is the paradox of belief; the inexplicable power of the weak to face the strong and triumph over them is the ancillary insight revealed in the paradox. Is it the strength of belief itself? Is it a power granted to man from the heavens?

In any case, there is a certain, straightforward tangibility to the sense of grace on which a believer depends. There are wondrous moments. There are moments when the miracle is a perfect certainty. Nor do these happen only at times of historic decision; rather, they occur in daily life, too, when the desire of a believer who set outs out on an enterprises succeeds; when something, even something small, is set right. The distance between what had appeared initially as a possibility and what has been achieved gives the believer the feeling that a helping arm has been extended to him, the power of God has been added to his own so that what appeared to be impossible becomes an actuality. God does help those who help themselves. The knowledge of this reinforces the believer so that he persists and hopes despite failures that lie in ambush along the way.

Belief is not an illusion if one does not construe it to be passive expectation, or limited activism in the arena of ritualistic religion. It is not an illusion when one sees it as an active position that employs all the tools available to man at a given historic juncture in order to realize the commandments, and this includes the very same tools that evil and malevolence employ in order to achieve their aims. For a believer who does not separate himself from the totality of sinful humanity, who does not place himself only in the midst of the sufferers and the unjustly persecuted, it is eminently possible to reiterate *ashamnu*—we have all sinned. He thereby recognizes that the punishment meted out to mankind, as a whole, is measure for measure because of its sins, both vis-à-vis God and vis-à-vis itself. Still, it is not merely acknowledgment of guilt based on a consciousness of moral responsibility, nor an atoning plea that will save him in the midst of his people and in the midst of all those who suffer because of humanity's sins. It is the readiness to act against evil and on behalf of that which is good and just, using all the tools employed by evil in its drive to rule the world. It is only this daring aspect of belief that can validate and preserve belief in its endeavors.

In modern times, when the fate of the Jewish people among the nations is viewed in this perspective, one concludes that Zionism alone was a believing answer to the suffering of the Jewish people in exile. Here is a people who, by its own initiative, exploiting its own meager resources, stood up to its enemies and persecutors in order to defend itself and create the foundation for its life as an independent nation. There was great daring in the establishment of the State of Israel precisely because to achieve this independent initiative, scientific, technological, and political instruments of other nations were adopted. There was the arrogance of belief in revolting against the fate of exile and against the routine forms of its life. It is no wonder that the devoutly orthodox, who guarded the routine forms of exilic life and the routine forms of expressions of faith in exile, regarded it as heresy. But this heresy contained a greater belief than the belief of its detractors because it dared to face up to historic reality and wrestle with it. Anyone who contemplates the circumstances of world Jewry at the beginning of organized Zionism cannot ignore the miracle of people devoting themselves to such an endeavor. In the second half of the nineteenth century, the Jewish people gave no indication that it could achieve such a task.

What bridged the enormous gap between the utopian vision and its realization? Was it the force of belief in itself, or was it a power delegated from above? When the State of Israel emerged, when it was victorious against its enemies in the War of Independence, when it absorbed a mass immigration and developed the country, when it repeatedly overcame its enemies without suspending its determination to consolidate itself and grow stronger—even those who did not regard themselves as believers could not, in the face of all this, deny a miraculous dimension. For believers, the State of Israel is a response to the suffering of the Jewish people in contemporary exiles, even the Holocaust. This is not because it is an ostensible *compensation* for such suffering, but because Israel, by its very existence, testifies to the fact that when—out of belief—will is harnessed to action exhausting everything that is within man's power to do, it can withstand all evil intent and repair something in the world. Because even in moments of weakness, one can shake off dejection and act so that, in acting, one senses the growing power that will achieve the goal.

The significance of these observations is not limited to the Jewish people or to Zionism. From this standpoint, one can observe the struggles of other peoples and the struggles of mankind as a family of nations. The answer to the many faces of human malice does not apply only to the Holocaust, and the response to man's prideful departure from the bounds of his moral capability and the limits of his responsibility is the same answer that perceives of belief as a dynamic mode that commits itself to action, using the tools available to man at the time. People who submit their will to God's will can, by their deeds, reintroduce divine Providence into the world from which it departed because of malice and hubris. They can make their Creator's will synonymous with theirs.

To summarize, Holocaust Day marks a new departure in the consciousness of the Jewish people as a nation among the nations, and as a people vis-à-vis its God. By virtue of nation's deeds, it also marks a new departure in recognizing the human situation from the standpoint of its capability to conduct itself and face up to lurking dangers. For the Jewish people, Holocaust Day is first of all a milestone in the history of exile. The temporary hostel that the people built for itself outside its land after the destruction of the country, Jerusalem and the sanctuary, has now been destroyed too and has no future. Furthermore, the forms of response to exile that were devised for days of national mourning, especially Tisha B'Av, are no longer suitable to the circumstances of the Jewish people's fate. The notion that suffering is punishment for the nation's sins, or that it is a trial that ensures that salvation will come from on high, no longer accurately explains either the historical experience, or directs the people to action that will enable its existence while preserving its uniqueness among the nations.

On Holocaust Day, the nation takes spiritual stock of the active response that manifested itself through the Zionist enterprise: the daring to act by means of its own strength, even if at first the goal appears to be beyond the realm of the achievable. The responsibility for the nation's life, its security, the entire breadth of its creativity rests on itself alone. It is only by utilizing all the tools available to it that the power to turn that which seems to be impossible into the possible will be revealed. Daring to perform the commandment—which appears to be eminently necessary, yet harder and greater than man's capability—is the answer of consoling belief to the nation's suffering and to the suffering of mankind. The Jewish people is part of humanity; its spiritual accounting in the Holocaust is part of the spiritual accounting of the humanity that perpetrated the Holocaust and that repeatedly commits holocausts against other peoples as well. On Holocaust Day, a universal truth is expressed in which the Jewish people assumes its portion: only mutual responsibility that is undertaken by partners for the fate of humankind in a readiness to take stands against evil and lay the foundation for a different human reality, which exists in keeping with the dictates of belief, can save humanity from the annihilation it is preparing for itself. Faith is will that submits to commandments even in a world that denies their existence.

At this point a cautionary note must be added, which applies particularly to the national spiritual accounting of the Jewish people in this generation. Jewish educators and thinkers, especially those who are Zionists, tend to point to the Holocaust as evidence of the correctness of Zionism, not only as a testimony to the unfeasibility of existence in exile, nor only from the need to undertake independent initiative, but also as an irrefutable argument regarding the identity of individual Jews with their Jewishness. Why remain Jewish? Why choose Judaism if the way to assimilation is open? To this trenchant question, raised not only by young people born in the exiles of the Free World but also by young people born in Israel, Israeli educators generally counter with a supposedly irrefutable answer: the ability to choose is illusory. The Holocaust shows that we are perforce what we were born, that Hitler oppressed not only those who were identifiably Jews but those who had become utterly assimilated. There are people who phrase this idea in a more delicate and profound way.

The important Jewish philosopher, Emil Fackenheim, asserts that anyone who remained alive after the Holocaust that was intended for the entire Jewish people is a Holocaust survivor, and as survivors we have a moral obligation to those who were destroyed to preserve their memory. We have a moral obligation to bear witness against the Nazi malignancy. We may not grant Nazis a victory after their defeat for if the Jewish people disappears, it will be the triumph of Nazism. This moral pathos is understandable particularly in someone who personally experienced the Holocaust, but under no circumstances can one build on it, certainly not on it alone, either the structure of Jewish education or the need to identify as Jews. It is not the hatred of other nations that makes us Jews, nor does their violence oblige us to historic loyalty.

The reason for a nation's existence is that its sons love it and their traditions, because they identify with their culture, values and symbols. Only those children of the Jewish people who know their heritage and live the fullness of its content—those whose Jewishness is their involvement in the community of peoplehood, participation in its ways of life and its creativity, will continue as Jews. Holocaust Day takes place between two great holidays—Passover and Yom HaAtzmaut (Independence Day). Only those individuals who inform their national, spiritual account with a historic memory that shapes the national heritage and its ongoingness—symbolized by Passover—will, through that identity, undertake the task of positive construction, the structuring of our people's political autonomy—symbolized by Yom HaAtzmaut.

ELEVEN

SPIRITUAL FREEDOM
AND POLITICAL FREEDOM
(PASSOVER AND INDEPENDENCE DAY)

THE PROBLEM OF POLITICAL FREEDOM

In the modern era, Israel Independence Day stands as the primary expression of the Jewish people's triumph over adversity. Though the verse, "More than one has risen up against us and tried to destroy us," is still read, the question arises, can today's Jews continue its recitation to the end of the verse—"The Holy One, Blessed be He, saved us from them"—as it has been read throughout the generations? The phrase, which is said at Passover, reflects an identification with the powerful trauma Jews experienced as they moved from exile to exile. On Independence Day, however, Jews are aware that exile's temporary hostel has been irreparably destroyed; this time the people were saved from unprecedented disaster because of their courage in acting on their own behalf. From the depths of weakness, the Jews gathered their remaining forces, grew in strength, and returned to their land where they settled and established a state. This achievement, which would have seemed inconceivable just one generation earlier, spurs a sense of wonder and gratitude. It may be that there is something of a miracle in the establishment of the State of Israel but, even if this is so, it is a different kind of miracle from that which occurred during the exodus from Egypt. The idea of freedom celebrated at Passover is distinguished from the idea of freedom celebrated on Independence Day by the changes the Jews have undergone in modern times. These changes have once again brought to a head the dilemma that consistently troubled the people as they dwelled in their own land but that disappeared during exile: the problem of political freedom.

The State of Israel is the enterprise of the Zionist movement, a movement established in reaction to changes in the external and internal condition of the Jewish people in modern times. A people is a historical entity that exists through the continuum of historical consciousness, and through the continuum of cultural values passed from generation to generation. As a national movement, Zionism was also a movement of continuity; it saw itself as the successor to messianic movements that sprang up in every generation. Zionism relied on an unbroken link with the Land of Israel, adherence to Hebrew as the people's language of creativity, and on the hope of returning to the Land of Israel to find redemption there. Zionism sought the realization of the hope in its own way, and "its own way" meant an independent initiative on the national, political, settlement, and societal levels. No longer would Jews long for Divine mercy, seeking to bring redemption closer through repentance and prayer. Zionism is a secular movement, which does not look to Divine leadership in the affairs and destinies of nations. Its aim for the Jewish people was to re-establish the political, social, economic, and military means enjoyed by every *normal* people. In this respect, Zionism was not only a transformation from the reactive pattern developed in exile, but a bold and bitter rebellion against it.

Zionist ideology interpreted the concept of *Shlilat HaGolah*, Negation of Exile, not only as a negation of exile itself; it was as well a negation of the distorted behavior that had come about as Jews adapted to exilic reality: a restricted, deprived ghetto life that focused on an inner light of Divine proximity through prayer, study of Torah, and the commandments between human beings and God. Zionism called for a "return to history"—that is, a return to the comprehensive national responsibility of Jews for all areas of their life. Paradoxically, this rebellion against the very essence of exile could also be seen as a form of continuity. Indeed, Zionism sought and extracted ancient layers and historical memories that predated the traditions born of exile; it looked to the wars of Joshua, the Judges and David, the Hasmonean revolt, the Zealots, and the Bar-Kokhba rebellion; to the life of the Jewish people as an agricultural nation

living on its own soil and close to the nature of its land. Not coincidentally did Zionism focus on Hanukkah, revive Lag B'Omer, and renew Tu
B'Shvat and Tu B'Av.

In all these measures, one can see a deliberate, creative effort to seek a
distinctive tradition beneath that of the Diaspora, one of a nation
struggling for political independence and a full, natural life. Emphasizing
the early tradition that had been obscured by exile was a clear indication
of the Negation of the Diaspora, and it necessitated a deliberate change
from the mold cast by the Sages and their pupils regarding the laws,
symbols, and ideas of these festivals. The festivals were renewed and
reshaped by the Zionist movement—Hanukkah in a version that stressed
the Hasmonean victory as one of a national movement, the miracle of the
cruse of oil pushed aside; Lag B'Omer as a commemoration of the Bar
Kokhba rebellion; Tu B'Shvat as a festival of setting down roots in Israel
through the ceremony of planting; Tu B'Av as the holiday of the grape
harvest and dancing in the vineyards. All these festivals are in contention
with the Diaspora; they set up a new tradition that relies on the ancient
past, which consciously skip over links to the continuous past of the
Jewish people. It is precisely in this point that the problem lies, becoming
more profound as it reopens a principled question for honest and
thorough examination: How does the Torah relate to the idea of political
freedom and the experience of sovereign independence?

The festivals of the traditional Jewish calendar did not give any real
expression to the idea or experience of political freedom. The concept is
not mentioned at Passover; it is deliberately obscured at Hanukkah; it is
hinted at ironically at Purim. What does this mean? Does the Oral Law
tradition disapprove of the idea and form of a nation-state? Has the
Zionist rebellion against the Diaspora placed it in confrontation with
tradition, advancing a notion that is foreign to it, whose origins are
external? In examining the distinctions between Independence Day—the
festival of national/political independence, and Passover—the festival of
spiritual/religious freedom, the full range of aspects regarding the question
will be probed.

FROM SLAVERY TO FREEDOM

At Passover, freedom is perceived first and foremost by the exodus from
the yoke of tyrannical rule. The joy of Passover is the relief that comes
after the chains have been removed. Travail is over and the threats, fear,

and persecution are gone. The feeling of relief is accompanied by a sense of revenge unleashed against the enemy who must suffer for the evil that was wrought on the now-liberated people. Along with revenge, there is the certain knowledge that the One who broke the shackles and took vengeance on the tyrants loves His suffering people. In any case, the range of emotional reactions to the change in the external situation are all linked to negative circumstances—the yoke is removed, the chains are opened, the oppression is lifted. There is an inherent element of freedom in the sense that *in principle* the people can act according to their own determination without external limitations. The feeling precedes any particular action for although the people has been freed, it has not yet decided what to do; hence there is the sensation that everything is open. When the people does decide, it will act on its own. At this stage, then, freedom is defined as a completely unimpeded prospect, as a state of facing an undefined expanse of space. This, it would seem, is the sensation on Passover eve—that is the last night of slavery, the first of redemption. On this night, fear of the rulers is dispelled and revenge loosed upon them. Gathered together by families, the people experience the surety of their existence—no one will harm them or disturb their peace—and they look forward to the morrow. The future is a completely open expanse, blank and vacant. They are still not required to take any particular action but they are ready to act, aware that now they have the potential of will and can act according to that will.

Naturally, this feeling is only an initial impression. The moment that the released slave must actualize the potential inherent in freedom is the moment when the question of the essence of freedom emerges as a problem. He must now define specific possibilities and choose between them. When this happens, given that no particular possibility imposes itself on him, there is a sense of distress at the need to choose and confusion as to what and how he will choose. In this second moment, freedom is seen as a heavy burden; now the desert is not a symbol of liberation from external restriction but a terrifying void with no saving grace. It is hardly surprising that at this stage there is an urge to return to Egypt, to realize freedom by taking a one-time decision to forego it. To escape this innate contradiction in the idea of freedom, a certain element of direction is needed to effect a positive definition of the actions that embody freedom. This is the answer given by the Torah. The exodus from Egyptian bondage is the act of both leaving slavery and moving toward the giving of the Torah at Mt. Sinai, and the people begin to receive commandments as soon as they set out. In the language of the Sages, the

Tablets of the Law are the freedom granted to the people; that is, the people only become truly free when they accept a particular program for life, which they have been commanded to follow.

Freedom is expressed in a willing acceptance of the commandments and in the content of the commandments, which directs the Children of Israel to achieve their destiny, to do what they should do according to the standard of what is right and proper. From here on, acquiescence to the commandments is liberty; rejection of the commandments is enslavement to desire. To return to the historic point of the night of exodus from slavery to freedom—a point to which Jews return each year at the seder service—it should be underscored that the main element of freedom at Passover, as seen by the Sages, was the knowledge that God kept His promise to His people, providing protection from persecutors and tyrants and drawing the people closer to His worship. In worshipping God and in obeying and studying the commandments of Passover, the people draw closer to their God and experience the freedom inherent in doing that which is proper. In so doing, the Jewish people is promised that just as they were redeemed in the past, so they will be redeemed in the present. One can see, therefore, that the freedom of Passover is the experience of togetherness felt by the family and the community who provide protection for their individual members (who are themselves sheltered by God who guides them) discovering freedom as they realize their proper destiny through the worship of God.

At this juncture, one finds a surprising fact: the idea and the experience of political freedom are not even mentioned. One finds the family, the community, and the people, and the web of interpersonal relationships between them; but there is no political framework to unite the people against other nations. The people stand alone in the desert, and the social and religious relationships within the people fully encompass the arena for its freedom. One could, of course, claim that even if sovereignty is not mentioned, it is implied. On the one hand, there is the destruction of an oppressive regime; on the other, the alternative and future destiny of the people to reach its own land. The Children of Israel are not, after all, destined to remain in the desert forever. Moreover, how is the giving of the Torah at Mt. Sinai to be understood? Is this not the occasion on which the Jewish people accepted God as their King? Is this not the moment in which they received an entire constitution for life? Nonetheless, Passover does not express political freedom. According to the biblical narrative, such freedom is a distant vision. Moses does not lead the Jews directly into their own land because the people are not yet ready to struggle against other nations for their patrimony and sovereignty. So, by a roundabout route, he leads them into the desert. There, the people receive the Torah and continue to wander for another forty years until they are ready, until they are prepared to take their land and to establish a political framework for life. In the traditional Passover service, political freedom is implied as a messianic event that will come in the very near future, which is beyond the moment and always defined as "next year."

Accordingly, existence in the desert symbolizes a situation of incomplete national freedom. The people is still not capable of taking full responsibility for its existence, either in terms of its economic livelihood or in terms of its ability to stand up to other peoples against whom it will be obliged to compete. As long as it is not capable of discharging this responsibility, it is far from political independence and, of course, far from the trials of independence as well. It is true that in some respects this circumstance of wandering in the desert may seem to be the ideal state of freedom—freedom from the burden of responsibility for a full personal/national existence in which nature and history are actually confronted. This is the ostensibly ideal freedom of adolescence. Mature responsibility is still a vision, and as a vision it has a wonderful wholeness. No hand has yet sullied it with the inevitable imperfections of life under the conditions of nature and human history. During adolescence, a youngster lives under the protection of his parents, dreaming of adulthood; so, too, there is the dominion of God as He leads His people in the desert. The prophet Jeremiah comments aptly on this state:

> Thus saith the Lord: I remember the affection of thy youth,
> The love of thine espousals;
> How thou wentest after Me in the wilderness,
> In a land that was not sown.
>
> Jeremiah 2:2

The Haggadah considers the comments of the prophet Ezekiel to refer to this same period in the life of the people:

> I cause thee to increase, even as the growth of the field. And thou didst increase and grow up, and thou camest to excellent beauty: thy breasts were fashioned, and thy hair was grown; yet thou wast naked and bare. // And when I passed by thee, and saw thee wallowing in thy blood, I said unto thee: In thy blood, live; yea, I said unto thee: In thy blood, live.
>
> Ezekiel 16:6–7

Once again, the exodus from slavery to freedom is described as the festival of spring, or the festival of youth—a vision of future maturity under the loving protection of God.

According to the biblical narrative, the period of maturity begins when the Israelites enter a cultivated land and settle it. On the one hand, entering the Land of Israel symbolizes the purpose of wandering in the desert, as the people at last reaches its home. On the other hand, entry into the Land of Israel is only the beginning of a long path, strewn with setbacks, on the way to political independence. At this point, the manna ceases to fall from the skies, and the people eat "from the crops grown on land"—that is, the Israelites must sustain themselves through nature and by their own labor. From now on, there is no pillar of fire or pillar of cloud; the people themselves must fight for their country, take possession of it, defend it, and they must do all of this under the natural cultural and political conditions that prevail. Seven different nations lived in the land then, each with its own organized pagan sovereignty. Surrounded by pagan peoples, the Israelites had to cope with them even as they lived and defended themselves, and continued to survive among them. The problem raised by this conflict quickly becomes apparent.

From the story of the exodus from Egypt, particularly from Moses' conflict and argument with Pharaoh, one can see the extremely critical view the Torah takes of a pagan kingdom. By enslaving the Jewish people and refusing to let them go free, Pharaoh represents the internal logic of a pagan regime, which made not only the Israelites but the entire country of Egypt into a "house of bondage." It is an inevitable consequence of the fundamental aspiration of pagan dominion: the attainment of absolute sovereignty. This ambition, the Torah teaches, is fated to enslave the people to the regime, and the rulers to their own dominion. Thus, in addition to its national significance, the exodus from Egypt takes on a level of universal meaning as the protest of the believer and the prophet against pagan and pharaonic tyranny. If, after slavery, the Israelites intend to establish their own regime in their land, it should be a different kind of regime—one that is not based on the desire for absolute human sovereignty, that does not turn its country into a prison and its people into slaves. The regime should be faithful to the idea of freedom.

In this respect, receiving the Torah at Mt. Sinai symbolizes the people's vision. Accepting God as King, they negate the notion of the absolute sovereignty of human dominion. In giving His own constitution, God places His laws above those of rulers, restricting their power, which is the meaning of the short phrase used by the Sages to explain the biblical phrase "The children of Israel are slaves onto me" (Leviticus 25:55). They are slaves to God, not to men. The Torah does not provide the constitution for a state; it does render the vision of a state in which the relationship among the people, its land, and its kingdom is established through a limitation on the ownership of property. It makes property conditional on mutual social and ethical responsibility; on equality between people in terms of their status as free men vis-à-vis one another, and in terms of a just legal system they shall enjoy.

Such a vision is indeed found in the Torah. This is not a political constitution, but it is a vision—or a utopia—designed to guide the people as it settles its land and develops as a nation. The system it establishes in its land needs to be genuinely different from the one it abandoned when it left the house of bondage. The people is repeatedly commanded to remember its past and to learn from the experience of slavery in Egypt as a negative pattern. It is repeatedly commanded to keep the vision of God's dominion before it as a positive vision toward which it should aspire.

The question that arises here, of course, is to what extent the people of Israel has succeeded in realizing this vision, and to what extent it could have realized it given the internal and external realities of history. It is the penetrating question that underlies the actions of the prophets throughout their endeavors, from the earliest stages of settlement of the land through the destruction of the First Commonwealth; the same penetrating question accompanies the Sages throughout the testimony of the mishnaic and midrashic periods, from the Return to Zion in the time of Ezra and Nehemiah through the failure of Bar Kokhba's revolt. Is it possible to build a dominion that serves the goal of adequately defending the people from surrounding pagan nations and enables it to sustain itself through nature and the fruit of its own labor without this dominion copying the fairly efficient model of pagan dominions? Is it possible to realize the utopia envisioned by the prophets and the religious literature as a sovereignty of freedom under the Divine constitution?

A decisive turning point in understanding the tradition of the Bible on this question is the well-known story concerning the dispute between the prophet Samuel and the elders in I Samuel 8:4–7. "Then all the elders of Israel gathered themselves together, and came to Samuel unto Ramah. And they said unto him: 'Behold, thou art old, and thy sons walk not in thy ways; now make us a king to judge us like all the nations.' But the thing displeased Samuel, when they said: 'Give us a king to judge us.' And Samuel prayed unto the Lord. And the Lord said unto Samuel: 'Hearken unto the voice of the people in all that they say unto thee; for they have not rejected thee, but they have rejected Me, that I should not be king over them. According to all the works which they have done since the day that I brought them up out of Egypt even unto this day, in that they have forsaken Me, and served other gods, so do they also unto thee.'"

Certainly the leadership of the Judges and of Samuel can be seen as an attempt to realize the concept of Divine kingship—an attempt that was ultimately unsuccessful not only because Samuel's children did not follow in their father's footsteps, but also because the people felt the need for a more efficient government that would enable it to be "like all the nations" and to resist the danger of being taken over by its stronger neighbors. Samuel states his opposition to this outlook in his notable speech: "And he said: 'This will be the manner of the king that shall reign over you: he will take your sons, and appoint them unto him, for his chariots, and to be his horsemen; and they shall run before his chariots. And he will appoint them unto him for captains of thousands, and captains of fifties; and to plow his ground, and to reap his harvest, and to make his instruments of war, and the instruments of his chariots. And he will take your daughters to be perfumers, and to be cooks, and to be bakers. And he will take your fields, and your vineyards, and your olive-yards, even the best of them, and give them to his servants. And he will take the tenth of your seed, and of your vineyards, and give to his officers, and to his servants. And he will take your men-servants, and your maid-servants, and your goodliest young men, and your asses, and put them to his work. He will take the tenth of your flocks; and ye shall be his servants. And ye shall cry out in that day because of your king whom ye shall have chosen you; and the Lord will not answer you in that day'" (I Samuel 8:11–18).

There can be no mistaking the forthright words. Samuel rebukes the elders, arguing that the request to have a king "like all the nations" is a request for slavery. The king who rules as in "all the nations" will strive to achieve the domination of power. The power structure that he establishes will enslave the people to him, despite the fact that he is supposed to serve the people. It is worth noting the precise phrases used at the end of this short and concise speech: "Ye shall be his servants," "and ye shall cry out in that day because of your king," "and God will not answer you"—these are clear references to the people's situation in Egypt. When Pharaoh made the people of Israel his slaves, the people cried out because of their labor and God heard them and responded. This time, however, if the people itself chooses slavery, it will cry out, but God will not answer. The demand for a kingdom "like all the other nations" amounts to a return to the starting point of slavery. It is an utter renunciation of the destiny of the Jewish people.

Samuel does not yield completely. As he realizes that the people's demand for a king is due to particular circumstances, Samuel reaches a compromise. Idyllic Divine dominion cannot be realized in its purest form; therefore a way must be found to draw nearer to it without rejecting reality. The compromise that is reached is rule by a sovereign king whose power is limited and who is subject to Divine command through the office of the prophet. In this way what follows—the coronation of Saul, the trial of the war against Amalek, the rift between Samuel and Saul, and the coronation of David—can be understood. In Jewish tradition, the figure of David is cast as that of the ideal king, based on the supposition that, despite his sins, he was faithful to the restrictions placed on a king's sovereignty by Divine will. It is quite possible that this image of David developed at a later stage as part of messianic hopes for the future. Whatever the case, the ideal image of David was the outgrowth of an attempt to realize Divine dominion as closely as possible given historic reality.

As the Bible shows, the tension between the prophets and the kings of Judea and Israel continued even after the concept of the monarchy had been accepted. Most of the kings are described as sinners who do "that which is evil in the eyes of God." They copy the ways of the surrounding pagan monarchies, intervene in foreign wars, and pervert social justice in domestic affairs; they oppress the weak and commit violence in order to glorify their regimes. Ultimately, when first the dominion of Israel and subsequently that of Judea is destroyed and exiled, the prophets see in this the punishment for the sins of these regimes.

After the Return to Zion, the contrast between spiritual leadership and political leadership again becomes evident. The struggle reaches its climax during the period of Alexander Yannai after the Hasmonean kings consolidate their rule. Although they came to power as the result of a popular rebellion against the attempt made to force Jews to abandon their law, the Sages saw these kings, both in internal and external affairs, as imitations of pagan Greek monarchs. The result was a division between the spiritual leadership of the Sages and their religious courts, and the political/military leadership of the kings. Hanukkah—which had been intended as the Hasmonean "independence day"—came to focus on the symbol of the cruse of oil, the renewal of worship, and the return to God through study of Torah and performance of the commandments within the narrow confines of ritual, home, and community. The regime that took power after the collapse of the Hasmonean dynasty was already seen by the Sages as foreign rule in every respect. Following yet another outbreak, which began with partial consensus and ended in a schism in the period of Bar Kokhba, there was to be no Jewish sovereignty until the establishment of the State of Israel in 1948.

It is true that from time to time a leadership arose that fulfilled limited political functions and consolidated a measure of political authority, such as the *nesi'im* in the Land of Israel and the Exilarchs in Babylon. The Jewish people, however, no longer had the institution of a monarchy wielding sovereign power in domestic affairs and embroiled in power struggles between nations. The Jews were subject to foreign regimes in which they had the status of exiles, living their lives in the restricted circles of Jewish society—the synagogue, the religious seminaries, and the family. Dominion became no more than a memory and a hope, illuminated by an enthusiastic idealization—the memory of the monarchy of David and of Solomon, and the hope of the monarchy of messiah who would lead the people back to its land and rule them according to the Torah. It was a very distant vision though anticipated every day ("this day, if only you heed My voice"); it transcended the limits of historical reality, and its realization was made conditional on a revolutionary change in the order of nature, and in the nature of humanity in particular.

The result was that it no longer seemed possible, given historical reality, to realize the aspiration of putting into practice a Torah ideal of freedom within the framework of a nation-state. The aspiration took on an *other-worldly* character. Although Jewish thought generally recognized the obligation to sanctify the secular and to seek to enable holiness to be present in worldly acts, the broad range of secular roles played by a state continued to be outside the sphere of national responsibility of the Jewish people. The messianic future was perceived as a purposeful perfection that could never be achieved in the present era—any present era.

Which explains the fact that the traditional calendar does not include a festival intended to mark the achievement of political freedom. The reason is not a principled objection to political freedom; on the contrary, the messianic vision elevated the idea of political freedom to the acme of longed-for eschatological perfection. Yet it would appear that it was this very desire for perfection, or for the integration of the Torah/prophetic concept of freedom into a mundane political framework that caused an ambivalent attitude toward statehood—an attitude that was at one in the same time essential, problematic, and disappointing. Any actual regime, since it adapts to the natural drives of humanity and to pagan tendencies, cannot meet the test of the moral and religious demands made by the spiritual leadership, by the prophets and the Sages. Even the willingness to reach a compromise that strikes a balance between the powers, does not guarantee that in the long run the goal of moving closer to the desired condition will be achieved. Compromise demands an extraordinary effort of moral will; consequently, non-failure is a one-time achievement that comes at history's rarest moments.

For the most part, the state, which by its very nature exists as a mechanism of power, seeks to achieve pagan sovereignty with all that this implies in domestic and foreign affairs. When the Jewish people achieves its own sovereignty, it must stand up to other sovereignties in the region, which it will come to resemble. There is no escaping this dilemma other than to rest on an undefined future, clung to with all one's might and yet forever kept at arm's length. In this respect, Passover is a classic symbolic expression. Memory of the past points to a vision of the future, the messianic vision whose arrival will be heralded by the prophet Elijah. It is a vision that is always just about to come true—every year, and always next year.

The establishment of the State of Israel in 1948 was an extremely significant turning point—the realization of a great expectation of Torah and prophetic tradition yet, at the same time, the overturning of this expectation. What had been experienced in the dimension of the perpetual future suddenly moved into the present; achievement and disappointment were both felt to the full. The Jewish people needs its State. In the reality of the modern era, the people could not have continued to exist without adopting the same instrumentality as that which is available to all nations. It was a necessity of life, and behind the political and mundane necessity lay the moral and religious imperative. This is the basis for rejoicing in the establishment of the State, which symbolizes the promise of life. However, the State actually exists in the real circumstances of time and place, established so that the Jewish people could respond to its enemies on the basis of equal strength; it is no longer a messianic vision. The State of Israel is a modern nation-state based on the model of contemporary democracies. Can it be seen as meeting the ideological expectation of Torah and prophetic vision, even by way of the tense compromise seen above? The tension rises once again, together with the joy at the achievement of the State as it stands and at the spiritual and religious significance it embodies, and the question is asked once again: Does this State, the Jewish state, do nothing more than return the Jewish people to the family of nations? Does it have, should it have, a unique character as a Jewish state? These are the questions that lie behind the fluid, still unconsolidated forms of Independence Day.

THE SYMBOLS OF INDEPENDENCE DAY

We turn now to the patterns and symbols of Israel Independence Day. The first element that strikes one is that the secular nature of the holiday distinguishes it from all other Jewish festivals. This is true as well for the religious community, which has added a number of religious and traditional elements to the festival such as the recital of the *hallel* prayer with accompanying blessing, a special reading from the Torah and Prophets, and the recitation of Psalms. Independence Day is an inherently secular event, initiated by the institutional authority of the political state in order to express joy at the achievement of its own existence. Therefore, it is clearly not a day sanctified by a prohibition of work; indeed, taking note of the day in the synagogue is marginal to its content and character. It is a holiday that focuses on what happens outside the synagogue. Yet Hanukkah and Purim—festivals co-opted into the tradition at a relatively late stage—were also not sanctified by a prohibition of labor, and they include a secular element. However, the significance in the secularity of Independence Day is quite different if only because the activity that stamps its public observance would not be possible if work was prohibited. The secularity of Independence Day marks it as the festival of a public that defines itself largely as secular. It is based on secular authority and expressed through activities that can only be undertaken if one is permitted to work. Even if a dimension of sanctity is added, the festival remains primarily secular.

What, then, are the themes and activities that diverge from traditional patterns? First, it should be noted that from the outset Independence Day was an outdoor event—for the street, the stadium, the field; anywhere where the public could gather together in unison. And this sets it apart from the traditional pattern of holidays, which centers on home and synagogue. It is true that on occasion, at Simhat Torah for example, festive joy may overflow into the street. Nonetheless, the core of the festival takes place indoors. By contrast, Independence Day festivities may move into the home or the synagogue for a few moments, but its core remains outdoors. The people display their exhilaration in great throngs that go beyond divisions of family and community. In and of itself, this requires secularity with its concomitant permission to work. Gatherings and activities on such a scale are not possible without the use of technological paraphernalia that are defined in Jewish law as "labor." In any case, to remove the mass scale character of the festival would be to remove its heart. The state is the framework for the public nature of the people, the unity of the crowd; joy at the existence of the state is therefore the joy of the masses, which is experiencing the power of its unity as a nation.

Which leads to the second difference: Independence Day provides the people with symbols of their unity. The flag, the procession, the military parade, the display of national achievements, the raised presidium from which the leaders speak to the people—by their very nature, these symbols represent both external and internal national unity; they are intended to lead the populace toward a common goal. Symbols of this kind consolidate the feeling of communality among the throngs of people; they express the presence of the nation. In a sense, since they bring into the individual's consciousness the recognition that he or she is part of a unified whole with a clear direction for action, the symbols serve to bind the individuals together as a people.

A third difference is that Independence Day marks achievements made by the people through the initiative of its leaders and through the use of its own power. Admittedly the religious population says the *hallel* prayer, offering thanks for a miracle. But for those who identify with the establishment of the state as a framework for national power and see it as a miracle, it is no longer the miracle of the cruse of oil, or the miracle of the reversal of the lottery in Shushan; even less is it the miracle of exodus from slavery with signs and wonders and the parting of the Red Sea. Instead, the miracle is the renewed strength of a weak nation—the miracle of this people's daring and success in its own initiative, given the conditions of exile and the forces that opposed it.

One of the most powerful expressions of the recognition that, this time, it was the people who took the initiative and changed its own fate is the direct link between Memorial Day for Israel's fallen soldiers and Independence Day. It is a bond intended to reflect the fact that, above all, thanks are offered to the children whose utter devotion and heroism gave the people national independence. The same idea is seen in all the ceremonies that emphasize the status of national leadership—the president, the government, the Knesset; the agencies that embody the organized power of the people, the army, and police; and simultaneously, the settlement movements; and large economic, scientific, and cultural enterprises. In brief, this is a festival designed to demonstrate the strength of the people, to anchor the sense of achievement into the consciousness of the nation, and its neighbors.

A fourth distinction: Independence Day marks an existing achievement and rejoicing affirms the value of the achievement. In this respect, the nature of Passover as the experience of being at the threshold of redemption should be recalled. At Passover, the people gather on the eve of redemption and look forward to the event to come; on Independence Day, the people celebrate the crowning event of many years of struggle. Each year the people celebrates not what is anticipated but what has already come about, what appears to be a given fact: an existence that the people support, and on which it can rely in times of trial. Once again, the demonstrative character of the festival should be noted—the appearance of national leaders before the public; the show of symbols that represent institutions of power and authority; the military parade to display the components of the nation's might; the review of attainments in all fields; and the award of prizes for excellence in avenues of cultural activity.

All these activities appear to make their mark on the nature of joy at Independence Day; it is the important and qualitative distinction between this festival and traditional festivals. On traditional festivals, joy is a commandment—"You shall rejoice in your festivals," and the focus is on the commandment itself as the cause of joy, "the joy of fulfilling a commandment." The implication is that each individual actively causes himself to enter a state of joy, and all the individuals jointly create public rejoicing. This is not the case on Independence Day. This is neither "the joy of fulfilling a commandment" nor the commandment to be joyous incumbent on each individual. The joy of Independence Day is presumed to be the natural and spontaneous response of the soul to the bountiful good which it sees in the existing achievement. The sensations of enjoyment, satisfaction, and assurance at what exists banish fear and anxiety, arousing an internal surge of vital forces. This surge is natural joy. Such joy is expected on Independence Day and, to ensure that it will indeed occur, efforts are made to engender it through external stimulus and action. In other words, instead of the animated initiative of individuals commanded to cause themselves to enter into a state of joy, the authorities that represent the achievement being celebrated promote activity that causes joy. On Independence Day the institutions of the State generate happiness—they display achievements, they appear before the people, they march in splendor and glory, they erect platforms for the people to dance and be entertained. And, of course, they expect the population to respond to all this by being swept away in an outburst of gladness expressed in song, dance, and merriment.

It is not difficult to realize that all these features of Independence Day, including the nature of the rejoicing, are directly derived from similar festivals that mark the establishment of other nations. Most European peoples celebrate the founding of their country in this manner—each people, naturally, expressing its own unique history, its struggle for independence, and its cultural achievements. In these terms, Israel's Independence Day clearly has a uniquely Israeli character. The unique character, however, occurs within a framework of similarity. On Independence Day the singularly Jewish dimension is actually reflected in the intense emphasis—after many generations of *abnormal* existence in exile—on the desire to become just like any other nation. Like all nations, Israel also wants this kind of jubilation—happiness at visible power and at the high tide of existence. The tension between the significance of Independence Day and the significance of a traditional festival such as Passover is abolished. At Passover, the Jewish people experiences its freedom as a "chosen people," while on Independence Day it experiences the freedom of being a political nation like any other. The different characteristics and symbols, and the profoundly different nature of the rejoicing, concretize this divergence, which is both ideological and existential.

CELEBRATING NATIONAL SOVEREIGNTY

Thus, in an affirmative way, Independence Day marks the transformation in the status of the Jewish people in the modern era. The reasons and factors that called out for a new approach and the initiating—or perhaps secular—act of entering historical reality were discussed in the previous chapter. Such a secular stance is justifiable in spiritual and religious terms because it is only by using all the tools of civilization, which trespass the realm of God's leadership in nature, that humanity as a whole or a particular people, can again give meaning to the revelation of God's will in human history. Of course, this is dependent on the manner in which a nation shapes its actions as it struggles to master the new political and civilizational tools. Will the Jewish people be successful in binding the mundane to the sacred? Or will it alienate the one from the other creating an ever-greater gulf among its cultural heritage, the temper of its national organization, and the way of life that stems from it? This is the question that looms most intensely in the social/cultural reality of the State of Israel. Will there be a unique Jewish character to the Jewish state?

It is a question that arises at different points in the social and cultural life of the state; it is raised as well in reference to the complex of themes expressed on Independence Day. In the early years of the state, a military parade was the highlight of the festival—a common tradition on the independence days of nations that have won their liberty after a war against foreign rule. The idea is simple and obvious: the army is the organized national force that fought for and gained independence and that continues to guarantee independence against foreign enemies. So the festival is also the army's festival. As it parades before the people, the army represents the power of the regime in totalitarian states. In democracies, the army is the people or the representative of the people; an organization designed to unite the nation and consolidate the power needed to defend its political freedom. In Israel, the military parade acquired an unusual emotional significance. Universal compulsory military service was introduced at the very beginning of statehood along with extensive reserve duty obligations that continue until a relatively advanced age. Consequently, in a real as well as symbolic manner, the army is the people. The thousands of spectators lining the parade route saw their sons, brothers, relatives, and friends marching and, in effect, saw themselves marching with them. The strength depicted by formation marching with weapons mirrored the strength of their desire for independence. Moreover, there was something not commonly Jewish at the sight of a Jewish army marching through the streets of a Jewish city in the State of Israel in light of the long road of Jewish history and of the immediate past.

The unbelievable success in securing the same political/national status that other nations take for granted: the march of the first Jewish army "in two thousand years"; the march of the Jewish army after years of dispersion, discrimination, and oppression; the march of the Jewish army after the Holocaust; the march of the Jewish army after the War of Independence, the 1956 War, the Six-Day War, the Yom Kippur War; the march of the Jewish army given that the Jewish people still does not enjoy full peace in its land. The military parade—the symbol of a political independence like *all other nations*—actually came to reflect the spiritual significance of the transition achieved by Zionism. By virtue of its own will, the Jews were transformed from a weak people to a strong nation that has begun to take responsibility for shaping its own destiny.

It might be asked whether the military symbolism used to express political freedom does not contain an element of *militarism*—the admiration of overt force as a value in its own right. And if this is the case, does it not represent a form of paganism? Demanding questions that cannot be ignored. Admiration of a war machine that possesses an enormous capacity for destruction, placing such a machine at the center of the experience of national freedom, entail serious moral and spiritual dangers. Even if the army is essentially a defensive rather than an aggressive force, it tends to institutionalize destructive power and depict it as a value; there can be no doubt that this is paganism. During the first years of Israel's existence as a state, most of the nation and its leaders were not sensitized to this danger. On the contrary, as a symbol of the transformation that had occurred, the military parade was a source of great excitement. The army was the bulwark between the people delivered from the Holocaust and the dangers that still lay ahead; it was the emblem of the flight from impotence to a position in which the nation could defend itself. The joy at the sight of the marching army was a genuine and spontaneous outpouring, and the people could not be denied this satisfaction.

In the course of a few years, however, doubts began to be heard. Many felt that there was something wrong in the military parade being made the center of the festival. And there was a practical aspect to this feeling. Unlike the armies of countries whose independence has been recognized for years, countries that enjoy peace with their neighbors, the Israeli army is not merely ceremonial; it bears a heavy burden of defense. The imposition of a ceremonious role on the army with additional demands for large investments of budget and manpower was questioned. Moreover, because of the arduous burden of security tasks it is required to perform, the Israeli army commands a much greater proportion of time from citizens than other democratic countries do. Is there a justification for imposing further reserve duty on the public for the sake of organizing a parade? Should the army, in any case, be given even greater attention than it receives in everyday affairs?

There were those who argued it would be wiser to balance the Independence Day picture by concentrating public attention on creative and peaceful activity in which Israel can take pride. The ideological consideration behind the practical argument is easy to follow: while the Jewish state continues to struggle for its existence and is required to invest enormous efforts in order to defend its security, it nonetheless aspires to a creative social and cultural life, and therefore it would be worthwhile to avoid a practical, emotional, or conceptual indulgence in the defensive military burden. Vital as such effort may be, it must not be presented as a goal in its own right. The purpose of the nation transcends the military, and this should be emphasized on Independence Day as the positive meaning of national independence. Indeed there is a grave and intrinsic danger in portraying the security effort as the primary national activity that unifies the people; eventually, this is bound to lead to a distortion of values and to a loss of the raison d'etre of the state. Precisely because the army plays such a real role in Israeli reality, it should be removed from the central position it has occupied on Independence Day and be replaced by representative civilian activity.

Interesting to note, army officers were no less sensitive to these considerations than political leaders, thinkers, and educators; they too asked that the military appearance be subdued as the main content and chief symbol of Independence Day; this was the harbinger of change. In recent years, the military parade usually has not been held. The army appears in the commemoration ceremonies for the fallen of Israel's wars, and in the ceremony that formally opens Independence Day; thereafter, it retires into the background, replaced by various displays of national accomplishments or by excursions and outings into the landscapes of the homeland. These activities have not, however, crystallized into a clear tradition and are far from filling the day with adequate and convincing content. The military parade had a strong, clear message; it had the power to excite citizens and was common to all sectors and strata of the people. The activities that have replaced the parade are inadequately distinguished from ordinary leisure activities; they lack the element of monumentality that creates a joint experience for an entire people. As a result, there is a sense of emptiness that can only be filled if a national culture emerges that has common social patterns of expression—in other words, a consolidated national tradition. This has not happened yet. Its creation is an important focus of deliberation and effort in ensuring the uniquely Jewish character of the State of Israel.

The lack of a clear socio-cultural message is evident in the nature of the popular celebration on Independence Day. As it is neither the joy of fulfilling a commandment, nor in itself a commandment to be joyous, the festival is characterized by the anticipation of the celebration and the opportunity for jubilation in reaction to that which exists, the state. Experience shows that popular joy does well up spontaneously and reaches a wonderful excitement on those Independence Days that fall soon after major national events—the War of Independence, the 1956 Sinai Campaign, the Six-Day War. The tension and anxiety that built up before and during wars are released at the festival; the sense of success is direct and striking; and the elation bursts out in parades, singing, and dancing. The picture is very different when Independence Day falls in *normal* periods, particularly in years when the national mood and self-image are at a nadir due to social and political crises. The expectation that spirits will be lifted is still present, and the relevant government institutions provide the technical means for the nation to celebrate: platforms and entertainment troupes, loudspeakers, orchestras, amusement parks, picnics sites, and so on. Crowds of people flow through the streets of the cities and towns, looking for revelry. They watch firework displays and listen to dance music. Here and there groups of youngsters break into dance, but the anticipated excitement fails to materialize. The sense of disappointment, initially internal, turns outward. Why are those responsible for bringing joy to the nation unable to provide it?

Perhaps this is the basis of a popular custom that, over the years, has become one of the main tokens of Independence Day, the plastic hammer. Children began using the toy, and gradually adults adopted it. Holding the hammer, the player vanishes in the crowd, then suddenly appears in order to hit an unsuspecting celebrator on the head. Although the hammer barely makes contact, it emits the sound of a blow. The person who has been *hit* turns around, but the assailant has already merged into the jostling crowd and cannot be found. If the *victim* wants to retaliate, he must buy a hammer and act the same way. Obviously this is only a game but, like all games, there is a seriousness behind it. One sees the classic reaction of the frustrated individual in the midst of an anonymous crowd that blurs his distinctiveness. One could see as well a way of interpreting the sense of freedom or a protest at the disappointment of failed expectations. The individual who blends into the crowd discovers the apparent advantage of complete anonymity. Since he is anonymous, he can't be held responsible for attacking anyone. Others do not see him; the victim does not see him; he is therefore freed from the obligation to see himself. The action of total strangers hitting one other with plastic hammers makes a statement about freedom in its uncontrolled sense; that is, I can do anything I want, I don't have to explain anything, not even to myself.

Naturally, this is possible only in the context of a game. A *serious* blow could reveal the identity of the assailant. But within the limits of a game, the symbolic message is clear, as is the feeling of disappointment that breeds this form of anarchic satisfaction. People adopt such a mode of behavior out of a sense of emptiness, to hide an expectation of rejoicing that has gone unmet. Individuals go out into the streets longing for joyousness; the streets are filled with the anticipation of jubilation.

Someone has taken this on as an obligation, and those who go into the streets expect that the promise will be kept. They expect their hearts to be filled with joy—that it will flow through them like wine, without their having to make any effort. They listen to music, watch dancing and fireworks, but they are swept away in the anonymous crowd, and their hearts remain without joy. They need to do something but their protest becomes an empty act intended to save them from emptiness. Anarchy takes on the form of merriment to fill the vacuum left by the absence of joy.

This is the problem inherent in the anticipation of a joy that is supposed to be the spontaneous reaction to an existing achievement. On occasion, joy does burst forth, is even overflowing. But these moments cannot be programmed or legislated; they are created by historical or biographical events. Ordering joy to come at a fixed point on the calendar is possible only if individuals are willing to bring themselves to a state of joy through a deliberate and voluntary act. This is another kind of joy, the joy of commandment. If one reflects on the matter, it become evident that a commanded joy is not the spontaneous response to an existing achievement; it is rather a conscious direction that goes beyond what exists to a vision of perfection that no existing achievement can parallel.

There is still another dilemma that recurs at Independence Day—the emotional transition from the grieving atmosphere of Memorial Day for the fallen of Israel's wars to the joyous atmosphere of Independence Day. The transition is extreme as one day immediately follows the other, separated only by the sound of a two-minute siren. In the same evening, memorial ceremonies end, and festive ceremonies commence. There are many, particularly among the families of the fallen, who feel that this transition is too rapid. The sorrow is too real to be shaken off in an instant before going out into the cheerful streets. It is a simple, easily understood position. The opposing argument claims that the link between Memorial Day and Independence Day is meaningful and organic. Precisely on the day when Israel rejoices in political independence, those who gave their lives for the victory and defended it must be remembered; there must be a connection between mourning and joy. Then why the apparent conflict? Can one take for granted that mourning and joy are two contradictory emotions, which can never touch or exist in juxtaposition?

A serious examination of these questions indicates that the answers depend on the manner in which joy is expressed. It is certainly true that mourning cannot be juxtaposed with the merriment of an entertainment that tries to disengage from all ties. One cannot leave the cemetery only to begin dancing in a carnival-like procession; one cannot rise from personal grief in an instant to be driven by *spontaneous* joy at bountiful good in the next. On the contrary, surely the knowledge that loved ones have given their lives so that others might enjoy the bountiful good, which they themselves have not been fortunate enough to know, can only engender the deepest sense of guilt in the midst of rejoicing. But spontaneous joy that seeks the cheer of entertainment is not, perhaps, the sole form of joy. It may be that there are forms of joy not essentially in opposition to deepest sadness.

It is worth noting again that the regular joy of the commandment on the Sabbath and the festivals, particularly the three pilgrimage festivals, is combined with the *Yizkor* memorial prayer in which the individual merges with the memory of departed loved ones, and the community as a whole merges with the memory of holy communities that perished as they sanctified God's Name. In the modern period, particular attention is given to the memory of holocaust victims. The atmosphere in the synagogue is one of profound mourning; weeping can be heard. In this case, mourning occurs not in the context of a transition from one day's ceremonies to those of the next, but within the continuous fabric of holiday ceremonies and prayers. Despite this, there is no sense of artificiality in the mandated transition from joy to mourning and from mourning to joy; on the contrary, the mourning is needed to complete the joy since there is a profound emotional and conscious link between sadness and joy, and between mourning and a holiday. These emotions can dwell together when the joy emerges as a genuinely spontaneous reaction to a great achievement that has just occurred. The public that celebrated the first Independence Day after the War of Independence, or the first Independence Day after the Six-Day War, did not forget its mourning in its joy, nor did it forget its joy in its mourning. The emotions blended together because they were an integral part of the occasion.

The same applies to any event that marks a human achievement. The inevitable suffering and sorrow on the path to great human achievement are an integral part of the joy. Joy and sorrow—mutual forces powered by a single life energy—are bound together as emotions that confirm human existence as it strives toward its destiny. There cannot be a joy that does not spring from some sorrow as in the case of struggle and victory; and there cannot be a sorrow that is not tempered by anticipated joy, which is the measure of its profundity. If, therefore, the joy of Independence Day appears to remove sorrow from its direct context, or to be tawdry, one should suspect the authenticity of this joy. In light of the above, it is not difficult to recognize that it is only when joy is seen as the refuge of oblivion or as a release from the tension of coping with life's predicaments, that it appears to contradict feelings of sorrow so that the transition from a day of mourning to this kind of joy seems forced and artificial. Joy that stems from the victory of life's inner forces carries mourning within itself, and rather than obscuring it, it overcomes the mourning and gives it meaning.

Three problems have been discussed with regard to shaping the content of Independence Day: the problem that results from focusing on a military display; the problem that stems from the characteristics of an institutionalized celebration, which nonetheless is supposedly spontaneous; and the problem that results from the close proximity of mourning ceremonies to a joy that tends toward mere entertainment. None of the problems are the result of poor organization; they are *natural* expressions of the unique nature of Independence Day; that is, the significance of the establishment and existence of the state and of political sovereignty in the life of the people. Regarding the first problem, the point has been made that the symbols of sovereignty, as well as its founders and defenders, need to appear as a central theme in the day's festive events; in the second instance, Independence Day is celebrated in the midst of the public so that the public is made conscious of its unity through the sovereignty that motivates and guides it; and finally, there is an essential link between mourning for those who fell in the wars to achieve and secure independence and the joy of the festival. Subsequently, however, it was pointed out that it is precisely the aim that seems to be called for by the special nature of the festival that may miss its target. At certain historical moments, the people does know real joy and a lifting of the spirits on its festival. But when the festival is celebrated as a standard event, routine produces disappointment and frustration, which—even from the point of view of the existence of political freedom—can lead to phenomena that are negative and somewhat dangerous.

In considering ways to mend these defects there has recently been a trend in the direction of suggestions to fill in aspects missing from the festival. Already mentioned are the curtailing of the military display (there are now exhibits of civilian attainments in place of a large parade); the awarding of the Israel Prizes, the World Bible Quiz, presentations of economic achievements, etc. There is also a clear change in emphasizing activities for the public in family or community settings that are not on a mass scale. Festive meals that include Haggadah-type recitations have been introduced; trips and family or communal outings to nature spots are commonplace. For the religious public, a prayer book for the festival has been developed for use in the synagogue. Similarly, it would be worthwhile seeking ways to imbue the joy of this festival with the joy of the commandment. This depends on changing the approach to political achievement, seeing it as a joyous accomplishment not only in terms of what it already encompasses but as the foundation of a more complete creativity and style of life for the nation, a purpose that individuals would take upon themselves to consummate. A commandment is a type of undertaking, and the joy of the commandment is the joy of a future achievement based on the conscious decision to act toward the undertaking. The destiny and vision that individual members of the nation place before themselves and toward which they aim is carried within the joy of the commandment.

In considering what direction to take to fill in those elements the festival now lacks, it is possible to become better aware of the primary cause of the problems and defects discussed above. Revisions and additions would be based on activity, social organization, and creativity that go beyond the defined areas of the political establishment and its idea of sovereignty. Providing activities for the family and community, emphasizing cultural achievements, utilizing traditional and *halakhic* symbols, defining the destiny and vision from which commandments are derived—none of these is the direct function of the political establishment per se. The establishment can only serve these goals by creating appropriate conditions and protecting them from being devalued. It becomes apparent that the source of the problems and flaws lies in the presumably natural tendency to emphasize those national and political dimensions exclusive to Independence Day, thus isolating it from the overall structure of familial, social, traditional, and cultural themes expressed on the Sabbath and other festivals. Indeed, it was natural to isolate the theme of political sovereignty and celebrate it in its own right—not only because that is what the day was intended for but also because in the political victory the Jewish people saw a decisive turning point in its history, a fitting response to the central problem it faced in modern times.

However, while at particular historical moments there is sufficient content here to fill hearts and lead to a great uplifting experience, it is not enough in and of itself; permanently severed from the totality of the people's lives and from the organic, familial, and communal structure of national society, the content dwindles considerably and may even be distorted and perverted. At moments when the nation is fighting for its very existence, the sovereign state, its leaders, and the army become a symbol which the individual directly identifies with his family, friends, community, and nation. History and culture are experienced at the junction of the existential struggle and individuals sense this, even if it is not overtly stated. In fact, the enormous throng that gathered on the sidewalks to watch the parade after the Six-Day War was not a crowd since the interpersonal encounter did not set off a sense of anonymity or alienation. On the contrary, because of the powerful ordeal that had been experienced by everyone, people who had never met saw each other as brothers. Facing the parade, the people met itself on the high peak of history, from which both past and future could be seen.

In ordinary times, however, such an experience cannot be orchestrated unless creative forms of expression are used that enable each individual to act in a conscious and self-commanding manner. To this end, one must move beyond the area of activity defined as belonging to the national establishment with its personification of sovereignty. The special theme of Independence Day is obviously national and political independence, and the symbols of sovereignty must plainly be given a central role in festive ceremonies. But it is a grave error to emphasize these symbols to the exclusion of other themes. It may be that beyond this error lies a mistaken perception of the value of national sovereignty. Or it may be that there is a mistaken application of the concept of sovereignty not only in the festival but in the structure of government and society, and the relationship between government and society. Thus, once again, the people face the internal tension between a vision of national liberty and the nature of the dominion that realizes and complements this vision.

THE JOY OF ACHIEVEMENT AND OF VISION

Having begun with a discussion of the ambivalent attitudes in the complementary/contradictory relationship between the desire of the Jewish people to live in its own homeland and sovereignty—like other nations, and the concept of moral and religious liberty espoused by the Prophets and Sages, we have come full circle. On the one hand, sovereignty is destiny; only under its own sovereignty can the nation and the individuals within it, perform all the commandments incumbent on it. On the other hand, sovereignty as a power structure tends by its very nature to admire power as a supreme value. This is paganism and if successful, it subjugates the people under its dominion. The Jewish people, having returned to its land from its wanderings in the *desert* of nations, and established its state in order to be as other nations, faces the problem in its modern manifestation. As a structure of unity and national might, the state is a necessary instrument not only for independence and the comprehensive responsibility for the people's needs, but for the people's very existence. The state and the army are the protective wall between the people and annihilation. They are the only safeguard of the people since it is clear that in modern times only national might can protect a people from the heinous intention of nations backed by tremendous and powerful civilizations. In these conditions, the establishment of the state is a prerequisite without which the people would be unable to perform any of the commandments that are incumbent on it as a nation.

Nonetheless, the danger to the moral and spiritual heritage of the people from the state's natural tendency as a power structure remains as distinct as ever, emphasizing an essential problem of political existence per se. The veneration of power in its own right, subservience to material aspirations in their own right, the tendency to abjure the individual's personal responsibility for society and to place this responsibility at the feet of the national framework—all these may crush the people's moral and spiritual tradition, creating an alienated mass society and ultimately losing the very point of inner freedom that was the goal of the struggle. The problems that have been examined in the development of Independence Day themes and symbols as a festival of freedom that is essentially different from Passover reflect the accumulated tensions of everyday life in the State of Israel. What is the relationship between society and the state? What is the relationship between the people's cultural heritage and the behavioral patterns set by the power structure? In what sense is the State of Israel a Jewish state?

Shaping Independence Day according to the pattern that mimics the national festivals of other nations points to one solution in solving these questions—a centralism that emphasizes the mechanism of power and completely blurs the status and nature of organic social frameworks such as the family and the community. This approach is evident not only in the planning of Independence Day ceremonies, but also in everyday reality. Symbols drawn from the tradition do appear, but they define a limited and fixed *common denominator* between two publics—the religious and the secular—that have become mutually and diametrically institutionalized in political terms. The customs and symbols unique to the festival are foreign to tradition, and this fact, too, is evident in the everyday reality of the

State of Israel. Thus it can be seen that Independence Day symbolizes the trend of defining Israel as a Jewish state in a purely national and political sense; that is, Israel is a Jewish state by virtue of the fact that most of its population are Jews, and that they hold sovereignty. As such, of course, the state is responsible for promoting the national interests of the Jewish people and, above all, its security and welfare. Since Israel is unique in its nature as a state intended for a people most of whom still do not live within its borders, the state is also—according to this perception— Jewish by virtue of its Zionist policy.

Is this sufficient? Does this situation reflect the true relationship between the state as an institutional system, and the people as the continuity of cultural transmission from generation to generation, as happens among other peoples? There is, and surely should be, an intimate connection among the social structure, ethos, cultural creativity, and religion of a people and the processes of government in its state, a fact that is evident when one observes states founded on similar principles that are significantly different from each other. The difference between the British democracy and the democracy of the United States, for example, reflects significant differences in the social structure, ethos, and cultural creativity of the two peoples. One might argue, therefore, that the State of Israel cannot be as all the other nations unless it, too, reflects the unique social and cultural character of its people. One might wonder as well whether Israel can survive if it seeks no more than to be a state like any other, if it does not allow its society to aim for a vision beyond that of political goals. This is an old question, though in modern guise.

In a Jewish state, simply a Jewish majority that implements Zionist policy is not sufficient. The Jewish nature of the state should be reflected in its embodiment of the social and communal ethos of its people as it developed in the patterns of traditional communities throughout the Diaspora; it should be reflected as well particularly in the innovative frameworks of Zionism's first period of fulfillment—the rural settlements of the *kvutzah*, the *kibbutz*, and the *moshav*. Moreover, Israel should be Jewish insofar as the legislation of its sovereign institutions rests on the national legal tradition of its people—the *halakhah*, just as the legislation of most states of the world draws on the legal tradition of their peoples. Even all of this is not enough. In a Jewish state, it is taken for granted that the national language of the people who are the majority and wield sovereignty is given the status of the primary official language, and the state should nurture and encourage national cultural creativity, above all through educational institutions. As a Jewish state, the State of Israel must place special emphasis on this area because of the process of assimilation that Jews have undergone in recent generations, a process that is currently reaching its peak. As a state that gathers in expatriates who have experienced rapid assimilation, Israel must devote much greater attention to encouraging the means of ingathering, and to rehabilitating the common cultural heritage that united the people in the past and that, if renewed, embodies themes that can unite it in the future.

In this context, the status of religious tradition in the consolidation of Israeli public life and school education must be re-examined. The unity symbolized by granting legal and juridical force to the *halakhah* in certain areas (such as the registration of Jewish national identity and laws relating to personal status) seems increasingly external and fictitious at a time when the public itself is divided; that is, part of the public defines itself as religious even as it turns its back on humanism and secularism, while the other part of the public limits itself to humanistic and secular themes, rejecting the values and symbols of Jewish religion, the essence of Jewish heritage. The bonds of unity are gradually unraveling, collapsing along with cultural themes that are no longer adequate for a complete national life—according neither to a religious nor a secular version. A Jewish state needs to reflect its Judaism in a conscious cultural effort of renewing and inculcating its heritage, and should strive to achieve a broad, multi-faceted common denominator of culture for the Jewish people.

All this requires another important dimension: the State of Israel is unique in that it faces the task of renewing and reviving a people dispersed in the Diaspora, in the throes of assimilation and collapse, with a unique culture. Since this task is still far from accomplished, the State of Israel cannot yet celebrate its existence as a given achievement. Even that which has been attained is still far from secure unless the state strives to complete its work. Accordingly, Israel must continue on its path, a journey it will not be able to traverse without a great vision that guides the public in its acts and in its way of life. What is this vision to be? From a national and political viewpoint, it is the redeployment of a dispersed people into a nation living on its own land like all other nations.

However, from the outset, Zionism's dream of becoming like other nations encompassed a vision of uniqueness rooted in the ancient Jewish heritage. The return to the Land of Israel symbolized the messianic destiny of a society guided by justice and truth, charity and mercy. This is the reign of God among His people since only divine grace can draw humans toward transcendental perfection. Such grace responds to the desires, choices, and efforts of human action. Destiny must be interpreted in consonance with contemporary circumstances and justice implemented according to contemporary circumstances. That which requires reform must be defined and solutions found to the individual and societal questions that arise in each generation in different garb. If, therefore, the unique nature that Israel, as a Jewish state, ought to adopt is defined as one that is messianic, the intention is that this state will not present sovereignty as an end in its own right, and dominion as a value, and will not see what it has already achieved and institutionalized as being perfect and complete. The vision is always beyond that which has been achieved, even beyond that which can be achieved. A constant effort of reform and perfection is required.

As a state with a purpose, Israel must take on the task of constantly re-examining the need for reform in internal societal relations and in external international ties; it must strive to cope with the moral and spiritual problems that result from conditions of life in the highly developed and complex culture of modern times. In other words, existing achievement is subordinated to envisioned achievement, and political sovereignty is subordinated to moral and spiritual vision. In Israel, as in any state, there is a natural tension between the tendency of the regime to emphasize its symbols and institutions as values in their own right, and freedom as a moral vision that the state must serve. As a state with a goal, Israel must constantly search for a balance between its tangible needs for mundane achievement and the absolute requirement of the moral impera-tive. Will it be successful in finding a balance? As it did in the First and Second Commonwealth periods, the answer to this question will deter-mine the future of Israel as a Jewish state, perhaps even the very existence of the state.

The topic here is not the development of practical policy and patterns of everyday life, but the content, patterns, and symbols of Independence Day. Independence Day ought to be developed as a festival that reflects the aspirations of the people for its state, and as an occasion that educates the people toward the realization of its goal. To this end, alongside the emphasis on statehood, it is important to emphasize the function of family and community as the foundation of the state. In all aspects of the festival, the new national culture should be more pronounced and traditional forms of expression should be found that are not confined to those who go to synagogue on Independence Day for special services. Above all, the festive ceremonies must not only mark achievement but set forth a vision and designate an undertaking that strives to realize this vision. It is only joy at a future reality, which exceeds that which has already been achieved, which is based on determination of will and strength of faith, that is the joy of the commandment.

INDEPENDENCE DAY AS PART OF THE CONTINUUM BETWEEN PASSOVER AND SHAVUOT

In the previous chapter, the unique nature of Holocaust Memorial Day was discussed and, in the context of comparison to Tisha B'Av, a profound change was noted in the self-perception of the Jewish people in modern times, and in the people's relationship to the religious viewpoint that shapes its tradition. The conclusion reached was that in the circumstances of modern reality the Jewish people cannot respond to persecution as a nation—is no longer entitled to respond to persecution as a nation—by conforming to the Diaspora patterns of Tisha B'Av. The people must return to history, becoming a nation like any other. It must take independent initiatives and use all the tools that modern civilization makes available in order to develop national strength. This was the conclusion drawn by the Zionist movement in its profound analysis of the condition of the Jewish people in the modern era; it was to the practical realization of this vision that the Zionist movement devoted itself. The State of Israel as a modern, democratic national state is the great achievement of the Zionist movement. But even as the festival marks the establishment of the political state, it also symbolizes the spiritual process embodied in its establishment.

A look at the content and symbols of Independence Day shows, however, that when the festival is focused exclusively on equating Israel with other nations so that the values, symbols, and vision of tradition and continuity are severed, the festival could become devoid of content, and joy give way to disappointment. As long as the national instrumentality is seen as a goal whose very existence requires struggle, the people regard this mechanism as a lofty symbol of all that can be achieved, and the joy at its advancing achievement is a genuine joy consonant with moral and spiritual dimensions. But when this mechanism is seen as in place and finished, as the embodiment of all that was hoped for, it no longer symbolizes anything other than the power inherent within itself. It is still vital but it no longer has purpose, and to put it forward as a purpose is *idolatry*. The positive achievement inherent in the state directs one again to a consideration of traditional themes. Without maintaining the heritage and without renewing it in the context of political existence, the state cannot lead the people to its destiny.

On Holocaust Memorial Day, national stocktaking raises the need for a fundamental change in the continuity of Jewish thought and action in modern times. No longer can the Jews be a Diaspora people in a Diaspora that isolates itself from other nations, eventually becoming their victim. Independence Day marks the beginning of the Jewish people's integration into the family of nations and the beginning of the consolidation of actual national power. The national stocktaking reflects the need for this state to be anchored in cultural and historical continuity, which seeks to realize something that transcends political achievement. Nor should a change in Jewish destiny be seen as a discontinuity. On the contrary, the new framework will draw into itself themes of the heritage, reinterpreting them as a network of actual obligations rather than mere ceremonials. Independence Day will reflect the unique event of the establishment of the state not as a festival that replaces Passover, but as one that mirrors and complements Passover within the continuum of meaning that links Passover to Shavuot, and that represents the Torah vision, which the people undertook to fulfill as it dwells on its own land. In this way, the state becomes the symbol of a binding present on the continuing path from the past of memory to the future of hope.

TWELVE

REPAIRING EXILE: THE PEOPLE, THE LAND, AND THE TORAH (SHAVUOT)

THE GIVING OF THE TORAH—A VERITY THAT SHAPES JEWISH LIFE IN THE LAND OF ISRAEL

The aspiration of the Jewish people to settle its land and dwell in it, just as every nation lives in its own land, is reflected in the Festival of Shavuot. Settling and maintaining the Land of Israel is the fulfillment of a conditional undertaking made in the Torah in which the Land was promised to the Jewish people; that is, the people can dwell in its own land in prosperity and peace providing that they observe the commandments that relate to the land. Shavuot reflects the experience of the Jewish people (who were commanded to celebrate the festival in the Torah, particularly in the Book of Deuteronomy) living in its land within this ideational framework. As the festival developed in the Oral Law, however, it came to be seen as the Time of the Giving of the Law. This distinction between the biblical festival, and the nature of the festival as it developed in later tradition, is an indication of the tension (discussed in previous chapters) between the ideal destiny of the Jewish people and its actual historical situation on the long path from exile to homeland, from homeland to exile, and once more from exile to homeland.

It bears emphasizing again that the Torah does not refer to Shavuot as a festival that marks the giving of the Torah on Mt. Sinai. The fifty days counted from Passover (and the exodus from Egypt) through Shavuot are the fifty days required for the harvest; they link Passover as the Festival of Spring to Shavuot as the Festival of the First Fruits. They are days replete with tension and anticipation from the first ripening of the fields until the crops are ready to be harvested. Thus the festival marks an agricultural season. If a symbolic meaning is sought for the fifty days counted from spring until the first fruits, it can be found in the name of the festival, Shavuot—that is "weeks"—seven weeks to the fiftieth day, reminiscent of the concept of the jubilee. Indeed, there is a profound bond between Shavuot as a festival marking the Jewish people's settlement of its land, and the idea of the Sabbath, the sabbatical year (when the ground lies fallow), and the jubilee. Nonetheless, nothing more than simple inference is needed to detect the biblical basis for the notion that Shavuot marks the giving of the Torah. The narrative in the Book of Exodus relates that approximately fifty days passed from the exodus to the time the Israelites stood at the foot of Mt. Sinai and received the Torah. So the fifty days could also be interpreted as linking these two events, as symbolizing the path taken by the people from the starting point of redemption through the high point and culmination of the exodus from slavery to freedom—the granting of the Torah.

There is no contradiction between the two interpretations; each encompasses the basis of an early festival of nature on which an ideational and historical structure is developed. The conjunction does produce an especially significant inner tension if one realizes that there are two possibilities for shaping a historical structure on the base of a nature festival. On one hand, it is possible for the festival to portray the giving of the Torah as the purpose of the exodus from Egypt; on the other, there is the possibility that the festival represents the settlement of the Land of Israel—according to the Torah, of course—as the purpose. The first instance stresses the unique and singular occurrence at Mt. Sinai in the heart of the desert; the second marks the cyclical (hopefully repeated) pilgrimage to Mt. Moriah in Jerusalem to appear before God. Be that as it may, it is instructive to note that according to the Torah, the Children of Israel were not charged with making a pilgrimage to Mt. Sinai, nor to mark the event that took place there in a festive framework.

Rather, they are commanded to make a pilgrimage to the place where the Temple of God shall stand in their own country, and to bring two loaves of bread to place before the Holy Ark as a sign of gratitude for the fruitful land, which they have been given as an inheritance. The revelation at Mt. Sinai is no more than a station along this way, and it was not at that point that the exodus from Egypt achieved its purpose; rather it was realized on the occasion for which the Children of Israel prepared themselves as they wandered through the desert—their entry into the promised land. The completion of the exodus from slavery to freedom will be fulfilled when the Israelites become a people dwelling on their own land like all other peoples; a people that draws bread from the earth by its own labor. The Torah aims to guide the people toward such a destiny.

Evidence of this perspective can be seen in the "Song of the Sea" (*Shirat HaYam*), which is found in the story of the exodus, following the parting of the Red Sea and before the Children of Israel reach Mt. Sinai.

> Thou stretchedst out Thy right hand—the earth swallowed them. Thou in Thy love hast led the people that Thou hast redeemed; Thou hast guided them in Thy strength to Thy holy habitation. The peoples have heard, they tremble; Pangs have taken hold on the inhabitants of Philistia...Till Thy people pass over, O Lord, Till the people pass over that Thou hast gotten. Thou bringest them in, and plant them in the mountain of Thy inheritance, The place, O Lord, which Thou hast made for Thee to dwell in, The sanctuary, O Lord, which Thy hands have established. The Lord shall reign for ever and ever.
>
> Exodus 15:12–18

The "Song of the Sea" does not refer specifically to the giving of the Torah on Mt. Sinai, only that God has led His people through the desert and brought them to the place of His "holy habitation." The story of the exodus is firmly fixed in its purpose of planting the people in "the mountain of Thy inheritance" and the institution of the Temple by God. Moreover, in developing the Shavuot image, the Bible returns to this literary context. The main references are found in the portion of *Ki Tavo*, in the Book of Deuteronomy, which discusses the general commandment regarding the bringing of first fruits.

> And it shall be, when thou art come in unto the land which the Lord thy God giveth thee as an inheritance, and dost possess it, and dwell therein, that thou shalt take the first of all of the fruit of the ground, which thou shalt bring in from the land that the Lord thy God giveth thee, and thou shalt put it in a basket and shalt go unto the place which the Lord thy God shall choose to cause His name to dwell there. And thou shalt come unto the priest that shall be in those days, and say unto him: "I profess this day

unto the Lord thy God, that I am come unto the land which the Lord swore unto our fathers to give us." And the priest shall take the basket out of thy hand, and set it down before the altar of the Lord thy God. And thou shalt speak and say before the Lord thy God: "A wandering Aramean was my father, and he went down into Egypt, and sojourned there, few in number; and he became there a nation, great, mighty, and populous. And the Egyptians dealt ill with us, and afflicted us, and laid upon us hard bondage. And we cried unto the Lord, the God of our fathers, and the Lord heard our voice, and saw our affliction, and our toil, and our oppression. And the Lord brought us forth out of Egypt with a mighty hand, and with an outstretched arm, and with great terribleness, and with signs, and with wonders. And He hath brought us into this place, and hath given us this land, a land flowing with milk and honey. And now, behold, I have brought the first of the fruit of the land which Thou, O Lord, hast given me." And thou shalt set it down before the Lord thy God. And thou shalt rejoice in all the good which the Lord thy God hath given unto thee, and unto thy house, thee, and the Levite, and the stranger that is in the midst of thee.

Deuteronomy 26:1–11

In essence, the perspective is a present in which the purpose of the exodus is fulfilled. The people has already arrived in its land and settled it. The people has managed to bring forth bread from the soil through its own labor, and realized that the land is indeed, as was promised, "a land flowing with milk and honey." On this occasion it remembers the exodus from Egypt and offers thanks to God for the mercy that is self-evident in the comparison between the state of slavery and the state of redemption. The people give thanks by making a pilgrimage to the Temple and bringing the offering of the first fruits to the priests. In this context, the pilgrimage is seen as a kind of symbolic repetition of the historic narrative; that is, symbolically, the people once again enter their land, re-experiencing each year the grace of redemption. Notice that the passage quoted above does not include any reference to the giving of the Torah at Mt. Sinai. Certainly this does not imply that the granting of the Torah is not recalled. The supplicant could not possibly overlook the fact that through his act he is obeying a commandment of the Torah, particularly since the declaration reminds him not only of the exodus from Egypt and the settlement of the land but also of the condition that applies to settlement and to the bountiful plenty that the land has brought forth for him. The condition is the observance of the commandments: compliance with the covenant founded at Mt. Sinai according to the Torah. So, one learns, the giving of the Torah is to be marked not as a one-time event but rather as a verity that shapes the way of life of the people in its land. The one-time event endures within the permanent sequence of this way of life, a sequence repeated year after year.

INHERITING THE LAND

If this is the case, a precondition for understanding Shavuot is a more detailed explanation of the way in which the people settles the land in accordance with the Torah. The commandment of offering the first fruits is contained within a cluster of commandments defined by the Sages as "commandments contingent on the land" (that is, commandments that cannot be performed outside the Land of Israel). The commandments reflect the way in which the people must interpret the quality of ownership they enjoy since all the commandments relate to a title of inheritance. A closer look at the commandments establishes the following. The land is given to the people so that they may draw forth bread from it. The land is divided between the tribes, and the inheritance of each tribe is apportioned equitably between its various families. The Torah takes pains to emphasize that no tribe or family will be placed at a disadvantage in the division of the land, that the entire nation will be able to earn a livelihood from the land; this includes the tribe of Levi, which did not receive an inheritance of its own but was sanctified for the service of God; and those who did not have an inheritance for various other reasons—the orphan, the widow, the poor, or those like the stranger who by their very nature could have no inheritance.

In order to ensure the equitable division of the fruit of the land, the Torah limits the individual rights of ownership that may be inherited. Ownership is not absolute, and the yield from a given portion is not the total and unlimited chattel of the settler since he must share the yield with those who have no inheritance, or who were unable to subsist from their portion. This is the basis for the system of tithes for the priests and the Levites, as well the commandment to leave gleanings, forgotten stands of grain, and the corners of the field for the poor. The same perspective, that possession of land is not absolute, is also seen in the laws of the sabbatical and jubilee years: the land returns to its *original* owner, God the Creator. Ownership is suspended for a year; aftergrowth—the fruit of God's blessing—springs up by itself and serves once more as an endowment for the needy. The land is then divided again on an equitable basis so that those who were unfortunate and had to sell their inheritance can repossess their portion after the sabbatical or jubilee year. It is a clear and simple concept, stressed in the Torah. As they dwell on the land, the people must remember that it belongs to the Creator. It is given to them as an act of divine grace in order that they may live on it with the express condition that they not relate to their inheritance as unlimited property; they must recognize the divine ownership of the land through the equitable distribution of its yield and by preserving the equitable division of the land among the tribes, families, and households. If the people uphold this constitution and refrain from treating the land as exclusively theirs, they will continue to own the land; if they come to see it as their absolute property, the land will be taken from them.

The commandment to bring the first fruits is part of the same conceptual framework. The offering of the first fruits in the Temple symbolized the recognition that the yield does not belong to the settler who works the land but to God, the Creator of heaven and earth, who guards the people and Land of Israel with particular care. Needless to say, this ritual is intended to ensure that there will be another bountiful yield in the next agricultural cycle, and in this respect one recognizes an agricultural festival of nature similar to those celebrated by all the peoples who lived alongside the Children of Israel. However, and as is usually the case, the Torah makes a distinction between itself and the pagan pattern of ritual. In place of a magic ritual coupled with myth, there is the symbolic act that relates to a historic story of moral and religious portent. It is not the offering itself that appeases God and ensures the bounty of the yield, it is compliance with the moral proviso that establishes both the relationship between God and the people, and the moral order within the people. The pilgrimage that takes place amidst the multitude of the people presenting itself before God to give thanks and rejoice in the inheritance of the land, the condition of ownership that has been observed by the people—this is the content of Shavuot according to the Torah.

RUTH THE MOABITE AND THE POWER OF MERCY

This content of this tradition pattern could not be maintained after the destruction of the Temple except through memory and study. The pilgrimage and the offering of first fruits ceased, as did the passing of two loaves of bread in front of the Holy Ark. Naturally, in the absence of all these elements, the Sages sought appropriate themes that could be drawn from the Torah to imbue the festival with experiential meaning. Before discussing the content the Sages chose, however, the manner in which even the later traditional pattern preserved the original ideational basis of the festival should be noted, specifically the book of the Bible selected as part of the Shavuot Service—the Book of Ruth. Reading the book, the worshippers return, albeit in their imagination, to the landscape of their homeland. The question of maintaining the relationship between the people and its land is raised to its full, relevant meaning—relevant even for those living in exile.

There is no need for a protracted explanation of the connection between the Book of Ruth and the Festival of Shavuot—the connection is evident from a straightforward reading of the text. Naomi and Ruth return to Bethlehem during the wheat harvest at the season of Shavuot. The climax of the story takes place at the end of the harvest during the encounter between Boaz and Ruth on the threshing floor. The narrative stresses Boaz's observance of the commandments that relate to the land; his care to leave the gleanings, the forgotten stands of grain, and the corners of the field for the poor—the cause of his success and wealth. The land responded to him. In contrast to the famine that drove Elimelech's family to live in Sde Moab, for Boaz it had truly become a land flowing with milk and honey. Those who observe the commandments concerning the land live to dwell in the land and pass it on as an inheritance for generations to come. The Book of Ruth's interpretation of this special connection between the people and its land therefore needs to be examined in greater detail.

In terms of literary genre, the book can be described as a fine novella depicting the origins of the house of David as well as the people's attitude toward its land. It was David the King who united the Tribes of Israel, overcoming neighboring peoples who had oppressed and, several times, even enslaved them. David expanded and secured the borders of settlement, thus completing the process. During the life of his son, Solomon, the people lived on the land in keeping with the ancient promise found in I Kings 5:5, "And Judah and Israel dwelt safely, every man under his vine and under his fig tree, from Dan even to Beer-sheba, all the days of Solomon." In the people's memory, the image of David remains that of the ideal king who ruled according to the will of God and His commandments. David brought the story of the exodus from slavery to freedom to its intended climax. So it is proper that a king who is descended from David be the messiah who gathers the people into the land at the end of days, renewing the monarchy. Assuming this is so, the

Book of Ruth proposes to show why David was chosen for this role, by virtue of what elements he could bring it to completion; in other words, what path ensures that the people will dwell on its land as an independent and free nation among its neighbors? In the Book of Ruth, the story of the settlement of the land is coupled with that of the establishment of the Jewish monarchy, and this monarchy—if maintained as prescribed by the Torah—is redemption completed.

The time-frame of the story that precedes the monarchy is set as the period of Judges, a period in which the people of Israel is still struggling for its land. The people were far from united, its hold on the land still uncertain. At times the nation is enslaved by enemies; only then does it unite, still only partially, and save itself. There is no permanent monarchy, however, and large areas of the promised inheritance are still not held by the nation. This is the time of initial preparations for unification and stabilization of the monarchy. A study of the details of the story shows that the Book of Ruth interprets the situation during the period of Judges as a trial in which the people develops the characteristics necessary to dwell in its land. The literary expression of this trial is the famine that caused Elimelech's family to quit the land. It is a recurrent motif in the biblical story. The land of Israel is always watched over and this providence is reflected in the provision of rain, or its denial. The resulting drought and famine are either punishment for sin, or a trial. The way in which the people cope with the punishment or trial determines whether or not they are entitled to dwell in their land.

From the context of the story, it is evident that the decision by Elimelech's family to leave because of the famine was interpreted as a failing and a sin. This can be seen in the terrible punishment that befalls the family in Sde Moab—the sons marry foreign women, do not have children and, as the divine punishment by premature death is meted out to them, die without heirs. Their very names bear witness to their circumstances—Mahalon (from the word for sickness) and Kilayon (from the word for ruin). In this respect, there is a clear allusion to the story of the patriarchs in the Book of Genesis, particularly Jacob and his sons. Because of famine, Abraham went to Egypt; because of famine, even Isaac, the only patriarch not to leave the borders of the country, moved to Gerer; because of famine, Jacob and his sons also descend to Egypt. There is a literary parallel, but the differences are surprising and significant. In the Book of Genesis, there is no suggestion of sin related to the decision to leave the land due to famine, and in Egypt the Children of Israel are not decimated. On the contrary, in Exodus 1:7 we read, "The Children of

Israel were fruitful and increased abundantly, and multiplied and waxed exceeding mighty; and the land was filled with them." Moreover, even when slavery begins, verse 12 goes on to read: "But the more they afflicted them, the more they multiplied and the more they spread abroad."

However, in the Book of Ruth, the decision to leave the land because of the famine is seen as a transgression and is severely punished. The family of Elimelech did not stand up to the test. It was deprived of its inheritance, cut off from the people and brought almost to the edge of total ruin. Naomi, returning from Sde Moab, to the place she had left, no longer sees herself as Naomi. She is the bitter "Mara"—living testimony to the terrible punishment she carries because of the act of treason against the land. Yet in her acceptance of the judgment, one sees the beginning of repentance that is an act of restoration. It emerges, however, that alone she cannot correct that which has been distorted. The decree cannot be reversed unless something unexpected happens to break its force.

This unexpected occurrence is the act of Ruth the Moabite, and subsequently the actions of Boaz in responding to her. The positive element of the story begins here, the rediscovery by the people of its birthright. Again, the contrast with the Genesis story is interesting. According to the Torah, return to the Land of Israel is an act of divine grace for those who withstood the test of exile. Settlement of the land in the Book of Ruth, however, is accomplished through an act of human kindness—kindness to one another and before God, since the people did not withstand the trial. More precisely and profoundly, the transgression committed by Elimelech's family is basically the sin of lacking faith. The family moves to the breadbasket of Moab, leaving a land where the bounty of the harvest is contingent on the grace of God who responds to the people's actions. The family does not have faith in the divine promise. Thus repentance comes through an act of kindness—an act committed for its own sake, without expectation of reward.

The story of Ruth is the story of mercy that overcomes justice. The extent of that mercy is immediately seen in the opening of the story though a comparison between the behavior of Ruth and that of Orpah. Orpah acts according to the attribute of justice. She performs all her duties toward her mother-in-law, but goes no further. When, as she should, Naomi implores her daughters-in-law to return to their home, Orpah responds and goes on her way. By contrast, Ruth does more than she is required to do, without expecting any reward. Her mother-in-law is a childless and penniless woman. In an act of pure love, Ruth identifies with Naomi, her people, and her God. This, then, is the measure of grace—a measure that goes beyond duty and is based on faith. Thus it is able to correct that which lack of faith has distorted.

The grace that Ruth performs for Naomi inspires mercy in those to whom Ruth comes. This is the reward for mercy, a reward that is unexpected and, precisely because of this, without parallel. In her concern for Ruth, Naomi discovers the attribute of grace that is beyond legalism. Boaz goes still further, repaying grace for grace. Ruth returns his kindness by visiting him on the threshing floor; he returns her mercy not only by providing her with more help than is required according to the law of leaving the corner of the field for the poor, but by his devotion to the redeeming deed. Once again, the story reverts to a comparison between behavior that conforms to the attribute of justice and behavior that conforms to the attribute of mercy. In addition to the comparison between Orpah and Ruth, there is now a comparison between Boaz and the kinsman—close to Ruth—who is willing to marry the widow of his brother as the law requires of him. But when Boaz points out to him that he must forgo reward since the deceased's field must remain in his name, the kinsman is dissatisfied.

He sees no advantage to himself in taking such a step so he exploits the legal loophole and backs down. His failure to act with mercy and his refusal only serve to emphasize the significance of Boaz's actions, which are an even more profound grace since he is only in second place to the kinsman. Not only does Boaz not hide behind the kinsman who should be the first to redeem the widow, but without any expectation of reward Boaz hastens to do more than the law requires him to do, out of love. The combined actions of Boaz and Ruth thus correct what has been distorted by the sin of Elimelech's family, and the sentence of destruction over the family is rescinded. Their possession reverts to them, and a son is born to continue the line, the son who will write Israel's name on his inheritance for eternity.

It may be assumed that the internal background to the Book of Ruth is the feeling that pervaded the period of Judges in Jewish history: a sense that the people's tenure on its land was not sufficiently secure. From time to time, this hold seems to have required some act of great devotion that took the form of a trial. What lay behind this feeling? Famine? Drought? Enemies? The Book of Ruth confines itself to the general term "famine." To plumb the question in depth would require dwelling on the precise period in which the Book of Ruth was written—a topic that is the subject of extensive research. For our purpose, however, this is not necessary. Anyone reading the Book of Ruth, as the festival is being celebrated, need only recall that this feeling was not limited to the ancient period but has been experienced at different times in Jewish history. Alongside love for the Land of Israel, the land of the patriarchs, the land flowing with milk and honey, there have been repeated tests and trials. It is difficult to hold to the Land of Israel, and the temptation of foreign granaries is great. This has been true in every generation including the current one, which faces the dilemma in its own way. The Book of Ruth teaches a profound yet simple lesson: only devotion born of love, beyond the call of legal requirement, can repair the sins of the people that has failed its tests and quit its land. The return to the land and its possession for eternity require more than mere compliance with obligations based in a faith that binds the people to its fate and its way of life; loving mercy is also required. At this point, it immediately becomes apparent that the story of the Book of Ruth possesses something radical within it—something that is almost a paradox.

Earlier the analogy was noted between the actions of Elimelech and the actions of the patriarchs who went to Egypt because of famine. And the differences between these stories was also pointed out. It is not difficult to appreciate that this analogy encapsulates a harsh, although muted, criticism of the patriarchs' deeds. The decision to leave the land because of famine is a sin; it leads to assimilation, which is the essence of Elimelech's sin. It brings his sons to marry foreign wives, moreover wives from a nation whose members were prohibited from mingling with the Children of Israel for ten generations. Thus the Book of Ruth does not regard exile, as one finds in the Genesis narrative, as God's will in accordance with some predetermined plan. Exile is a sin on the part of expatriates; it is also the terrible punishment for this sin. It is hardly an exaggeration to perceive the lesson in the Book of Ruth as a warning to Israel that it should not regard the actions of its patriarchs as a model. It was David who enabled the people to settle securely in its land since his family personified a direction opposite to that taken by the patriarchs who had wandered from country to country. In taking up this point, one seizes on a latent motif that runs through the Book of Ruth. If this motif is pursued, it will be seen that mercy, as an act that goes beyond legal requirements, sometimes borders on breaking the law and—precisely in doing so—corrects that which has been distorted by acts of the patriarchs!

This observation relates to two key incidents in the story of Ruth. In terms of narrative structure the incidents are parallel and extremely prominent, although the innocence and poetic beauty of the story almost serve to mask the wonderful daring they embody. One episode concerns Boaz and the other, Ruth; both are background to the meeting that serves to correct and bring redemption to that which has been distorted. If Elimelech sinned when he moved to Sde Moab, and his sin grew when he took women from a foreign, forbidden nation for his sons, did not Boaz commit the same sin when he took Ruth the Moabite, who was forbidden to him according to the law? In other words, Boaz's act of mercy not only went beyond the requirements of the law, it was actually a transgression of the law and verges on the very sin that it came to repair. Naturally, the fact that Boaz's intentions were diametrically opposed to those of Elimelech should not be ignored. Elimelech removed his sons from their people and effectively became part of a foreign nation; Boaz brought a woman, who came to shelter under his protection, into the people of Israel. Thus far the action of Boaz.

As for Ruth, her action is no less surprising. The emotional and ideological climax of the story is the encounter between Ruth and Boaz in the middle of the night. Ruth comes of her own accord to a man sleeping alone on a threshing floor, and remains with him—the two of them alone. One might see this as a wonderful act of innocent love, and indeed this is how it is seen by Boaz. "Your latter mercy is greater than your first." Boaz feels that her bold step reflects Ruth's devotion to her purpose, both as a woman and as someone who has taken it upon herself to repair that which has been damaged by the sins of her departed loved ones. From an objective viewpoint, however, the law of the time saw this act as verging on licentiousness. Through sin she comes to repair that which was damaged by sin! From the standpoint of the story, it is evident that Boaz's position is the correct one. Ruth did not go only of her own accord. Naomi sent her to prepare Boaz so that he might understand the act of grace expected of him. Had Ruth not come to him, he would not have thought of it. In these terms, what is seen is not a sin but an act of total and innocent devotion to destiny. Mercy overcomes law in order to achieve the purpose of law itself.

The significance of this surprising motif is worthwhile contemplating in the context of the relationship of the people to its land. Is one to draw the conclusion that the redemption of the people in its land can take place only through that grace which sometimes breaks away from the strict letter of the law? If the answer is yes, as hinted in the Book of Ruth—coming as it does on the day that has emerged as the occasion on which Jews mark the giving of the Torah—it carries a tension laden with a conceptually audacious paradox. It is as if two opposing sides of the same truth are being presented. The Torah is a lacework of edicts, laws, and commandments that seeks to guide the people and provide a fixed framework for its actions. The Book of Ruth, by contrast, discloses a grace that breaks away from this fixed framework and, in doing so, enables the people to return to its land and securely possess it.

The paradox leads one to ask what the nature of this grace is—not only in terms of its external attribute but also in terms of the inner motive that is revealed. The question of the nature of mercy, in its inner sense, goes back to the notion of liberty. From the story of the exodus, one learns that freedom is seen first of all in its external sense, the removal of the yoke placed on the people by others. The person who leaves slavery can now act as he wishes. Immediately a question regarding the positive content of liberty arises. What *should* the individual do? What *should* he choose? The granting of the Torah on Mt. Sinai gives the theological answer to the question. The commandments of the Torah direct the Children of Israel toward those actions which are in keeping with their destiny. If they comply with the commandments, they will not be subject to human enslavement. Consequently, the Sages expounded on the verse ". . . and the writing was the writing of God graven upon the tablets" (Exodus 32:16), saying instead of *harut* (graven), one might read *herut* (liberty), granting liberty on the tablets of the law.

If the question of liberty is examined from the standpoint of the need to choose between that which is good for the individual in terms of his own destiny and those selfish urges which enslave a human being to his desires, then this is an adequate answer. However, it still leaves something undefined. The initial experience of liberty is seen as a direct and externally unfettered expression of human selfhood. Liberty is the spontaneity of the soul, and this is not necessarily compatible with obedience to an external authority. Thus far, not a particularly grave line of thought. Those who interpret liberty as doing that which an individual should do will point out that the commandment liberates the spontaneous moral will of the individual precisely by putting a brake on instincts and urges that disturb him from within. In this respect, response to the command is not a submission of ego, but rather the undisturbed flow of the positive force that directs the individual toward that which is good in the human soul.

In any case, the Torah sees this force as the real selfhood, and as man's destiny. But a way of life that is established according to what is engraved on the tablets of the law quickly tends to become routine, taken for granted. Then the individual is once again unable to express his positive spontaneity; there is rather the mechanical, and undoubtedly comfortable, act of habit. Moreover, a way of life established according to what is engraved on the tablets of the law perpetuates forms of behavior established in the past on the basis of certain experiences and may prevent the positive forces of the individual from responding spontaneously to one-time events in current situations, particularly when these deviate from past experience or daily occurrences.

In such situations, a gesture of obedience to the fixed order of the commandments may obstruct both the spontaneous autonomy that springs from the one-time *here and now*, and that which an individual feels he should do from a moral standpoint. This is the dilemma faced by the faithful believer who is utterly devoted to his destiny so that, on these exceptional occasions, externally his response may appear to be close to a sin. Yet when man sins he gives vent to a selfish drive that injures those around him, whereas when he acts with mercy he exhibits a loving autonomy, completely devoted to its beneficial deed.

Thus mercy is a direct and spontaneous manifestation of positive and loving human autonomy. It is an act that does not cling to the strict letter of the law, since by its very nature it springs from within and turns directly to its object, without direction or guidance from the law. For the same reason, it always verges on breaking the law. It does not draw on past experience in justifying its action, but chooses its action according to that which is perceived as appropriate in the present, at the current, unrepeatable and one-time juncture at which it occurs, by the singular individual who performs it and at the specific time at which it is performed. This one-time moment may be a turning point, in which case the act of mercy will break a pattern of behavior that has ceased to be applicable and replace it with a new pattern of behavior. In other words, it is only if the attribute of mercy goes beyond the set framework of the commandments that liberty will not sink into a routine of engraved words.

To return to the story of Ruth and Boaz—both of them react from their deepest and most spontaneous feelings to the current, unique situation they face, without the mediation of the attribute of justice. Boaz chooses Ruth the Moabite according to what she is and what she does. He does not see her as a Moabite, the daughter of a foreign people whom Jews are forbidden to marry. For Boaz, Ruth is a loving woman who is utterly devoted to her destiny. Her one-time act of grace arouses his mercy. And from this attribute of mercy, taking Ruth as a wife is not only justified, it is even mandated from within. All other considerations are overruled by this inner affirmation. One might argue that Boaz is not breaking the law since it is not the law that he is confronting. The law applies to a completely different stratum of human or social behavior, the stratum that conditions contemporary events according to the accumulated experiences of the past. It cannot compete with the absolute force of an inner obligation in the present. Like Boaz, Ruth also acts out of complete loyalty to her destiny, and her actions are direct and simple. She is not held back by the law since it does not apply to her one-time moment, a unique moment that dictates her fate and that of the generations that will proceed from her. Why, precisely, is this the act that corrects what has been spoiled in the past? Precisely because it is the act that represents a new beginning. It starts from scratch as if nothing had gone before. The moment of mercy is a moment of creation.

If one wishes to examine the significance of the story of Boaz and Ruth in the context of King David who secured the people of Israel in its inheritance, the renewing nature of the moment of mercy as a moment in which a new way of life is forged must be considered. The intentions of the Book of Ruth on this point cannot be more than speculation. Nevertheless, it is notable that the text refers to the great moment of mercy in which the Davidic dynasty is founded; it is also the moment of innovation and change. David is a believing king who fears and loves God, yet he is also an initiating personality who seizes the moment to secure change. Nor are the dramatic changes David achieves in the life of his people only external; the internal attitude of the people to itself and its surroundings is also completely transformed. A people divided into tribes, whose hold on its land had been weak and tenuous since the period of the Judges, even at the time of Samuel, is reconstructed under David's leadership into a nation that lives in its own land and is bound to it, united and organized according to the principles of a monarchy. The change not only encompasses action that goes beyond the strict letter of the law—namely, those laws by which the people lived before the establishment of the monarchy—but includes, as well, actions that are a transgression of that law. Only a gifted and purposeful personality such as David could bring about such a dramatic reformation at the precise moment of grace predestined for this purpose.

CELEBRATING THE GIVING OF THE TORAH

As noted, the transformation of the Festival of Shavuot from a harvest festival marking the settlement of the land to a festival celebrating the giving of the Torah came about as a result of the destruction of the Temple, the cessation of the pilgrimages, and the abandonment of the land. During exile, the Jewish people maintained their connection to the land but it was primarily on a spiritual level, an attachment marked by sorrow and longing, by hope and vision. What fed this strange form of attachment so that it was not erased by cycles of apparent prosperity or genuine sorrow during life in exile? The sustenance was the Torah, the testimony that bears unfailing witness to the irrevocable promise of the Land of Israel to the people of Israel; it is what shapes a way of life in which the Land of Israel is constantly recalled. When the people were physically removed from the actual land so that, seemingly, they returned to wanderings in the desert, a portable Mt. Sinai replaced Mt. Moriah, and the community's way of life took the place of arrangements of the monarchy. The Land of Israel once again came to be seen as a vision from afar, and the Torah was the path to that vision. The transformation in the character of the festival was quite natural, almost self-evident. Moreover, it was simple enough to find a theological and *halakhic* justification for the transformation. The Torah, after all, relates that it was about fifty days after the exodus from Egypt that the people arrived at the foot of Mt. Sinai.

Nevertheless, it is fascinating to note that no special commandments were introduced into the festival to mark the precise time of the giving of the Torah at Mt. Sinai. All the commandments particular to Shavuot relate to the settlement of the land and, although these could no longer be performed, no others were placed in their stead so that the Jewish people might feel what was lacking and long for its renewal. How, then, could the new content be introduced into the framework of the festival? By deliberately shaping the general patterns of worship. These patterns offer a wide scope of themes that take in the entire range of experiences embodied in the way of life guided by the commandments. Through the introduction of appropriate emphases, the new connection is forged with the original commandments and the desired content emerges on interpretative and homiletic levels through the unchanging themes. And, as will be seen below, the conceptual themes of the pilgrimage were drawn into the ritual that marks the giving of the Torah.

Designing the day as a commemoration of the giving of the Torah begins with the formal declaration embodied in the text of the *kiddush*, the sanctification. The *kiddush* for the three pilgrimage festivals contains an express sentence for each festival. In the case of Shavuot, the festival is described as "the time of the giving of our Torah." The next section of the prayer service, which can be adapted according to the occasion, is the Torah portion and accompanying *haftarah*. Selected for this day are sections appropriate to the theme of the giving of the Torah; taken from Chapters 19 and 20 of Exodus, they relate the story of the revelation at Mt. Sinai. The *maftir* section is from Numbers 28:26–30 regarding special offerings made on Shavuot. The *haftarah* is from Chapter One of Ezekiel, with the addition of line 12 from Chapter Three, and relates to the appearance of the chariot; the connection with the revelation at Mt. Sinai will become apparent subsequently. During the early Middle Ages, a special poem written in Aramaic was added to the Torah reading. Entitled "Akdamot" (introductions) the poem has been sanctified and is regularly read in Ashkenazi congregations. This addition ought not be seen as an exceptional commandment relating to Shavuot since it is no more than a custom that uses set forms of prayer. The addition of poems to regular prayers on the festivals was customary from earliest times. In this instance the poem is recited before the reading from the Torah rather than during the *amidah* portion of the prayer service, a reflection of the nature of the day as commemorating the giving of the Torah.

Only at a still later stage did the form of the service spill over to include a distinctive innovation to commemorate the giving of the Torah. The seventeenth-century mystics of Safed who left a vivid mark on the development of many of the festivals as they are celebrated by most traditional Jews to this day, instituted the concept of *Tikun Leil Shavuot*, the midnight study session. The homiletic excuse for this innovation is found in the legend that recounts that the Children of Israel were unable to keep from dozing during the night on which the Torah was given. In order to compensate for the infringement of holiness on that occasion, it is now customary to remain awake all night and study Torah according to a fixed sequence of chapters established for this purpose. Since the Torah is the link between the upper spheres and those below, night-time study (particularly at midnight, which is when the heavens open so that the *Shekhinah*, the divine presence, can unite lovingly with the Supreme Source) repairs the rift that developed between Israel and the Creator because of Israel's sins. This is the way to overcome exile while still in exile, and this is the way to bring redemption closer.

The conceptual contributions of these elements in shaping the Festival of the Giving of the Torah are examined below.

THE *AKDAMOT* POEM

The *akdamot* poem is the first element encountered during the festival. It offers an explanation of the importance of the giving of the Torah in the context of world history and the annals of the Jewish people. Written in a popular vein, the poem summarizes a number of themes from the Bible and the Sages, creating what one might term an ideological manifesto for the people of Israel during its exile. The poem begins by praising the Creator of the universe, basing its praise on the wonders of Creation, which bear testimony to the greatness of their Creator. The entire universe was created only to worship the Creator and give thanks and praise to Him. The people of Israel—sanctified above all other peoples—was chosen in particular for this role. Other peoples are jealous of the Children of Israel because God selected them as the chosen people. They persecute the Jews and embitter their lives, yet the people of Israel persist, secure in the promise given to them of a better future yet to come. God will overcome His enemies and avenge His people's mistreatment. He will set a banquet table for His people, and all the nations will be in awe of His presence. All this is promised to the people of Israel in the Torah given by God. The Torah is the refuge that keeps the Jews safe until the day of redemption. The poem ends by thanking God for favoring the people of Israel and giving them the Torah: "God, exalted from beginning to end, Was pleased with us and gave us the Torah."

Truth to tell, this poem is graced neither with esthetic beauty nor philosophical depth. Popular affection for the poem probably lies in its very simplicity and in the comfort it held for the people as they suffered the persecutions of exile. Jews could not help but wonder at a situation in which the chosen people were exiled and persecuted while the nations who worshipped false gods held dominion over the world and enjoyed prosperity and success. The poem offers a simple answer: the suffering of the Jews is the result of envy on the part of other nations. That is to say, other nations are aware of the greatness of the Jewish people and acknowledge it. Thus the suffering is no more than a trial; by withstanding the test the people will see revenge visited upon their enemies and will come to enjoy all that is good before their God. But how can the people give credence to such an expectation when reality seems to contradict it at every turn? The answer, of course, lies in the Torah. When the people look to the Torah, God's word, which they carry with them, they know with absolute certainty that God is with them. Situated between Creation in the past and Redemption in the future, the revelation at Mt. Sinai is the ongoing bridge that links these two points.

Understanding the importance of the Torah in the life of the Jews, one can also understand the significance of the reading of the Torah in the synagogue on every Sabbath and festival as a reaffirmation of the Covenant. But on Shavuot, as the time of the giving of the Torah is marked, the Torah reading has a heightened significance. On this occasion, one might see the reading of the Torah as a primal event; a symbolic re-enactment of the original happening. The people gather in their synagogues, receive the Torah, and bless it. The *akdamot* poem serves as a garland—decorating, emphasizing, and interpreting.

THE TORAH WAY OF LIFE

We come now to the Torah section and the accompanying *haftarah*. The revelation at Mt. Sinai is described in the Book of Exodus as the occasion on which the covenant was established between the people and God. The people undertook to accept divine dominion. God undertook to lead the people to its land and settle them there in security. Naturally, the mere fact that a covenant is forged between a people and God is an exceptional event. The people must cleanse and purify themselves. As directed in the prohibition not to advance beyond a certain point, they stand at the foot of the mountain in awe. They may not ascend the mountain, but only stand at its foot, the distance reflecting their humility. The appearance of God on the mountain after days of preparation is described as an astonishing and terrifying event. A spectacular thunderstorm breaks out around the mountain and from within terrifying horn blasts can be heard. The entire mountain is covered in smoke. The details of the event disclose a surprising and paradoxical duality: God is revealed, though shrouded in cloud, just as the people draw nearer though still keeping their distance. God's presence is witnessed by awesome sounds, but before He is revealed on the mountain, smoke descends on it. God remains beyond; only His word reaches the people. His presence is felt in all its force by its very veiling. At the same time, the people are granted the proximity of mystery and the recognition that the proximity of God is precisely that awareness of the absolute distance that separates them.

It is interesting that the same paradoxical duality characterizes Moses' encounter with God at the burning bush, when Moses is drawn to the wondrous sight but is commanded to stand afar. The words come to him from beyond an unbridgeable divide. This revelation should be seen as preliminary to the revelation at Mt. Sinai. At Mt. Sinai, in contrast, Moses is required to penetrate the mist that covers the mountain and is found worthy to draw nearer in order to bring the word of God to the people. The proximity is, however, only relative. Later, when Moses asks for a more intimate demonstration of God's essence, God replies by covering His presence once more, so that it is His speech alone that reaches Moses.

Speech, too, is a presence between personalities, but the speech of God at all three revelations is confined to the task, to commands and instructions regarding proper behavior. In other words, the individual or the people who depart from everyday life to stand before God do so only in order that He might send them back to act in a specific manner; accordingly, they comprehend that the proximity of God comes through performing His commandments in the course of daily life. The occasion of awesome majesty is not an end in itself, but a means. What remains after the overt, explicit speech is not fear. The fear that had been is gone and only a memory that embodies authority and the living speech remains to guide the people and instruct it in its way of life. Conforming to this way of life, the people will enjoy proximity to their God. This is the content of the covenant forged between God and the people—a unity of action. Both sides, God and the people, mutually undertake to act in particular ways. The undertaking must be a free act of consent between them, and in this respect both sides are equal. Yet their inequality is evident even at this initial stage. It is God who initiates the Covenant. He chooses the people, He leads them out of slavery and draws them close to Him. He wishes to command them so that they may be a chosen people before Him. The people do not initiate, they respond; but their response is also an autonomous act. It is an act that reveals the people's free will, which is the basis for the mutual nature of the covenant itself. The people remains free to obey or to refuse, to perform the commandments or to break them. The people chooses to agree and in doing so recognizes that obedience to God's commandments is in its own best interests. Willingly they receive the yoke of the commandments. Only then comes revelation. God descends to the mountain in order to make His commandments, which are the substance of the Covenant, heard; that is, the constitution defining God's dominion over the people. It is only after all this that the ritual ceremony of the covenant is held, both sides joining in their mutual undertakings, which have been voluntarily accepted.

As noted, the enactment of the covenant is the event at which God is accepted as King of the people, and the dominion forged at the covenant has a clear constitutional force. Of course, not all dominions are identical. Some monarchies relate mainly to employment of the power/authority between the ruler and his people. Such a monarchy does require a constitution, but the constitution simply serves to identify the sovereign force to which the population must submit. This is the nature of authority as embodied in the relationship between a despot and his slaves; the former is arrogant and the latter submissive. There is, however, a form of monarchy that is principally benevolent. It too requires a sovereign, but sovereignty is solely a means for maintaining the purpose and aims of the constitution. The kingdom forged at Mt. Sinai belongs to the latter type and appears in contrast to the human domination endured in the Egyptian house of bondage by the Children of Israel. Here is the full significance of the event: God brings His people from slavery to liberty in order that by virtue of the liberty they have been granted they may willingly choose to accept a sovereignty in which the main focus is not domination, but the desire for good embodied in the constitution. The dominion of God is a constitution for life. It is maintained when it is willingly accepted, and the result is the genuine freedom of the people.

In the case of the first type of monarchy described above, clearly the act of coronation has an instrumental importance; sovereignty exists only when it is put into force. The people standing submissively in the presence of the ruler who appears in powerful majesty bespeaks sovereignty; such a sovereign places importance on the coronation ceremony and re-enacts it as the axis around which the life of the nation revolves. This is not the case with the second type of dominion. The Torah, as the constitution of the dominion of God among the people, does not sanctify the moment of its own revelation. It sanctifies the way of life that the people is to live in accordance with the commandments. Its time is every day and every hour that the people observes the commandments; every day and every hour that the covenant is observed. Only when the covenant is broken, or forgotten, is there a need to renew it through an event that reflects the primal memory of the founding moment.

The *haftarah* that accompanies the Torah section read on Shavuot appears to stress a different message, one that requires the giving of the Torah to be underscored as the content of the festival. The substance of the *haftarah* section is a description of God's appearance on the chariot before the prophet Ezekièl. What connection is there between this detailed description of the image of the chariot and the figure poised above it, and the revelation at Mt. Sinai? Though it may not emerge in an initial comparison, the connection is not difficult to find. If the revelation at Mt. Sinai is the occasion on which God is crowned as King of His people, His appearance on the chariot before Ezekiel is also the appearance of the King Himself—an appearance designed to sanctify Ezekiel and enable him to serve as an emissary among the people that has not properly kept its King's commandments. The analogy would be more obvious if one compared the vision of the chariot to that of the burning bush. Yet even by comparison to the revelation at Mt. Sinai, the connection is evident. Nonetheless, the tremendous difference between these two events cannot be overlooked. At Mt. Sinai, the main element is the voice that is heard, the word of God that reaches the people standing at its distance. The same applies to the burning bush. By contrast, in the case of the vision of the chariot, the main aspect is a visual one. God's presence is revealed to the prophet who transmits his impressions of the vision. The voice is heard at last, but the *haftarah* ends with a description of the vision so that it would appear that awe at the sovereignty present in all its immense majesty is the primary message the prophet is required to transmit to the people. Moreover, the revelation of the chariot contains neither the forging of a covenant nor the granting of a constitution. A perception of God's dominion emanates during the event itself.

Returning to the description in the Book of Exodus, one finds that the revelation at Mt. Sinai includes this dimension as well. There is a vision on the mountain, and God's presence is revealed in its awe-inspiring glory. Moving to the end of the description, in a section not read on this day, one finds that after the blood of the covenant is sprinkled on the altar and on the people, Moses and Aaron and Nadav and Avihu go up the mountain with seventy of the elders of Israel: "And they saw the God of Israel; and there was under His feet the like of a paved work of sapphire stone, and the like of the very heaven for clearness" (Exodus 24:9–10). This short sentence includes an image similar to one of the details in the description of the chariot that appears in Ezekiel. Thus the *haftarah* emphasizes this motif in the revelation at Mt. Sinai and draws the attention of the public, gathered for the festive prayers, to the nature of the occasion at which God's dominion—the central notion of the day—was established.

It is not difficult to detect that the experience of God's ruling and guiding presence is far from being an isolated occurrence in the Torah. This is the function played by the tent of meeting in the desert and later at the Temple in Jerusalem; it is as well the function of the sacrificial worship in both these places. All of this marks the existence of the Divine

Presence among His people. After God is revealed at Sinai, Moses goes up the mountain and is given detailed instructions concerning the establishment of the tabernacle so that God may have a permanent place in which to be known to the people. The tabernacle serves as a kind of portable Mt. Sinai, accompanying the people in their moves until they reach their land and settle it, and the Temple on Mt. Moriah takes the place of Mt. Sinai. The worship of God in the Temple perpetuates the moment when the people stood before their King. The worship itself is an acceptance of the yoke of dominion and of the decision to act according to the will of the Ruler.

There are two tracks in this path: on one, commandments that direct the people and each of its individuals in their everyday life so that they may live according to these precepts before their God; on the other, commandments that relate to those occasions when the individual stands in awe before God revealed on His throne—the Temple. The Torah way of life is the link between the two tracks, which are mutually supportive despite the tensions that sometimes prevail between them. The differences between the individual who emphasizes the ritual side and the individual who emphasizes everyday commandments may cause dissension. Which is more important? Which hold the main element? Which the purpose and which the means? The tension is observable in the interplay between the Torah section and the additional *haftarah* reading.

The commandment of pilgrimage, in order to appear before God at the Temple, undoubtedly stresses the experience of presenting oneself in awe before God, the King on His throne. However, it is the moral and social way of life one should follow before God that is emphasized in the festival commandments articulated in the Torah. The bringing of the first fruit offerings to the priests and Levites, and the affirmation made as the offerings are presented, are a clear indication of this. The people come to stand before their King in order to witness the fact that the covenant continues to apply from their side and from God's, and in order to renew the covenant so that it may endure for eternity. On Shavuot, however, which is seen as the "Time of the Giving of the Torah," emphasis is on the experience of standing before the King who gives the Torah. Though it is true that the Torah instructs the people on how to live their daily lives before God, it can also be seen as the means by which they can draw closer to the God who speaks and reveals His presence before them. Study of the Torah could be seen as a form of spiritual pilgrimage to the ethereal Jerusalem and the ethereal Temple, in place of the physical pilgrimage no longer possible.

TORAH STUDY AS REPAIRING THE FLAW OF EXILE

Change in the content and emphases of Shavuot should be understood within the context of the general spiritual development of the Jewish people during the Second Commonwealth period, a process that reached its climax following the destruction of the Temple. These developments are reflected particularly in the fact that study of the Torah was introduced as the prime religious value. Study of Torah for its own sake was the supreme religious value in the world of the Sages, defining their personality, way of life, and activity. Knowledge of the *halakhah* is undoubtedly a practical necessity in enabling a Jew to conduct his life, and the Sages ceaselessly demanded that the goal should be to learn in order to do. Despite this, study for its own sake is imbued with an intense religious value, so much so that one might see study itself as the most important religious act—the performance of a commandment which subsumes all other commandments. Study became a way of life to which the scholar, as the leading religious figure, devotes his life, attempting to serve as an example to his people by doing so. The individual is required to study Torah for its own sake, according to his ability. What is the source of Torah study, for its own sake, as a value? The answer lies in the sense of intimate proximity to God that scholars feel as they learn Torah. The experience of the *Beit HaMidrash*, the study hall, and that of the *Beit HaKnesset*, the synagogue, coalesce; together they fill the vacuum left by the destruction of the Temple and the cessation of worship performed there. In prayer and in study—and sometimes more in study than in prayer—the scholar senses that God is present and speaking to him. The more a person comes to understand the depth of the Torah and its multiple meanings, the closer he comes to God who gave the Torah, and the more he experiences God's love, His mercy, His comforting and strengthening proximity.

The Kabbalists developed this understanding of the value of study for study's sake, taking it to its most distinct and extreme level. They did not confine themselves to exhausting the *halakhic* or homiletic significance that can be garnered from each verse in the Bible. In addition to reaching every possible interpretation, including those that require the most far-reaching homiletic devices, in a flash of insight they saw the outcome of speech as the expansion of the speaker's soul, so that when speech is heard an actual contact is created between speaker and listener. The speaker places himself into his speech and through his speech brings himself to the person of the listener, which explains the Kabbalists' belief that the Torah, as well as being a series of words that expresses particular ideas, is also a series of names of the Holy One, Blessed be He. The Name, as distinct from speech that reflects specific themes, carries with it the personal and actual presence of God. The person who knows these names and distinguishes between the nuances that divide them experiences the divine presence that transcends speech. Through study, which reveals the depth and hidden profundity that lies concealed beneath the simple meaning of the words (the *Peshat*), the Kabbalist clings to his God. Removed from the mundane and everyday world around him, he soars to the higher spheres. A well-known analogy in the *Zohar* likens the Torah to a tower in which a king has imprisoned his beautiful daughter. The tower is closed on all sides, but it has a concealed window from which the daughter can look out at the world. All the suitors of the princess surround the tower and exhaust themselves if just to see her, but only the privileged few are aware of the window and look intently at it. They know that the princess may suddenly appear and glance out, and for a fleeting moment they will be able to see her exceptional beauty. Such is the study of the Kabbalist. In every word, even every syllable, they seek the concealed entrance through which they experience the presence of God. Thus the Torah itself is the presence of God among His people; through its infinite interpretations it fills the vacuum left by the destruction of the Temple.

This background facilitates an understanding of Kabbalist behavior on Shavuot. At the *tikun* study session, which the Kabbalists introduced as a primary element, they gather on the evening of the festival to study Torah all night—particularly midnight, the hour at which the heavens open. Through profound study, which seeks to reach the hidden spheres, they *repair* the flaw of exile. It is the act of repairing that bridges the rift between God and His people and the distance that has opened between them. Through studying the hidden depths of the Torah on the night of the festival, the Kabbalists manage to draw closer, to rise up to the spiritual level of the Land of Israel, Jerusalem, and the Temple. There is an actual act of spiritual pilgrimage in order to present oneself before God in His Temple. In this sense, one can say that the concept of Shavuot as the "Time of the Giving of the Torah" has reabsorbed all the content of Shavuot as the festival on which Jews brought their offering of first fruits to the Temple in Jerusalem. The theme of the festival has moved from the life of the people living in its own land according to the Torah, to the life of the people who stand before the uplifting experience of facing its Father and King in the heavens.

A FESTIVAL OF SETTLING THE LAND
AND GIVING OF THE TORAH

From the beginning of Zionist resettlement of the Land of Israel, particularly during the Second Aliyah period, the secular Zionist movement showed a clear tendency to *return* Shavuot to its origins as an agricultural festival. No longer would it serve as the "Time of the Giving of the Torah" but as the "Festival of the First Fruits." This return to the ancient source could be seen in the restructuring of the ceremony to celebrate a splendid bringing of first fruits before the entire community. Led by the children, the procession of those who brought the offering drew near to the stage. The ceremony was drawn from the Bible and the Mishnah and featured colorful dances and lavish singing and playing of instruments. This re-enactment was essentially a secular ritual that shaped the religious sources as a kind of metaphor. The content was overtly social and national. It reflected the joy of the worker who tilled the Jewish land that he had won through his labors; the joy of the people's return to their land to live a natural life; the joy of rooting oneself in the soil; the landscape and nature of the homeland.

Bringing the first fruits as a contribution to the ongoing endeavor of settling the land was the climax. Nor was it the priests who received the first fruits to place before God; rather, it was representatives of the Zionist institutions. The fruits were sold and the proceeds assigned to the Jewish National Fund to redeem and settle more of the Land of Israel. It is true that the ceremonies continued the ancient combination of an agricultural festival that expressed thanks for the bountiful harvest and a historical festival that related to the people's settlement of its land; indeed, one might claim that despite their emphatically secular tone, at least during the early years, these ceremonies had a religious and experiential basis. The return to nature and to a more natural life was replete with such images. In the thinking of A. D. Gordon, the religious element was overt: the human being is an inseparable part of nature; and nature is the unity of infinite forces, which derive from an absolute source. Joining with nature in order to draw out the harvest is not only an act of creation, it is also an act of devotion in the religious sense of the term. Labor, simple labor in the fields, is the labor and worship of God; it embraces a sacred element.

This perspective of the ceremony of the first fruits as a contribution to the building of the nation can be seen as a *midrash* on the ancient festival that is at once revolutionary and traditional. The ceremonies, incorporating allusions to moral and social themes concerned with the settlement of the land according to the commandments of the Torah, were held within a community of landworkers that sought—through settlement of the Land of Israel—to realize values of justice, cooperation, and equality. However, the events also entailed an intentional transvaluation of meanings, not only as compared to the Diaspora manifestation of Shavuot but also compared to the tradition that emerged in the Torah and the Mishnah during the early period when the people lived on its own land. The latter-day version was a secular festival; even its *cosmic* aspect was secular. It grasped the divine core as identical with the forces of nature, which included the natural forces of man.

The truth is that even in the early years there were some disturbing aspects already evident in the tension between the image drawn from religious sources and carrying religious meanings, and the secular national innovation. There was something artificial about the way first-fruit ceremonies were designed as a recollection of the Temple, and there were those who felt that the ceremony had a touch of artifice or even pretense. Although they represented the people and the vision of its redemption, the institutions of Zionist settlement could not take the place of the priests in worship. Only a high measure of national enthusiasm and idealistic devotion to the process of rebirth could bridge the gap between the material concept and the religious or spiritual symbol. During the initial period, this enthusiasm was maintained, but it began to wane when the pioneering efforts realized their main material achievements— extensive settlement and prosperous agriculture. The tradition of the first-fruits festival as an agricultural event has been preserved in the agricultural settlements of many *kibbutzim* and *moshavim*, but its form has changed considerably. Today it is held primarily for and by the children, and the ritual relating to events in the Temple is invariably omitted. In its place, the harvest and achievements of the settlement are presented so that the public can see and rejoice in the fruits of its collective labor. The religious dimension of a return to nature also seems to have disappeared as social games, dancing, and picnics now characterize a day that has become an ordinary holiday.

Against this backdrop one can appreciate the recent phenomenon of drawing more intensively on traditional post-biblical and Mishnaic sources, especially in celebration of the pilgrimage festivals. In the Passover seder, this trend is seen in a growing dependence on the traditional Haggadah; at Shavuot, liberal interpretations of the *tikun* format mark the celebration of the festival as the "Time of the Giving of the Torah." The all-night study sessions relate to various issues from traditional and modern sources, and an effort is often made to clarify questions regarding the nature of a Jewish way of life and Jewish cultural identity. The considerable level of reflection on such issues, which are discussed throughout the year, is thus imbued with an institutional character; so far the solution to the problem appears to lie in the very fact that it is addressed in a framework of study and discussion.

This brings us back to questions discussed in the previous two chapters. On Holocaust Memorial Day and Independence Day there is a conscious deviation from the outlook and view of reality espoused by tradition, whereas in the modern shaping of the Festival of First Fruits—a pilgrimage holiday—one now observes an inner spiritual need to *repair* the deviation. The aim here is to infuse renewed patterns and symbols with traditional content, and the moral and spiritual experience with traditional themes. The rebellious trend has been replaced, however hesitantly, by a desire to maintain a continuity with tradition and to stay short of the breaking point.

This is not the place to enter into a detailed analysis of the reason for the change, but the following are some of the main factors involved. Tradition per se provides a vital infrastructure for the individual and for a cultured society. Without tradition there is no continuity, and without continuity there is no identity. Tradition preserves that which is enduring within changing circumstances. Tradition may limit and restrict, but in its absence the living memory from which innovative creativity springs evaporates, the sources of creativity dwindle, and innovations quickly become empty gestures—superficial and meaningless changes. This fact has now become quite clear even to that segment of the public that once enthusiastically adopted the constant innovations typical of what is dubbed modernity. There is something threatening in the rapid break-down of behavior patterns, ceremonies, symbols, and accepted forms of expression. Within the whirlwind of informal changes, in which emotional and conceptual content has been impoverished, people long for stability and permanence, and for the emotional and conceptual weight these carry. This is defined as "the search for roots."

It would appear, however, that what is longed for in the tradition is not only roots, patterns, symbols, and content, but also an authority that can be trusted and relied on when setting those objectives, which, when achieved, provide meaning and value for the individual's life. It may be that an individual is capable of identifying a direction or trend in his feelings and thoughts, some longing that supersedes all other desires and which he sets as his objective in life. However, he realizes very quickly that the strength to persist in this objective and incorporate it within the objectives of society as a whole does not lie within himself, but beyond. Without the presence of an authority that establishes structured and purposeful individual and societal lives, there cannot be a unified personal and social destiny. Tradition emerges as the direct agent that embodies this authority, even if it is only the authority of previous generations whose actions serve as a prelude to the generations that follow. The demand for continuity that derives from these actions is their authority.

Rediscovery of the need to rely on the establishing and guiding authority of tradition brings with it another discovery. The destiny that gives meaning to human and societal life is not only in realizing the creative ability of the individual, nor even the combination of all the individuals into a society. Destiny rooted in an establishing authority exceeds individual existence, or the existence of society as a combination of individuals. The demand for continuity is inherent in this authority, and it invokes those who follow into the next generation. Thus tradition, particularly its authoritative establishing and directing dimension, embodies the human being's effort to reach beyond the borders of his own isolated, finite, and transient being and to be integrated into the infinite chain by standing in relationship to eternal existence. The desire for continuity is the desire for a life that *justifies* itself not only in terms of its own transient moment but also by offering purpose and meaning in terms of *eternity*. When the desire to be part of what lies beyond the individual self—unique but transient—re-emerges, the gesture of faith, which is the initial spark at the base of all tradition, is kindled once more.

If this analysis is correct, the polarity of dialectic tension created between Holocaust Memorial Day and Tisha B'Av, on the one hand, and between Independence Day and Passover, on the other, may reach its point of balance at Shavuot as the time of the giving of the Torah. The desire to cling to stabilizing tradition, to authority, and to the initial gesture of faith is equivalent to the aspiration to accept the Torah, which imposes the authority of its commandments on the current hour of Jewish history. It is clear, however, that a Torah that is anchored in tradition and imposes its authoritative commandments on the present will no longer be the Torah that guided the people of Israel in the Diaspora. Rather, it will be a Torah that turns to the people as it gathers once again in its land, there to live the life of an integral nation. In other words, in marking Shavuot as the time of the giving of the Torah, we should no longer gloss over the primal and original meaning of the festival as the settlement of the Land of Israel by its people. Indeed, it would now be desirable to relate in a tangible and ordinary sense to the elements evoked and absorbed during the Diaspora period by the ecstatic experience of the giving of the Torah. In place of the *spiritual pilgrimage* to the highest spheres that symbolize the Holy Land, one should now recognize the real, living, and committed contact between the people of Israel and the land, which is both its homeland and its destiny.

Thus the entirety of the themes of the festival can be rediscovered. Once again that section which describes the revelation at Mt. Sinai as the establishment of the covenant that prepared the path for the settlement of the land by the people should be emphasized. The central theme will not be the ecstatic experience of revelation, but rather the social order according to which the people hold its land and live a life of liberty and justice forever. Study of the Torah, which assuredly contains the possibility of *repairing* the flaw left in the national life of the Jewish people by their long period of the Diaspora, is a study of Torah that delves into the social, moral, and political questions that relate to the people's life in its own land. Such Torah study links the portion that describes the giving of the Torah with the commandments that relate to the Land of Israel, the offering of first fruits, and the laws of the monarchy and then moves on to the social and philosophical thought that has guided the people as it returned to its homeland, particularly in the modern era. This is the content of the renewed covenant that re-establishes the life of the people.

From an emphasis on the establishment of the covenant through the commandments, which are connected to the Land of Israel, there is a direct link to the philosophical themes that the Book of Ruth contributes to the Shavuot festival. These themes deal with an act of grace and devotion based on independent initiative. The recitation of these motifs brings the people back to its land, corrects the flaw of the Diaspora, and commemorates the generations that were cut off in the Diaspora re-establishing them on their land. Moreover, this grace is a reflection of the strength to cut oneself off from the past and begin anew; to change the patterns of the past in order to enable the people of Israel to live as a nation state. For the purpose of continuity, it is vital to begin from the beginning. Such thoughts must find suitable expression in the prayers of the festival, its symbols, and ceremonies. Innovations in prayer and ceremonial can articulate the effort to return to the Land of Israel— reflecting in particular the unselfish acts of the pioneers through whose devotion to their people and their land Israel is now able to stand as a politically independent state in its own land—and the burning desire of the people to embrace its nation and its independence and continue to live on its land. As in the declaration of those who brought the first-fruit offerings, these innovations will bear witness to the spiritual readiness to meet obligations and commandments without which the people cannot be constituted on its land.

Shaped in such a way, Shavuot, as a festival of both settlement of the land by its people and the giving of the Torah, could embody the trauma of dislocation undergone by the people in modern times, anchoring them once again in the continuity of tradition, which encompasses the wonderful and merciful ability to begin, recurrently, from the beginning. The intense polarization exhibited in the contradiction between Holocaust Memorial Day and Tisha B'Av, between Passover and Independence Day, could be mediated through Shavuot if the Jewish people breaks free of previous limitations: a Diaspora limitation when the festival was exclusively the "Giving of the Torah" without reference to the settlement of the land; and a limitation that occurred at the beginning of the pioneering period when the holiday was celebrated as a festival of settlement without reference to the giving of the Torah. If the Jewish people returns to the full range of themes that emerged from the early sources through to modern times, this gap, too, will be *repaired* in the innovating continuity of memory and hope.

THIRTEEN

The Individual
Enters the Covenant

GOD AND PEOPLE IN COVENANT

The yearly sequence of a nation's festivals is set by the calendar; the yearly sequence of individuals as they develop, mature, have families, and pursue their personal agendas is marked by private anniversaries. Most people have special days that are particular to themselves, though neither the form nor content of personal celebrations are fashioned solely by the celebrant. There are standard designs for such occasions, and the calendar accommodates them. In setting up societal patterns, the nation enables individuals to integrate their own special days into the overall time cycle; thus, the inner rhythm of changing generations becomes part of the internal flow of the life of the nation. Generations come and go, and the nation—progressing along its course, is sustained through its individuals.

There are several rites of passage that mark turning points in a person's life. Some of these are experienced alone, some in the company of family and friends, and others within the community or nation; but the form and content of the central events conform to a pattern. These rites of passage are an outgrowth of the natural life cycle and are mandated by the societal/civilizational matrix of man's existence: birth, maturation, taking responsibility for family and society, the birth of one's own offspring and their nurturing to maturity. Jews reflect this natural ebb and flow as they structure time through three festive milestones—introducing the eight-day-old son into the Covenant of Abraham by means of the circumcision ceremony, accepting the yoke of mitzvot at thirteen years of age, and undertaking marriage. The sequence ends when it begins anew: parents whose own parents brought them into the Covenant of Abraham, then bring their sons into the same binding contract. In essence, it is at these moments that the individual, each in his own turn, is formally invested and co-opted into the family, the community, and the nation. It seems appropriate, therefore, even before discussing the form and content of each of the ceremonies to consider a hotly debated contemporary question: the principle of the individual's integration into the Jewish people; that is, who is, a priori, a Jew? And how can someone who was not born Jewish become a Jew?

To start with, the question has a straightforward answer, which, at first blush, is no different than the accepted norm among other peoples. The Jews are a people and, as with all peoples, the ordinary process of inclusion, *of joining*, is simply to be born into the generational continuity. An a priori Jew is someone born to Jewish parents who are Jewish because they in turn were born to Jewish parents, and so on back to Abraham who is deemed the progenitor of the Jewish people. So it is with other peoples as well although, from a legal standpoint, there are variations about the qualifications required in doubtful cases; e.g., when both parents are not of the same people, is the determination matrilinear or patrilinear? Such legalities are not germane here because substantively it is the general principle that obtains: one enters the continuity of any people's life a priori through the natural process of birth. A people is an amalgamation of individuals based on kinship and on practices that have evolved over the generations.

In addition, every people, the Jews included, have a conventional way for outsiders to join. Generally this is by means of acculturation, the end product of which may be marked by marrying in. A foreign person adopts the language, behavior, and values of the host culture, simulates the environment to the degree he can, intermarries, and when children are born of the union, the joining is accomplished. It is a natural process and in essence one that a non-Jew, who wishes to join the Jewish people, undergoes, except that he is usually expected first to convert; that is, he needs to accept the Jewish faith and the obligations of the covenant, which have maintained Jewish unity over the generations. It bears emphasizing that the convert is not only required to accept the Torah, its beliefs, and commandments, but to regard himself as a child of the Jewish people. He is considered an "adopted son" and as such a son of Abraham. Nonetheless a convert is distinguished from those born into Judaism since he is referred to as a *ger*, a convert. The process of conversion is completed only through his children as they are born into Judaism. In any case, kinship is the primal relationship that constitutes peoplehood, binding its members; anyone born a Jew is considered a Jew by other Jews even if he alienates himself from the people, even if he converts to another religion.

Conceiving of kinship as the basis for belonging to the human collective grounds societal bonds in the natural stage—that is, the pre-cultural stage—in human development. However, in and of itself, kinship cannot be regarded as solely a *natural* process; it is unquestionably a cultural phenomenon. In other words, although they have roots in man's impulse-driven persona, the bonds of peoplehood are not the bonds of instinctual drives; they are mainly a matter of self-consciousness and will. For a family—or a people—to exist, its members must voluntarily choose to regard their kinship as the basis of their association in mutual multi-faceted cultural endeavor. It must regard the fact of kinship as the background for an obligating social unity. Should that assumption cease, the bond is broken, kinship is forgotten, and the natural sentiment allied to it disappears.

This means that volitional cultural shaping transforms the natural inclination of kinship into a binding moral norm. Family, tribe, and people assume that the continuation of the feeling of kinship is an ideal expectation and need of each individual: it is assumed that individuals will strive to preserve the bond, continuing it from generation to generation. Why expect the bond to be retained and continued? As it is formulated, the moral norm clearly has a rationale rooted in the collective will to survive as a group. This is manifestly a cultural issue, but through this issue the inherent sense of kinship becomes an internal life value. It symbolizes a fundamental given unity that serves as a permanent starting point of human socialization that is absolutely taken for granted. Thus the moral sense of social responsibility is born in the bosom of the sense of kinship. Man and woman are mutually obligated because fundamentally they are "one flesh." Brothers are mutually obligated because they are fundamentally connected through a single womb. Social empathy is perceived as a womb-like feeling that symbolizes feelings of motherhood. (In Hebrew, the words mercy and womb have the same root.) The mutual obligations people have for one another derive from the fact that they stem from a single entity. So an individual owes the person to whom he is attached as his own "flesh and blood," whatever it is that he himself aspires to. This appears to be the basis of the principle that remains constant in its potency, the forerunner of all moral legislation: "Love your neighbor as yourself" (Leviticus 9:18), because friendship, too, is a feeling of closeness; it assumes a person's identification with a member of his group, conceiving the other as part of his own self. Emphasizing such a feeling and maintaining it as an obligatory norm means that we must prefer it over contrary natural drives that can divide families when they regard relatives as competitors, even as detested enemies, who vie with one another.

Particularly apparent in the Book of Genesis, one is readily convinced that this is a primary source of social ethics in the Bible. Man and woman are "one flesh," hence their love, and hence their mutual obligations. Cain and Abel are brothers, sons of the same womb; therefore they must feel that fratricide is forbidden despite the fact that the law against it had not yet been specifically enunciated. It is not only God who utterly rejects fratricide; so does the very ground from which the blood cries out. Murder is understood as utterly opposed to the natural order because brothers, who are one by nature and origin, ought to protect each other. Transposed into an obligatory norm, the unity of a people is nothing other than a direct continuation of the same feeling of unity. The people is a unity of those born into it who are its ongoing generations. Their mutual obligations stem from this, and the responsibility of the people to protect its sons stems from this as well. The people is the *redeemer* of its individuals because each of them is "bone of its bone and flesh of its flesh."

Not only is this the basis of the moral sense that unites kin into family, tribe, and people but it is also the basis of the unity of generations that follow one another. The bond of natural procreation is seen as a symbol of the spiritual/psychological bond that is expressed in education and the transmission of values. In the way in which they function, creatures of nature embody the species' will to exist. They not only exist for themselves but for the procreation of the generation that follows; and they reach maturity when they are capable of procreation, which is their vital function. According to the Bible, man was meant to be fruitful and multiply, to fill the world and perpetuate his species. The significance of his existence is embodied in the continuity of his generations; every individual is identified and assigned according to his place on his family tree: father to son to grandson, and so on. Yet man born in God's image must stand on his own. The well-known dictum of the Sages when cautioning witnesses in capital cases clearly demonstrates this biblical notion, "This is because each person is born unique . . . in order to declare the glory of God: for man mints numerous coins in the same mold where each one resembles the other; whereas the King of Kings, the Holy One blessed be He, minted each person in the image of the first man, yet none of them resembles his fellow. Therefore each and every one is required to say, it is for me that the world was created" (Sanhedrin IV, 5).

The fact that each individual has a unique and intrinsic value does not contradict either the human will to exist within a generational continuity or the functions of begetting and bequeathing; on the contrary, it imparts an additional importance to this drive in the aspiration for eternity, which is rooted in the individual's consciousness of self. Man's eternity is found in the memory that remains with his children as they continue the legacy of his life, spiritually no less than physically. Indeed, in the view of the Bible and the Sages, children are really the eternal life of their parents. Parents need not fear death so long as they have children to whom they can impart a *blessing*; it is the consequence of their lives, which they bequeath to their offspring as their patrimony. So it is that the Patriarchs feared infertility and childlessness, why the most grievous punishment is the decree of *kharet*, being cut off without continuity—death without offspring who will be called by their parents' name. The continuity of generations transmitted by a physical, spiritual, and psychological legacy is the eternal life of each generation and each individual within each generation.

It would appear that it is only as against this basic feeling of continuity in which the singular value of each individual is maintained within the people that one can understand the covenant concluded with Abraham: through his seed he would become the father of a multitude of peoples. It is through the commitment of the fathers to obligate their sons, and the sons their sons, from one generation to the next that one can understand the assumption that underlies entry into the Covenant of Abraham. Just as an obligation between generations is assumed, it must be emphasized that the value of each individual and of each generation is also posited. Along with the sense of being obligated to one's parents and obligating one's sons, each person ought to volitionally enter and maintain the covenant. Every generation, and every individual within it, both continues and begins. Every individual Jew returns to stand in Abraham's place as he personally initiates his sons into the covenant; only thus can the continuity of generations maintain the unique, unparalleled value of the individuals who constitute it.

From this distinct meaning of man's intergenerational continuity, one discovers that beyond the natural, instinctual drive that binds parents and their children, a voluntary decision is required. Though it parallels the instinctual connection and flows from it, the spiritual, psychological bond that exists between generations (in the absence of which there is no societal unity of family, tribe, or people) is not the outcome of instinct. It is a moral norm. It does not exist of itself and the natural drives do not ensure it. The expectation is that one should choose the bond repeatedly, should want it repeatedly, should agree to it again and again. Just as morality does not necessarily flow from a feeling of kinship, but must be consolidated as an obligatory norm, so the intergenerational bond does not necessarily flow from a sense of kinship. Such a bond depends on an education to belonging and on a choice that must be renewed. Consequently, entering into the continuity of a people's life does not end with the natural fact of birth. It requires affirmation before the people so that the bond is elevated to a level of moral obligation, as well as being the contractual ritual expressed when initiating sons into the Covenant of Abraham. Jews are not simply members of the same people; by virtue of their belonging to the same people, they are mutually obliged, morally and legally. Jews are *b'nai b'rit*—that is, bound by a covenant.

The notion of covenant has been discussed in previous chapters but since it is the main element of everything that follows, it is necessary to reiterate briefly the scope of this concept. A covenant is an institutionalized ritual and legal undertaking between sides—private individuals, or groups such as families, tribes, or peoples whose collective unity is in turn based on a covenant. Such an undertaking is the initiating, constitutive step, which joins the parties into a social unit regarding matters to which they obligate themselves. Uniting into a social body does not cancel the individual status of each side entering the covenant. On one hand, the unity is *greater* than its parts; it is a framework in its own right whose orientation is the agreement between its partners. On the other hand, each of the parties to the framework remains an independent entity, and as such makes up the unified body. The concept is expressed in the legal institutionalization of a covenant. Each of the parties accepts the a priori autonomy of the other parties. They agree to respect the will and responsibility of each of them, granting each of them the status of sole decision-making vis-à-vis themselves; they stand behind their actions and pledge not to have recourse to any means of coercion in order to achieve their goals. Power struggles and attempts at coercion are replaced by voluntary agreement. This is the first step.

In the second step, all those who enter a covenant employ the autonomy they have been granted, and which they have accorded to each other, in a mutual obligation that ensures their independence within the common framework. In the mutual obligation of the covenant, observance by each of the partners obliges all the others to observe as well; nullification by one of the partners cancels the covenant for all the others. A legal framework is thus created, which is civilizational in that it goes beyond the natural order, though it parallels the unity of kinship and is based on it. In the logic of the partners' moral responsibility for one another, the natural and civilizational forms of association are completely merged. The members must consider each other as part of a single entity, each regarding the welfare of the other as their own. In actuality, it is likely that without the morally sanctioned model of the natural unity of kin, there would be no precedent for constituting a covenant; nonetheless, a covenant comprises a different type of unity, broader than natural unity and superior to it. It is the partnership of those who share a will to unity based on the essential freedom of man created in God's image.

The unity of kin is palpable and emotional, which is its advantage as well as its initial, indispensable basis. The unity of people who join a covenant seems at first to be an *abstract* legal matter, predicated on mutual, free consent. Such consent seems to depend on a willingness to renew the covenant from day to day; thus it seems to lack stability. In reality, however, no unity can exist as an actual guiding element in people's actions if it remains such an abstraction that is constantly dependent on personal attitudes and moods that are subject to daily change. For a covenant to be established and become a social actuality it must be accorded a tangible, objective status. This status is conferred at a public ritual. The bond and the establishment of a social entity are symbolically actualized by a sacrificial act. Even more important is the demonstrated consciousness of the mutual obligation undertaken in standing together before God as Witness and Judge. Standing before God who knows all that transpires, the commitment in the hearts of individuals attains a status that transcends the individual. What has been done cannot be undone. A change of heart alone cannot annul it. Just as individuals cannot unilaterally abrogate a contract except through specified modes and in accordance with certain rules, so annulling a covenant cannot be effected because of second thoughts on the part of those who entered into it. It would be considered a sin, a transgression against an existing presence to which God is guarantor as Witness and Judge.

Therefore entering a covenant is an agreement rooted in the free will of the individual, but having made the decision to enact the covenant, a person is in its grip and the obligation he has undertaken acquires the validity of objective reality. Jews stand together on the basis of their relationship to one another as one people before God in a covenant they undertook to be mutually responsible for each other and mutually bound to an agreed specific goal. One sees here the exceptional element that distinguishes this covenant from most other covenants. God is in the covenant, not only as Witness and Judge of the mutual undertakings between people, but as a Party to the covenant as well. Those who enter the covenant oblige themselves to Him even as they oblige themselves to one another; and He obliges Himself to them.

INDIVIDUAL COVENANT

What has been stated above brings us directly to the first ceremony through which a Jew enters the covenant that binds him to his people. All the elements of a covenantal ceremony are found in the chapter that pronounces the ongoing commandment of circumcision.

> When Abram was ninety-nine years old, the Lord appeared to Abram and said to him, "I am El Shaddai. Walk in My ways and be blameless. I will establish My covenant between Me and you, and I will make you exceedingly numerous."
>
> Abram threw himself on his face, as God continued speaking to him, "As for Me, this is My covenant with you: You shall be the father of a multitude of nations. And you shall no longer be called Abram, but your name shall be Abraham, for I will make you the father of a multitude of nations. I will make you exceedingly fertile, and make nations of you; and kings shall come forth from you. I will maintain My covenant between Me and you, and your offspring to come, as an everlasting covenant throughout the ages, to be God to you and to your offspring to come. I give the land you sojourn in to you and to your offspring to come, all the land of Canaan as an everlasting possession. I will be their God."
>
> God further said to Abraham, "As for you, you shall keep My covenant, you and your offspring to come, throughout the ages.
>
> Such shall be the covenant, which you shall keep, between Me and you and your offspring to follow: every male among you shall be circumcised. You shall circumcise the flesh of your foreskin and that shall be the sign of the covenant between Me and you.
>
> At the age of eight days, every male among you throughout the generations shall be circumcised, even the homeborn slave and the one

bought from an outsider who is not of your seed.—The slave that is born in your household or bought with your money must be circumcised!—Thus shall My covenant be marked in your flesh as an everlasting pact. An uncircumcised male who does not circumcise the flesh of his foreskin—such a person shall be cut off from his kin; he has broken my covenant."

Genesis 17:1–14

The story of the enactment of the covenant distinguishes between several stages in which the bond is established with Abram (designated the progenitor of several nations, especially the patriarch of the Jewish people) and God. In the first stage, Abram is commanded to "walk in My ways and be blameless." In effect this is a commandment that summarizes Abram's path from the moment he was commanded to leave his land, his birthplace, and his father's house to go to Canaan. Abram walked before God in the sense that all his acts were dedicated to the performance of God's will, declaring His nature to all. In the sense that all his deeds were done in whole-hearted faith, he was an innocent. Because he undertook the obligation and fulfilled it, God entered into a covenant with him; that is, an explicit obligation was forged whose maintenance is not only as a promise or an intent but as a reality that transcends the intentions of those who are mutually obligated to each other. "I will establish My covenant between Me and you, and I will make you exceedingly numerous." The covenant is *between* the parties. In other words, this becomes a reality that actually exists between them and joins them into a continuing compact. Of course this is not the first covenant between God and Abram. In the earlier covenant sealed at *Brit Ben HaBettarim* (the covenant between the pieces; Genesis 15), the commitment was made to bequeath the Land of Israel to Abram. Now there is a pledge regarding offspring as God commits Himself to fulfilling His promise. Abram will become a father, further concretizing the relationship between God and Abram. A symbolic but tangible act is performed during which God changes Abram's name to Abraham. This change, "And you shall no longer be called Abram, but your name shall be Abraham," is the symbol of the promise.

The change of name symbolizes the change of Abraham's inner status. He is, from this point on, a new man. With his name changed, he stands before God as someone who has had the promise fulfilled in him; he *is* already, in full actuality, a patriarch of many peoples. The second stage follows as an unbroken progression of the first. Since, in the sight of God, Abraham already enjoys the status of patriarch of many peoples, he can engage in a covenant with God regarding his offspring. Abraham obligates the children who come after him. In the act that is performed on Abraham himself, and on his seed, the covenant is once again personified. It is an act performed actually on the body (not on a sacrifice that serves as its substitute). Moreover, the substantiating act is performed on the same organ that pertains to the substance of the covenant: God pledges His assurance that Abraham's seed will never perish, even as Abraham pledges that his children will observe what he himself has undertaken, namely to walk before God. Although the obligation of only one commandment is encompassed in this ceremony, it is the commandment that embodies the covenant.

Abraham's seed will observe the commandment of circumcision, an observance symbolic of many observances: as he circumcises his son, every father of Abraham's seed stands in the place of Abraham who circumcised himself and then his sons, and undertook to walk before God in all His ways. How could the covenant actually be maintained in Abraham's seed? At this stage, there was no answer because Abraham was still only symbolically the father of many nations. The time to interpret the specific commandments expected of Abraham's offspring would come when the promise was fulfilled in practice, and the multitude of Abraham's seed would become a nation. At such time, the pledge made at the *Brit Ben HaBettarim* would be fulfilled. The people enters its land and undertakes the commandments that are dependent on living in the land. The third stage of the covenant is not amplified in this story. It is a potential that exists as an allusion of things to come.

In any case, the people is founded when a single man presents himself as a father, and enters into a covenant with his God, introducing his seed into that covenant, and this action, which is repeated for each individual who is born to that lineage, maintains the continuity of the people from generation to generation.

BRIT MILA—CIRCUMCISION

The ceremony by which the individual Jew enters the Covenant of Abraham remains the same as that which was formulated by the Sages in the Oral Law. The event described in the Book of Genesis, including all the inferences, is well-represented in the ritual. But, in the style characteristic of the Sages, one does not find a re-enactment of that first ceremony but its continuation, which was formulated once the promise had been fulfilled: Abraham's seed has grown and become a people, a people that has been given the Torah, has entered its land, experienced exile from it, and awaited redemption. The historical reality of the people, if only in general, is also in the ceremony that now speaks of a people obligated by a covenant, having experienced joys and sorrows, that now welcomes a newborn into the chain of its generations.

The audience, usually made up of family members and friends, assembles at the synagogue or a hall set aside for circumcision ceremonies. The infant is brought in from an adjacent room to the guests who await him—the first ritual step. The audience welcomes the infant, saying "Baruch HaBa" (Welcome). The father, who is in the expectant audience, says a verse from Psalms 65:5, "Happy is the man whom Thou choosest, and bringest near, that he may dwell in Thy courts," and the audience responds, "May we be satisfied with the goodness of Thy house, the holy place of Thy Temple." Only after the audience welcomes the infant into its midst does the father begin his role of bringing his son closer to the "courtyard of God," to the sanctified circle, and the audience, which responds to the invitation, turns to the father who wants to dedicate his child to sanctity. The infant is placed on a special chair known as the throne of Elijah. Once again the father calls attention to the significance of what is about to happen: "This is the throne of Elijah of blessed memory." The prophet Elijah is thereby made a symbolic witness to the covenant to be enacted. Along with the symbolic presence of Elijah, the history of the Jewish people is recalled, the essence of a people attempting to remain loyal to a covenant.

Now the mohel, the person who performs the circumcision, begins his role. He undertakes to be the father's emissary and continues what the father has initiated. (The mohel, it should be emphasized, is not an independent figure but an intermediary in the ceremony. The commandment falls basically on the father; the mohel is merely a professional who represents the father and acts in his name.) "O Lord, I hope for Thy salvation. I wait for Thy deliverance, O Lord, and I do Thy bidding. I delight in Thy promise, like one who finds abundant wealth. Abundant peace have they who love Thy Torah, and there is no stumbling for them. Happy is he whom Thou choosest to dwell in Thy courts close to Thee." This is a personal dedication by the person about to perform the important task. The first stage of the ceremony reaches its peak when the mohel declares and those assembled repeat after him, "Hear O Israel, the Lord our God, the Lord is One. The Lord reigns, the Lord reigned, the Lord shall reign forever and ever. O, Lord, deliver us. O, Lord deliver us. O, Lord, prosper us. O, Lord prosper us. Happy is the man whom Thou choosest, and bringest near, that he may dwell in Thy courts. May we be satisfied with the goodness of Thy house, the holy place of Thy Temple."

This part of the ceremony is opened and closed with the same verse. When it is said the second time, a situation has been created that incorporates its meaning because a group of individuals has now consolidated into a congregation, and the congregation merged into a community that is bound in a covenant. It is the community of Israel, which shoulders the yoke of divine sovereignty; as such, it represents the whole of Israel throughout the generations and the figure of Elijah—who symbolizes absolute, radical loyalty to the Covenant—bears witness to this. The prophet Elijah entered Jewish folklore as a figure symbolic of the Jewish people's power of survival to surmount all obstacles. Elijah is not dead. He lives and exists; he reappears periodically; and in the name of the unity of the Jewish people throughout its history, he welcomes the newborn son into the community of Israel, as a member of the covenant. The congregation that has assembled at the sacred court stands ready, whereupon the circumcision ceremony begins.

The father, on whom the commandment to circumcise his son devolves, now declares, "I am ready to fulfill the commandment to circumcise my son as the Creator, blessed be He, has commanded us." And the mohel who is about to perform the commandment in the father's stead, recites the words which recall the source of the commandment and its substance. "The Lord, blessed be He, said to Abraham: Walk in My ways and be blameless. I stand ready to perform the commandment which God commanded me to circumcise my son." The mohel recites the blessing and performs the circumcision, then repeats the blessing "to introduce the child into the covenant of our patriarch Abraham" upon its completion. He also blesses the occasion, "Blessed art Thou O Lord our God King of the universe Who has kept us alive, sustained us, and brought us to this season." The assembled guests bring the second part of the ceremony to its conclusion as they recite the blessing that precedes the last segment, "Just as he has entered into the covenant, so also may he enter into the blessings of Torah, of marriage, and of good deeds." At this juncture, the father stands in Abraham's place, recalling the past—the inaugural event in the people's existence; at the same time those assembled invoke the future—the future of the child, which is also the future of the people.

The third segment of the ceremony is made up entirely of the blessing made by the mohel as the father's emissary. He recites the blessing over wine, saying: "Blessed art Thou O Lord our God, King of the universe

Who sanctified beloved Israel from birth, impressing Thy statute in its flesh, and marking its descendants with the sign of the holy covenant. Because of this, for the sake of the covenant that Thou didst impress in our flesh, O eternal God, our Stronghold, deliver our dearly beloved from destruction. Blessed art Thou, O Lord, Author of the covenant." Up to this point, the blessing is over what has already taken place, and a hope that the child who has entered the covenant will live and be part of the eternal generations. A specialized portion of this segment of the ceremony follows. "Our God and God of our fathers, sustain this child for his father and mother. Let his name in Israel be _____ the son of _____ . May both husband and wife rejoice in their offspring as it is written: 'Let your parents be happy; let your mother be filled with joy.' As was inscribed: 'I passed by you and saw you weltering in your blood. Live through your blood—I said to you—Live through your blood.' And it was said: 'He remembers His covenant forever, the word which He pledged for a thousand generations, the covenant He made with Abraham, and His oath to Isaac. He confirmed the same to Jacob as a statute, to Israel as an everlasting covenant.' And it was also said: 'Abraham circumcised his son Isaac when he was eight days old, as God had commanded him. Give thanks to the Lord for He is good, His mercy endures forever.' May this child, named _____ , become great even as he has been introduced into the covenant, so may he be introduced to the Torah, to the marriage canopy, and to a life of good deeds."

The most important part of this blessing is naming the child, an act that confers his identity in the community. His own pathway now begins; it is the pathway of a unique individual, of integration into the community: to build it and to continue its chain of generations. This is a rehearsal of what occurred to Abraham, but it is in reverse order. Abraham, who entered the covenant as a father, was first called by his new name and later circumcised. The infant that enters the covenant as a son is first introduced into the covenant and subsequently named. He is considered a defined and identified individual by virtue of the covenant.

Afterward, the ritual proceeds to a feast that is, in essence, a continuation of the ceremony. This is a festive, religiously sanctioned meal with a reference in scripture: Abraham conducted a great feast for his guests when Isaac was weaned. Such a festive meal denotes joy and is unparalleled in giving expression to the community's sense of togetherness. At the communal meal, it is as though the community grows in strength, extending its security and, in turn, feeling more secure. The joy

is gladness in the stability of existence, which has just been proven
through the introduction of a new son into the chain of generations.

BAR/BAT MITZVAH

For the father, the ceremony of initiating his son into the Covenant of
Abraham closes a cycle in which his parents performed the same ritual for
him in his own infancy. For the child, it is only a token of what is to come.
The future will determine if he lives up to what is required of him and
what had been hoped for at the hour of the ceremony. The family looks
to the future; that is, toward the two voluntary events in which the grown
child further enters the covenant: the ceremonies of *bar mitzvah* and
marriage.

There is a parallel between the dual structure of holidays in the general
Jewish calendar and the dual structure of events in the personal growth of
the individual. A nature festival is at the substructure of the holidays that
commemorate historic events; historic symbols embody the stages of an
individual's natural maturation. Circumcision is performed on the eighth
day after birth when it is apparent that the infant is sturdy and will
survive; when a boy reaches thirteen years of age, when the incipient
signs of sexual maturation are evident and one can say of him that he is
viable from the standpoint of being able to procreate; one also notes the
beginning of spiritual maturity. The young man undertakes the yoke of
the commandments when he is considered an intelligent person, capable
of distinguishing right from wrong and in control of his drives. But he is
not considered an adult or an independent personality from all societal
and legal aspects. According to the biblical concept, which is the basis for
the Sages' concept, full maturity is achieved when a man marries a woman
and establishes a family.

Only then is he considered a substantial citizen, carrying full responsibility for all the social roles of an adult. All of which indicates a
cognitive structure. Over time, the highly complex societal reality gives
rise to detailed legal provisions, which make allowance for a great variety
of individual circumstances. Achieving adulthood or full legal responsibility in society is, in actuality, a highly complex process that frequently
depends on the circumstances and the developmental process of each
individual. This discussion does not deal with legal status and the changes
that occurred in it throughout the generations under the impact of
historical, social, and cultural processes; rather, it is concerned with the

principal symbols expressed in the important ritual events that demarcate the stages of a Jewish life. From this standpoint, what has been stated remains valid to this day. There is a clear and educationally important distinction between an individual's initiation into the sacred congregation of Jews—that is, his responsibility for the commandments that organize the relationship between man and God—and the initiation of an individual Jew into society in its broadest sense, which include interpersonal relationships and an individual's relationship to his society. This is the basis of the essential, as well as symbolic, difference between the bar mitzvah ceremony and the marriage ceremony.

The content of the *bar mitzvah* ceremony, as it has been shaped by tradition, is simple and clear. There are two foci for the ceremony—home and synagogue, and two values that stand at its core—study of Torah and performance of the commandments. Of course these are clearly linked. At home, there is a festive meal and according to the traditional custom that emerged in the Middle Ages, the *bar mitzvah* boy delivers a homily during the meal, which generally revolves around the laws of *t'fillin*, the phylacteries. In this homily, the young man must show that he has achieved a certain degree of independence in the study of Torah, particularly on a topic that now pertains to him. When he becomes *bar mitzvah*, he is required to put on *t'fillin* and pray three times a day as a member of the sacred congregation. This reflects the viewpoint formulated by the Sages (and mentioned in previous chapters) that study of Torah was considered an independent, spiritual value; it is an individual commandment that lays the proper foundation for the observance of the remaining commandments of the Torah. From the standpoint of responsibility for performance of the commandments between man and God, the individual considered to be an adult must *prove*—or express—his changed status by moving from the study of a mitzvah to its performance.

At the synagogue, the *bar mitzvah* celebrant is called up to the Torah on a Sabbath close to his thirteenth birthday. He reads from the Torah according to the cantillation, and then reads the *haftarah*. It is on this occasion that the youth becomes an adult from the standpoint of his membership in a *minyan* of worshippers; he is now considered one of the quorum and all the obligations that devolve on a member of the quorum apply to him as well. Just as the moment of reading from Torah and Prophets on the Sabbath is symbolically the moment of renewal of the covenant at Sinai, and just as the moment when the sacred congregation took upon itself the commandment to worship God is constituted anew in the synagogue—so this is the appropriate time to have the maturing youth join the congregation. He enters the covenant of his people of his own free will. As for the youth's legal status, the transition that stems from this is expressed in the short benediction his father recites at the ceremony, "Blessed is He who has released me from the responsibility of my son's deeds."

Until the *bar mitzvah* ceremony, the father was liable for the acts of his son in whatever pertains to man's relationship to God. As his sire and mentor, the father who initiated the boy into the Covenant of Abraham was required to lead him in the ways of the Torah. If the son transgressed, the father was guilty for not having discharged the commandment to properly educate his son. Although according to one interesting version, there is an opposite meaning to the ceremony: it is the son who is released for he no longer carries the transgression of the father (in accordance with the verse, "visiting the iniquity of the fathers upon the children") rather each person is responsible for his deeds alone. ("Everyone shall die for his own iniquity.") Still it seems clear that the change in the legal status of the son can be found in what was said earlier: having reached an age at which he exists in his own right, is intelligent, in control of his deeds, and able to study Torah, the youth is consequently responsible himself in all matters relating to the service of the Lord. In this sphere he is already a completely mature person, a "legal entity."

As we have noted, this tradition was fashioned over many generations and as with all holidays and ceremonies, it too has undergone change. The chief determination that thirteen is the age of maturity comes from the Mishnah, and it is the literature of the Tannaim that defines the age and its obligations. There is literary evidence of rituals that mark maturity and the age of responsibility for the commandments that date to the period of the Second Commonwealth, but the formulation of the tradition practiced today is much later, principally the late Middle Ages. It is possible that the tradition was heavily influenced by the non-Jewish environment and the practices in different Jewish communities, which are linked to the common core of the ritual reflect the customs of a variety of cultural environments. From a contemporary standpoint one ought to bear in mind two issues whose impact has been most palpable both in the essence and shaping of the ceremony. The first issue relates to the significance that this ceremony holds for that Jewish public which perceives of Judaism as a culture and aspires to maintain a traditional core of that culture, but does not regard itself as obligated by the command-ments of the Torah in the manner that was accepted by Jews for generations. The second issue relates to how the family and community marks a daughter's arrival at the age of fulfilling mitzvot.

In general, it would be correct to say that the ceremony of entering the Covenant of Abraham in its traditional-religious-formulation is observed by everyone who is Jewishly identified, whether Orthodox or "secular." The same holds true for the ceremony of entering the age of responsibility for the commandments, except that here the traditional form has been opened to formations that reflect opposing world views. The non-Orthodox religious streams have introduced far-reaching changes in both the external forms of the ceremony and the nature of the homily; the most apparent ideational dimension that has been added to the ceremony is the ethical dimension. The maturing youth is still not considered a personality that holds social, legal responsibility for all his deeds, but he is regarded as bearing full ethical responsibility for his social relationships with members of his family, his friends, and society as a whole.

From *bar mitzvah* on, this moral responsibility vis-à-vis others is perceived as the principal religious commandment that applies to him before God. According to this religious view point, love of one's neighbor and responsibility to society is the true worship of God while the commandments between man and God have been relegated to symbols whose function is to shape a world view and educate toward the observance of moral commandments. Since this is so, preparations for the *bar mitzvah* ceremony, as well as the ceremony itself, include deeds and symbols that express moral obligation as religious content. The public that identifies itself as "secular" manifestly equivocates. There are those who chose to routinely observe the traditional ceremony: putting on *t'fillin*, going up to the Torah, and enjoying a festive meal, which largely takes on the character of a grandiose birthday party that reflects the parents' social status; and there are others who prefer to take something from the social/ethical fundamentals formulated by the non-Orthodox religious streams.

These approaches are indicative of a confusion with regard to a definition of maturity at this age because even the non-Orthodox public speaks about physical maturity and spiritual values still considered pre-adult from a social and legal perspective. It appears that the same ambiguity also relates to the Orthodox public, which continues to celebrate the traditional forms. The Orthodox adolescent who becomes *bar mitzvah* does not simply enter a worshipping quorum. One would therefore expect to find a greater variety of symbolic patterns with their attendant meanings and a reshaping of traditional forms so that along with the earlier meaning expressed by joining a *minyan*, there would also be an integration of moral responsibility into the Orthodox view of life.

The second issue relates to marking the maturity of a daughter. According to the traditional view, the girl goes from her parents' responsibility to the responsibility of her husband although she too is obliged by commandments. The most obvious expression of this difference between a son and a daughter is that a daughter is not obliged to study Torah; moreover, traditional society did not view the study of Torah by girls favorably, nor did it encourage it. Anyone who does not study Torah is not independently self-sufficient, even for commandments that one is obliged to fulfill. Such a person's adulthood is perceived as emanating from the adulthood of whoever is responsible for that person in the environing social framework; recognizing the time of a daughter's maturity in a ceremony similar to that of the son's was not practiced. The change that has occurred in contemporary Jewish society is obvious and widespread. It is found not only in secular society and non-Orthodox religious streams but in the Orthodox community too. The independent and equal status of women in society has changed their position in the family, bringing with it the need for a suitable expression of the stages in a girl's development toward maturity. Consequently there is an increasing tendency to celebrate *bat mitzvah*.

Even the Orthodox public, it appears, though anxious that its daughters remain within the fold, understands today's social/educational necessity to underscore a young woman's personal responsibility to study Torah and perform mitzvot. Open to innovation in accordance with personal preference, the forms of the *bat mitzvah* ritual are certainly far from a traditional formulation so that it is no longer possible to give a detailed analysis of the ideational essence represented. What can be said is that there is no essential difference between the *bar mitzvah* ceremony and the *bat mitzvah* ceremony for those who observe them. The absolute equality between daughters and sons embodies all that is new from the standpoint of the moral and spiritual responsibility that a person undertakes on reaching maturity. This development can be seen as a consummation of the tradition.

MARRIAGE AS A SYMBOL OF FULL MATURITY

From a social and legal standpoint full maturity is not achieved at the age of *bar mitzvah*. Symbolically, tradition accords men and women the status of full maturity at the wedding ceremony; that is, the goal of personal development is marked by the union that establishes an independent family.

To understand the thinking behind this traditional approach, one must return to the story of Creation in Genesis, Chapter 2. Following the description of man's creation from the dust of the earth—placing the breath of life within him so that he becomes a living soul, and after the description of the garden in Eden—placing man in the garden to "cultivate and maintain it," comes the commandment that forbids eating from the tree of knowledge that discriminates between right and wrong. It is in the context of this prohibition that the story of woman's creation is presented. "And the Lord God said: 'It is not good that the man should be alone; I will make a helpmeet for him.'" The tension between the prohibition on eating from the tree of knowledge and the declaration that "it is not good that man should be alone" is highly significant, particularly in light of the continuation of the story but also important in and of itself. The word "good" should be understood here as it is understood through-out the Creation story in the previous chapter: "And God saw that it was good." "Good" is used to testify and verify that the intended deed has been accomplished according to its purpose. The word is apposite to the thought that preceded it and indicates that the deed is worthy and the blessing is then given directly after the validation. The thrust of the blessing ensures the survival of life by means of its being bequeathed from generation to generation. If "it is not good that man should be alone," the task of creating man was not been completed in the sense that when he is alone man is neither whole nor can he survive and the blessing of ongoing existence could not apply to him.

Ostensibly, in this sense, there is no difference between man and all other creatures. Indeed, in Chapter I, in a general and non-specific way, it was said about man, "And God created man in His own image, in the image of God created He him; male and female created He them, and God blessed them, and God said unto them: 'Be fruitful and multiply and replenish the earth'" (verses 27–28). Yet even from this standpoint there is some difference between man and all other creatures. Initially, man was created alone—not "after its kind." Before he was given woman in a manner without parallel in the entire Creation story, God causes all the living creatures to pass before him so that he may give them names, and so that he may realize that he stands alone and solitary, differentiated from all other living things. Man requires a different consummation, one other than that found among the species of the animal world. "But for

Adam there was not found a helpmeet for him" (Chap 2:20), which means that man was not fully realized by virtue of his being a living creature. Though the quality of gender was inherent in him from the moment of his creation ("male and female created He them") man first had to become conscious of his need for a helpmeet, a helpmeet equal to him in status as someone created in God's image.

The story is strange and surprising. It has enjoyed many interpretations, not all of which can be encompassed here, but among these one interpretation stands out as the symbolic embodiment of the way in which the Bible conceives of the establishment of the first family. It is an illustration that subsumes the quality of family relationships and the nature of the law by which the family is established in both the biblical narrative and the statutes of the Torah. The family unit rests on a covenant consecrated between man and woman before God. The covenant joins man and woman making them singular and distinctive to one another not only by virtue of gender but also as individuals. In essence, the story of the creation of woman represents the covenantal ceremony that takes place in the persons of those entering the covenant, and as such it symbolizes a transformation in the essence of man and the woman as they are joined. God bisects man, severing the initial physical union inherent in the natural physical passion between male and female; He reintroduces the two halves as belonging to one another in a mutual social bond, which reveals them as the converse of one another.

The physical reunion is re-established between them as a natural drive that is the quintessence of creation, "Therefore shall a man leave his father and his mother, and shall cleave unto his wife, and they shall be one flesh" (Genesis 2:24). But this union does not sweep aside the separate status of each individual; beyond the sexual attraction, there is a social, ethical meaning to the alliance. They undertake a mutual obligation sanctifying themselves to each other, establishing a family in which children are not only born but are educated to maturity, persons in whom "the image of God" is engraved. This then is the consummation man requires in order that "it is good" may be said of him. From this standpoint, the narrative of Eve's creation and her presentation to man is the enactment of a covenant that transforms man's physical and spiritual essence.

This is a ceremonial severing. The self is cut into its components as man and woman confront each other as persons, each innately an individual, autonomous personality. As such, they merge with one another as helpmeets for one another. The word k'negdo (which is rendered "for him" in the English translation of the Bible) infers the equality of status between woman and man. By establishing a social relationship that replaces pre-social, physical, and instinctual relationships, the family is therefore the first alliance to raise man to his special status. An ethical relationship is superimposed on instinctual drives and sublimates them. It would not be an exaggeration to say that the description of Eve's creation and her presentation to Adam is, in effect, a primal marriage ceremony that symbolizes the completion of man's creation as a person as he achieves physical and moral maturity and enters family life.

This interpretation is reinforced in the legal status that biblical law grants the family. According to the contemporary concept every individual adult (that is, a person who has completed his childhood and adolescent years and has arrived at an age that is considered mature) has full legal status in the community, a status not dependent on starting a family or joining an existing family. According to biblical law, personal legal status depends entirely on family status in the sense that the individual does not stand by himself before institutions of the community, the tribe, or the people but within his family and in accordance with his status in that family as one of its components: father, mother, sons, and daughters (brothers and sisters). Admittedly, within the family the husband/father is most prominent, and in his absence, the eldest son. The father is head of family, but the role does not inhere in him as an individual. He is rather the representative of the family; his rights are those of his family and his obligations are those of his family, and he stands as the protector of each individual in the family.

Hence the special sensitivity the Torah has for the stranger, the orphan, and the widow—all individuals whose family has been destroyed. They are defenseless; therefore the entire community must extend its guardianship to them. The husband/father status does not grant a man despotic control over his family. On the contrary, the family is a partnership built on a covenant of mutual responsibility that grants every individual a personal status as part of, and according to, his place in the family. The differences in legal status among members of a family are a reflection of their differing roles, yet each one of them has and grants rights to and from all, is responsible to all, and all are responsible to him.

It is self-evident that the family's legal status does not relate only to its inner functioning but also to those functions that serve to integrate it into the environing society. No family is self-sufficient. In order to exist, a covenant of families is necessary, and this covenant requires another that is yet broader, which will be the guarantor of the legal status of all its components. This is a progression of covenants based on one another that are mutually supportive: the paternal family, the tribe, the people, the state. As the network of alliances broadens, the units that make it up are strengthened and they secure each other's viability. Consequently, an individual who establishes a family by virtue of his obligations to his wife and children enters into social responsibilities that ensure the conditions of his family's existence while acquiring a status in the environing society, a society that is the context for existence. This is full maturity. Now the maturing person becomes responsible for issues of property and work, competition and mutual support, fraternity and enmity, war and peace. He is now obligated in an alliance of paternal families, community, tribe, and people.

There is, therefore, a highly significant difference between entering the yoke of commandments for the worship of God or moral and interpersonal responsibility, and entering the yoke of commandments for social obligations at their broadest level. Nor is this difference merely a quantitative matter. Membership in the covenant of a sacred community is ideal and symbolic. It is accompanied by an actual obligation, but it is graver regarding divine laws than it is with reference to interpersonal laws. The public that assembles as a quorum for prayer is the symbolic embodiment of a utopian society; where there are implications for daily social life (as we have seen in the chapter dealing with the Sabbath), they are limited to a circumscribed set of interpersonal relationships. This is not the case for belonging to a paternal household, tribe, people, or state. Here responsibility is not symbolic and relationships are far from utopian ideals. They reflect all the limitations and difficulties inherent in man's instinctual nature and in the conditions of material existence, which require effort, labor, and competition. The broader the scope of societal relations, the more they are based on property and forms of ownership: ownership of land and inheritance, ownership of house and property, ownership of the means of production. All these influence orientation. Every society solves the problems of ownership in accordance with the circumstances of its life and its values; far from idyllic, these reflect ongoing struggle. Since the family is entwined in the societal and institutional network, it is also affected by it, not only in terms of its exterior station but with regard to internal relationships as well.

The family too has property, which ensures the provision of its needs. Bride and groom bring various properties with them into the marriage and enhance these properties through their labor. The right of use to this property is an inseparable part of the agreement that sets the nature of the relationship among members of a family, as well as between the family and their environment. This fact necessarily influences the shape of interpersonal relationships in the family, impacting particularly on the position of each family member and the role definition of husband, wife, and children in daily life. It is clear that the socio-economic and political structures, which of course change from time to time, have had a decisive influence—for good or for bad—on forms of family relationships and the significance attached to them. The most intimate relations between members of a family can also be defined in terms of property, in the sense that obligations between family members can be seen as rights over one another that they can employ, or ownership they have of one another.

In this way, an acute tension is created between the earlier ideal description of the family as a covenantal unit based on love and a sense of moral responsibility, and the legal social/historical description of the family as a contract based on property rights; this is true regarding both family property and members of the family themselves. Relationships in families was always shaped by this tension. One can also understand from this the transformations that have taken place over time in the social character of the family. Currently, the family is undergoing a far-reaching transformation in its institutionalization both from the standpoint of property and the assignment of roles. All the more reason to stress the interplay of these two elements—love, the ideal and constant element; and property, which is conditioned by historic reality and to a great extent also by the personal character of the members of a family.

A symbolic articulation of the tension between these two elements can be seen once again in the biblical narrative. After the ideal marriage, which places man and woman as equal partners united in a loving union, the story of sin looms, transforming the relationship between husband and wife to an alliance of property, even enslavement. What is the quality of the desired alliance? The answer that emerges from the story in Genesis is quite explicit. However, both in the Bible and in the Oral Tradition, the legal pattern of the family is set as an outcome of the tension between the ideal and the reality of historic society as it has changed over time. As the marriage ceremony evolved it reflected these two elements, including the internal tension that occasionally appears as a contradiction.

THE MARRIAGE BLESSINGS

A single ritualized ceremony does not suffice to highlight the great importance marriage has for the two individuals involved, their families, and their communities. The union of a couple is a complex and extended process; it requires preparation, ripening, and maturation. The appropriate social and personal background must be provided, a fact expressed in a long sequence of ceremonies that sometimes begin long before the wedding day itself. But since the concern in these pages is for the value-laden and ideational elements enacted in the ceremonies, we turn our attention now to the primary and definitive ceremonial event that encompasses the complex significance of initiation into full social adulthood that is inherent in the establishment of the family.

The first part of the ceremony is sanctioned by law. Once married, the man and woman undertake certain obligations to one another, and these are set in the *halakhah*. The process begins with the man asking the woman to marry him. Should she agree, she takes on an obligation regarding marital relations, maintaining a household, and raising children. The man also undertakes obligations to his wife regarding those same responsibilities. Breaking these obligations by either of the parties can serve as grounds for seeking the dissolution of the bond; however, the couple cannot dissolve the bond between them by themselves since at the wedding ceremony it is evident that the couple commit themselves in the presence of a legal authority that stands beyond and above themselves. The decision to marry, even if others such as parents and relatives are involved, is essentially the decision of the couple. Hopefully they agree to the bond between them of their own free will. Once married, however, a framework is established that has an objective legal status, and therefore its dissolution is not the prerogative of either party nor even both of them jointly. Only a judicial institution that represents the law in the life of that society which originally sanctioned the marriage can terminate the marriage if either of the sides demands it, and if the grounds for the demand are accepted by the legal authority as being sufficient and justified. At this point, it is not germane to examine such dissolution in detail for it is highly complex and influenced by the social reality at any given period.

Our aim is to observe the general structural character of such alliances, and to point out the symbolic expression given to the alliance in a ceremonial ritual: the signing of the *ketubah* (the marriage contract) by the man in the presence of witnesses, the reading of the *ketubah* aloud in the hearing of the couple and those assembled, and entrusting of the written contract to the woman. The content of the *ketubah* is traditional. Though it no longer spells out the complex legal obligations involved in married life, the ceremony does have a symbolic importance for the legal ritual. It is meant to impress on the consciousness of the couple the fact that their decision, which initially depended on both of them, will become an objective reality that their society attests to and guarantees as soon as the contract is concluded. Ostensibly there is no clearer illustration of an individual's integration into society. With the establishment of a family, the two individuals have left their individual status. They build a new unit, are responsible for it, and are defined by it.

The second part of the ceremony is the sanctification of the marriage. The union between both parties is accomplished by a symbolic deed that depicts the bond between them, establishing and concretizing what has been agreed to in advance with the signature of the *ketubah* and its bestowal on the bride. Accordingly, establishment of the bond is a concretization of ownership: the groom brings the bride under the wedding canopy, which symbolizes the "authority" of the groom—or his house, the area of his domain. Before witnesses, he then gives the bride a ring worth at least one penny, and recites the definitive sentence, "With this ring you are sanctified to me in accordance with the laws of Moses and Israel." Once more this is a matter of ownership by means of a symbolic payment (giving a ring is a relatively late development and the symbolic value of the ring effects ownership). It should be noted particularly that ownership is effected according to a specific law, the same law that the *ketubah* represents. With the recitation of this verse, the bride virtually becomes the property of the groom in accordance with detailed formulations of the *halakhah*. Of course, the *halakhah* also stipulates property rights that the bride has vis-à-vis the groom. Nonetheless, in the course of enacting the symbolism that certifies the property agreement, a spiritual and emotional significance, from completely different spheres of human experience, is superimposed on the legal aspect of the ceremony. First, one notices that the definitive sentence that establishes the bond between the couple does not say "You are my property," but says instead: "You are consecrated unto me." Though the wedding canopy is symbolic of the groom's domain, it also symbolizes entry into a joint home, the guardianship of a kin and protector, and the providence that hovers over the couple as they unite to create a new family in the house of Israel.

The marriage ceremony gives absolute and binding validity to the feelings of love between a man and a woman, and the purpose of betrothal is to bring these feelings to full fruition. This consummation goes beyond the natural attraction between a man and a woman to encompass a mutual, moral obligation to one another as specific individuals because sanctification implies separation from all others in order to fully and exclusively devote oneself to the other. Sanctifying the betrothal as an ongoing obligation of complete mutual devotion fills the "prosaic" mold of a legal action with a spiritual and emotional content that is entirely one of inner feelings. The substance of the relationship that establishes the family is a love that has reached the stage of union; so long as this exists, the legal framework remains an external bond that is not experienced as a constraint. It is only when the relationship is weakened that the essential function of the structure is discerned. In any case, the internal content of family life is determined by the personal way in which the couple interpret the sanctified bond between them.

This does not mean that they are consecrated to one another alone. On the contrary, they stand in the midst of family, community, and people. The public, which has assembled, witnesses the consecration, and rejoices in the happiness of the couple. A new Jewish home has been established, one that is reinforced by the Jewish people and, in its own turn, builds the Jewish people. On this plane, the consecration is also conceived as symbolizing the special status of the Jewish people as a people consecrated to God. The complete devotion of the couple to each other symbolizes the utter devotion of the Jewish people to its God, and the God of Israel to His people. One should not forget that man created in the image of his Creator bears an aim that was intended for him by his Creator. When he becomes fully adult, when he establishes a family of his own, he has also potentiated his ability to bear full responsibility for the purpose for which he was intended. He enters the covenant of the people—all the obligations of the covenant sealed between the people and its God—to fulfill the original purpose for which man was created. The emotional and ideational peak of the marriage ceremony wells up from this meeting of the personal, national, and universal spheres that are now symbolically concretized. With the recitation of the seven blessings of the marriage ceremony, one returns to the original and eternal foundation that is renewed whenever a new couple establishes its home, the latent infrastructure of the narrative in the Book of Genesis.

The third part of the ceremony, the recitation of the seven benedictions, begins with the blessing over the wine, which marks the special joy of the celebration. Afterward, the blessing recited for the creation of the world attests to the glory of its Creator. The third blessing notes the uniqueness of man among all the creatures of the world. The entire world was "created" whereas of man it is said that he was "fashioned," and it is the fashioning that sets him apart. God fashions man in His image. This is attested to by the fourth blessing, which bears witness to the fashioning of woman from Adam himself. In the words of the blessing, "And did for time everlasting shape woman out of his form." The fifth blessing spells out the previous blessing even more specifically. Woman is for man, "for time everlasting" because together they establish a new generation. The woman represents all of the children meant to be born; this is her joy.

A characteristic ambiguity should be noted in the fifth blessing, "May Zion exult at the joyful reunion of her children in Jerusalem. Blessed art Thou, O Lord, who causes Zion to rejoice in her children"—this formulation is redolent of Hannah's ode in Psalms, "Who maketh the barren woman to dwell in her house as a joyful mother of children," and from this standpoint that indeed is the intention of the verse, the continuation of life through birth; but the end of the blessing points in another direction as well: "Blessed art Thou O Lord who causes Zion to rejoice in her children." The barren woman also means Zion, and the ingathering of her children is not only the homecoming of the exiles at the time of redemption, as one hears in Isaiah's words about Zion, "Then thou shalt say in thy heart, 'Who hath begotten me these seeing I have been bereaved of my children and am solitary, an exile wandering to and fro? And who hath brought up these? Behold, I was left alone; These, where were they?'" (Isaiah 49:21). The bride standing under the wedding canopy is "the barren woman" about to become the "joyful mother of children" (also a symbol of Zion), one of the mothers who ensures the survival of the Jewish people.

The sixth blessing returns the ceremony to the flow of the biblical narrative as it recalls Adam and Eve in the Garden of Eden. This is the beginning of their shared journey in the sense of being "beloved companions." At that point, everything was set out before them for their pleasure and the gladness of their hearts. The blessing projects a luminous beam from that primal situation to the wedding couple, a light that is actually renewed for each person and each new couple as they build their home. From this standpoint, the wedding ceremony is both aspiration and destiny, rejoiced in for its own sake. Upon marrying, the couple has achieved wholeness, and rejoicing is an expression of the consciousness of that wholeness. Therefore, the bride and groom under their wedding canopy are compared to Adam and Eve in the Garden of Eden. It should be noted that this is an additional interpretation of the notion that it is through marriage that man builds a structure "for time everlasting." According to the previous blessing, the meaning of continuity of life is children who will yet be born, whereas according to the sixth blessing the reference is to a sense of paradisiacal eternity that husband and wife experience together in this, their time of love. They have arrived at a unity that has raised them to a sublime eternity.

The final blessing combines the content of all of the blessings with a special clarity. God, who created the world and man, also created joy, love, harmony, and companionship. Joy, love, harmony, and companionship are feelings that are expressive of wholeness; marriage is the loftiest symbol embodying those feelings. Marriage, thereby, parallels the Sabbath of the Creation story. This could perhaps be formulated as: on the day of his marriage, man reaches the Sabbath of his life. Man's creation is completed and perfected when he weds. An allusion to this interpretation is also seen in the enumeration of seven blessings, which parallel the seven days of Creation where the seventh blessing is analogous to the Sabbath. But along with denoting the perfection of the life of individuals, the seventh blessing also bespeaks the perfection that radiates to the entire Jewish people at the marriage ceremony. The joy of the couple is also the joy of the people, and the Sabbath of the couple stands for a future Sabbath that awaits the whole people, the Sabbath of redemption when the betrothal covenant between the people and its God will be fulfilled. "The sound of mirth and gladness, the voice of bridegroom and bride" (Jeremiah 33:11).

KLAL YISRAEL—ALL OF THE JEWISH PEOPLE

1. The way in which the cycle of generations organizes time finds expression in each individual's life cycle, though it cannot be set into the calendar. Still, just as individuals integrate the course of their lives into the sequence of their people's festivals, the people integrates itself into the cycle of each individual's special days. Klal Yisrael—the totality of the Jewish people—(represented by the minyan) is the societal framework in which the festivals, that have been described throughout the book, occur. Klal Yisrael is present at every ceremony, integrates individuals into itself, and joins in their rejoicing; in this way individuals' time becomes the people's time, and the anniversaries of the people—historic events as they unfold from Creation to Redemption—become the anniversaries of individuals. The individual's life cycle of birth, maturation, marriage, and childbearing, as well as the sequence of generations as they unfold and maintain the people, ostensibly belongs to nature's cyclical ordering of time. This would be the case if individuals stood alone at the anniversaries

that mark off their personal development. But they do not stand alone. *Klal Yisrael*, which participates with individuals in their special days, carries them along in the flow of history and infuses the dimension of linear, historic time into their individual, natural cycles. This is perceived at every stage of the wedding ceremony.

In the legal part of the ceremony, the tenets of Jewish society as they have changed over time are expressed. Undoubtedly, in our age there will be changes in the formulation of the *ketubah* because of far-reaching changes in the sociological character of the Jewish family, particularly in the definition of the roles of men and women in the context of maintaining the home and the education of the children. It would be appropriate if the new historic reality were to be expressed, not only in legislation but in a symbolic representation during the wedding ceremony. Conceivably such a change would transpose notions of property into notions of covenant and mutual responsibility in the second part of the ceremony too; that is, the definitive and substantiating part of the ceremony. In this second part, historic reality is articulated in the common practice of including a homily whose substance is to elucidate the significance of the ceremony for the young couple and those who are assembled. The rabbi or one of the parents or one of the close friends speaks in the name of the public, and since those assembled at the ceremony represent the Jewish people, it would be appropriate that what is said should be from the vantage point of a people that aspires to flourish through its children. In any case, the homily is an important medium for expressing the societal situation that serves as a background for the wedding ceremony and the particular responsibility that the couple undertakes within its society and people.

In the third part, historic consciousness is depicted in an all-encompassing manner. It has already been seen that the marriage, which is a kind of Sabbath in an individual's life cycle, symbolizes the Sabbath intended for the entire Jewish people. In its union, the couple represents a future redemption. From this standpoint, every new family that builds its home within the Jewish people is not only a reinvigorating force in the biological cycle of the people's generations, but it is also a milestone on the road to the aspiration and destiny that extends from *Lekh Lekhah*, "Get thee out of thy country . . . out of thy father's house to the land that I will show thee" until the vision of "the end of days." The holidays and festivals set into the calendar of the Jewish year are landmarks along the individual's path among his people, and the people's path amid the nations.

FOURTEEN

AFTERWORD:
COMMENTARY ON THE HOLIDAY

JEWISH LITERARY WORKS

This book joins an extensive collection of works—written from various viewpoints—on the Jewish calendar, its Sabbaths, holidays, and festivals. In early Jewish literature, holidays were studied in the religious context and systematic foundation of the *halakhah* ; that is, holidays were discussed from the standpoint of rules that determined people's patterns of action. Inasmuch as the Sabbath and holidays claim an important place in a life determined by the commandments, naturally entire chapters were devoted to the topic. The significance of the theory behind commandments was elucidated by *halakhic* discussion, by stories set on the background of the holiday; by interpretive *midrashim* on a particular moral that could be drawn from a commandment, a quotation, or a story. Though the stories and *midrashim* can be woven into a colorful composite picture, the source material itself makes no attempt at a systematic observation or study about the overall significance of the commandments concerning the Sabbath and holidays. Even in the Middle Ages, when there was already a separate, well-defined branch of Jewish thought set apart from *halakhic* literature, there was still no systematic study of holidays as a separate topic. Such

Jewish thinkers as Rabbi Yehudah HaLevi and Maimonides, who did make systematized studies on the reasons for the commandments, dealt with holidays in a broader context, making do with general comments without attempting to fully encompass the ideational content of a particular holiday.

It would appear that they felt no need for such an exhaustive approach, and it is not difficult to imagine why. Living within a Jewish community that loyally practiced a way of life prescribed by the *halakhah*, they knew the continuity of celebrating the Sabbath, *Rosh Hodesh*, the pilgrimage festivals, and other holidays as tangible and steadfast, almost as taken for granted as the changing seasons of nature. This was such an organic whole, so clearly understood, that there was no need to describe it in detail. Therefore it was left as the unmediated context for discussions of specific details that did prompt special attention because of historic or personal experiences or for some innovative school of thought. In any case, in this literature too, alongside *halakhic* summaries, one can find occasional rays of illumination about a wealth of details without fully covering the topic.

In modern times, scores of books have been written about a certain holiday, or on the totality of the calendar, so that there are now comprehensive works that deal with holidays as an independent topic. Besides books that summarize *halakhic* rules in detail, which of course continue to be published, one now comes across a wide range of treatises that deal with holidays from the standpoint of historical research or from the standpoint of what their image ought appropriately to be in the cultural reality of the Modern Era. The appearance of these works aims to fill two perceived needs. First, the new educational requirements that arise because of modern literary and historical research; this is a cultural necessity that constantly renews itself in order to recognize and understand reality by employing those tools that appear to be most reliable. Second, the need to overcome the growing distance made by large sectors of the Jewish people from a traditional way of life. A Jewish way of life is no longer axiomatic or taken for granted by this public, which has undergone a sweeping process of secularization, so that even when a certain knowledge about patterns of behavior, practices, commandments, and symbols are acquired these are never more than chance combinations of fragments rather than part of an encompassing Jewish life experience. The operative calendar for these Jews is no longer the Jewish calendar; at best they straddle two calendars. In such a situation, educators or thinkers who seek to prevent a complete split can no longer depend on partial enlightenment; they are obliged to immerse their readers in the context of that totality, which was taken for granted by their predecessors. A tremendous effort must be made to recall and retain the memory of a situation that once was, so that through an understanding of meanings that were relevant in the context of the past, meanings that are still relevant can be found at least on the level of theoretical insight.

The most cogent expression of this need can be found in anthologies. Many of these include historical research about a holiday bound in the same volume as stories, songs, and poems, which describe the holiday atmosphere as a cherished memory; often there is a detailed explanation of rules and practices pertaining to the holiday and brief theoretical interpretations of its meaning, for past generations as well as for Jews in the modern period. These collections mostly reflect a desire to keep precious memories from oblivion while providing a range of material that can be used by those who would like to choose selections that they find relevant, minimally enabling them to retain some historic reference to what once was. In other words, this is literature about the holiday that celebrates it by discussing it.

Analyzing the selections in an anthology, one finds a broad assortment of essays about the holiday as it was in the distant or more recent past. A prominent place is given to belles-lettres. In the classics of modern Hebrew literature, descriptions of holidays are a favorite topic. Sabbaths and holidays serve as foci of events; important turning points take place on holidays and their symbolic meaning is drawn from the holidays. The reason is clear. Frequently the central figures of this literature are young people caught in a dilemma between the traditional world and the seductions of the secular world. The holidays, representing as they do the internal continuity of Jewish life, naturally become a focus of their indecision and uncertainties; subsequently the holidays act as reference points for nostalgic recollections, which serve to tie the person who has crossed over the threshold of his father's home. Of course these are stories and poems for which the holiday serves as setting and background rather than the central thrust of the writing, though at a later stage one does find stories that were deliberately written to retain the atmosphere of what had been while clinging nostalgically to the past. Such stories are the most prevalent sources recycled in anthologies.

A second category of works about holidays consists of historical studies that trace their origins: primarily their background in ancient Middle East culture during the biblical period, their reformulation in the biblical literature, and what has been added or changed in the tradition of the

Oral Law and in the cultural ambiance of Jewish communities. Some general studies deal predominantly with a given holiday; others address practices that relate to little-known historical events. There is now a well-grounded and comprehensive view of the way in which Jewish holidays evolved as well as the background for the emergence of most of the commandments, symbols, and practices that surround the holidays. This knowledge enables one to understand the importance of each mitzvah, symbol, and custom in terms of its period. Beyond the desire to understand and the value of research for its own sake, researchers apparently think that a clear knowledge of the way in which the holiday was celebrated throughout the generations is the correct way of transmitting the heritage, and that drawing on treasures of the past contributes—even if indirectly—to renewed cultural creativity. Study exposes the student to an understanding of such treasures, making them available to him. There are some who even regard the very activity of studying a holiday as virtually experiencing it, for to know is to experience.

A third type of reading related to historical research is about the folklore of holidays—customs, popular art forms of various kinds (particularly the fashioning of special implements and utensils), and folk songs, as well as foods and games. The early literature did not deal directly with these topics, mentioning them, if at all, when they were the subject of a *halakhic* discussion. In the contemporary era, monographs have been written first so that these themes could be collected for purposes of preservation, and subsequently so that, using the tools of historical research, their sources, meanings, and the extent of their geographical spread could be uncovered. One also discovers the perspective of another kind of distance in these studies: as it begins to be forgotten, folklore becomes an object of collection and classification. When the accumulated material is studied, and so becomes a new creation, it is no longer folk art but a retrospective and sophisticated art form. The great affection attached to folklore in holiday literature stems from the problematics of a non-religious public, which nonetheless seeks a cultural link to tradition.

This public is attached to folklore, as distinguished from the commandments and the overtly religious rituals, as a stratum of culture that is a quasi-secular dimension of the holiday and a stimulus to renewed cultural creativity that does not raise troubling questions of belief. Folklore is not an expression of the holiday's sanctity but rather an evocation of an aesthetic experience: the sense of ease, the sense of refinement and exaltation; it is precisely these aspects of celebration that are so appropriate to the "secular public" in its popular outlook and expectations. For this public, the holiday at its best is an aesthetic experience in which it takes part both as observer and active participant. Of course there is a close bond between literary expressions about the holiday and its folklore. Nostalgic descriptions of holiday atmosphere are steeped in folklore, and one can readily see how the holiday is shaped through a reflexive, sophisticated, and aesthetic reworking of the folklore in order to nourish a following that no longer experiences the holiday as part of a direct continuity of its content.

A fourth type of book—collections of holiday sermons—reflects the characteristic development of religious movements in the Modern Era, particularly movements that tend toward renewal. Admittedly this writing is a continuation of a much older tradition but its re-establishment and the new stylistic elements it employs reflect a spiritual need that has made itself felt especially in the contemporary period. Through instruction and interpretation, the role of the sermon now is to bridge the distance brought about by lack of knowledge or misunderstanding or a sense of alienation on the part of a congregation that is assembled at the synagogue to celebrate a holiday, and the commandments, rituals, symbols, forms of recitation, and prayer dedicated to a given holiday. Even groups whose affiliation is to modern Orthodoxy have felt a certain estrangement growing between certain portions of the commandments and holiday rituals, and between an outlook that stems from an involvement in modern secular culture. All the more so for groups affiliated with innovative religious streams. The sermon serves to interpret what is unavailable and to make that which is distant more familiar. It is intended to reveal the luminescence of the early traditions in terms that are relevant for a public caught up in modern reality. Granted this is a priori a rhetorical creation that requires a certain kind of dramatic presentation, but it is precisely because of the careful staging that it is quickly transformed into a literary genre. The sermon delivered in a synagogue is essentially a written presentation; as such it is readily available for the medium of print. A rich literature has been created composed of collections of sermons, and the best of these serve as comprehensive explanations of entire dissertations of holidays, or an exposition of an entire outlook of Judaism through an interpretation of the content of holidays.

A fifth type of work includes the pedagogic literature intended primarily as an instructional aid for teaching holidays in schools. These books are adapted to the curricula of Jewish schools in Israel and abroad, and they generally include a selection of chapters from the Sources in addition to didactic instructions or discussions about the holiday. They are meant to be a reader for students, or an interpretive aid for teachers on how to use the reader and how to develop discussion based on it that will forge an intellectual and emotional bond to the tradition.

The sixth type of work contains essays that deal with a theoretical and philosophic analysis of the content of the holiday. These essays were written on the assumption that the holidays incorporate an entire world view that shapes the uniqueness of Jewish culture. They propose a philosophic interpretation of this encompassing world view, attempting even to examine the validity of such views from the standpoint of a contemporary thinker. This is still not a highly developed literary form. Though there are collections of sermons for the holidays somewhat allied to this type of work, systematic philosophical essays that relate to holidays are few in number. Among these, Franz Rosenzweig's *Star of Redemption* is particularly notable. The problematic distance that has opened between the way in which large segments of the Jewish people perceive their reality and between the living tradition can be seen in the reflexive style of the writing. However, unlike works that focus on literary description, historical research or holiday folklore collections, the philosophic/ theoretic *midrash* aspires to an integrated view that reconstructs the overall ideational context of the culture represented by the holiday through its symbols. Through observing the totality, the philosophic *midrash* seeks to expose anew symbols that had become unavailable to an immediate or direct understanding; that is, the reflexive view strives to bring distant aspects closer and inject the original forms of the holiday into expressive instruments that speak to the sensibility of modern Jews. This is therefore a literature that labors for a re-orientation of the modern Jew to his heritage while motivating new creativity that draws on the complete compass of the tradition so as to devise full integration.

THE HOLIDAYS—
A COLLECTION OF HISTORICAL MEMORIES

To which of the above categories does this book belong? Having arrived at this Afterword, the reader can judge for himself. The author believes that the work has content and forms of expression drawn from almost every category mentioned above, though it does not belong exclusively to any of them. The book draws extensively on historical research but it does not relate any but the most general conclusions in order to establish a perspective for observation. There is much *midrash* and philosophical study as the book seeks to serve as a reference work for teachers and students of Jewish holidays and thought in general. But it is not a book of sermons on the holidays, nor does it belong to pedagogic literature; it most nearly approximates the sixth category as it strives to place an overall philosophic study alongside the main primary sources.

The book had its beginnings in a series of lectures taught at Tel Hai College in 1980. Directed mainly at teachers and coordinators of cultural events in rural settlements in Israel, the lectures were a response to a natural interest that this public had. It was quickly apparent that the interest was not part of a need for professional or in-service training, but was primarily the result of recognizing the extreme importance of the topic from both educational and socio-cultural standpoints. This was a learning community, animated and aware of the pressing spiritual need of national/secular Israeli society, particularly the younger generation, to renew its nourishing connection to the more profound sources of Jewish culture in order to fill a distressing void. There was no need to prove to this public that learning and experiencing the holidays was one of the most suitable instruments with which to confront the problem. This public was highly aware of what it itself lacked, both from the standpoint of familiarity with the scope and breadth of the material, and from the standpoint of understanding the significance of major aspects of the material, which stemmed from traditional ritual and ceremony, and from Orthodox thought. Could such content be relevant for a group whose self-identity is secular? In itself, the question was an a priori assumption, but the students understood that they could not allow this consideration to get in the way of learning the material before coming up with an answer to the question.

Perhaps this was because their extensive experience had shown that previous answers that portrayed a holiday only through folklore or literary and artistic descriptions, or even historical research, were inadequate. These were costumes from which the actual body of the holiday had simply slipped out along the way. One had to revert to examining the actual body of the holiday, if the true spiritual problem was to be confronted, despite the ideological difficulty inherent in the customary tension between "religious" content, on the one hand and a "secular" world view and life style, on the other. If one has recourse to the essence of the holiday and that essence equals ritual symbolism and prayer, then it would be proper to examine the meanings inherent in such ritual and prayer.

Perhaps not all of them will appear to be "irrelevant" as was first assumed; perhaps there is a way in which these meanings touch upon the existential and cognitive centers of anyone conscious of the full range of his cultural life.

The goal of the participants in the lectures was simply and directly defined: to rediscover those sources that fill the traditional image of Jewish holidays, to become acquainted with the contents and plumb their most profound meanings, and only then to raise the question of whether and to what extent they could be presented to pupils as study material and to adults as the underpinning of the holidays. At this point a workshop technique with the appropriate methodology was employed. First, an inventory was called for regarding all the material connected to each holiday; for instance, what commandments, symbols, prayers, and recitations combine to make up the holiday? After that, the various strata of the material had to be examined and placed in reference one to another. By what process is material amassed with components following one on the other? What does each component contribute to the total context of the holiday? Were there meaningful changes, and if so what was the reason for the changes? And finally, what experiences were these contents meant to effect, and what core questions in an individual's life were meant to be addressed in personal, interpersonal, and societal/national contexts?

The point of departure for the study was an inventory of the traditional holiday as it came down to us through all of its historic transformations; the first question was, how is the holiday celebrated today in the image of a full historic tradition? The determination is critical for an understanding of the methodology used in writing this book. We did not initially approach the topic as scholars of history who describe the development of a holiday in its transformations from one generation to the next; instead we went directly to the outgrowth of the historical transformations as they have been consolidated to the present period. Clearly even a non-professional student of history can perceive traces of historic development in contemporary models. But someone celebrating the holiday today is not aware of differences between early and late developments, seeing rather the various components as a complex unity, all of which are equally available to him. It is only by becoming aware of the internal tensions that exist between the contents that a historical perspective can be gained. It is an experience not unlike that of an individual who, in recalling his past, experiences the tension between past and present as an internal perspective of the present.

Undoubtedly there are readers who will question the decision to describe the inventory according to its traditional image; that is, according to the image the holiday now holds in the way of life of observant Jews who are Orthodox. Such readers will argue—and justly so—that meanwhile other traditions have consolidated that have winnowed out material from the traditional content, discarded quite a bit, changed particulars and added new ones, and fashioned holidays whose image is not Orthodox, and as a matter of fact is not at all religious. Why not begin with these traditions? Or at least why not describe their inventory alongside the traditional one? Actually these new traditions were not overlooked; indeed a great deal of attention was devoted to them, particularly when considering holidays that express modern Jewish thought and experience. Yet one ought not overlook the fact that the holiday in its traditional garb is itself the starting point of new traditions, traditions still not fully ripened so that they could be placed as wholly developed practices alongside, or in opposition to, the early traditions. Uncertainty and feelings of incompleteness are still the lot of those who celebrate according to new traditions; they still scrutinize what they have fashioned by comparing it to the early tradition and define their problems according to its yardsticks. The intention is to encourage the creative process concerning new holiday traditions but apparently, precisely to that end, one has to continually confront the picture that is held up by the standing tradition in order to assess the problems that stem from its definition in today's Jewish reality. One needs to examine how the reconstructed answers gain validity not through detachment from the heritage but by regarding it as a source for renewed creativity.

As we have indicated, we are dealing with historical perspective as an internal dimension created by tensions of style, feeling, and thought among the different strata that make up the unity of the traditional holiday. Of course it must be understood that although the background is not explicit in the content of the holiday, once one distinguishes among the various strata, the question of the historical background of each individual layer rises. Against this background one can imagine what the character of the holiday was in early periods, and appreciate the meaning of each stratum's themes in relation to the time of its creation. Though class discussions touched upon this aspect of historical research, it bears emphasizing that this was done only when it could contribute something to an understanding of the internal perspective of the holiday as it has come down through the historical tradition; even then no need was seen to go into detailed findings of scientific research. A vast literature on this topic exists and is available for a reader to refer to. In any case, the concern was not for an emphasis on historical research for its own sake but on historical dimension from the standpoint of the major content of the holiday itself. After reading the chapters of this book, the reader will have no difficulty in understanding that "the holidays mark historical memories and crystallize a consciousness of one's being within the course of linear historic time." It can therefore be seen that in the stratum of content, holidays store up the historical memories of various generations, and this historic message—for all its tensions and contradictions—is the very essence of the holiday.

Still, it is worthwhile to return for another look at the tension that arises between an understanding of each holiday's content in its historic context, (namely, in the context of its original literary source) and an understanding of the same content within the totality of the literary material composed for the holiday. For example, the readings from the Torah, the *haftarah*, and the *megillah* that were assigned to each holiday can be interpreted in their original literary context as well as on the background of what is known as a result of research about a particular period. In addition, these same portions can be interpreted in the light of how they are paired to each other, or from the flow-through of the prayers that are recited before them and follow on them. The confrontation between expressions of feelings and thoughts from various periods and historical/cultural circumstances gives rise to a wealth of ideas, and these create an interpretive stratum which overarches the strata that are compared. This interpretive stratum is intended to create a unity of all of the ideas; at the same time, it adds its own intrinsic contents to the rich variety that, in turn, will sustain the next interpretive stratum that follows. Once we are alert to the tension between an understanding of each separate layer of the holiday in its individual historic context, as opposed to understanding the holiday in the context of its overall content and totality, we become aware of the secret of organic continuity in the holiday's development. This is the secret of the *midrash*, which discovers and rediscovers themes in the Sources in order to draw from them a spiritual creation that expresses the experience and thought of Jews in every generation. By its very essence, the *midrash* is not merely an interpretive technique; it is also an essential approach to the Sources.

It is basic to the assumption of a primary harmony between the eternal themes of a binding Scripture whose authority is objective, and a subjective understanding of individuals and of the group, which seek to extricate an eternal content through the temporary and changeable instruments of each generation. So it is only natural that not only do cognitive interpretations change, but the very forms of *midrashic* thinking change. Every generation has its *midrashic* modes. This generation confronts the contents of the Sources equipped with the tools of research and a scientific way of thinking, an unavoidable outcome of a consciousness of history that was formed as a result of experiencing such quick and frequent changes that historic continuity was broken. If one wants to bridge this fracture, one can no longer posit continuity as a given; instead, the difference between the experience and thought of previous generations—each in the circumstances of its own period—and the thought and experience of this generation must be defined. Only then will the connecting thought be found.

This means that the bridging *midrash* of our time cannot approach the varying strata in the Sources in an unmediated way, interpreting them without a prior reckoning of their significance in their original context. The use of an unsophisticated *midrash* is no longer viable. Scientific research must be a basic component of the *midrashic* thought process; only then can a *midrashic* effort be used to consciously create a new layer of meaning. In other words, taking historical perspective into account now becomes a necessity of the spiritual process for the creation of forms and symbols that express the historic experience of this generation.

Finally, it must be noted that *midrash* is not an artistic tool of sages who created a work of art while concealing the tools they used. Admittedly there are *midrashim* of both law and legend that deal with rules of the holiday, which, while not an integral part of it, are studied as a preparation for the holiday. But even here *midrashic* thought has a presence in the holiday experience; all the more so when the *midrash* itself is incorporated, either as a reading or a prayer, or as an actual learning experience. There are times set aside during the holidays for *midrashic* study and thought as an accompanying intellectual observation of the mitzvot, the symbols, the prayers, and the biblical readings. In other words, there is no celebration that is not accompanied by an intellectual interpretation, which unifies all the variegated activities and interprets them. Thus it was in the past and so it is in the present. Only the component of studious observation of the holiday as it renews itself can bridge the deep chasm that separates the experience of Jews in this generation from the tradition, which is why it is important to assess the methodological basis of *midrashic* interpretation and transmit it as a skill and an ongoing practice to those who want to participate in the holiday experience.

LITERATURE FOR THE HOLIDAYS

What strata are found in the traditional inventory?

1. The literary layer, whose source is the Bible, is present in the traditional holiday in three ways. First, a reference to the commandments for the holiday is made through a reading of the appropriate verses from the Torah; second, specific Torah sections and the corresponding *haftarot* from the Prophets are read; third, there is a reading of a particular *megillah* from the Writings. Individual psalms, which make up part of the daily prayers, are added to these three. There are special psalms dedicated to holidays (the reference here is to *hallel* recited on certain festivals). However, since there are no sections devoted specifically to each holiday, an analysis of the Psalms as a source from which a holiday draws its special content is not called for. These chapters should be dealt with in the context of ideational themes in the prayer book. Though only a direct biblical presence in the holiday has been mentioned, there is an indirect presence as well. Prayers and liturgical hymns are a checkerboard of biblical verses extracted from the original context and applied in new contexts. The Bible is the seedbed from which the holiday grew, and from which it continues to draw its renewed themes.

2. The literary layer whose source is the Oral Law. First of all, there are detailed rules that set the framework for the holiday, the time and way each mitzvah, specific to the holiday, should be performed, and occasionally an explanation of the reasons for it. There is also the formulation of prayers whose source is in the literature of the earlier and later Sages, bearing the imprint of the Sages' *midrashim*. In this connection, the notion that has emerged throughout all the chapters in this book should be recalled: in effect, the form and content of Jewish holidays were consolidated through the *midrash* of the Sages, which was based on biblical foundations.

3. Despite the reservation made about it, the prayer book ought to be considered as a literary work that bears discussion because it is a uniquely crystallized literary creation in its own right. Indeed, the prayer book remains open-ended. It absorbed literary creativity that expressed the experiences and feelings of the past generations, and it continues to do so.

4. Lastly, one should note the literary sources that are not an integral part of a holiday, but whose impact is felt in the way Jews direct their hearts and minds when they perform the mitzvot of the holiday. The reference here is to the literature of thought in its broad diversity beginning with the midrashim of the Early Sages through the essays of

medieval savants such *The Cuzair of Rabbi Yehudah HaLevi, The Guide to the Perplexed* and *The Mishnah Torah* of Maimonides, and continuing on to more recent books such as *Cycles of the Year* by Samson Raphael Hirsch and *Star of Redemption* by Franz Rosenzweig. This body of literature is a part of the education for the holiday, and its influence is sometimes seen in the prayer book in such liturgical hymns as "Adon Olam," "Yigdal," and "Keter Malkhut," "Shir HaKoved," and others.

CONTINUING IN THE CREATION OF THE HOLIDAYS

After examining the available material and differentiating its various strata, the workshops required an analysis of the contribution of each layer to the pool of the holiday's content. Each contribution needed to be examined in two ways: the variety of the literary sources from which the various sections came—the Bible, Mishnah, *midrash*, prayer book, liturgy, and literary thought; and the unifying dimension that the holiday itself imposes on the selections. Clearly these two dimensions are not separate. It is likely that the chapters selected by thinkers of later generations from source literature that preceded them are the very chapters whose influence shaped the traditions on which the Sages were nourished. While this later thought derives from the tradition, it is not identical to it. What was emphasized in the selections, due to their original literary context, differs from what is emphasized when they are transposed into a specific holiday framework. Concentrating on these significant differences enables contemporary students of holiday thought to employ a two-pronged intellectual approach: setting up a historic perspective as it is embodied in the holiday tradition; and selecting those ideational links that appeal to the feelings and thinking of a contemporary person so that he can fashion the nature of thought about the holidays that best expresses the way he identifies with tradition.

The interests and aims of each student will decide which of various directions will be taken. There are students who will tend more toward the historical track, asking, What remains today of the holiday as it was celebrated in the biblical era, at the time of the Tannaic literature, and so on? What is the difference between the way we celebrate the holiday today and the way our forefathers celebrated it at various times? What have we received from the tradition and what have we rejected? This approach places greater emphasis on scientific research, both historical and philological. It has recourse to a great deal of evidence that is external to the tradition embodied in the holiday itself so that it is able to break down the unified image of the festival in order to discover the historic components. But even in this approach one is not restricted to mere archeology because research whose starting point is decidedly the present contributes much to the self-understanding of a modern person vis-à-vis his heritage. Clearly one can put greater emphasis on the synthetic aspect, an approach that traces the total content of the holiday as it has been consolidated in tradition to the present day. Such an approach is less inclined toward research, and more toward the methodology of philosophic thought through the student's systematic, cognitive tools, which is why it has an element of creative interpretation. These two approaches do not contradict one another nor are they mutually exclusive. On the contrary, by combining them they serve as checks for one another, and are thus perhaps complementary.

A reader of this book quickly notices that its thinking leans decidedly in the second direction. It certainly would have been possible to devote an extensive part of the beginning of each chapter to a summary of the historic research that has been conducted in the development of the holiday from the biblical period onward and by means of this research describe the holiday picture in several decisive periods, and only after the scientific description move to the interpretive, literary/experiential discussion. Nor would this have gone against the general approach of the book. It was not done because of the following considerations. First, as stated earlier, research literature on the holidays is extensive and available to any student. There was no reason, therefore, to rehearse it again, thereby needlessly expanding the scope of the book. It would only have been tedious for the reader. Second, literature that seeks to compile a synthetic picture of the holiday is still very sparse, whereas in the educational process of teaching holidays, and the creative process of fashioning the holiday in families and communities that are not ultra-Orthodox, it is precisely the synthetic compilation that is most needed. This book is intended to fill that vacuum and therefore the synthetic orientation is emphasized. This is also the reason for stressing a creative interpretation whose modes and whose openness to study of the authentic Sources has already been mentioned. Our hope is that this study will serve not only as information about holidays, but the beginning of a spiritual process in which one moves closer to the holiday so as to experience it and thereby continue in its creation.

MIDRASHIM FOR CONTEMPORARY JEWS

Consequently, the final stage for a modern Jew participating in such a workshop who, because of his life experience and outlook, finds the tradition problematic, is the attempt to reconnect with the holiday as he draws the holiday's content closer to his own position within the history of his people. This is the stage in which a new *midrash* is created that relates to the entire gamut of content in the tradition of the holiday. This is the stage in which the individual finds something to grasp by which he can construct an integrated picture where the long perspective is neither broken nor disappears, but expresses the experience and the thinking of this generation.

The difficulties are obvious. Ours is a generation in which the majority is far from the continuity of the tradition, a generation that cannot be regarded as having been educated by the tradition; indeed if at all, then only partially. Much of the contemporary individual's daily activity and experience derives from, and is directed by, a culture that is external to the tradition and is foreign to it. For this generation, furthermore, important historic circumstances put into question central tenets of belief basic to the tradition, that are expressed by the structure and symbols of the holidays. To these two dimensions of distance, one must add an alienation from the procedure and interpretive style used to bridge differences, even contradictions, between previous generations. For a Jew brought up in the scientific/ philological/ historical tradition of the New Era, *midrash* appears to be a foreign, not to say peculiar, style of interpretation and thought on several counts: the authoritative approach to the Sources, and the ostensibly subjective liberty with which a *midrashic* interpreter permits his own ideas to be injected into ancient texts. From both these standpoints, the *midrash* in its traditional garb is a coercion of critical thinking, on the one hand, and a forcing of the written sources, on the other. This is not a trivial methodological difficulty. It indicates a double distancing from the continuity of tradition as well as from the basic assumptions of faith on which the tradition stands. But it would appear that precisely because of this, if this book can show that a modern *midrash* could be designed that does not run counter to the methodology of modern interpretation, it could also show that a return to the Sources is possible in order to derive vital and relevant content from them.

The chapters of this book embrace an array of *midrashim* that combine into a comprehensive *midrash* concerning the broadest aspects of Jewish holidays and the Jewish calendar. What is the basis of this *midrash*? First, the belief that despite the double distancing from tradition there is an inescapable human need for cultural resources and roots in tradition; in fact, this need is one of the strongest and most spirited factors in the cultural creativity of our generation. True, a general feeling of longing for "roots" does not necessarily attest to the link with a specific tradition, or with a specific content; sometimes it points only to the existence of an oppressive emptiness that is without any specific attachment to a certain culture. Nonetheless, the perceived need to anchor oneself and to belong indicates that the very awareness of Sources and tradition, the very awareness of their function in human life, is not foreign to those schooled in a modern culture that uprooted itself for the sake of "progress." In examining the existing cultural foundation, one may discover that it is still carries much of its former tradition despite the fact that the modern consumers are not aware of either its specific source or its original meaning. They only sense that their culture is *drawn* from a certain forgotten source. In any case, just as the life experience of a contemporary Jew creates a distance between him and Jewish tradition, it also impels him to rediscover it as the explanation for his distinct cultural identity.

If an individual wants to respond to the impetus that springs from the essence of human cultural existence, first he is required to adopt an affirmative attitude to his former historical tradition and its content. This may sound so obvious as to be superfluous, but in the spiritual reality of contemporary Jewry, particularly in the State of Israel, it must be determined and declared. Modern Jews are particularly ambivalent toward their tradition; although the impetus to anchor oneself in it is quite strong and a distressing emptiness continues to be troubling. There is alongside this a deeply rooted intellectual and emotional opposition. The Zionist enterprise in Israel was born on a wave of revolt against the exilic image of the Jewish people and its culture, and in its extremism this revolt railed against the entire network of a *halakhic* way of life. There is indeed a dialectic to the rebellion for it draws something from the essence of what it revolted against, but this is a dialectic that leads to separation. However, if one feels that the need for roots is stronger, it is proper to make a special effort at reorientation in order to initiate a counter-dialectic that will bring both the elements of revolt and attachment into a positive and continuing relationship. In any case, a sophisticated educational effort is necessary to overcome the sweeping rejection of traditional and religious topics in order to create an attitude of affirmative acceptance to the study of these themes, and to examine their essential meaning and validity.

The desired change is expressed in empathetic study, which can be

achieved through employing the tools of research and literary analysis.
But empathy calls for more than mere curious interest. It demands a
psychological investment through a directed effort of the imagination,
which gives rise to emotions. That is, the student has to enter into
situations that are shaped by symbolic deeds, to imagine them, to think
and feel them. Experience shows that this is possible, and the fact that it
is possible shows that man's nature responds to symbols that point beyond
his established world view, drawing from a vast emotional potential that
is never wholly conscious. Conceivably, therefore, empathetic learning
can teach us something about our still undefined spiritual resources, which
may connect us to profound strata in the cultural language that raised us
and shaped our personality. Conceivably we will also realize that the
internal drive that directs a return to the Sources wells up from those
latent strata within us that inarticulately demand expression. In any case,
empathetic study may reveal the multi-faceted aspects of man's personality and the fact that it is nurtured from beyond the modern "now" that
gives voice to a very limited range of spirit, feeling, imagination, and
thought.

This is primarily true with regard to feelings of religiosity. An
empathetic study of prayers and ritual symbols that express religious
feelings will uncover psychological inclinations that thirst for the realm of
sanctity in man. Not that a person becomes a religious believer or one
who actually prays because of this. But prayer and religious observance are
then perceived by him as experiences within his cognitive horizon; they
enrich his inner spiritual life and prepare him to understand the culture
from which he sprang as well as intensify his own distinct world view. It
would appear that we will only be capable of infusing a continuity of
cultural creativity into the contemporary rebellion against certain elements in the Jewish people's tradition of faith when we discover the fact
that human existence is as multi-layered as the culture from which we
stem, that our personality "recalls" early strata of our culture and responds
to them, and that without activating these internal strata there is no full
personal life and there is no complete spiritual creation. The crisis of
belief so characteristic of the modern period will then no longer be a
decree that severs the vital sources; instead, it will be a moment within a
historic/cultural process possessed of a past as well as a future.

The realization that the crisis of faith does have a past and a future is
the underpinning for a creative *midrash* with a potential for the renewal of
the holiday. Such a realization brings a contemporary thinker closer to the
thought patterns of the early *midrash* : purposeful anchoring in an early

source in order to extract a verification from it. The same realization also differentiates the *midrash* conceivable for a contemporary Jew from the earlier *midrashim*. It is no longer a naive *midrash* that unquestioningly equates the subjective explanation with the meaning originally intended in the source that is being examined. Instead, it is a critical *midrash* both vis-à-vis the source and its own content; this critique distinguishes clearly between the learning stage that strives for objectivity and employs philological and historical research to that end, and the learning stage that aspires to a subjective interpretation and employs the methodology of philosophic inquiry to that end.

This is another way of saying that *midrash* does not necessarily negate scientific interpretation. On the contrary, scientific interpretation can prepare the *midrash* and make it fruitful if we are rigorous about the special role of each of these two disciplines: study that wants to understand the Sources from within their historic context, and a discipline that chooses a vantage point for an interpretation that reflects the student's questions with reference to the cultural/historic context of his own thought. Since we have before us a multi-strata traditional creation that emerged through the process of an extended *midrash* that integrates many conflicting elements into a multi-faceted unity, then the potential for many current midrashim is very great; and there is no difficulty in discovering directions along which one can extend the content of tradition as a continuity, reaching a variety of solutions, each of which differs from the others yet each at the same time reflecting the totality of the tradition.

The chapters of this book include many such *midrashim*, particularly philosophical interpretations of sections of the Torah, the *haftarot*, and the scrolls that are read on the holidays. Certainly these interpretations are not scientific; they are philosophical *midrashim*. Nonetheless, the author of these *midrashim* feels that they cannot be faulted for forcing the text, nor do they stand in contradiction to a scientific understanding of the text. An understanding of the manifest level of the text in its scientific sense underlies all of them. The *midrash* emerges as the student redirects the thrust of his studies and puts questions that rise from his interest as a person who belongs to the culture of his time to the text he is confronting. Such a confrontation with the Sources raises certain salient points from the text, in its entirety, and submerges other points that appear to be less salient without having the totality of the chapter disappear from his attention.

This is not unlike the perspective of a person who observes a wide-scale landscape from the top of a mountain. Certainly his vantage point places an emphasis on particular points of concentration and obscures others; no less certain is it that another vantage point would cause other points to be emphasized. Nonetheless he may be looking at the same landscape, and his observation is equally encompassing in both cases. The creator of the *midrash* concentrates on important aspects from his point of view; he concentrates on such aspects, joins them into a totality, and develops the ideas inherent in them as a response to his own questions; yet in no way does he force the text. But it is clear that he requires a certain ideational choice of texts, and it is also clear that his choice is influenced by his interests and needs.

Since this is so, it is apparent from at the outset that such *midrashim* neither exhaust the content of thought inherent in the Sources nor do they claim to be ultimate or exclusive interpretations of the Sources. The creator of a *midrash* knows full well—and this was known by people who wrote *midrashim* from earliest times—that endless additional *midrashim* are conceivable alongside his own *midrash*, and all of them are correct according to the same criteria. Anyone who studies such *midrashim*, standing alongside the author at the same vantage point, will derive these responses as answers to his questions. A person who stands at another vantage point discovers how the landscape is seen in the eyes of the other, and perhaps also learns what latent wealth can be found there, and how it can be extracted. If this is done with regard to the content of holidays, the individual will find himself immersed in the creative process by which the holiday moves from thought to deed. Such a person will soon find himself celebrating the holiday.

THE PURPOSE OF THIS BOOK: TO SHOW THE SEEKER A DIRECTION

The intent of this book is summarized in combining two disciplines: an acquaintance with the traditional contents of the holiday and the desire to find the place and significance of such contents in the Jewish reality of our time. This duality can be presented differently: the combination of a philosophical approach—that is, an understanding of basic problems of traditional Jewish thought in light of the experience and thought of contemporary Jewry along with an attempt to formulate this experience into a Jewish world view that confronts basic questions; and a pragmatic goal—that is, a renewal of the tradition of the holidays as a network of commandments and symbols, which grants them meaning and direction in the way of life of a contemporary Jew. Just as study and *midrash* are intertwined, thinking and the pragmatic formulation of symbols and customs are connected to one another. We will not have a genuine holiday, in the sense of a day replete with symbolic moves that structures a whole ordering of one's life during that day, if we do not confront anew basic questions on the outlook of belief that sets the Jewish people apart. Profound confrontation, however, is not an abstract matter. It is tied up with the effort to find a behavioral expression for a way of life as well as basic values of the inherited culture. Anyone who wants to educate—not merely teach—must merge all these levels of activity, study, inquiry, thought, and expressive deed in his work.

Many of the readers of this book will find that the philosophical, emotional, and practical problems that emerge from the intention to find a link to the tradition in our time are more difficult and more principled than what was at first assumed. For those who come to such a conclusion, this is important in and of itself. The magnitude of the challenge must be correctly evaluated in order to prepare for it. If real answers are desired, profound questions must be asked. In any case, this book was not written to respond to all the questions that are asked. No contemporary book that lays claim to anything more all-encompassing than answers to a single questioner will succeed. Such a statement may not seem modest, yet it requires saying because it is appropriate to the time: it is the intention of this book to show the seeker a direction, even as he strides forward.

INDEX

About the Author

Professor Eliezer Schweid is Emeritus Professor for Medieval and Modern Jewish Philosophy at the Hebrew University, Senior Professor at Schechter Institute for Jewish Studies in Jerusalem, and Vice-President of the Jerusalem Center for Public Affairs. He received his doctorate in Jewish Philosophy and History in the Hebrew University. He is the author of numerous books and articles including: *Judaism on the Cross-Roads, Democracy and Halakhah, Searching for Meaning in the Thinking on the Holocaust,* and *History of Jewish Thought in the Twentieth Century,* which were also published in English. Professor Schweid is the recipient of the 1994 Israel Prize in Jewish Thought and Education. He resides with his wife Sabina in Jerusalem and has three children and ten grandchildren.